D0915440

Trading Nature

Trading Nature

Tahitians, Europeans, and Ecological Exchange

Jennifer Newell

University of Hawai'i Press

Honolulu

15 14 13 12 11 10   6 5 4 3 2 1

Library of Congress Cataloging-in-Publication Data

Newell, Jennifer.
Trading nature : Tahitians, Europeans, and ecological exchange /
    Jennifer Newell.
        p. cm.
    Includes bibliographical references and index.
    ISBN 978-0-8248-3281-0 (hard cover : alk. paper)
    1. Animal introduction—French Polynesia—Tahiti (Island)—History.
2. Plant introduction—French Polynesia—Tahiti (Island)—History.
3. Tahiti (French Polynesia : Island)—Commerce—Europe—History.
4. Europe—Commerce—French Polynesia—Tahiti (Island)—History.
I. Title. II. Title: Tahitians, Europeans, and ecological exchange.
    QL345.T3N49 2010
    578.09962'11—dc22
                                            2009034058

University of Hawai'i Press books are printed on acid-free
paper and meet the guidelines for permanence and
durability of the Council on Library Resources.

Designed by Josie Herr

Printed by The Maple-Vail Book Manufacturing Group

For Mark

CONTENTS

PREFACE

I cannot help thinking that our late voyage would reflect immortal
honour to our employers, if it had no other merit than stocking
Taheitee with goats, the Friendly isles and New Hebrides with dogs,
and New Zealand and New Caledonia with hogs.
  —George Forster, 1777

They [the people of Tahiti] think that because there are no breadfruit, cocoanuts nor plantations in England, that there cannot possibly
be any food that is good there; and they say, that we come here on
account of their sweet food, as they are pleased to call it.
  —Rev. Charles Wilson, 1803

This book tells stories of "ecological exchange"—the movement of
plants and animals across cultural divides. It investigates the ideas
and expectations that brought Tahitians and Europeans together, in the
volatile years between 1767 and 1827, to trade and give away their animals,
birds, fish, seeds, and crops. It explores the often surprising consequences
of those exchanges for the surrounding landscapes and cultures. It is both
an environmental history and a history of cross-cultural engagements. Tracing the dynamics between an island, its inhabitants, and its visitors, *Trading
Nature* makes clear the potency of exchanging species.

Many people, in Oceania and beyond, have contributed to this project.
Colleagues, curators, archivists, editors, friends, and family generously supported the researching and writing of this book and the doctoral thesis
from which it grew. I give warm thanks for the guidance and collabora-
tion of John Knott of the History Program, Australian National University.
Thanks also to my advisors, Iain McCalman (ANU), Anne D'Alleva (University of Connecticut), Lissant Bolton (British Museum), and Bronwen
Douglas (ANU).

I was privileged to have had an apprenticeship in Pacific history and anthropology with Nicholas Thomas at the Centre for Cross-Cultural Research, ANU. His creativity and originality have always been inspiring, and I thank him for his friendship. Anne Salmond and Jonathan Lamb have also been very important to me—I give them both heartfelt thanks for their pioneering scholarship, for generously agreeing to assess the manuscript to two different ends, and for the improvements they contributed both times. Nicholas Thomas, Iain McCalman, Tom Griffiths, Libby Robin, Paul D'Arcy, Michelle Hetherington, Frances Steele, Stephanie Jones, Rachel Eggleton, and Bernadette Hince commented very helpfully on portions of the manuscript. I have fond memories of the late Greg Dening: the wonderful conversations, challenging graduate programs, and the visit to consult his impressive card index of Pacific mariners.   '

For opening up vistas into an endlessly fascinating region, I give thanks to the artists, scholars, and friends from across the Pacific who worked and spoke with me at the ANU and the British Museum. For advice and insights in Tahiti I am particularly grateful to Celestine Vaite, Mama and Turia Vaite, Miriama Bono, Véronique Mu-Liepmann, Tara Hiquily, Robert Koenig, Michel Guerin, and Fortuné Teissier.

I owe particular thanks to Lissant Bolton, curator of Oceania, British Museum, for her support throughout. I am also grateful to British Museum colleagues Jill Hasell, Brian Durrans, Andrew Burnett, Jonathan King, J. D. Hill, and Jonathan Williams for their help and interest. Thanks to history and anthropology friends for stimulating discussions, particularly Makiko Kuwahara, Stephanie Liau, Jane Lydon, Kalissa Alexeyeff, Ian Coates, and the late Minoru Hokari.

I give lasting thanks to Stephanie Jones and Oliver Morris for their intellectual engagement and practical and moral support, and for the cheer of my goddaughter Charlotte. Special thanks for support from Mavis Pilbeam, Morwenna Lawson, Anne Forsyth, Caroline Clayton, and Hugh and Miranda Morris. Writing while at Hugh and Miranda's idyllic Ferry Cottage was as easy as they hoped.

I thank the staff of the National Library of Australia (Canberra); Australian National University Library (Canberra); State Library of New South Wales (Sydney); Archives Territorial (Pape'ete); Centre ORSTOM de Tahiti (Pape'ete); Musée de Tahiti et ses Îles (Puna'auia, Tahiti); Bibliothèque Nationale (Paris); British Library (London); Public Record Office (Kew); Special Collections Reading Room at the School of Oriental and African Studies (London); Centre for Anthropology Library, British Museum (London); Library of the Royal Society (London); Museum of Natural History

(London); Caird Library, National Maritime Museum (London); Polynesian Visual Arts Project at the University of East Anglia (Norwich); and Cambridge Museum of Archaeology and Anthropology (Cambridge). I am grateful to the ANU for a PhD scholarship that funded the first two years of my research.

The manuscript was revised while I was a research fellow at the Centre for Historical Research, National Museum of Australia, and I give thanks to Craddock Morton, Peter Stanley, Maria Nugent, Anna Edmundson, Anne Faris, and the rest of the team for intellectual and practical support. The fine maps are by Mark Gunning. Thanks to Julie Ogden of the NMA Press for her enthusiasm. I appreciate Drew Bryan's skillful copyediting and Robin Briggs' index. I have been fortunate to have Masako Ikeda and Cheri Dunn of University of Hawai'i Press to skillfully guide the book through production.

Thanks to my family for support and good cheer throughout: to my father, Barry Newell, and Katrina Proust; my mother, Dawn Hollins, and Ivan Hollins; my parents-in-law, Brian and Marion Gunning; to Denise and Ralph, Patrick and Libby, David and Debra, Kanthi and Richard, Ben and Melissa, and all my nieces and nephews. My brother Tim followed the progress of the project keenly, despite everything. He is missed. Thanks to my darling sons Ben and Tom for their patience with it all.

Finally, my husband Mark Gunning has been a phenomenally supportive partner to me and this book. His encouragement, insights, magnificent computer support, and his endless good humor made completing the book not only possible but enjoyable. I dedicate it to him.

ABBREVIATIONS

Australian National University, Canberra	ANU
British Library Additional Manuscript series	BL (Add. Ms)
British Museum, London	BM
Church World Mission Archive	CWM Archive
Historical Records of Australia	*HRA*
Journal of Pacific History	*JPH*
London Missionary Society	LMS
National Library of Australia, Canberra	NLA
Natural History Museum, London	NHM
National Maritime Museum, Greenwich, London	NMM
New South Wales	NSW
Public Record Office, Kew	PRO
Royal Botanic Gardens, Kew	RBGK
Royal Society Library, London	RS Library
School of African and Oceanic Studies, London	SOAS
South Sea Journals	SSJ
State Library of New South Wales, Sydney	SLNSW
University College London	UCL

Figure I.1. *Breadfruit trees, Point Venus, Matavai Bay. 2003. Photo: author.*

Introduction

A few years ago I met a Tahitian writer at a workshop on contemporary Pacific literature. Celestine Hitiura Vaite had recently published a novel, titled *Breadfruit*. Breadfruit had a lot of significance in Tahiti, she said. I told her about my research into Captain Bligh's breadfruit voyages and she told me about the huge breadfruit tree in her mother's garden on the island, planted by her great-grandfather. It was, like all breadfruit trees, a reliable producer of large, useful fruits. Ever bountiful, it had been bearing fruit, season after season, as her family's generations passed. In 1983, after a major cyclone hit, Celestine's family came out of their shelter and found everything—the house, the garden—was gone. Except the breadfruit tree, which was standing there still. Celestine also told me the old legend of the creation of breadfruit. Long ago, in a time of famine, a father decided he could not bear to see his family go hungry anymore. He went outside in the middle of the night and turned himself into a breadfruit tree, saying, "I will always be there for you."[1]

By the late eighteenth century, this understanding of breadfruit as a reliable stand-by in times of need had been carried beyond the Pacific, to take root in Britain. Captain Bligh's breadfruit saga, the most widely recognized episode in Tahitian history, began when British plantation owners in the Caribbean, desperate for cheap, dependable food for their starving slaves, settled on breadfruit as the solution. With the support of the British scientific establishment, they successfully lobbied the Admiralty for an expedition of transplantation from Tahiti. The image on this book's front cover is a 1796 tribute to the successful breadfruit transfer that had been initiated on the shores of Matavai Bay four years earlier. A Tahitian is directing operations, wearing the barkcloth robes that Maʻi ("Omai") wore when Reynolds painted his portrait in London. The project of transplantation brought Captain Bligh to the island twice, brought a Tahitian chief, Tu, a large quantity of European goods and weapons, brought mutineers to settle on the island and embroil themselves in local politics, and carried

1

two Tahitian gardeners to the Caribbean. The breadfruit project prompted just some of the many exchanges of ideas, relationships, and goods moving back and forth between Pacific islanders and Europeans at the time. It was only one of a series of visits by Europeans during the late eighteenth and early nineteenth centuries directed at making use of the resources contained within Tahiti's natural environment. The implications of all these visits for Tahitians and their island were extraordinary.

This book is an exploration of the exchanges between Tahitians, Europeans, and their natural worlds. It is based on the premise that the natural environment is inextricably woven into the unfolding fabric of human histories. As Geoff Park has said, "the ecology of a stretch of country and its history are far from unrelated. They work on one another. . . . If you go in search of one, you are led to the other."[2] Seeing nature as separate to human culture is a deeply rooted Western habit of mind, and, as William Cronon has said, it is a false dualism; nature is "much less natural than we think," being perpetually reshaped by us as well as being seen through "the lens of our own conceptions."[3] The landscape and its living ecology are integral to the physical context, the daily lives, spiritual relationships, conflicts, economies, political machinations, mythologies, and imaginings of human communities.[4] Plants, animals, and other aspects of a natural environment do not only have a presence in the perceptions, decisions, and actions of societies—plants and animals are themselves historical agents.

The story begins with the first meeting between Tahitians and Europeans: the arrival of Captain Samuel Wallis and the crew of HMS *Dolphin* in 1767. It ends in 1827, with the bedding down of a series of major political, social, and religious changes on the island. 1827 marks the end of a particularly volatile period of ecologically significant trade with the Australian colonies, the first year of the reign of the young, chiefly woman Aimata, and the start of a new era in which French colonial rule radically altered the Tahitians' ability to control their environment. Tahiti is the focus of this book, but the story includes other islands, primarily the other Society Islands: neighboring Mo'orea, the Leeward Islands to the west—Huahine, Ra'iatea, Taha'a, Porapora ("Borabora")—and a set of islets and atolls: Tetiaroa, Maupiti, Me'etia, and others.[5] The people who occupy these islands are the Maohi, the "people of the land."

This book focuses on the point at which cross-cultural relations and environmental relations coincide. It is first and foremost a historical project, centering on historical texts and using historical frameworks to explain the dynamics of a particular human and environmental conjunction. Environmental history is an important part of our ability to create nuanced, dynamic understandings of how humans have shaped and have been shaped by their natural world. These understandings, and the stories we tell about them, are crucial for addressing our current global need for greater environmental intelligence.[6]

The project also focuses on the point of intersection between two culturally distinct groups. It is at such intersections that especially dynamic, influential, often unexpected events and relationships occur. Around the world and throughout history, it is the meeting of cultural groups that has caused changes to many of the world's ecologies. Whether in the context of traveling, trading, colonizing, or warring, cross-cultural encounters carry a burden of ecological impact.

A focus on cross-cultural engagement is a relatively recent development in the scholarship of the Pacific.[7] Early histories of the Pacific were narratives of triumphal European exploration and empire. These were overturned from the 1960s by the mournful exposés of the damage of European impact, from A. Grenfell Price's *Western Invasions of the Pacific* (1963) and Alan Moorehead's well-known *Fatal Impact: An Account of the Invasion of the South Pacific* (1966, 1967, 1987), to A. Mitchell's *The Fragile South Pacific* (1989). The Pacific has also featured in this mode within global environmental histories, such as in Alfred Crosby's *Ecological Imperialism* (1986), which looks to early European colonizers taking over the environment of the New World with their exploitative appetites and invasive "portmanteau biota."[8] By these domineering practices, Crosby argues, the Old World weeds, viruses, and herds engulfed those ecologies and created "Neo-Europes" in the southern hemisphere. As K. R. Howe has said, after telling the history of the era of Enlightenment voyages, the "single most dominant metaphor for the subsequent history of the islands, and Tahiti in particular as a symbol of all others, is 'paradise lost'."[9] This perspective perseveres in many popular conceptions of the Pacific today. Both the "imperial" and "fatal impact" historians present an image of powerful European actions being brought to bear upon a passive Pacific.[10]

Since the 1980s, historical anthropologists and ethnohistorians—most notably Greg Dening, Nicholas Thomas, Anne Salmond, Douglas Oliver, and Marshall Sahlins—have been addressing the active engagement between Pacific islanders and Europeans. They have sought evidence of indigenous metaphors, ritual practices, oral histories, and material culture, through which islanders made sense of the eighteenth-century newcomers. K. R. Howe and historians at the Australian National University have been providing Pacific-centric histories that recognize the more dynamic, islander-driven stories of continuity and change in Oceania.[11] Their research

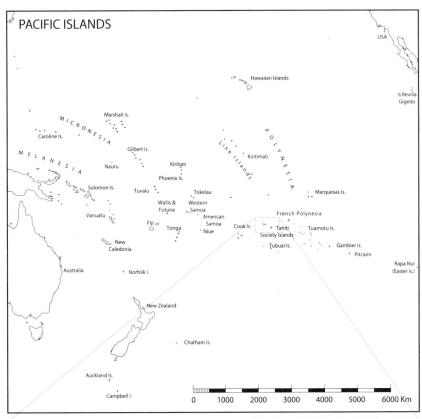

PACIFIC ISLANDS

USA

Hawaiian Islands

Is.Revilla
Gigedo

MICRONESIA

Marshall Is.

Caroline Is.

MELANESIA

Nauru

Gilbert Is.

POLYNESIA

Line Islands

Kiritimati

Kiribati

Phoenix Is.

Marquesas Is.

Solomon Is.

Tuvalu

Tokelau

Wallis &
Futuna

Western
Samoa

Vanuatu

Fiji

Tonga

American
Samoa

Niue

Cook Is.

French Polynesia

Tahiti
Society Islands

Tuamotu Is.

New
Caledonia

Tubuai Is.

Gambier Is.

Pitcairn

Australia

Norfolk I.

Rapa Nui
(Easter Is.)

New Zealand

Chatham Is.

Auckland Is.

Campbell I.

| 0 | 1000 | 2000 | 3000 | 4000 | 5000 | 6000 Km |

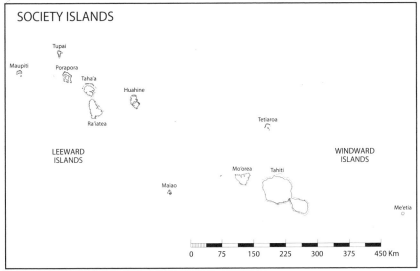

SOCIETY ISLANDS

Tupai

Maupiti

Porapora

Taha'a

Huahine

Ra'iatea

Tetiaroa

LEEWARD
ISLANDS

WINDWARD
ISLANDS

Mo'orea

Tahiti

Maiao

Me'etia

| 0 | 75 | 150 | 225 | 300 | 375 | 450 Km |

Map I.1. *The Pacific and Society Islands.* © *Mark Gunning (AHHAdesign.com), 2009.*

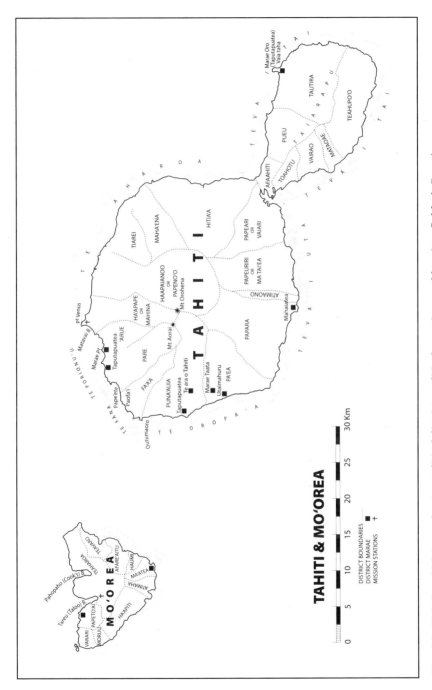

Map I.2. *Tahiti and Mo'orea, showing political districts, political groupings and key sites.* © *Mark Gunning (AHHAdesign.com), 2009.*

into indigenous perspectives combines with rigorous examination of European documents to return to the historical actors a sense of the uncertainties and complexities of the engagements on the beach, achieving credible insights into the meanings of those experiences for those on both sides of the encounter.[12]

Importantly, historians and writers such as Albert Wendt, Epeli Hauʻofa, Vilsoni Hereniko, and Teresia and Katerina Teaiwa have opened up new, ocean-centric perspectives to their more landlocked colleagues. Their histories are often centered on a nexus of place and identity, and they employ storytelling, theater, dance, and film, modes of communicating and commenting on the past that draw on long traditions of oration and staged performance of historical narratives.[13] These academics have often worked with the same impetus that inspired Epeli Hauʻofa's influential essay "Our Sea of Islands" (1994). Hauʻofa calls for the Pacific to be conceived of as Oceania, a region of islands interconnected, rather than isolated, by their ocean. Recognizing this, says Hauʻofa, can galvanize the overturning of colonial narratives of division and dependency.[14] Greater historical understandings are needed of the world of the ancestors, Hauʻofa states, "in which peoples and cultures moved and mingled, unhindered by boundaries of the kind erected much later by imperial powers."[15]

This project joins with the impetus of these scholars (both within and beyond Oceania) in underlining the mutuality of agency across the cultural divide. Neither islanders or Europeans had a monopoly on action, authority, competency, sensibility, or moral high ground. Across that cultural divide, Europeans and islanders communicated, traded, challenged, inspired, entertained, alarmed, teased, supported, and defrauded each other. They were, in fundamental ways, changed by one another.

As Tahitians and Europeans began meeting each other, they tried to establish some shared words and communicative gestures, tried to find out how the other did things, which gods they lived under. They traded for the intriguing and useful things the other made. They negotiated with each other for special assistance: Tahitian chiefs asked to borrow European manpower and ammunition to assist in wars against neighboring islands; European captains asked for islander navigators and translators. There was also plenty of sexual contact between the European crews and island women.[16] These exchanges proceeded at a rapid pace, between members of all classes of Tahitian society and at all levels of each ship's crew. Despite the cultural differences, all their physical contact, bartering, and giving of gifts ran relatively easily, especially when compared to other Pacific islands where less value was placed on connections to the visitors and their possessions.

During the eighteenth and early nineteenth centuries, most of the meetings between Tahitians and Europeans took place on the island itself. However, Society Islanders also traveled on British and French ships around the Pacific and, in some instances, visited Europe. The high priest and navigator Tupaia (c.1725–1770) guided and translated for Cook on the *Endeavour.* Ahutoru (c.1733–1771) voyaged with Bougainville to Paris, and Ma'i (c.1753–c.1780) became a celebrity in London before returning to the Societies with a collection of British weapons and technological curiosities.[17] It was an era of mutual fascination and experimentation.

Among these interactions, there was a particular type of exchange that involved specific kinds of material. The Europeans were asking the Tahitians each day, repeatedly, for things from the island's natural environment. The crews wanted fruit, coconuts, fish, shellfish, tubers, chicken, and pork. They wanted fresh water from the island's streams and timber from groves of trees. The islanders were generally willing to supply these things. They traded and gave them away in surprisingly large quantities.

It is particularly intriguing that the Europeans wanted not only to take plants and animals away from the island, but that they wanted to leave their own. When Captain Samuel Wallis became the first European to land at Tahiti in June 1767, he left a British flag on shore. He also gave Purea (chiefess of the Teva-i-uta people, Papara, in the island's southwest) three guinea hens, a pair of turkeys, a pregnant cat, and a garden planted with peas.[18] Captain Louis-Antoine Bougainville of France, Captain Cook of England, and Commandante Boenechea of Spain all planted vegetables, grains, and fruit and gave breeding pairs of cattle, goats, sheep, and poultry to the local chiefs.

What goal could have been so important that these captains were prepared to share the ships' limited spaces and resources with livestock for six to twelve months before reaching their island destination, only to give the animals away? On the other side of the shoreline, what was prompting the islanders to give up great quantities of important resources, including their immensely valuable, often spiritually significant, pigs, trees, and fish to the visiting strangers?

When reading accounts of the decisions, statements, and actions made by those involved in the meetings across the beach, one can at times founder for an explanation of their motivations. Whether looking at the phenomenal effort a captain expended to carry cattle to a remote Pacific island or a chief's apparently casual trading away of a previously sacred animal, the rationale is often opaque. As Robert Darnton has shown, it is at these points of opacity, when we as contemporary readers cannot find our way into a past worldview, cannot explain the actions or get the joke, that are most valuable to the historian.[19] They indicate the greatest conceptual distance between the historian and the historical subject. It is at these points that the historian of mentalities starts to question most actively and tries to uncover the traces of a past mental world. The decisions and actions taken by Tahitians and Europeans during the last half of the eighteenth and early nineteenth centuries over the treatment and trade of ecological elements is one such point of fruitful perplexity.

As plants and animals were passed between people, there were ripples of impact on the surrounding people, conceptual frameworks, and environments. Moving plants and animals across cultural and environmental borders had exceptionally deep and wide-ranging impacts on Pacific islands. I call this set of exchanges "ecological exchange."

Introducing Ecological Exchange

I define an exchange as "ecological" if it encompasses an exchange of species—living or once living—which has the capacity to impact, however slightly, the ecosystems those species are entering or leaving. So an islander providing a pig to a ship's officer in return for an iron nail is an ecological exchange even though an ecological element forms only half of the exchange.[20] Taking the pig out of the local system removes that animal's foraging, predating, and breeding functions from the system. The impact is especially clear when a single exchange of a food, animal, or plant is multiplied to many such transactions in a day in a small geographical area. The crew of British ships, anchored in Matavai Bay for several months, routinely consumed a thousand coconuts a day.[21]

The passing of animals and plants between islanders and Europeans during the Pacific voyaging era has been mentioned by various writers of Pacific history. The most considered and detailed treatment of the topic to date has been Nicholas Thomas' discussion of James Cook's fascination with the introduction of animals to the Pacific.[22] However, no sustained attention has previously been given to how these transactions operated as a powerful, cohesive, and ongoing context of exchange. The broader implications of ecological exchange for the individuals, communities, conceptual frameworks, and ecologies involved have been largely unconsidered.

I have come to three central conclusions about ecological exchange. First, and most fundamentally, the exchange of plants and animals is a process that contributes to the course of human histories. Ecological exchange has extensive cultural and environmental consequences. Second, ecological exchange is shaped by and contributes to the operation of cross-cultural relationships. Finally, one of the dynamics that operates within ecological exchange in a cross-cultural environment is that the inhabitants of a landscape retain substantial control over the exchange. In Tahiti, islanders, particularly islanders of high rank, managed the import and export of plants and animals to their own ends. Europeans who engaged with the island held a greater battery of weapons, but they did not hold the greater portion of power.

The history of Tahiti is one that has been particularly shaped by its living environment. This is not because the island's inhabitants were more or less "at one" with their natural world than members of other societies were. Since Pacific islanders occupied the islands of the eastern Pacific, moving from Samoa into the Marquesas, Society Islands, Hawaiian archipelago, and Easter Island from about 200 BC to AD 800, they established a range of socially codified means for ensuring sustainability of the flora and fauna upon which they relied.[23] They also overexploited natural resources for short-term purposes and caused extinctions, habitat loss, and soil erosion. There is nothing essential in indigenous communities that renders them environmentally enlightened. The Maohi of the Society Islands did live lives closely intertwined with the physical world on a conceptual, practical, and ceremonial level. This meant that ecological changes tended to have broader and more immediate implications for paradigms, social practices, spirituality, politics, and economics than usually experienced by urban or industrialized societies.

To fully understand the history of a place and its people, we need to trace specific histories of ecological exchange. Histories of ecological exchange allow us to see the mechanisms by which an environment has come to be constituted. The continued introduction of exotic species and overconsumption of existing resources remain among the greatest challenges facing Pacific islands.[24]

Observing Islands

On an island, people generally bring in and take out plants and livestock on clearly observed occasions. Islands have long been used by scientists and anthropologists as testing grounds for theories.[25] Researchers from Johann Reinhold Forster to Charles Darwin to Margaret Mead have found islands useful sites for observing environments and societies. They are ideal locations for discerning how societies work within and against their environments. As Richard Grove, J. R. McNeill, Patrick Nunn, and others have ably demonstrated, islands are ideal sites for the work of environmental historians.[26] Small and specific, cut off from the leveling effects of broad continental processes, the workings of islands are more visible. On a continental land mass, plants and animals can migrate, self-sow, move gradually into new territory. During the eighteenth and nineteenth centuries, seeds, roots, seedlings, cuttings, cages of birds, and animals of all sorts could be transported, traded, and smuggled on foot or by cart, carriage, train, or boat. By contrast, the species reaching Tahiti during the same period included sea birds and plants blown or flown in as seeds, but those brought by human agency were carried by the sole medium of ships.

Because of this, the flow of plants and animals in and out of Tahiti was easily witnessed. European naval officers and the missionaries who came soon afterwards were both institutionally required by their various admiralties and missionary societies to carefully, regularly, and precisely document what they experienced and transacted.[27]

Exchange Systems in a Cross-Cultural Context

> Exchange relations seem to be the substance of social life.
> —Nicholas Thomas, *Entangled Objects* [28]

Exchange is a powerful analytical category. A social operation that encompasses communication, gift giving, and trade, exchange relations do not just allow economic systems to turn—they are the fundamental means by which relationships between individuals and between groups are formed and maintained. As Nicholas Thomas has said, they can be seen to constitute social life. In a cross-cultural context such as Tahiti in the late eighteenth to early nineteenth centuries, exchanges between Europeans and islanders gave shape to the social life of both groups. The giving and trading of plants and animals operated within this broad and active context of exchanges. The difficulties that ran through the broader context of their meetings—the expectations of fair returns that went unmet, the asking for more than the other deemed just, the unwitting insults given—were difficulties that also complicated ecological exchanges.

At first, the Europeans and islanders who met on Pacific beaches made connections across the cultural divide by offering food and objects. The acts of offering and accepting created links when there were few words in common and minimal comprehension of each others' intentions, priorities, or beliefs. Through these first transactions of food and goods, tentative relationships were established. More fully developed relationships were established from the 1770s as more involved exchanges of property became routine. A familiar pattern settled over the trade for plants and animals as these things were translated into scientific specimens and commodities. Both sides knew basically what the other side wanted and expected. The trade was, nevertheless, troubled by persistent discord.

For Europeans of the eighteenth century, gifts were marked out clearly from items used in trade. In their eyes, gifts were precious items, presented with specific etiquette and suitable ceremony on a particular, clear occasion for maximum impact. Certain morés surrounded how these gifts could be spoken about, a delicacy surrounding the unvoiced but integral bond of obligation created by the gift. The trade of food for provisions on island shores, on the other hand, was a commercial proposition and was conceived of as barter, involving an overt discussion of value. The Polynesian practice of gift giving and trading was not so clear-cut. It operated as a continuum rather than as a distinction. Gifts were given frequently, casually, and with an open expectation of a gift to be given in return. Douglas Oliver has suggested that particular forms of gift exchange within Maohi society were a way of managing the surpluses of fish, fruit, and other produce that an individual would acquire from time to time.[29] The receiver was under a social obligation to accept the gift, and a return could be called in later, when the giver was in need. There were subtle graduations defining the value of plant and animal products as property. Greater or lesser exchange value attached to these depending on how much labor was required to produce them. The needs and resources of the parties involved were also taken into account when determining an exchange, rather than just the value of the goods. Europeans initially discerned very little of this hierarchy of values.[30]

The disjunction between values placed on property and definitions of gift and trade were a frequent source of tension in Matavai Bay. Captains were affronted by the "forwardness" of the chiefs asking for presents. The Tahitians were frustrated when the usual, fluid play of goods between associates became mired. James Morrison, after living on the island for months following the *Bounty* mutiny, stated that Tahitians considered it "no disgrace for a Man to be poor . . . but to be Rich and Covetous is a disgrace to Human Nature":

> should a Man betray such a sign and not freely part with what He has, His Neighbours would soon put Him on a level with the Poorest of themselves, by laying his possessions waste and hardly leave him a house to live in—a Man of such a discription [*sic*] would be accounted a hateful Person.[31]

The Maohi would have noted the Europeans' apparent stinginess and seen their failures of reciprocity as flawed generosity or, more significantly, as an unwillingness to enter fully into a relationship. Tahitians found European property attractive, considered most of the Europeans' possessions as fair game, and would seek the assistance of Hiro, the god of thieves, in acquiring it. British captains and officers dealt severely with Tahitians who breached the British code of legitimate exchange: they were shot at, hauled out of the water with boat hooks, flogged, had their ears lopped on Captain Cook's order, or their district's canoes and houses set alight. Property, as Jonathan Lamb has argued, underpinned virtually everything in British experience.[32] Civility itself was founded in the notion of property. Captain Cook's increasingly violent fury over the Tahitians' light-fingered approach to his ships' tools and fittings sprang partly from anxiety over his ability to properly carry out his expeditions, partly from the affront it represented from a people with whom he thought he had established a friendly bond, and partly from the necessity he felt to protect the property of his majesty's ships,[33] the only means by which the authority and civility of British voyagers was maintained.

Figure I.2. *William Hodges, "HMS* Resolution *and* Adventure *with Fishing Craft in Matavai Bay." 1776. Oil on canvas, 54 x 76 in. (137.2 x 193.2 cm). Painted for the Lords Commissioners of the Admiralty. © National Maritime Museum, Greenwich, London (BHC1932).*

Tahitians, in turn, were affronted and alarmed by the British freely taking fruit out of groves, fishing in privately owned locations, or cutting down trees without permission from the owners.[34] Some Tahitian men attacked one of Cook's crew when they saw him picking flowers from a sacred plant at a *marae*. It was a serious, shocking breach of the laws of respect for sacred property, with severe repercussions for the people of the district, and the crewman was lucky to escape with only a blow to the head.[35] When islanders and Europeans met, they were accompanied by their conceptions of the living world around them, and these conceptions shaped much of their encounter.

Meetings of Ecologies and Cultures

> Human beings are inextricably bound to the natural world, travel with more of it than they know, and often underestimate its independent historical influence.
> —Tom Griffiths, *Ecology and Empire*[36]

The "classic" exchanges that we are used to reading about in connection with the eighteenth-century Pacific—exchanges of ideas and knowledge, of manufactured goods, of labor, of sexual contact—all had social, cultural, economic, and political implications. Ecological exchanges carried these implications too. But they had the additional potential for permanent repercussions for the environments involved, and this in turn had implications for the people who lived within them. The offspring of the cats Wallis and Cook gave to Tahitian chiefs as diplomatic presents ate several of the island's bird species to extinction. Bligh and others took pains to plant guava bushes at Matavai Bay, and the plants soon became, and remain, one of the Pacific's most invasive weeds. When Cook sailed up to the coast of Taiarapu on his second voyage, the islanders could be seen running up into the hills to hide their pigs. But by the early 1800s chiefs were ordering their people to trade away pigs by the shipful.

Historians of the world's natural environments have long been demonstrating the crucial, historically determining operation of interactions between people and their land. However, there are as yet few studies of the Pacific that recognize the dialectic between ecological elements and human histories, and even fewer that address the recent, rather than archaeological, past. Geoff Park's *Ngā Uruora, The Groves of Life: Ecology and History in a New Zealand Landscape* is a powerful exploration of the intertwined history of people and ecology in particular forests, rivers, and valleys, telling stories that matter, often about landscapes that are no longer there.[37] Paul D'Arcy's *People of the Sea* is an insightful study of the role of the ocean in shaping the lives of Pacific islanders. D'Arcy focuses on "Remote Oceania" (the region of widely spaced islands roughly analogous to the regions classified by nineteenth-century Europeans as "Polynesia" and "Micronesia").[38] His project is a contribution toward Hau'ofa's vision for greater historical understandings of the interconnections within the world of the ancestors.[39] As Hau'ofa says, "we cannot read our histories without knowing how to read our landscapes (and seascapes)."[40] D'Arcy demonstrates the extent to which the ocean has bound islanders together across great distances and formed the medium of so much of everyday conceptual and spiritual existence. It is a work that recognizes, as Anne Salmond and Douglas Oliver have in reference to Tahiti, that for most of their history, Pacific islanders conceived of a world in which the substance and actions of people, animals, plants, insects, fish, gods, ancestors, rivers, rocks, and sea intermingled. The border between people and nature was less significant than the flow across boundaries between worlds of the living and dead. These nuances are important but illusive.

When I was one year into my research project I traveled to Tahiti to obtain not just archival records but a sense of the place about which I would be writing, to better ground my approach to the Tahitian past through the present landscape and living inhabitants. I took a bus to Matavai Bay, walked with mounting anticipation toward Point Venus, where Cook's observatory had been set up, to view the bay and the setting of so much of the action the voyage journals described. Stepping out from the edging of palm trees, I looked down the bay's curving stretch of black sand, toward the volcanic peak of Orohena, the waves breaking gently on the reef behind me. Little had visibly changed since it had been described in 1767. It was possible, standing there more than 230 years later, to feel some connection to the vision of the voyagers who formed part of my ancestral heritage, the imagery, language, and stories I had been steeped in all my life. But how was I to make the leap of imagination into how a Tahitian of that era could have seen this bay? It is all very well to look for points of opacity within past mentalities as an entry point, but what to do when it is all opaque? Accessing Maohi chants, oral histories, early records of conversations and actions, descriptions of uses and communication with the world of the living and the dead, have all contributed to my attempt to grasp how Maohi made sense of their world. I remain an outsider, and I remain tantalized by how much more there is to learn.

The chapters of this book focus on key instances of ecological exchange.

In the book's first part, "New Shores," I address the formation of the ecological exchange relationship between Europeans and Tahitians. Chapter 1 traces the establishment of an exchange relationship through the provisioning of ships. Chapter 2 examines the way Europeans and Tahitians viewed and valued landscapes. At issue is how these conceptions shaped the way the two groups engaged with each other and each other's ecological elements. In the book's second part, "Into Tahiti," I explore the introduction of plants and animals to Tahiti. Chapter 3 addresses the motivations behind these introductions, how the islanders managed them, and the impacts they had. Taking the example of a specific introduction, chapter 4 compares the importation of cattle into Tahiti and Hawai'i. Finally, "Out of Tahiti" investigates ecological exports from the island. The motivations, management, and impact of exporting Tahitian plants and animals are explored through two examples: the British project of transplanting breadfruit seedlings from Tahiti to the Caribbean (chapter 5), and the unsettling consequences of nineteenth-century trade of Tahitian pork to New South Wales (chapter 6). The chapters are arranged in an approximate chronology. Appendix A provides a compact chronology of events, ships' visits, and the reigns of key chiefs. Appendix B lists instances of species introduction to Tahiti.

Roots of Maohi Ecological Exchange

A long tradition informed the Maohi's practices and proprieties of exchange. The exchange of plants and animals operated between islands of the Pacific from the first launching of oceangoing canoes. As small groups moved out from Southeast Asia, across the western Pacific, and eventually through to the islands in the eastern Pacific, settlers took on board carefully wrapped tubers and breadfruit seedlings, live chickens (*mo'a*), dogs (*uri*), and pigs (*pua'a*). They established these plants and animals on new shores. Once settlements, stocks, and crops were flourishing, trade routes were developed between islands. Many people on coral atolls established trade relations with a more fertile volcanic island group within a few days' or few weeks' sailing in order to secure food plants and soil for gardens. Inhabitants of high islands relied on other islands and atolls to supply the particular foods, timbers, cloth dyes, and pearls and other specialist commodities. Long-lasting social and cultural links accompanied these trades.

Trade kept island groups in contact, encouraging the mutual inspiration of artistic styles, religions, technologies of food production, and the exchange of kin through marriage. As we shall see, trade with the Europeans was equally creative. However, as powerful as the new experiences of the eighteenth century were and as influential as the exchanges with Europeans became, it is important to keep sight of the islanders' beliefs, processes, and products that did not change. Among all the new contacts, new species, new opportunities, and pressures arriving in Tahiti during the voyaging era, there was still a framework that chiefs, priests, landowners, and commoners worked within and kept in place. A large proportion of everyday life, systems of trade, relations of power, and sacred practices persisted. Some practices only changed in their outward form. The red feathers that were traditionally attached to the woven coconut fiber cover of a *to'o*—a figure designed to attract and contain a god[41]—might be replaced or supplemented with red English cloth, but the significance and the potency of the red material remained.

The Pomare Clan

Once European ships started arriving, some people benefited more than others from the enhanced trading environment. One of Tahiti's families in particular, the Pomares, capitalized on the new opportunities. The Pomares were a chiefly lineage based in the northern districts of Pare and 'Arue. In the years following the first arrival of Europeans they managed to win dominion for a short period over the whole of Tahiti-nui ("Big Tahiti," the main part of the island, as distinct from the peninsula, "Little Tahiti," Tahiti-iti or Taiarapu), and later the island as a whole. That the Pomares' lands were on the northern coast ensured that their fortunes would improve more conspicuously than any other chiefdom on the island. It was there, in the sheltered harbor of Matavai Bay, that the greatest number of ships came to anchor and to trade. Bougainville had landed on the east coast in the Hitia'a district, and the Spanish stopped three times in Vaitepiha Bay on Taiarapu, but the British, who visited the island repeatedly in this period, quickly made Matavai their main port of call. The chiefs (*ari'i*) of each district did what they could to turn these visits to their advantage. From at least the last half of the eighteenth century to the 1840s there were six main tribes on the island (Te Porionu'u, Te Aharoa, Teva-i-tai, Teva-i-uta, Atehuru or Te Oropa'a, and Fa'a'a. See map I.2). Within and between these broad groupings, there were complex rivalries and alliances of *ari'i*, including tussles over the role of paramount chief (*ari'i rahi*). The island was divided up into territories (as many as twenty-one in our period), the boundaries lying largely along topographical boundaries or denoting work groups or areas of cultivation.[42]

The British met several generations of Pomare *ari'i* (see appendix A). By the time Wallis arrived, Teu, born around 1728, had established considerable authority in the Pare-'Arue district.[43] He managed affairs with the assistance of his brother-in-law, the powerful priest Ha'amanemane. Around 1750 his first son, Tu, was born. The title of *ari'i rahi* passed to the boy.[44]

Tu was about fifteen when the *Dolphin* arrived. He was, in adulthood, a tall man, ambitious and rather nervous. Like any chief, he adopted a succession of names. He had received the formal name Tu-nui-e-a'a-i-te-Atua at birth, commonly shortened to Tu. This is the name I will use. By the time Bligh arrived in 1788, Tu had married his primary wife, 'Itia (formally Tetuanui-reia-i-te-Ra'iatea), a woman of strong character and intelligence with useful family connections on Tahiti and the nearby island of Mo'orea.

Figure I.3. *John Webber, "King Pomare I of Tahiti." Portrait of Tu, 1777. Oil on canvas board, 14.2 × 11 in. (36.2 × 28 cm). Alexander Turnbull Library, Wellington, N.Z. (G-697).*

When they had their first son, around 1782 or 1783, Tu gave his title to his child and adopted the name Tina.[45] Another name associated with the chief and his lineage was Pomare ("night cough"). The British used this as a dynastic name. They called Tu's son Pomare II, the name I will use here. As the embodiment of the lineage's divine potency, Pomare II's subjects accorded him all the necessary marks of respect: uncovering their upper bodies when in his presence, surrendering up the support and goods he requested. He was carried on his attendant's shoulders to avoid his sacred ancestral power (*mana*) damaging his people's land and buildings. While he was young, his role in the region was as a spiritual figurehead; his father retained the reins of effective political power.[46] One of the key features of Maohi chiefly rule was the distinction that existed between, on the one hand, an individual's hereditary right to rule (which in a chiefly lineage stemmed from descent from the gods) and, on the other hand, the right to wield political, operational power, a right which had to be earned.

Early British visitors to Tahiti were confident they had identified the local leaders. Purea, and then Tu and his family, clearly had the authority to call in the trade goods of their region and dispose of them for their own ends. They could give goods as showy gifts to the visitors, make sumptuous feasts, and lay them up in piles on the altars at the island's sacred, ceremonial sites (*marae*). A typical gift from the Pomares to a captain comprised pigs or roasted pork, along with breadfruit, plantains, and other fruits, coconuts, taro (*Colocasia esculenta,* similar to a yam), and lengths of pale, fine cloth made of beaten paper mulberry bark. The Pomares' ability to command the land's produce was the kind of expression of power the British could readily recognize and understand. The earliest captains to visit Tahiti assumed the Pomares were monarchs of the island, and referred to them as kings and queens.

Marks on the Landscape

By the end of the eighteenth century, the northern districts of Tahiti were marked by the decades of supplying Europeans with local resources. One can extrapolate from the records of consumption European visitors made while at the island and imagine the resulting prevalence of tree stumps and the reduced populations of many animal species. But it appears there was, then, no deep change to ways of living and working on the land. Alan Moorehead's presentation of "fatal impacts" on Pacific environments misses the crucial point that despite the introduction of European livestock, plants, and parasites into islands like Tahiti, for a long time much remained fundamentally unaltered.

This is because Tahitians regulated the introduction of new ecological elements and the heightened levels of consumption. Chiefs set constraints and there were clear boundaries on the use of the natural world. Many of the new species being brought into the island were not valued and were accidentally or deliberately destroyed. There were also controls integral to the Tahitian environment. Local species tended to curb the invasion of exotic species. Tahitian dogs, for instance, attacked and killed introduced livestock, and local pigs rooted up carefully planted European gardens. It was largely because of these controls that the ecology and the cultural roles of many Tahitian plants and animals remained stable. Some of these roles remained in place over the centuries that followed. Walking around Tahiti now, a tall, dark green breadfruit tree stands protectively in the garden of almost every house. Breadfruit trees shade urban pavements and parking lots. The tree is employed visually in print media and in the corporate identities of companies wanting an image of dependable fruitfulness: the Banque Socredo logo is an *uru* branch with leaf and fruit. Despite two hundred years of exotic arrivals and in the face of newer, foreign significances overlaying the fruit's history, it remains an everyday staple and a symbol of solid reliability.

Along Papeʻete's bustling harbor promenade today there are busy flocks of sparrows and loud, strutting mynah birds. Dogs, mostly mangy mongrels, patrol the yards and streets. Gardens sport rose bushes, lilies, tomatoes, potato vines, pumpkins. In the mountains and along fences, silvery-bark eucalypts and South African flame trees are common. The miconia bush, an ornamental with heavy green-purple leaves, was introduced to Tahiti's botanic gardens in 1937 by the American botanist Harrison Smith. Miconia is now ubiquitous, forming a choking forest understory covering more than 60 percent of the island. It continues to spread throughout the Society Islands.[47]

The casual visitor may find these landscapes attractive, tropical, a little messy, perhaps "spoiled," yet a pleasant enough backdrop to a beach holiday. People who live in Tahiti—now not just the Maohi but also the long-established Chinese population, the resident French, and recent migrants from Australia, Japan, America—all have their own relationships with and understandings of the environment in which they live and work. Most of the island's inhabitants can offer some explanations for the current form of Tahiti's environment. Some know that Captain Cook and Captain Bligh

Figure I.4. *"Stop Miconia." Poster, Ministère de l'Environnement, Pape'ete, 2001. Photo: author.*

brought oranges and pineapples to the island.[48] Many are aware that recent avian immigrants such as the mynah and bulbul are aggressively supplanting indigenous birds. People may be conscious of these things, but there is no widespread sense that these bits of information actually matter.

The environmental issues of greatest concern to Tahitians have been pressing and present: primarily the French nuclear tests at Muruora Atoll, not far east of Tahiti. Pollution of the sea is also a major problem and receives substantial government and media attention, highlighting the effects on fishing grounds, the pearl industry, and tourism. The rise of sea levels is causing rising concern. However, questions about the island's bio-diversity—why there is so much guava, or why there are so few Polynesian pigs compared to other islands—are, for most people, less troubling.

The island's changing species profile has implications for the health of the island. Ecological exchange continues in modern-day Tahiti and continues to have broad-ranging cultural, social, economic, political, and ecological consequences for the island. The continued trade and transplan-tation of species in and out of the island profoundly affects the ability of Tahitians to fish profitably, to maintain an environment tourists still find appealing, and to retain the birds, food plants, fruits, and flowers that are integral to Tahitian life and Tahitian identity. Although there are increasing governmental controls, ecological exchange will continue. The importa-tion of seeds, plants, and livestock continues to be used to assist agricultural development. The island's main export industries, of cultured pearls and horticultural products such as vanilla, will continue to be important sources of revenue.[49]

In recent years the Ministère de l'Environnement of French Polyne-sia has raised awareness of the problems caused by introduced species. Pamphlets picturing noxious weeds have been distributed. High-profile campaigns about curbing the miconia plant appear frequently in newspa-pers and on television. Competitions run by the Ministère capture popular attention: a feature in *Dépêche* in 2003 highlighted for each day for a month ways to protect the Tahitian environment. One of the double-page spreads pointed out that the Society Islands has 825 indigenous plant species and more than 1,700 introduced species, many of which are highly invasive.[50] The experiment of introducing the red-vented bulbul at the end of the 1970s to tackle the fly population has been recognized as a disaster for the island's indigenous birds.[51] The government is unlikely to make fur-ther attempts at this type of biological control.[52] When anyone travels to French Polynesia by airplane they are warned before touchdown of bans on bringing in seeds, bulbs, roots, flowers, and animals into the island. There is a growing acknowledgment that moving plants and animals from one ecology to another is a serious act. Understanding histories of ecological exchange highlights the necessity of carefully managing the human trans-fer of species, particularly into and out of islands. Such histories reveal how intimately people and ecologies are entangled.

Part I

New Shores

Amusemens des Otahitiens et des Anglais.

"*Amusemens des Otahitiens et des Anglais,*" *frontispiece to Jean-Pierre Bérenger,* Collection de tous les voyages faits autour du monde *(Paris, 1788–1789), vol. 8.*

CHAPTER 1

"No Country More Capable"
The Provisioning Trade in Tahiti

> There cannot be a more affectionate People than the Oteheiteans, nor is any Country more capable of affording refreshments of various kinds both Animal & Vegetable to Ships long at Sea nor any people more ready to part with them & all for ye trifling Barter.
> —Arthur Bowes

I met with Robert Langdon, a scholar of Pacific history and ecology, in 1999 to discuss some of the issues raised by my doctoral thesis on ecological exchange.[1] When I described the sudden, high consumption of pigs, other animals, fruits, and vegetables in Matavai Bay whenever a ship pulled in, he shrugged and said, "but so what?" The pigs and chickens would breed again. There were plenty of coconut palms and taro fields and they would continue to produce. This gave me pause; perhaps I was assuming too much. Maybe the Tahitians around Matavai Bay were affected very little in a material sense by the outward trade in fresh food, water, and other ship's provisions. More mouths to feed for a few weeks or months might have stretched resources in the short term but not seriously impaired the Tahitians' ability to feed themselves. Perhaps there was not much impact on the everyday functioning of island life once the visiting ships sailed away.

But something did not ring true. What of the difficulties voyagers periodically reported in finding enough food at the island? What of all the measures Tahitians routinely used to prepare and store their own sources of food against times of hardship? There were times when staple plants and animals were unavailable. And what about the comments that reveal that although the Tahitian populace did trade on their own account to some extent, their chiefs controlled most of the exchanges with Europeans? The local chief's demands on his people to surrender their crops and stock would have been more frequent and unpredictable every time a ship pulled in. There is also the basic point that the island's ability to provide provisions was the reason that the ships were there at all. The new materials, ideas, and relationships the Tahitians engaged with as a result of the provision trade could hardly fail to have a lasting impact.

In this chapter I will demonstrate that supplying animals and plants to Europeans did make a major difference to Tahiti. The trading and giving of food was central to relations between Europeans and islanders. It drove first contacts and shaped many of the negotiations that followed. The ecological exchanges of the provision trade did bring substantial changes to the complexion of life and the way people related to the Tahitian environment at the end of the eighteenth century. This chapter is my response to Langdon's thought-provoking "so what?"

Provisioning Voyages

On a long-distance voyage, dried and salted provisions alone could not keep a crew alive. If a journey across the vast Pacific Ocean was to be managed without the men dying of illness, fresh food had to be found at regular intervals. Europe's fascination with the Pacific began in the early 1500s. Basca Núñez de Balboa was probably the first European to catch sight of the ocean when he reached the west coast of South America in 1513. Not a pacific man himself, he stepped past the bodies of slaughtered Embera Indians to view the immense expanse of water his local guides had been telling him about, and named it for its apparent calm. He claimed this ocean for Spain, including all the lands it washed against. Spain's expansion of its national ambitions and its navies during the sixteenth century was soon followed by other European powers: Holland, France, and Britain. As each heard of the great stretch of sea, their leaders planned expeditions to map and secure their own corner of this tantalizing new region. The right to trade any newly discovered spices, timbers, minerals, jewels, furs, and rare foodstuffs would go to whoever could reach them first. Seven years after Balboa, the Spanish royal family sent out a ship under the captaincy of Ferdinand Magellan in search of lands of gold. The crew sailed nearly four months across blank ocean, catching few fish, becoming ulcerated and raw with scurvy, and eating rats, sawdust, and sea-soaked leather to try to stay alive. By the time the collapsing ship finally landed at Guam on the far western edge of the Pacific in 1521, much of the crew had died of starvation.[2]

Throughout the seventeenth and eighteenth centuries, Pacific voyages often lasted two or three years. The ships were small and crowded with sailing and anchoring apparatus, with casks of water, hencoops, and other stores lashed to the decks and stored below.[3] British ships carried barrels of salt beef, salt pork, butter, oatmeal, and rum, along with bags of bread and boxes of condensed and dried "portable soup."[4] James Cook and other captains loaded sauerkraut, vinegar, and essence of lemons to help prevent scurvy.[5] The provisions often did not last the distance. Bread moldered; grains were eaten by weevils and rats. Some casks, if poorly prepared, spoiled shortly after leaving England. There was livestock on board to supplement supplies. Chickens were used for eggs and meat, goats for milk. But keeping the animals alive was not easy; they, like the sailors, fell victim to seasickness, scurvy, and storms. As the animals provided the only fresh food on the ship, losing one was a particularly hard blow. Cook recorded at one point that severe gales had not only broken one of the *Endeavour*'s rigging plates and washed a small boat overboard, but, he said, "drown'd between 3 and 4 Doz^n of our Poultry which was worst of all."[6]

Even if provisions and provision animals survived intact, quantities were limited and never enough to keep a circumnavigation provisioned. Finding a safe place to take on fresh food and water was crucial. Captain Samuel Wallis, sailing across the Pacific, found such a place in June 1767: Tahiti.

Meeting Tahiti

Before leaving England in August 1766, every part of the twenty-four-gun frigate HMS *Dolphin,* even the steerage and stateroom, had been filled with provisions, stoves, and other "necessaries."[7] Captain Samuel Wallis, accompanied by Phillip Carteret in the storeship HMS *Swallow,* took five months to reach the tip of South America. When the supplies of butter and cheese ran out in October, Wallis started serving the ship's company daily with oil and with fortnightly doses of mustard and vinegar.[8] They then spent four months navigating through the Straits of Magellan, losing the old, leaky *Swallow* on the way. The *Dolphin*'s crew finally made it through the Straits in April 1767 into the open ocean. They kept an eager lookout for a new coastline. The secret instructions Wallis had received from the Admiralty were to look for the lands "of great extent" that were theorized to lie between Cape Horn and New Zealand, "in Climates adapted to the produce of Commodities useful in Commerce."[9] European philosophers argued that a huge land mass should exist here, to balance the weight of the continents in the northern hemisphere. As they progressed westward, privation and illness slowly set in. The rations of soup and antiscorbutics were no substitute for fresh, vitamin-rich vegetables or fruit, and the crew "began to look very pale and sickly, and to fall down very fast in the scurvy."[10] Their joints would have started to swell, their skin become ulcerated, their gums rot, their nerves become painfully oversensitized.[11]

They weathered another few weeks before a seaman finally sighted land on the horizon, on 18 June. Late the next day, with the captain sick in bed, the officers navigated the *Dolphin* toward this coastline, which had no presence on any of their charts. It could have been the edge of an island or a peninsula of a great southern continent. Whatever it was, it lay green, lush, and inviting before them, high, forested peaks in the center, running to foothills. A smaller, peaked island lay off to one side. The master said "we now looked upon our-selves as relieved from all our distresses."[12] As they drew closer, though, they could see this paradise was not entirely straight-forward: the beaches thronged with people. The *Dolphin*'s officers would need to negotiate effectively and quickly with these people, the cultivators and possessors of the island's food resources, to secure the sustenance they needed.

The islanders looking out on this tall, single-hulled vessel would have been transfixed.[13] They would have had unavoidably in mind the prophecy made by the priest Vaita in the 1750s.[14] One day, invaders from Pora-pora cut down one of the sacred trees at the great Ra'iatean sacred site, Taputapuatea, and Vaita the priest went into a trance. He declared that a different kind of people would come to the land:

> *The glorious children of Te Tumu*
> *Will come and see this forest at Taputapuatea.*
> *Their body is different, our body is different*
> *We are one species only from Te Tumu.*
>
> *And this land will be taken by them*
> *The old rules will be destroyed*
> *And sacred birds of the land and the sea*
> *Will also arrive here, will come and lament*
> *Over that which this lopped tree has to teach*
> *They are coming up on a canoe without an outrigger.*[15]

The *Dolphin*'s arrival was a turning point. This outriggerless canoe carried the threat of change. Other European ships had traveled near the island group, and islanders in the Tuamotus passed on news of meeting violent, white-skinned visitors in 1765: Captain John Byron and his crew on their circumnavigating expedition (1764–1766). For the Tahitians, though, the men of the *Dolphin* were the first non-Pacific peoples they had encountered. Their meeting would last several weeks. Like so many of those that would follow, the engagement was sustained by the travelers' need to secure fresh food.

As the early morning fog lifted from the *Dolphin* on 19 June, just off the island's rocky southeast coast, the seamen found themselves surrounded by a fleet of about a hundred canoes.[16] The ship's master, George Robertson, revealed the nervousness of the moment when he described the canoes having stopped "a pistol's shot away."[17] The islanders were calling out from their canoes and some stood to offer plantain leaves and speeches.[18] One of them, "a fine brisk man," paddled to the side of the ship, hoisted himself up the side and climbed rapidly up onto an awning where he was out of reach of the crew. He stood, laughing and staring down at the Englishmen. He would not take any of the "trinkets" being offered up to him but waited for his companions in the canoes to throw some plantain branches on deck, symbolic of human bodies and thus standing for a human sacrifice of appeasement.[19] This achieved, he was prepared to take gifts and to shake hands. A few more islanders came on board. George Robertson, who wrote a detailed account of the *Dolphin*'s stay, vividly described this first negotiation between Europeans and Tahitians:

> They seemed all very peaceable for some time, and we made signs to them, to bring off Hogs, Fowls, and fruit and showed them coarse cloth, Knives, Shears, Beads, Ribbons etc, and made them understand that we was willing to barter with them. The method we took to make them Understand what we wanted was this: some of the men Grunted and Cried like a Hog, then pointed to the shore— others crowed Like cocks, to make them understand that we wanted fowls. This the natives of the country understood and Grunted and Crowed the same as our people, and pointed to the shore and made signs that they would bring us off some.[20]

So it was through the cries of animals and gestures of barter that the two sides had their first functional communication. The animal calls could have been interpreted in any number of ways on the other side of the deep cultural divide, but instead of wondering if the visitors were displaying some sort of affinity with the pigs and chickens on shore, the Tahitians picked up their inherent request and accurately translated the gestures as an offer to swap goods. It was not long before they brought out the requested animals. But the ship's provisioning needs were a long way from being fulfilled. Continuing northward up the coast, looking for a sheltered anchorage, they were overtaken by sailing canoes hurrying ahead with the news. The next day, on the northwest edge of the island, the crew sighted a large, calm bay protected by a partly exposed reef with a clear entrance. This was Matavai Bay. It had a long, curving black sand beach shaded by coconut-laden palms, backed by hills covered in fruitful-looking trees, and a fresh spring to one side. The thatched houses visible through the trees were larger here than on the east coast.

Despite these inducements, the officers argued about whether they should risk an anchorage. Huge crowds were gathering on the beach. Some officers feared losing "our lives, Ship or Boats"[21] and advocated leaving immediately for the Spanish-colonized island of Tinian, in the western Pacific, where "all sorts of refreshments" were available. They decided to try to anchor in the bay, a fortunate choice for all those on the sick list: Tinian was 4,246 miles (6,833 km) away.[22]

Several days passed with skirmishes between the two sides. Flotillas of canoes would attack, throwing stones and trying to ram the English boats when they tried to sound for an anchorage or to get fresh water.[23] The sailors fired on the Tahitians, causing consternation when a man was shot and could not be made to sit up again. The islanders' first experiences of gunshot did not convince them to pull back from engaging with the strangers. Large groups of islanders persisted in coming alongside the boats, offering fruit, coconuts, chickens, and "fine fat Young Pigs" in return for hoop iron, nails, beads, and other small items.[24] Landing on shore was a different matter. Whenever the *Dolphin*'s men attempted it, great crowds, as many as a thousand people, gathered on the beach. Groups of women lined up, calling out, jeering, lifting their skirts.[25] The sailors pulled back to the safety of the ship. With a thick pall of incomprehension lying between them, establishing a relationship was no easy task. The English, however, could not retreat. Below decks the sick were getting worse.

The men on the *Dolphin* assumed the aggression directed at them was about defending the island, about the desire to take the boats, their goods, and, before long, the ship itself. The Tahitians were unlikely to have welcomed the prospect of the pale-skinned, strangely dressed creatures coming on land. They were beings ominously matching the "different kind" prophesied, and could be expected to have come to bring retribution and deep changes to the island.[26] Anthropologist and historian Anne Salmond sees the Tahitians' actions in this light. Furthermore, the dances the sailors saw as provocative were, she says, actually derisory, a performance of scorn usually directed at enemy warriors. Women's power was more *noa*, profane, than that of men, more closely connected to the dangerous, dark world of the dead, able to nullify men's more *ra'a*, sacred, power.[27]

Historian Greg Dening has suggested an alternative reading: rather than trying to repel the strangers, the Tahitians approached them through the metaphor of their relationship to the war god, 'Oro.[28] The beguiling presence of dancing girls and offerings of food were, argues Dening, the forms used to attract the attention and physical manifestation of 'Oro, who was the primary god being worshipped in the region at the time. When these acts failed to bring 'Oro to the sacred *marae*, the site where priests could present appeals and demands to the gods, aggression was one powerful response. Throwing stones at the embodiment of a spiritual force is one way to attract its attention, attention that can be then directed to specific purposes.[29] It is likely that the prophecy was guiding the Tahitians' responses to the strangers, and the Tahitians' aggression was directed at controlling the potency they expected the strangers to carry—whether by repelling it or by directing it to their own ends, in the same way they would direct the terrible power of 'Oro.

The Tahitians were still prepared to trade their fruit, pigs, and chickens in return for nails, but now if they attempted to "defraud" one of the mariners, the latter had only to point a musket—or a handheld telescope—at them and they would rapidly return the nail or deliver up the food.[30] With the stakes now much higher, the British seemed to have finally gained an advantage.

The next episode would be arguably the most influential of all the early encounters with Europeans on the island. On 24 June, after soundings had been made and the *Dolphin* guided into anchor, the marines were amazed to see a mass of about three hundred canoes approaching the ship. One was particularly large, powered by a substantial set of rowers and boasting a tall, ornamented prow. A woman and plenty of fruit and other produce were in each canoe. Some trading for provisions went on. Suddenly, all the women stood up naked in the canoes and began "practicing allurements"[31] until all the sailors were standing agog at the ship's rails.[32] When a signal was given from the "grand canoe," the Tahitians reached under the cover of fruits and leaves and started pelting the sailors with stones. In the mayhem on board, orders were barked out, muskets found and loaded, cannon readied and, with a huge cacophony, let loose. Many Tahitians were killed. The bodies of men and women floated beside the splintered canoes; the survivors pulled the casualties with them as they struck back for shore. A horrified stillness fell over the bay and neither side knew what to expect next (fig. 1.1).

It had been a shocking incident for all. Some of sailors had been injured by stones but they escaped relatively lightly. They had been able to make a useful display of their cannon. This was important. When traveling in the Pacific, European explorers were not in the strong position that we now tend to assume. Like most European crews, the "Dolphins" were vastly outnumbered and vulnerable. Although several later British illustrations of the

The Natives of Otaheite attacking Capt.ⁿ Wallis the first Discoverer of that hospitable Island.

The Interview between Capt.ⁿ Wallis and Oberea, after Peace being established with the Natives.

Figure 1.1. *W. Grainger, "The natives of Otaheite attacking Captn. Wallis the first discoverer of that hospitable island" and "The interview between Captn. Wallis and Oberea after peace being established with the natives." Engraved for* Bankes's New System of Geography *(London, c.1790). Based on J. Hall's engravings for John Hawkesworth's* Account of the Voyages, *1773.*

battle grandly depicted the ship surrounded by small canoes with three or four islanders in each, this was an understatement. The larger canoes were more than 90 feet (27 meters) long, each of them powered by some forty warriors.[33] A sixth-rate frigate like the *Dolphin,* like other Royal Navy ships sent to the Pacific, was not substantially bigger at 113 feet (34.4 meters), with 130 crewmen. Pacific islanders had nothing to equal the *Dolphin*'s great guns, but European firepower was by no means reliable. Muskets frequently failed in the thick of battles on island shores; the guns were too prone to failure when damp and too slow to reload when faced with sling-stones.[34] If it came to combat at close quarters, the ship's crew could be easily overpowered, even if armed with cutlasses.

Despite an awareness of their vulnerability, after repulsing the attack the crew began to feel some confidence. Ship's officers landed on Tahiti on 26 June, protected by marines waiting in boats close by. No one met them. They were able to stand together on the beach, turn a sod of earth, plant a flag pole, raise the English jack, and "take the island" in the name of King George III.[35]

A small group of islanders watched the officers' proceedings. They approached slowly with plantain branches and pigs. An old man came forward, making a speech. The lieutenant in charge accepted what he read as the Tahitians' "Emblems of Peace" and gave them some nails and trinkets in return. Master Robertson reported that after filling the water casks safely, they rowed back to the ship and "now thought ourselves very happy, and made very little doubt of getting all sorts of refreshments soon."[36] The group of islanders went up to the flag with caution, took it down, and carried it away. The red pennant would later be sewn onto the most potent embodiment of temporal and sacred power in the Society Islands: the *maro 'ura* (a feathered sash or "girdle") named Te Ra'i-puatata.[37] The *maro 'ura* was made from sections of finely woven netting covered with red and yellow feathers, to which a new length of feathers was added at the inauguration of each new *ari'i maro 'ura*. This object was a centerpiece over which bitter wars between the main chiefdoms of the island had been fought and would continue to be fought.

The morning after the flag planting, on 27 June, the Matavai war fleet gathered in the bay and a group of "several thousand" men were seen on the shore carrying the flag.[38] Alarmed, Wallis ordered a heavy round of fire into the fleet, the crowd on the beach, and on a hill some distance away.[39] It is not known how many were killed. Among those wounded was a young man called Ma'i. He would later get to know the British and their homeland well, meet the British royal family, and acquire more marks of

European contact in addition to the gunshot wound on his hip. For the Tahitians at Matavai Bay there was no mistaking the importance of appeasing these unpredictable visitors. They worked to repair the chasm that had opened up, and they chose to do this in the most effective way they knew: presenting the British with gifts normally given to gods.

Eight large pigs, four piglets, "two fine fat Dogs" trussed up ready for butchering, a dozen chickens, fruit, and six large bales of *tapa* (barkcloth) were laid out on the beach. A lieutenant went to collect the gift, picking up the part he and his countrymen valued most: the food. He let the dogs free and left the *tapa* where it was. He placed gifts for the Tahitians and rowed back to the ship, watching through his telescope. The Tahitians would not pick up his gifts. They continued to wave plantain branches and carry themselves with anxiety until the ship sent another boat to collect the cloth. This done, the islanders could see that the exchange had been properly enacted; the gift of appeasement and bond of obligation had been accepted. There was "Joy in every one of the Natives' faces."[40] They were then prepared to take the British gifts and more pigs and fruit were brought to the beach. It was from this point that a settled exchange relationship was established.

Wallis and his officers set up a system for managing the trade. The ship's gunner took up occupation on one side of the Matavai River and indicated with gestures (no doubt including the leveling of muskets) that no one was to cross without permission. He allowed only a minor chief of the region, Fa'a, and a younger man thought to be his son, to be the purveyors of Tahitian foods. This had the effect of alienating the higher-ranking chiefs, who refused to send anything from their districts, and encouraged the locals to sell only their inferior produce, leaving once they had secured the trade goods they wanted.[41] The daily haul was meager. The *Dolphin*'s attempt to control the trade was failing.

The situation was resolved when one of the island's most influential women, Purea, arrived from the southern district of Papara. Purea was the former wife of Amo, *ari'i* of Papara, and although she was related through marriage to some members of the Pomare clan, she was operating in competition with them. Purea could see the possibilities these potent visitors offered for her project of building up the props of sacred power to establish her son as high chief—*ari'i rahi*. She took the radical step of establishing a Tahitian bond-friendship with a European, making Wallis a *taio*, binding him and his crew to her family.[42]

The *taio* system in operation in the Society Islands was a long-established means of integrating people from other islands, severed from their own family connections, into the fabric of local society. A Tahitian man who adopted another man as a *taio* would have acquired in essence another brother, someone with whom he shared tasks, obligations of mutual assistance, material possessions, and usually his wife, if she was willing. The relationship involved trading names and genealogies, and enacted a kind of integration of identities.[43] It was not just chiefly men and women and captains who enjoyed these bonds. Landowners and others created *taio* friendships with midshipmen and seamen. Being adopted as a *taio* gave the visitors an entrée into Society Islands life. In most cases a *taio* provided protection and useful contacts for diplomatic arrangements, in addition to supplying provisions and arranging large gift exchanges. When a bond was formed between a chief and a ship's captain, as between Tutaha and Captain Cook in 1769, it created a pervasive and long-lasting strengthening of the community's involvement with the visitors and their material possessions. The Europeans often recognized the responsibility and at least some of the significance of the role of a *taio*.

Purea's presentation of gifts to Wallis clearly displayed her authority to the visitors. Wallis welcomed Purea's gifts of food, cloth, and friendship and gave her a return gift of exotic goods. They assumed she was the queen of the island. It was a major strategic achievement for Purea, one the Pomares had failed to make. The significance of her act was neatly turned on its head in the first published image of the occasion, in John Hawkesworth's 1773 account of the voyage. This engraving, titled "The surrender of the island of Otaheite to Captain Wallis by the supposed Queen Oberea," was later printed with a caption describing the scene more aptly: an "interview" between the two after peace had been established (see fig. 1.1).

Purea started directing operations, and the trade flourished into a warm relationship and a ready flow of goods. After she visited the ship on 20 July, Robertson reported the ship had received more provisions in one afternoon than in the previous three days. "In all," he said, "we got forty-Eight Hogs and pigs, four dozen of fowls, and a great Quantity of all sorts of fruit."[44] With the increased quantities of fresh food, the captain and crew recovered. Here at last was the kind of trade they had been hoping for, and it had come about through the decision of a local leader. The ship had become crowded with pigs and chickens, enough for Wallis to feel confident about leaving some of the ship's English livestock behind as part of a gift to continue the good relationship with his *taio*. On 24 July he sent Purea:

> two turkies, two geese, three Guinea hens, a cat big with kitten, some china, looking-glasses, glass bottles, shirts, needles, thread, cloth,

ribands, peas, some small white kidney beans, called callivances, and about sixteen different sorts of garden seeds, and a shovel . . . and other things.[45]

The *Dolphin*'s men planted a range of seeds in a garden for her, and they "had the pleasure to see them come up in a very flourishing state."[46] The planting continued. John Gore arranged an excursion into the Papeno'o Valley, led by Fa'a and including marines and twenty-four armed seamen. They saw houses with pigs and chickens around them, fenced gardens and grounds of a "very pretty appearance," neat plantations of breadfruit and *vi*—a fruit like an apple—in rows, all irrigated and growing in a "rich fat earth." Gore planted peach seeds, cherries, plums, limes, lemons, oranges, and other garden seeds where he thought they were likely to thrive.[47] The visitors were already augmenting the land, imagining return journeys and future provisioning. On 27 July 1767, farewells were made, and the visitors raised anchor and sailed for England with news of their discovery.

During their brief three-week encounter the Tahitians had learned that any attack on the visitors would result in a swift and deadly response. They also realized the inadvisability of coming together in very large groups within sight of the ship. They would certainly have had no doubts that what these visitors hungered for was food and they had a ready interest in women. The British for their part had learned that the islanders were forceful warriors and challenging tacticians. While many of the Tahitians' actions remained inexplicable, they had demonstrated a persistent willingness to barter and give gifts of food that kept the British optimistic about the usefulness of the island for meeting their immediate and future needs.

A Climate for Commerce

Giving and trading food would be central to relations between Tahitians and Europeans over the next half-century. Ecological exchange in the form of gift giving, bartering, and the provision trade would continue to bring them into uneasy contact, forging relationships and substantially shaping their experience and understanding of each other.

As the early voyagers started to witness the structures of Tahitian society, they saw structures they felt they could comprehend. Both the English and French were from hierarchical societies with an ultimate leader surrounded by a court and a politically powerful priesthood, an aristocracy, a tier of landowners, supported by commoners. They recognized analogous divisions within Maohi society. The visitors were also part of a maritime establishment that operated in a strict hierarchy of power, and they were particularly attuned to discerning and according respect to those with rank. While this assurance meant the early voyagers missed the complexities of Maohi power structures, the result was that Tahiti's attractiveness as a provisioning stop was heightened as the visitors felt they could engage with rulers and their supporters and have some expectation of a predictable outcome.

The Maohi lived in family-based households (*'utafare*), sharing not just a house but a cookhouse, garden, and a small sacred ground—a *marae*. The people lived in chiefdoms (*teva*) (see map I.2) under the direction of a chief—an *ari'i*, who could trace descent back to the gods. The *ari'i* had a separate residence from the populace and possessed exclusive regalia and rights. An island would also normally support an *ari'i rahi*, a paramount leader who was the sacred head, not necessarily possessing ultimate political power. Each *ari'i* possessed a retinue of men and women of noble birth, *teuteu*, attending on his (or, sometimes, her) desires. Chiefs did not have to touch food, being fed by retainers, and they required respect from their people as well as "tribute" payments of food and materials. Chiefs were *ra'a* (sacred), and their *mana* (sacred power) was hereditary, passed down through generations from the originating gods of creation. Most *ari'i* were male, but there were also chiefly women, with powerful lineages behind them and abundant personal power, employing this to manage the potency of their lineages stretching ahead of them.

A number of Society Islands also supported the *'arioi*, an aristocratic society whose members bore tattooed marks of status and devoted themselves to dance, song, and sexual performance in their worship of the god 'Oro. They had large lodges built for them and when they traveled between districts or islands, performing and feasting along the way, the locals were obliged to support them. British commentators pointed to aspects of the *'arioi*'s sensual decadence and exploitation of social inferiors as parallels to the aristocracy back home. *Tahua*—priests—occupied a place that European observers would have found familiar, at the right hand of the monarch, managing communications between gods and chiefs and holding considerable power in the affairs of state. Below all these high-ranking individuals were the *ra'iatira*, a class of landowners, who oversaw people to work their lands and maintained, whenever possible, amicable alliances with the seats of secular and sacred authority. There were classes of high-status warriors and highly skilled specialists: master carvers, doctors (*tahua ra'au*), professional fishermen, tattoo specialists, orators. And at the base there were the commoners. These people, the *manahune*, were the primary workforce in food production and on building projects. They were, to varying degrees, *noa*, ordinary or profane. They often held little property of their own and little attention was paid to them by those at the top of society.

In April 1768 the *ari'i* and people of the Hitia'a region on the east side of Tahiti received the island's next European visitors when the *Boudeuse* and *Étoile* anchored nine months after Wallis' departure. The local *ari'i*, Reti, and his people had heard from the people of Matavai Bay about the risks attendant on this kind of visitor, as well as what kept them happy. Being on a different part of the coast and staying only ten days, Captain Louis-Antoine de Bougainville did not hear or see signs of Wallis' visit and assumed he was the first European to reach the place. He too took possession of the island in the name of his king.[48] Like Wallis, the Frenchman was scouting for territory that would be useful to his government, either for establishing a colonial outpost or gleaning new commodities for trade.[49]

The islanders greeted the crew by offering fruit and pigs. They also sent out a woman wearing a ceremonial gift of finely beaten barkcloth (*tapa*), which she let fall once she arrived on board, releasing ancestral power through the act of unwrapping.[50] After negotiation Reti granted the crew use of a patch of land for a limited period of fifteen nights. The sailors ran riot and helped themselves to the island's pleasures. The ship's naturalist, Philibert Commerçon, judged the air on the island to be particularly "pure and healthy"; the men suffering from scurvy "were cured there in five days."[51] Their recovery was assisted, he said, by the "many simples, plants, and trees which promote good health," including "cardamine, a great antidote to scurvy."[52] He also decided the climate was suitable for growing the fruits and vegetables already being grown in France's South American colonies. On the hills he sighted thick plantains more impressive than those growing in Martinique and noted that "the islanders raise pigs, goats, and chickens, which are about the same there as in Europe."[53] His inclusion of goats in the list is intriguing; a goat is a hard thing to mistake. He may have remembered incorrectly when writing up his report, or perhaps Wallis had left some of his goats behind, although the crew would surely have recorded such a substantial loss from the ship.

Bougainville had arrived during one of the harvest seasons (*ta'a'oa*, moving into *au-unuunu*), and although the season of scarcity was approaching, the islanders were still able to supply plenty of fruit, fish, and shellfish. To obtain all this food the crew offered "axes and other kinds of utensils, nails, locks and pieces of iron of all kinds."[54] Commerçon was glad to report that the islanders would:

give a pig in exchange for a single [nail]; they would offer chickens and fruits in profusion for the smallest scraps of iron which they found so useful in holding their canoes together.[55]

Bougainville described the many charms of the island's resources and people, concluding, "This country is finer and could be wealthier than any of our colonies."[56] He decided to embellish the island's usefulness by asking that a patch of Reti's ground be cleared for a garden. Reti was "greatly" pleased by this suggestion and helped with the clearing. Bougainville reported, "We sowed in the presence of [Reti] the cacique and to the great satisfaction of the people, wheat, maize, beans, peas, lentils and the seeds of various vegetables."[57] While Commerçon wrote:

> Mr de Bougainville made them plough a small square in which he planted wheat, barley . . . lemon and orange seed (which were absent in this island) with many other domestic seeds such as cabbage, salad, rape, lettuce, chervil, parsley, etc. We showed them how bread was made with wheat . . . In case these seeds did not succeed the first time, we gave them a second set of all the seeds.[58]

They also made a "very precious" gift of a pair of turkeys (leaving no more on board), explaining that they were for breeding, not killing.[59] Bougainville named the island Nouvelle Cythère, finding it suited his imagining of the birthplace of Venus. The overall picture he presented, of friendly islanders, lush vistas, delicious foods, sensuous public performances, and attractive women, readily available, was of an island stopover ideally suited for weary mariners. He said it was "the true Utopia."[60] This was despite the frequently tense situations that flared up over thefts, to which the soldiers responded by shooting people at point-blank range or attacking them with bayonets. Peace was brokered, however, and when the French weighed anchor five days short of their allotted fifteen, Reti asked that they take as a passenger Ahutoru, a man of about thirty-five or forty, who was a chief's son and Reti's *taio*. He traveled with them to France, becoming the first Pacific islander to reach Europe. He enjoyed the pleasures of Paris and soon verified the voyagers' accounts of Tahitian amiability, the "natural" charm of their manners, and their titillating sensuality.[61]

Despite the enthusiasm for the place, the French did not immediately follow up on the potential identified in Tahiti. The ill-fated du Fresne and 1785 La Pérouse voyages, neither of which made it to Tahiti, would be the last French expeditions to the Pacific for some time. With political unrest and revolution erupting at home, the Pacific slipped out of focus.[62] There were no further French visits until Jules S. C. Dumont d'Urville's scientific expedition stopped at the island in May 1823.[63]

Meanwhile, in England, the Lords of the Admiralty had decided the island could be immediately useful. A scientific expedition to the Pacific was already in planning by the time Wallis returned in 1768. The main aim was to make observations of the transit of the planet Venus across the face of the sun, a rare astronomical event that, when accurately timed, would enable astronomers to calculate the distance of the Earth from the Sun.[64] The Marquesas islands, which had been vaguely located by Alvero de Meñdana in July 1595, had previously been selected as the observation site. News of the discovery of Tahiti, well-charted, with ample provisions and welcoming inhabitants, redirected the voyage's trajectory. Joseph Banks, a lively young naturalist of the Royal Society and one of the expedition's primary supporters, was particularly glad to hear of this safer and more charming site for his researches. The *Endeavour* expedition, commanded by James Cook, set sail in 1768. Cook's orders called on him to carry out astronomical observations in Tahiti, stock up thoroughly on provisions, then continue Wallis' search for the southern continent. They stayed from April to July 1769. After the negotiations over the use of land to set up their astronomical observatories, all the gift giving, *taio* friendships forged, trade, and tussles over thefts, the British and the Tahitians were able to establish a more complex set of relationships, stronger bonds, and a deeper comprehension of each other.

Managing Europeans

The Tahitians capitalized on their visitors' demands for fresh food. They used the desire for provisions as leverage to manage relationships with the Europeans and to negotiate for valuable trade goods in return. The fish from the reef, the fruit on the *vi* tree in the garden, the taro in the field, and the chickens around the house could be transformed into a range of benefits, material, political, and spiritual.

The chance to secure exotic commodities from Europe in return for the everyday produce of the island was an extraordinary opportunity. The items the islanders traded for were often made of materials otherwise unobtainable on the island, such as iron and glass, and were practical, often status-laden objects. They ranged from iron nails, scissors, ribbons, mirrors, glass bottles, or small, transparent beads of varied colors to iron axes, woven cloth, clothes, storage chests, and, most potently, muskets, ammunition, and powder. When a ship arrived, the people rapidly gathered up armloads of food, filled canoes and paddled out to meet the hungry crews.

As ships arrived erratically, and stayed for unpredictable amounts of time, the islanders wasted little time starting up the trade. Arthur Bowes of the convict transporter *Lady Penrhyn,* when arriving in July 1788, gave a (somewhat hyperbolic) description of the degree of enthusiasm for engaging in exchanges:

> By break of Day, the canoes were alongside in great numbers & frequently we had not less than 500 on Board at a time, they stuck about every part of the rigging & Ships Sides like Ants upon a Mole hill.[65]

Iron nails provided the islanders with finer, more resilient points for carving, drilling, and tipping fish hooks than coral, stone, or wood. Compared to stone blades, iron axes and adzes made lighter work of cutting wood, preparing food, and digging. Ready-made clothes and lengths of cloth were durable and had a vibrancy of color or a fine, smooth whiteness that made them peculiarly attractive. Preparing, beating, and bleaching a length of thin, white *tapa* from the bark of the paper mulberry tree (*Broussonetia papyrifera*) was five or six days' work. It was a valuable possession, but it could be torn and soiled quite readily.[66] The officers' white bedsheets and lengths of European trade cloth were useful alternatives.

The new trade items Tahitians were obtaining were valued not only for their practicality; they also inspired creative innovations. As historian Anne D'Alleva has shown, women decorating sheets of *tapa* experimented with English scissors to create intricate new designs, cutting sheets with vandyked edges and pasting striking, finely detailed geometric shapes of a darker *tapa* over the top of a lighter ground (fig. 1.2).[67]

Tahitians incorporated European goods into their internal trade systems and gift exchanges. Traditional courting gifts from a man to a woman comprised baskets of white, half-opened *tiare* flowers (*Gardenia taitensis*), puddings, or some leaf-wrapped fish.[68] After European goods became available, elders started advising young men that a suitable gift would be scissors and trade cloth.[69]

Many of the imported objects carried particular weight as claims to status. Possessing a marine's scarlet jacket, a naval officer's cocked hat, a kaleidoscope, or a knife demonstrated a relationship with the powerful, well-armed visitors. The meanings these clothes and other items carried for the islanders were largely opaque to the Europeans. The goods acted as trophies of politically powerful allegiances, symbols of material wealth, and high-status adornment. All these values created a fashion for things European. Women wore white sailors' shirts, European hats, ribbons, and

Figure 1.2. *Detail of a late eighteenth-century Tahitian* tapa *tunic with scissor-cut designs of dyed* tapa *on a bleached ground. Full size 89.7 x 46.2 in. (228 x 117.5 cm). © The Trustees of the British Museum (Oc,Tah.102).*

shoes when they could obtain them. At one formal dinner on board the *Providence,* George Tobin described the attire of the "royal family." With the exception of Tu, who "seldom put aside his native dress for european finery," the chiefly family wore their recently acquired gifts in a distinctively Tahitian style. 'Itia wore a "crimson coat with gold button holes," a present from Bligh to Tu, with a sheet wrapped around her like a skirt, taking the place of a traditional *pareu* of *tapa*. Her sister wore a blue dress jacket and a tablecloth *pareu*. In Tobin's eyes 'Itia looked "truly ridiculous," but 'Itia knew the value of this innovative style on shore.[70]

High-ranking visitors to the ship's great cabin for a meal typically studied the cutlery, crockery, and furniture. Some Tahitians arranged for local versions of these to be made to furnish their own houses so they could receive their British guests in a style they felt was suitable.[71] Tahitians would ask ships' carpenters to make them wooden chests like those owned by the sailors to store the important goods they had collected. By 1792 George Tobin was able to state that most people had their own chests for valuables. Beyond objects of utility or of dress, the islanders also sought out objects they simply found interesting. Tobin, a collector of intriguing paraphernalia himself, was entertained by seeing a parallel urge amongst Tahitians: "they have at *O'tahytey* their *Collectors,* and their cabinets of *European curiosities.*" He said that the high priest Ha'amanemane:

> was in possession of a volume of the 'Statues at large', which he had procured from a vessel that had touched at the Island, on which he placed as much value as some among us do, on a . . . petrified periwinkle, or . . . a stuffed baboon.[72]

This was the distinct practice of obtaining objects with the intention of keeping them, as opposed to that of acquiring objects for consumption or trade—it was "collecting" in its most essential sense, a practice usually assumed to be the preserve of Europeans.[73]

It is important to note that some of the most effective trade goods the British brought with them were things that mirrored the Tahitians' own valued tools and objects. We need to be cautious of generalizations, as Nicholas Thomas has warned, and wary of seeing islanders as engaged in trading away their island's resources because of an irresistible captivation with frivolous European things.[74] When Tutaha visited his *taio,* Cook, aboard *Endeavour* in 1769, he asked the captain to open all the drawers in the great cabin so he could select the presents he wanted. After he had picked out a pile of objects, he spotted a Tahitian-style adze, made of English iron. He immediately gave back everything else and asked for this single object.[75] Another powerful example lies in the fact that initially, the most potent trade valuable a European could bring was something not from Europe but from other Pacific islands: red feathers. Red was a favorite color of the gods, and bird feathers drew on connections between gods and birds. Red feathers, used in a ceremonial context, were seen to be particularly useful for catching the favorable attention of a god. Members of Cook's crews were only able to obtain a few of the dramatic, elaborate Tahitian mourner's costumes (*pare*), on the second voyage, when they at last arrived with a trade item worthy of the exchange: red feathers from Tonga.

All these items brought in through the agency of European voyagers were crucial to the smooth running of the provision trade.

Were it not for the Tahitians' interest in obtaining those goods, the trade in provisions would have foundered, as it did for Cook on the southeast coast of Australia in 1770, when Gweagal and Dharawal people opposed Cook's landing party and did not accept any of the gifts they offered.[76] Without a way of setting up a trading relationship, Cook despaired of being able to secure sufficient provisions and quickly moved the *Endeavour* further north. Society Islanders were keen to negotiate and encouraged their visitors to stay and keep the trade going for as long as possible.

Governing Provisions

Motivated by a range of factors which included an acknowledgment of the material and political advantages brought by outsiders from other islands and beyond, Polynesians, particularly the Maohi, generally worked to keep relations with visitors on an even keel, mend breaches of trust or respect, and extend the existing *taio* system to include the newcomers in the operation of local relationships.

In other islands where leaders did not enact formal friendship bonds, captains and their crews were much more at risk from rival political and religious leaders. During Cook's stay in Tonga, for instance, where no bond of friendship had been established with the captain, a local leader apparently (it was reported some years later) had plans to kill Cook and his officers in order to secure the ships and their crews.[77]

A pastel drawing composed by an unknown artist after Bougainville's return from Tahiti shows the magisterial captain, seated and receiving a bowl of fruit from a bowing islander. It would have been an appealing image, reflecting the paternal relationships Bougainville had portrayed in his account, reflecting the advantages of the settlement he had suggested. But it was a fanciful presentation of the power relationship. It ignored the complex of power relationships, the necessary negotiations, that outsiders could not sidestep, particularly if they wanted to obtain food.

Captains and their officers could attempt to manage the provision trade, but too much lay in the hands of the *ari'i* and other stakeholders for such attempts to be completely successful. Soon after arriving in Vaitepiha Bay in August 1773, George Forster and his companions hungrily eyed up the pigs they saw on their excursions inland, but the locals "were always

Figure 1.3. *Anon., Tahitians presenting fruits to Louis-Antoine de Bougainville, attended by his officers. Undated (1768?). Pencil and watercolor on paper, 3.6 x 2.7 in. (9.2 x 6.9 cm). National Library of Australia, Canberra (nla.pic-an6045157).*

careful to hide them in low styes, covered over with boards, forming a kind of platform, on which they sat or lay down." Although they offered all manner of trade goods, the "constant answer" was that the animals were the *ariʻi*'s property.[78] *Ariʻi* had formal mechanisms for controlling the use and distribution of their district's resources, as did the owners of specific fishing places, groves, plantations, and taro fields, systems that had been practiced for generations beyond number. Tahitians managed their own "provisioning" carefully.

The Maohi managed their production and consumption of the living elements in the landscape around them through a detailed calendar of seasons charting the growing, fruiting, and harvesting seasons of the year. The activities of plants, fish, and other animals gave shape to each season. According to the calendar described by the *arī'i* Tu in 1818, the Tahitian year was divided into thirteen moons and adjusted locally according to food supplies. Late June to early July was the season of 'Apa'apa, the "descent into the time of scarcity," when the leaves of plants yellowed. It was followed by the season Paroro-mua ("first fall"), when several plants, including turmeric and ginger, stopped producing.[79] So, as 'Apa'apa approached, the islanders started to hold back, keeping food to sustain them in the leaner time approaching. As each season arrived, the relevant gods and spirits were engaged, "first fruits" were offered as each new crop arrived, and the fertility of the next crops were ensured through appropriate ritual and offerings. The subtle mapping of seasonal scarcities and abundances of specific fruits, seafoods, and root crops helped to ensure a sufficient supply to keep families from starving. The time to make and preserve breadfruit paste was carefully observed to ensure enough food to last through September and October, the season of Hia'ia—"Cravings."

During Cook's first visit to the island, provisions were abundant for the first part of the stay, but from late June to their departure in mid-July, they "got very little refreshments of any sort."[80] He found it was difficult to get breadfruit, he could only provide the crew with two pork meals a week, and the islanders were reluctant to part with their fish. Few chickens were in evidence. At first Cook thought that his capture of some of the islanders' canoes in an attempt to force the return of a stolen piece of equipment had made them unwilling to come out to barter. But, he later admitted, "it was not wholy owing to this but to a scarcity; the season for bread fruit was wholy over and what other fruits they had were hardly sufficient for themselves."[81] It took time for the Europeans to recognize these fluctuations. Wallis' and Bougainville's visits were too brief to allow cycles to be discerned but long enough to gain some understanding that an overflowing abundance was not the island's perpetual state. Each new voyager noted the quantities available, and as the Tahitians and Europeans learned more of each others' languages, the Tahitians could communicate about fruiting seasons and competing demands on foods, which gave the Europeans a better understanding of the rhythms of food production. Later voyagers could determine the production cycles of the highly important staple, breadfruit, and take this into account when planning their voyages.

The Maohi knowledge of the world, recorded in chants, stories, and explanations handed down through generations, enabled a powerful understanding of the ebbs, flows, and requirements of the living parts of the world. Fish, for instance, were a fundamental part of the Maohi world. The island itself was originally a fish, hauled up out of the ocean by the demigod Maui. British observers in the 1770s noted that Tahitians were able to name 150 types of fish, at least 48 of which were edible.[82] Techniques for catching fish were highly refined, based on generations of careful observation, ranging from the types of fishing to be carried out under each phase of the moon (whether to fish from the reef or from a canoe, which types of light to use, and how particular kinds of fish would be moving)[83] to naming particular congregation spots of tuna.[84] Specialized types of hooks were made for specific types of fish, and nets for shallow lagoons, reef fishing, deep water fishing, up to the huge salmon nets (*upea ava*) that several communities would collaborate on constructing.[85]

Fishermen had their own sacred *marae,* and in addition to making prayers and offerings there, some fishermen had rights to employ a *tapu* stone or coral object called a *puna* to control the movement of marine creatures. A heavy, torpedo-shaped form of polished basalt at the British Museum is a possible example of a fish *puna,* and an abstract turtle form in coral at the Musée de Tahiti et ses Îles has been identified as a *puna honu* for managing turtle.[86] Turning the head of the *puna* inland would bring the relevant fish or turtles to the shore; turning it out to sea would send them away.

Maohi techniques for storing foods, protecting breeding stocks, and ensuring staggered ripening patterns provided some insurance against droughts, cold seasons, and the destruction of groves by hurricanes. As we will see in chapter 5, the process of preparing and preserving breadfruit paste was finely regulated to protect it from physical and spiritual contamination.

Ari'i managed the resources of their regions to ensure their own political and spiritual security as well as the well-being of their people. One of the *ari'i*'s most effective means for managing exchange was the placing of a formal restriction—a *rahui*—on the consumption of particular natural resources. The system worked to retain certain groves or specific types of animals for privileged, usually sacred purposes. Food was regularly required by *ari'i* and landowners for making offerings to gods, holding feasts on ceremonial and social occasions, and for rebuilding stocks after a destructive rampage by enemy warriors. Some *rahui* were cyclical, regularly restricting consumption in a district over a recurring seasonal period or ceremonial phase.

Rahui could also be called when a proprietor wanted to bring a temporary halt to consumption of a particular resource. For instance, the principal owner of a rock-cod or albacore tuna congregation spot could install a tassel of bamboo leaves on the nearby reef or on a recognized place on shore to indicate its restricted status.[87] The restriction may have been enforced simply through the proprietor's personal influence or the possibility of physical retribution, but it is also likely that the proprietor's spirit associates (spirits of ancestors particularly) would have been invoked to watch over the restriction.[88]

District-wide restrictions were also enacted in response to events, such as the death of a high-status individual. During the mourning period there would be a *rahui* on eating during the day, on launching canoes for fishing, and on lighting fires for cooking.[89] Such *rahui* were put in place after the mid-eighteenth century to control the use of food while a ship was at anchor. According to James Morrison, people from all around the island would flock to Matavai or Vaitepiha Bay when they heard that foreigners had arrived. They would typically arrive with some provisions but would soon barter them to the visitors and expect to be fed by the host district. Some *ari'i* took to instituting a *rahui* to stop the consumption, encourage the crowds to dissipate, and thereby avoid a local famine. An *ari'i* knew that neighboring districts could supply the ships in the interim.[90]

The *manahune* had ways to manage shortfalls in food. A single fruiting tree could be owned by several families, with the produce shared between them. As we will see in chapter 5, there were formalized systems in place to enable families to ask their neighbors for gifts of fruit when needed.

Tussles broke out from time to time over who had the right to cut down, pick, or collect particular resources and, when these were traded away, who had the right to keep the payment. One of the officers on the *Dolphin* devised a method of determining which trees a landowner was prepared to have cut: he would hammer a nail into each tree he wanted, and if the owner took out the nail and kept it, the tree would be felled. It was left standing if the owner returned the nail or pointed out an alternative tree.[91] In one instance, says George Robertson, a "great dispute" occurred after an elderly owner of a tree took out a nail in consent. A "stout well-looking man who seemed to be one of their chiefs" came up and took the nail, on which there were a "good many ill-natured words" between them. At that point Purea and her retinue happened to be passing and, hearing of the dispute, restored the nail to the old man, after venting her anger on the perpetrator of what she felt an inappropriate act of repossession.[92]

Governing Crews

The operation of ecological exchange is typically shaped by relationships of power, not only between the two sides entering the exchange, but internally within each group. Within Maohi society an *ari'i* could not guarantee complete control over the consumption and trade of plants and animals within his region. Despite the severe risks involved in transgressing a *rahui,* for instance, there are a few accounts of people doing so. One report includes a chief explaining the sudden death of one of his retainers by saying he had secretly eaten pork during a *rahui,* a useful explanation to have circulated.[93] The challenge of maintaining authority over the use of food and other ecological resources was one that was shared by European captains.

On arriving in Tahiti, captains endeavored to control their crew's trading. They issued orders to ensure that the provision trade was managed efficiently, orders the sailors initially tended to follow. They concurred on the importance of laying their hands on something to eat other than grimy salt beef and year-old bread. As James Morrison of the *Bounty* reported:

> Imediatly on anchoring, an order signd by Mr. Bligh was stuck up on the Mizen Mast, Prohibiting the Purchase of Curiosities or any thing except Provisions—there were few or no instances of the order being disobeyd, as no curiosity struck the seamen so forcibly as a roasted pig & some breadfruit.[94]

As the sailors became better fed, though, the orders became harder to enforce. Wallis was the first to discover the difficulties of maintaining discipline over the exchanges. There was little that could keep his men in check when they discovered that many Tahitian women were prepared to offer sexual hospitality in return for a piece of English cloth or iron. Some of the women took to indicating with unmistakable hand and finger gestures that iron nails of certain sizes could earn the sailors dalliances on a graduated scale.[95] Despite the captain's orders, backed up by floggings, the men traded away all the nails they could find, drawing out the large ones that had held up their hammocks and, as Wallis discovered with horror, even pulling out the cleats pinning the planks of the ship's hull.[96]

The market for provisions was at risk of collapsing if the crew satisfied the Tahitians' desire for European goods. George Tobin reported that sailors wanting souvenirs and exotic objects to sell on returning had disrupted the provision trade:

> A scarcity of cocoa nuts was observed about this time in the public stock, and other provisions were brought in but slowly. The eager demand for shells, ornaments and other *curiosities*, however publicly discouraged, occasioned this scarcity.[97]

If a captain was to ensure sufficient food for his crew in harbor and on the onward journey, he had to avoid the trade stalling like this. He also had to try to control the price of provisions. There was a high degree of agreement amongst the Tahitians, of all ranks, on the current value of any one item. Joseph Banks chose to give up on obtaining a pig offered at a high price soon after he arrived in 1769, knowing as he did "from the authority of those who had been here before that if we once did it they would never lower their price." [98]

The price of pigs rose steadily from voyage to voyage, and whereas a large nail could buy a pig "Sufficient to Dine 20 Men" in 1767,[99] by 1777 Cook found the Tahitians required an axe for a pig and "they would not now so much as look at" nails and beads.[100]

There were instances where collusion between a ship's crew and the Tahitians undermined or flew directly in the face of a captain's authority. When Captain Bligh started commandeering all the live pigs and pork brought onto the *Bounty* for ship's provisions, even those the sailors had bought personally, James Morrison reported that the Tahitians helped the men by waiting for Bligh to go on shore before paddling out to bring "provisions to their friends." [101] Bligh discovered this and ordered the mate to keep a book of the number and weight of all pigs brought onto the ship, but James Morrison reported with glee:

> the Natives took to another Method which was Cutting the Pigs up, and wrapping them in leaves and covering the Meat with Bread fruit in the Baskets, and sometimes with peeld Cocoa Nuts, by which means, as the Bread was never seized, they were a Match for all [Bligh's] industry; and he never suspected their artifice. By this means provisions were still plenty.[102]

Despite all the management measures employed by captains and chiefs, there was only so much that could be achieved. The back-and-forth of deals and persuasions over supplying provisions was, throughout the period, a complex, sometimes slippery process of negotiation. In addition to this, there was an element of unpredictability in the availability of provisions that would always evade management. Regardless of how enthusiastic an *ari'i* was to trade away the products of his region for cloth and iron, regardless of the pressure and enticements the Europeans brought to the meetings, there was only so much that could be done about the range of environmental and social circumstances that led to a crop to fail or the population of a food species to fall.

Implications of Provisioning

> *Where none contest the fields, the woods, the streams:*
> *The Goldless Age, where Gold disturbs no dreams,*
> *Inhabits or inhabited the shore,*
> *Till Europe taught them better than before,*
> *Bestowed her customs, and amended theirs,*
> *But left her vices also to their heirs.*
>
> *Away with this! Behold them as they were,*
> *Do good with Nature, or with Nature err.*
> —Lord Byron, *The Island,* 1823 [103]

There were repercussions for Tahiti's being drawn into the cross-hemisphere trading network for commodities. In the 1790s, with growing islander demands for the artifacts available through this network, a parallel unease grew in Europe. There were concerns about the speed at which Tahitians were giving up traditional ways of life. Commentators fretted about what they saw as a loss of innocence, an original, simple purity being sullied by the contamination of industrial, scheming, grasping, exploitative "civilization." [104] Images painted and drawn in Tahiti during the eighteenth century studiously avoid depicting Tahitians wearing anything but Maohi *tapa* or Maohi ornaments or holding anything but Maohi objects. The experimental integration of materials and styles described in texts were rarely permitted a presence in the artworks being created at the same time. John Webber, William Hodges, George Tobin, and others intended to capture for the audience back home the "true nature" of the place and its people. They were unwilling to show in their idealized visions the troubling evidence of change their own presence had sparked.

It was in journals and travel accounts where the realities of the changing Tahitian experience were aired and discussed. Bligh wrote of his dismay at the change he saw in the Tahitians by the time he returned in 1792. Every "blackguard expression" the sailors used had been picked up by the locals. They had discarded their elegant *tapa* robes for European "rags," and the shirts, waistcoats, and coats were shabby from long use and starting to disintegrate. They were, he said, "no longer the clean Otaheiteans, but in appearance a set of Raggamuffins with whom it is necessary to have great caution in any intercourse." He declared, "I would rather forfeit any thing than to have been in the list of Ships that have touched here since April 1789."[105] Writing in the early 1800s, George Tobin wondered, "What does the future promise?" Traders from British colonies were starting to arrive in growing numbers. These traders knew that for "a dozen Muskets and a good proportion of ammunition" they could get "an abundant supply of provisions."[106] The typical trader cared little, Tobin felt, for the destructive effects of these commodities and only wanted:

> refreshments and supplies, to enable him to prosecute, in this distant quarter of the globe, his greedy scheme of gain—and if Gunpowder, or pernicious enervating brandy, should be demanded in preference to the useful Axe or ornamental bead, will they not be given without reflecting on the consequences?[107]

The guns and brandy were European versions of existing Tahitian slingstones, clubs, and the debilitating narcotic *kava,* but—as we will see in the final chapter—on entering the island these imported commodities worked in ways that unsettled existing political relationships.

George Vancouver wrote in 1792 that the rapid adoption of iron tools had rendered the Tahitians "regardless of their former tools and manufactures, which are now growing fast out of use."[108] The speed and frequency of timber cutting increased, something that would have carried an environmental impact. Naturalist George Forster observed that between his leaving the island in September 1773 and returning six months later in April 1774, a fleet of 159 war canoes had been constructed in the Atehuru district (comprising Pa'ea, Puna'auia, and Fa'a'a), a feat which he guessed could not have been accomplished without the importation of iron tools.[109]

Tahitian women continued to make and experiment with *tapa* into the nineteenth century, but because of the increase in imported cloth, the decrease in demand for *tapa,* fewer people to tend groves in the wake of introduced diseases, and (as we shall see) increasing competition from imported plants, the prevalence of the groves of the paper mulberry tree dropped. In the early 1800s the missionaries reported that many of the former plantations had been abandoned. There is little *tapa* manufacture in Tahiti today.

The broader ecological impacts of provisioning primarily stemmed from the surge of consumption of the island's plants and animals every time a ship stopped by. When Cook's second voyage arrived at Tahiti's isthmus in 1773, they found a *rahui* had been placed on the local pigs. James Burney pondered the possible reasons behind the ban and in doing so took the unusual step of stopping to consider the impact of European consumption. He suggests that the "Hogs & fowls carried off the Island by European Ships within this 5 or 6 years must have greatly thinnd their number & made this prohibition necessary."[110] Since the arrival of Captain Wallis, he decided, the English and French ships that had stopped for weeks and months at a time must have, "at a moderate computation, consumed 2000 Hogs."[111] This was a modest guess, but a valid point. Islanders' consumption of pigs was generally restricted to ceremonial occasions. Sudden and intensive consumption of local species would have placed pressure on their populations. Occasional comments by voyagers do point to plummeting populations of food species, but it is not possible to disentangle pressure caused by those plants and animals being used as provisions and pressure caused by seasonal and climatic fluctuations or the impact of overconsumption by a visiting group of *'arioi*[112] or wartime destruction of stock, groves, and crops.

It can be safely asserted that increased consumption would have resulted in reduced resources for the local inhabitants. Households with fewer pigs, bare breadfruit trees, empty *fe'i* banana plantations, or diminished taro reserves would have had to manage their meager state until they could re-establish some stock. They could do this by calling in a return gift, trading with more prosperous neighbors in less depleted districts, or waiting for whatever remained of their breeding or seed stock to mature. In that transitional period, though, food for immediate consumption would have been scarcer, less would have been available for trade with other regions or islands for anything but essentials, and more work would have been needed for the cultivation of plants and animal husbandry. At a time when there would have been a greater need to call on the help of ancestors and other protective spirits, offerings of food to ask for assistance would have to be more modest.

This is not to suggest that the process of ecological exchange could not be managed; we have seen that the Maohi had enough experience of lean times to know how to cope. But the key issue is that those dictating the terms and the number of plants and animals to be traded away to provision ships were not usually those who had to do the work of raising the crops and animals. While provisioning was likely to cause hardship for the *manahune*, the island's elites had little to lose and much to gain. The ceremonies at the state *marae* that the *ari'i* needed to carry out could still be achieved through bringing in pigs and other food for offering from further afield. Turtles, dolphins, and sharks, the highest-caliber offerings, stood outside the foods required for the European commodity trade.

Finding Familiarity

As passing ships and visiting expeditions spent more time in Tahiti, its exceptional usefulness as a place to provision was cemented. As we saw earlier, British mariners gradually distinguished the graduations of Maohi society and saw in them analogues to their own social structures. The visitors were particularly attuned to identifying and relating to the world through a framework of rank. Their own identity was bound up with social class and status, and each also occupied a position within the clearly defined hierarchy of the maritime establishment. For them, it was a particular stroke of good fortune to have found a society in the middle of the Pacific—which could have been organized and governed through any perplexing means— that actually possessed many points of apparent comprehensibility. Perceiving a social hierarchy among the Tahitians provided the visitors with a way into Maohi society, suggested ways to proceed, and gave a leverage point to try to secure the food, goods, and sexual contact they desired. Some were particularly optimistic about their ability to manipulate the local situation. Joseph Banks, with Wallis' claim over the island in mind and a flush of elated confidence after his first walk around the Matavai district, said the scene before him "was the truest picture of an arcadia of which we were going to be kings that the imagination can form."[113]

The pattern of European ships stopping to engage with Tahiti's people and resources changed over the decades. During the 1770s they appeared reasonably regularly, every year or two. Then, without warning, after Cook's final visit to the island in 1778, ten years passed with no ships from Europe stopping by. The American War of Independence and the French Revolution occupied European attentions during the 1780s. This was the start of renewed period of European interest in and ability to pursue Pacific expeditions, particularly from Britain. In October 1788, three months after the convict transporter *Lady Penrhyn* left Tahiti, Captain Bligh arrived aboard the *Bounty*, wanting to trade not just for provisions but a shipload of plant seedlings. In the two years from 1791 to 1793, nine British ships visited in quick succession.[114] All stopped at Matavai to take on provisions and to engage in other exchanges, ecological and otherwise.[115] The importance of provisioning for bringing Europeans to Tahiti was to remain firmly in place into the nineteenth century. Governor King said in 1802 that Tahiti was "the only island that needs little or no precaution for the safety of those who visit it."[116]

Cosmological structures prevalent in the western Pacific and Australia created different sets of interpretations of the arrival of visitors to those common in the eastern Pacific. Island groups such as the Solomons and Vanuatu had long histories of rival groups arriving to attempt hostile take-overs and, from the 1500s, sporadic and destructive encounters with Spanish and French voyagers. Europeans who made landings in this region, often in the face of strident opposition from the locals, only stayed briefly and returned to Europe with stories of spear attacks, cannibalism, and disease, all of which acted to keep ships' crews wary of the western islands well into the nineteenth century.[117] The goods offered by Europeans were not valued in the same way throughout Oceania. Some trading for provisions in the Vanuatu archipelago was achieved during the second voyage, but relations were troubled. Cook came away with the conclusion that the ni-Vanuatu "seemed to have no notion of exchanging one thing for another."[118] The statement reveals how superficial the interactions had been and how wide the gulf in understanding had remained. Cook did not return.

The Tahitians, accustomed to the persistent requests from Europeans, looked beneath the statements from naval commanders, scientists, and missionaries about their lofty reasons for stopping by and developed a more down-to-earth assessment. Some Tahitians asserted that Europeans came to the island expressly for pigs.[119] In 1803 the missionaries, after years of making very vocal proclamations about their purpose, were dismayed to find that because England had no breadfruit or coconuts, the Tahitians assumed the missionaries had come to the island "on account of their sweet food, as they are pleased to call it."[120]

At the heart of the matter, whatever additional motivations Europeans had, many ships had indeed come, and continued to come, into Matavai Bay because above any other island they knew, Tahiti offered such "sweet food" so readily.

Conclusions

Ecological exchange—and provisioning in particular—did have an impact on Tahiti. Of all the islands in the eighteenth-century Pacific, Tahiti played host to the greatest number of ships over the most extended period. The early commencement and persistence of the provision trade meant the impact on this island was acute. The island is still noticeably affected by its long history of feeding the European maritime establishment.[121] Supplying quantities of pigs, fruit, fish, timber, root crops, and other plant and animal products to European ships created new tensions, new relationships, and new demands on the island's ecology. Being the favored Pacific provisioning post of British voyagers also meant the island was selected for a range of other ecological exchanges, bringing Cook with his livestock and Bligh in search of breadfruit. The social, ecological, and political implications of provisioning continued to make their mark on the island. As became increasingly clear in Tahiti, providing provisions did matter.

CHAPTER 2

Conceptual Landscapes

When Europeans came to Tahiti and looked out on the palms, hills, and clouded peaks, the landscape they saw was not the landscape the Tahitians saw. The breadfruit, pigs, and fish the Europeans took on board were different from the breadfruit, pigs, and fish the Tahitians were handing over. The two cultural groups had radically differing ways of conceiving how the world worked, the mythologies and deities that operated within it, and the role plants, animals, rivers, reefs, and storms had in relationship to themselves. These types of conceptions form the bedrock of how human societies operate. The Tahitians' and Europeans' conceptual landscapes shaped how they moved within and interacted with their own environments and how they responded to the living members of other environments. The visions, understandings, and expectations about Tahiti's landscape had a fundamental role in determining the exchanges and events that took place there.

The rights Europeans felt they had in Tahiti to move within and make use of parts of the natural environment, and their deliberate transgressions of cultural and religious boundaries in order to get to some desired resource, brought them up against Tahitian methods for responding to such transgressions. Conflicting beliefs about what was most important about the natural world kept islanders and Europeans frequently at loggerheads.

Captain George Vancouver and his crew arrived at Matavai Bay in January 1792 (three months before Bligh anchored there in the *Providence*). The ship's surgeon, Archibald Menzies, took a long walk into Tahiti's interior with several island men to guide him. On the way he became increasingly thirsty. As they descended from the slopes they walked near a coconut grove cordoned off with boundary markers, probably a pair of palm fronds placed in the ground with a coconut suspended from a stick between them.[1] Menzies goaded his guides into entering the grove. They told him they could not, as every tree in the grove was "under a particular interdiction." It was *tapu*—prohibited, sacred. Menzies understood this, but he was persistent:

Figure 2.1. *William Hodges, "Vaitepiha Bay, Tahiti." 1776. Oil on canvas, 36.4 x 54.4 in. (92.7 x 138.4 cm). Painted for the Lords of the Admiralty. © National Maritime Museum, Greenwich, London (BHC2396).*

> I used a good deal of persuasion with them to go up one of the trees, which one of them at last did with much reluctance, while the other remaind at the foot of it emplyd in fervent devotion, & the first Cocoa Nut that came down, he cut off the top part of it & placed it on a bush as an offering for Tee & gave me the other part to quench my thirst, whilst he still continued muttering his prayer, which in a short time had the good effect of removing any squemishness of conscience he might have entertained against the use of this forbidden fruit.[2]

Menzies saw the grove as a source of refreshment, set aside by a superstitious restriction that would do the Tahitian men no harm—and probably some rational good—to break. How did the Tahitian men see the grove? The marked-off space was potent, laden with presences, needing care to avoid the danger it contained. The markers were indications that the grove was the property of a powerful entity, a chief or a god.[3] It was a space protected by watching spirits and was not anything that a humble man of ordinary birth and insubstantial spiritual power could tamper with without severe consequences. One of the men called on the god Ti'i or one of his ancestral spirits (*ti'i*), giving an offering and prayers, asking for help in assuaging the anger from the beings watching from the realm of the dead.[4] The living essence of the coconut offered would have been welcome sustenance to spirit beings. It may have helped to mollify the more malignant spirits, encouraging them to remain content in their realm and not enter the landscape of the living to seek vengeance. The Tahitians who accompanied Europeans through that living landscape often needed to find ways to manage serious transgressions, limiting the potential repercussions for themselves and their families and ancestors.

The fundamental difference between the perceptions of the two groups was that for Maohi the world of the living was changing, active, and fluid in essence, while Europeans held a more rigid, tightly classified view of the "natural world." The key divisions of the European cosmos lay between the world of humanity, the world of nature, and the world of the spirit (of heaven and hell). While angels and saints could operate between spiritual and mortal realms, ordinary human souls were less mobile, making the journey to the spirit world once, on death. Any other movements that were seen to occur between the three worlds—a ghost returning or a man degenerating into animal-like behavior—were rare and disturbing, shocking overturnings of the natural order.

The Maohi occupied a world in which the fundamental cosmological distinction lay between the world of the living—the *Ao*—and the world of the dead, the *Po*. The dividing boundary between the two realms was highly permeable. It was constantly being crossed by powerful, often dangerous, spirit beings that flitted back and forth between the realms, occupying birds, sharks, pigs, trees, stones, creating a landscape that was responsive, volatile, and full of alarms.

Enlightenment-era Europeans visiting Tahiti were usually unaware of the significances Tahitians read into their landscape. On the occasions when they glimpsed the activity of Maohi spiritual beliefs, it was usual for them to dismiss it, as Menzies did at the coconut grove, as a curious superstition rather than a legitimate cosmological construction. The voyagers were, for the most part, too embedded in their own *habitus*, their own beliefs and cosmology, to manage anything other than a stray interest and amusement at the foreign ideas they encountered along the way.

Gentlemen of science,[5] naval officers, sailors, and missionaries all brought a set of standards with them by which they judged the significance, beauty, and productivity of the Tahitian landscape. They also judged the degree of civilization of its inhabitants, which they measured to a large extent by the way people occupied and cultivated the land. All these judgments carried extensive implications for the nature of European engagement in the island. They looked out on Tahiti's landscape as an exotic entity; the distance between it and themselves was palpable.

Journeys through Landscapes of the Mind

> Before it can ever be a repose for the senses, landscape is the work of the mind. Its scenery is built up as much from strata of memory as from layers of rock.
> —Simon Schama, *Landscape and Memory*[6]

The broad sweep of a culture's conceptions of the natural world is highly complex, discernible at many levels, and operating in many important ways within a society. Strata of cultural memory form each society's bedrock of conceptions about the world around them, and on this is placed layer after layer of perceptions and priorities specific to each social group.

We can take simple routes through the broad terrain of British and Tahitian conceptions by tracing the approaches of some representative individuals. The naturalist Joseph Banks, ship's officer George Tobin, and the Reverend John Jefferson and some of his fellow missionaries provide useful ways through. They were each profuse record keepers and members of a distinct class and professional group. Finding detailed contemporary sources for individual Tahitian conceptions of landscape is more challenging, but the navigator-priest Tupaia left insightful records, and 'Itia and her family, being people of high status, moved through the environment and through engagements with European observers in a more visible way than most of their compatriots. Each of their specific experiences can illuminate a way into the denser general picture.

The three Britons—Banks, Tobin, and Jefferson—saw the Tahitian landscape through frames that provided a basis for judging new vistas against particular aesthetic criteria, against particular moral standards, using economic judgments, and based on particular assumptions about their God's creation. The frame was part of their British heritage, constructed of deep-rooted emotional and imaginative associations that stretched back through generations of legends populated with faerie queens, elves, the cathedral grove, the noble English oak.[7] Early Celtic and pagan mythologies meshed gradually with Christian approaches to the world of nature, combining with new symbols of nation and eventually with Enlightenment philosophies.

Before the eighteenth century, a Briton's reading of landscape was imbued with the closeness with which most people lived among fields, pastures, stock, poultry, and the wildlife of hedgerows, in what was pre-dominantly a rural life. In 1700, more than three-quarters of the population lived in the countryside.[8] The gentry possessed large estates worked by tenant farmers and cottagers, and teams of gardeners and laborers tended the neatly landscaped parks. During the seventeenth and early eighteenth centuries, the most stylish of these were laid out in careful classical geometry. Areas of "wilderness" on country estates were well-ordered plantings of trees, kept free of undergrowth and intersected with linear pathways.[9] The countryside occupied the energies of most Britons. But changes were under way. Commercial centers were flourishing—London most vigorously. An increasing industrialization and rise of manufacturing throughout Britain drew people off the land into the promise of more lucrative, excitingly urban, livelihoods. By 1800, nearly 40 percent of Britons were living in towns and cities.[10]

By the late eighteenth century the natural world had become for England's growing urban working and middle classes not a place of life or work but a separate entity, a place to be visited on trips out of the metropolis for relaxation, and an escape from the grime, smoke, and sulphur.[11] A country landscape could be seen as distinct and definable—an aesthetic vista, land, water courses, forests, farms, and sky above working together visually. The land had become objective landscape.

On country estates, the landed gentry occupied themselves, as the eighteenth century progressed, with altering their landscapes to keep in step with changing aesthetics. While basic conceptions about the natural world did not shift, Europeans were re-evaluating the ideal degree of closeness to nature. People were increasingly questioning the value of detached Enlightenment rationalism, generalized abstraction, and mechanization.[12] Many were looking to the purifying, uplifting power of nature as a source of spiritual redemption for souls corrupted in the march toward an industrial world. A growing range of writers, artists, and designers found inspiration in a more naturalistic approach, a reconnection to the wildness of nature, of emotional reaction and imagination. This movement, labeled Romanticism, by no means led to a unified canon, but some key treatises, such as the Reverend William Gilpin's on the picturesque and the sublime,[13] were broadly influential. Wanting to create harmonious landscapes, landowners constructed interesting vistas with naturalistic plantings, lakes, follies, and ha-has and other earthworks to keep agricultural stock controlled, attractively in the middle distance.[14] Landscape painters created similarly layered views, completed by a backdrop of dramatic mountains to uplift the senses and inspire feelings of the divine.

For the Romantics, the aesthetic value of a landscape remained under-pinned by its value as a place of production.[15] Keeping the land productive was increasingly challenging in Britain with the rural population draining away, and there were new challenges attendant on providing food for large town and city markets. This added extra significance to the role, in the cen-ter of the national psyche, of the essential, civilizing, wholesome practice of agriculture. All these aesthetic and practical concerns were taken on board ships to the Pacific.

Joseph Banks: Botanical Dilettante

Joseph Banks (1743–1820) approached the Tahitian landscape as he approached any new stretch of land: as a potential source of new species and curiosities that promised scientific and commercial advance. His fam-ily's large fortune and estates gave him the liberty to explore within and beyond Britain and to continue the family tradition of effecting agricultural improvements.[16] Banks had been educated at Eton, Harrow, and Oxford and found plenty of time at all three to botanize in woods and fields (his social position, as John Gascoigne has said, spared him "the tiresome neces-sity of having to take a degree"[17]). As a young man, he moved to London, joined numerous gentlemen's clubs, joined scientific discussions, and expanded his natural history and antiquarian collections. He established fruitful collaborations with, most importantly, Daniel Solander, a natural-ist at the British Museum and a former student of the great systematizing botanist Carl Linnaeus.[18] On dining with Solander and other friends in 1768, shortly before the *Endeavour* was due to depart for the Pacific, Banks expounded on "the excellent opportunity I now had to improve science and achieve fame."[19] Solander was fired with enthusiasm for the project and arranged to join it as Banks' botanical collaborator.

On each island and continental shore they touched, Banks and Solan-der eagerly went out into the new environments with their eyes on the foli-age, the rocks, birds darting past, and insects hovering about them. The specificity of Banks' vision meant he often missed the broader view. "Dr Solander and myself go upon the hills," wrote Banks on arriving in Ra'iatea in July 1769, "in hopes of finding new plants but ill rewarded; return home at night having seen nothing worth mentioning."[20] On the more rewarding shores, Banks set to work with the others gathering up samples of birds, shells, and foliage with accompanying seeds or flowers, taking over Cook's great cabin with swathes of greenery where the expeditions' artists drew and painted the specimens. They then pressed and dried plant samples, bottled fleshy animals in spirits, sorted shells, and skinned the birds they had killed to best preserve them for the journey.

In New Zealand, a Maori boy watched Banks' and Solander's behavior on the beach and later described the peculiar activities of the "goblins" who "collected grasses from the cliffs, and kept knocking at the stones on the beach." [21] A few of the boy's family offered up stones and leaves to these creatures, and they accepted some and discarded others. It was unusual behavior, with no clear explanation, and the Society Islanders must have seen the actions of first the French naturalist Commerçon, then Banks and his scientific entourage in Tahiti, with as much initial perplexity as the Maori observers had. The naturalists' intentions were by no means transparent. At one point early in the *Endeavour*'s stay an *ariʻi* decamped rapidly with his "household and furniture" on seeing Banks and his bird-collecting team preparing their guns and bags for a duck-shooting expedition. [22] By the end of the *Endeavour* expedition, Banks was able to state:

> The Number of Natural productions discover'd in this Voyage is incredible: about 1000 Species of Plants that have not been at all describ'd by any Botanical author; 500 Fish, as many Birds, & insects [of the] Sea & Land innumerable. [23]

In addition to being delighted with introducing knowledge of a great range of Pacific flora and fauna to Europe, Banks expected the specimens to fulfill "considerable oeconomical purposes." [24] Of all those he collected he thought those most promising were "the fine Dyes of the Otaheitians, & the Plant of which the new Zealanders make their Cloth, of which we have brought over ye seeds." [25] On returning to England, Banks worked on cultivating these Pacific plants at the Royal Botanic Gardens at Kew. Not many of Banks' Tahitian plants survived, [26] but his collection of preserved specimens and ethnographic artifacts made an impressive gift to the British Museum. [27] The Botanic Gardens soon gave Banks a directorship, and the Royal Society made him president, the British Museum a trustee. Well established through these high-profile achievements as a "statesman of science," [28] Banks advised the king and government on experiments in agricultural improvement, industry, and botanical exploration at home and within Britain's steadily increasing radius. The Pacific ecological cargo he had negotiated for had set him in good stead.

An intrigued public viewed the wonders from the *Endeavour* not just in public collections such as the British Museum and Sir Ashton Lever's Holophusicon (or "Leverian," see fig. 2.2), but also in private museums and collectors' cabinets around the country. The European fascination with the

Pacific, and Tahiti in particular, continued as voyagers continued to return with captivating collections, accounts, and images. Andrew Kippis noted in the first published biography of Cook (1788), that Tahiti had "opened new scenes for a poetical fancy to range in." [29] Aristocrats could give free rein to such fancies in the creation of Tahitian scenes on their estates, impressing guests with their fashionable exoticism. Sir Richard Hill, in his mechanized confection of a landscape in Shropshire, included a "Scene at Otaheite": a low reed hut modeled on an engraving in the account of Cook's second voyage, filled with bows and arrows, horns of animals, "idols," caps of red feathers and shell necklaces to "distinguish the manners and occupations of the

Figure 2.2. *Sarah Stone, view of the interior of Sir Ashton Lever's museum as it appeared in the 1780s, London, c.1835. The museum contained 28,000 "natural and artificial curiosities" typical of the period, including Cook voyage collections. 15.7 x 16.77 in. (40 x 42.6 cm). © The Trustees of the British Museum (Centre for Anthropology Pictorial Collection, Am2006-Drg54-Sto).*

inhabitants."[30] At Wörlitz in Germany, the Archduke of Dessau designed a Tahitian garden boasting a *marae* and an "Otahitisches badhaus"—a Tahitian-themed bathhouse.[31]

Banks' and Solander's collaborative work continued, their efforts directed at mapping the extent of the natural world. Like other Europeans of their era, they were working from a basis of seeing the original effort of God's creation as having brought the entirety of the natural world into existence at once, a finished masterpiece. Uncovering and recording the great breadth and wealth of God's creation had long been a driving force of Enlightenment endeavor, seeking to extend human knowledge through the application of reason rather than continuing to accept proscribed, centuries-old understandings of the world from scripture and the writings of classical authors. A growing posse of traveling collectors (professional and amateur) in Britain, the Americas, Asia, Australia, and Africa were collecting and organizing evidence of every example of the creation they could find and sending it to philosophers and scientists across Europe. In Britain and on the continent, the search for workable systems to classify the growing mass of specimens and information continued. Classifying animals, plants, minerals, and natural phenomena became a key philosophical and scientific activity.

Carl Linnaeus centered his system of botanical classification on the sexual organs of plants. It was later extended to classifying animals through their reproductive and circulatory systems, then by their specific bodily characteristics. Binomial nomenclature proved more enduringly applicable and flexible than the other systems developed in the same period, which defined plants and animals according to their environment or by their relationship to humankind. These latter systems worked from the basis of dividing the natural world into "edible/inedible" and "useful/non-useful,"[32] or (as in Buffon's classification) by their domesticity or wildness.[33] The plant and animal specimens picked up in Tahiti in ecological exchanges contributed to the expanding conceptions of natural systems as well as philosophical debates about the determinants and universality of human interactions with the natural world. Engaging in ecological exchanges in the Pacific carried implications for the development of ideas in Europe.

A considerable portion of the animals and plants the Tahitians bartered away to collectors over the late eighteenth and early nineteenth centuries were handed over as live specimens. Some were shipped back to Europe alive, and some of these survived the journey. Wallis returned with two pigs, presumably the first animals to arrive in Europe from the Pacific. He gave them to the secretary of the Admiralty, and, though the sow died, the boar

was reported to still be alive by 1773.[34] Thomas Haweis, a missionary returning from the Pacific in 1799, wrote to Banks that he had "an Otahetian Boar
& Sow at your service, or of any friends of yours who would value them." [35]
Cook's second voyage returned with three Tahitian dogs, and a few blue
and white *vini* parakeets successfully made the journey to England, perhaps
on the early Cook voyages and certainly on the *Providence* (fig. 2.3). A pair of
vini, perched stiffly on a branch, were painted by Sarah Stone around 1785,
possibly as one of her series of illustrations of specimens and artifacts at
the Leverian Museum. Stone's paintings are useful tools for provenancing
Cook's voyage collections, as she painted before the return of later Pacific
voyagers. [36] In June 1792, while the *Providence* was anchored at Tahiti, Lieutenant George Tobin employed a local man to bring him live parrots, green
doves, and *vini* parakeets. After three days, the bird catcher returned with
about two dozen. Tobin acquired about forty before leaving. "Great pains,"
he said, "were taken to bring them to England, but with scarcely any suc-

Figure 2.3. *George Tobin, "Parroquet of O'tahȳtey—Vēney [Vini]." 1792. Watercolor,
page 13.7 x 10.2 in. (35 x 26 cm). Sketches on HMS Providence, SLNSW, Sydney
(PXA 563 f.53).*

cess." They all died within a few months. He was happy to report that the gunner saved one pair of *vini* by "uncommon attention" and these, he was fairly sure, reached Lady Banks.[37]

These Tahitian survivors joined the exotic animals from Africa, the Americas, and Asia in privately owned menageries being incorporated into the broadening discussions over the workings and classification of the ever-expanding natural world.[38] It is not possible to determine the extent to which Tahitian examples of birds and plants contributed to theories about the creation, variety, and distribution of species, but the simple drawing of comparisons between new and known plant and animal types was a stimulus to debates. Haweis admitted to Banks that the Tahitian boar and sow, "to speak the truth," appeared "not to posses finer features, or to grunt more musically than our own."[39] It was exactly these similarities between far-flung members of a single type such as the pig species (*Sus scrofa*) that would lead to some of the more productive conclusions on the origins and development of species.

"The ardent researches of the traveller": George Tobin in Tahiti

For the Tahitians, by the time the *Providence* arrived in Tahiti in 1792, the sight of a European picking up and peering at stones, leaves, and lizards was commonplace. The islanders had responded quickly to the unprecedented market for segments and examples of their flora and fauna. Collecting seashells, seeds, and flowers, catching insects and birds, and cutting clusters of leaves for trade could be managed by the locals relatively easily (especially once the relevant spirit bodies were quieted). This appears to have been a more straightforward process than arranging food items like breadfruit, pigs, or fish, which were often heavily relied upon locally and always belonged to someone. Providing collectors with live specimens opened up possibilities for especially healthy profits, as the *Providence*'s second lieutenant, George Tobin, reported:

> One fellow really deserved much credit as a sharper. I had bargained for four of the beautiful little blue paroquets called *Vêneys* with a promise to call for them on returning. In about an hour after, he came lamenting that two had escaped from the cage. As I did not doubt his veracity he received the whole price, which was no sooner done than a boy brought two more and sold them, but we soon discovered by the looks of those around that the whole was a scheme to get double pay for the birds.[40]

Collectors needed to stay alert, but with so much willing cooperation from the inhabitants, Tahiti was an easy place to gather natural history specimens. Tobin pointed out that there were few hindrances: no poisonous snakes or dangerous animals "checking the ardent researches of the traveller."[41] He was fascinated by the island and the islanders and enthusiastically documented his explorations and discussions, painting scenes depicting himself and the islanders who guided him, collecting birds and fish, and illustrating them.

Tobin was of a merchant family, with connections to Caribbean plantations, and like other young men of his background, the twenty-three-year-old had already met a considerable number of foreign landscapes. He had joined the navy as a midshipman at the age of twelve, served in the Channel Fleet and in Nova Scotia, then as a mate on an East Indiaman merchant ship trading to Madras and Canton.[42] He wrote of his "anxiety . . . to embark on a voyage to the South Seas,"[43] and was delighted with the appointment with Bligh on the *Providence*. Sailing eight months from Spithead, Tobin and his messmates cherished their expectations of delicious food, good drink, and most particularly that "dearest solace life affords," in the arms of Tahitian women.[44] His enthusiasm flowed over into his writing of a journal in addition to his official log. He would have been schooled, like any naval trainee, in rendering accurate records of coastlines in ink and watercolor, and he did paint coastal profiles in his log.[45] Unlike other officers, more in the tradition of young Britons on their grand tour, he also recorded himself in word and image in the landscape of the new places he visited: the Cape of Good Hope, Tasmania, and then, finally, at his "long wished for Island," Tahiti.[46] Tobin later worked up his journal into a polished account of three hundred pages, illustrated with his paintings. He worked on it off and on until 1831, apparently never finishing it to his satisfaction—or perhaps just failing to secure a publisher's interest. The public's appetite for accounts of the Pacific had started to wane by the early decades of the nineteenth century, as the region's people and places grew more familiar. Tobin died in 1838 with his work still unpublished.[47]

While in Tahiti, Tobin had ventured out with his pockets "filled with different articles to exchange for any thing curious," fully aware that his eagerness for natural history specimens would expose him to ridicule:

> The natives ever laughed at the avidity with which such collections were made and to shew their contempt some brought a stone, another a feather, and so on, being highly delighted with the tricks they were playing on us.[48]

The laughter marked the extent of the cross-cultural distance over the appropriate value to place on these elements of the Tahitian environment. When Europeans collected odd, seemingly stray bits of the environment with no apparent purpose, any random, insignificant stone or feather could well be what the Europeans wanted, and that was why it was such a good joke.

There were also differences of value within the shipboard community over this type of ecological exchange. J. R. Forster, official naturalist on Cook's second voyage, was driven to exasperation by the sailors' gathering great quantities of shells and other specimens before he had a chance to get ashore. He knew they were collecting for the personal profits they expected from selling the shells in England rather than achieving the noble improvement of human knowledge that he saw himself pursuing. He was furious when a sailor offered to swap six shabby shells in return for half a guinea's worth of brandy.[49] When exchanging ecological curiosities, value was so much in the eye of the beholder it became a game of seeing what the vendor could get away with.

Drawing Out Conceptual Exchange

Tobin's careful, formal illustrations of Tahitian birds, fish, and breadfruit (see figs. 2.3 and 5.1) were modeled on familiar works of natural history. They showed the animal or plant in a view that allowed the viewer to distinguish the key features determining its classification, with perhaps a few generic plants as backdrop or a nonspecific branch on which a bird could perch. While theories about species developing in response to their environments were developing at this time, only some scientific illustrators were responding to this through their work by including a carefully observed rendition of the specimen's environment.[50] Tobin was sufficiently interested in the Tahitian language to ask his informants for the Maohi names for the species he drew, adding these to his captions and the extensive vocabulary he included in his account.

He also enquired about planting, production, and cropping techniques. The food plants he noticed and included in his scenes made the vista more admirable and worthy of reporting. With his amateur's eye and straightforward, largely *plein air* compositions (rather than carefully reworked studio paintings), Tobin's views lacked the flourishes of atmospheric effect, chiaroscuro, or sublime, misty distances employed by his contemporaries more fully and formally trained in the visual arts. Like other Enlightenment travelers, Tobin was interested in conveying the attractiveness of a view, but he also concentrated on illustrating the resources in the landscape that were of inescapable interest to a British mariner.[51]

He wanted to capture these aspects as accurately as possible, rather than conveying, as Cook voyage artist William Hodges did, the wonder of specific tints of a tropical sky and its exceptional cloud formations, or the philosophical nuances, drama, and sensuality of an island scene (see fig. 2.1). Tobin aimed through his paintings and text to illustrate both the beauty and utility of the Tahitian landscape for those who could not see and judge for themselves.

There were few demonstrable exchanges of ecological ideas between Europeans and Tahitians over the last half of the eighteenth century. It was one aspect of ecological exchanges that did not run readily. Such exchanges required a more sophisticated grasp of each others' languages than either side possessed, and needed more openness and respect for alternative

Figure 2.4. *George Tobin, "The Watering place, Matavāi, in the Island of O'tahȳtey, 1792." Watercolor, page 13.7 x 10.2 in. (35 x 26 cm). SLNSW, Sydney (PXA 563 f. 49). A note Tobin penciled to himself in the left margin reads "Make English* Among *the Natives." A red "W.B." indicates that William Bligh had selected the image for inclusion in his planned, but unpublished, book of the voyage.*

approaches. There is, however, one particularly striking example of a cross-cultural exchange of ideas about landscape that did not rely on language.

In the British Library's manuscript collection is a set of unsigned drawings of Pacific people and scenes from the *Endeavour* voyage. Until the 1980s they had been thought to be by a member of the crew who was particularly inexperienced at drawing; Rüdiger Joppien and Bernard Smith suggested Banks as a possibility.[52] Then Harold Carter, editing Joseph Banks' correspondence, found one of Banks' letters that mentions a drawing of a Maori man exchanging a crayfish with himself (the image on this book's back cover). He said it had been drawn by Tupaia, the Ra'iatean high priest who accompanied the *Endeavour* to New Zealand and Australia.[53]

Tupaia was of a high-ranking family, a member of the *'arioi,* and, by 1767, Purea's lover and closest political supporter. He was a respected figure in the Society Islands and something of a virtuoso. He was a ritual specialist, skillful navigator, and negotiator. Cook and Banks, on the lookout for a guide, felt he "was the likeliest person to answer our purpose." He provided navigational advice and a map of islands in the central Pacific, and, on reaching New Zealand, he was able to understand and translate the Maori language, which was based on his own. Maori communities respected him, and he was able to ease relations between them and their British visitors. On the southeast coast of Australia he was not able to provide any help with deciphering Australian languages, but he established a trusting relationship with the Guugu-Yimithirr people in northern Australia. He had intended to reach England, but he and his young servant Taiata fell sick and died in Batavia in December 1770.[54]

Accompanying Tupaia's crayfish drawing are several others: a coastal scene, a Tahitian dancer, a chief mourner in costume, a group of musicians, a *marae,* indigenous Australians in a canoe, all of them recognizably by the same hand. Tupaia appears to have taken the opportunity—offered to him by Banks or the voyage artists Sydney Parkinson and Herman Spöring—of creating images in a new medium.[55] He experimented with a pencil and watercolor on paper, a departure from the modes of creating images he was familiar with: tattoo on skin, a chisel into wood or stone, or (in the medium reserved for women) dye designs on *tapa.* Over May and June 1769, Tupaia would have watched Parkinson and Spöring make sketches around Matavai Bay, and, adopting the European style of depicting a portion of the environment as discrete and visually unified, he drew several images that rendered a three-dimensional view into two dimensions. His innovation was also, as Nicholas Thomas has pointed out, to make images that were descriptive.[56]

Polynesian images had functions: indicating genealogy and rank, projecting power, or calling on gods. Creating representative copies of a visible world was not the aim.[57] One of Tupaia's drawings is a shoreline scene with a house and canoes, surrounded by vegetation (fig. 2.5).

His resulting landscape drawing provides unique insights into the conceptions and priorities of a Polynesian man of the late eighteenth century. The plants in particular are intriguing. He has drawn each plant as a spe-

Figure 2.5. *Tupaia, beach scene with* fale, *vegetation, and war canoes, Tahiti (and detail). Pencil, ink, and watercolor on paper, 10.5 x 14.4 in. (26.7 x 36.8 cm). From folio "Drawings from Cook's First Voyage,"* © *British Library, London (Add. Ms 15508, f.12).*

(Detail at right)

cific type—it is clear that the shapes of the leaves, trunks, and branches are intimately known to him and the parts of each that are most important are emphasized: the fruits are clear.[58] He shows the roots of the pandanus reaching down into the soil. Taro, the staple root crop, is shown in the soil in x-ray style, thread-like roots radiating out from the tuber. In Tupaia's process of creating a landscape drawing and Tobin's process of creating paintings that accurately reflected the place and its ecological components, both men looked out onto the Tahitian landscape with their own culturally determined vision. Tupaia was open to a European reduction of the visible part of a complex, extensive place into a single, bounded plane. Tobin asked questions to uncover local meanings in his attempt to render the landscape more meaningful to himself and his audience. It was in rare moments like these that some of the most creative cross-cultural exchanges—exchanges of concepts about the visible environment—took place.

Moral Landscapes

In 1773 in Dusky Bay in New Zealand's South Island, Cook voyage naturalist George Forster wrote a lengthy passage on the triumph of cultivation, and therefore civilization, over the wild New Zealand landscape. It is worth quoting at length:

> The superiority of a state of civilization over that of barbarism could not be more clearly stated, than by the alterations and improvements we had made in this place. In the course of a few days, a small part of us had cleared away the woods from a surface of more than an acre, which fifty New Zeelanders, with their tools of stone, could not have performed in three months. This spot, where immense numbers of plants left to themselves had lived and decayed by turns, in one confused inanimated heap; this spot, we had converted into an active scene, where a hundred and twenty men pursued various branches of employment with unremitted ardour.[59]

They widened the course of a stream, flattened some ground for an observatory, cut tall trees for planks, and cooked up the "neglected indigenous plants,"[60] in a steaming pot while the philosophers and artists gave their attention to noting the "differences and uses" of the local animals.[61] All around them Forster saw the "rise of arts and the dawn of science," for a temporary moment. It was here that he had some of his most rewarding meetings with a group of Maori and drew particularly sympathetic conclusions about their society, yet he was doleful about any future for the "salutary and useful" seeds he had planted. He was sure they would soon be smothered by weeds and the chaos would take over again. The spot actually remains visible in Dusky Sound. As Nicholas Thomas and Mark Adams have documented, the point still bears stumps and thin regrowth. Cold climate forests grow and break down slowly, and the forest has not yet reclaimed this site of Enlightenment industry.[62]

European philosophers had been increasingly engaged with determining the causes of human difference since seventeenth-century voyagers had started to return with descriptions of new societies on the other side of the world.[63] Discussions gained pace and increasingly attracted systematizing efforts in the eighteenth century.[64] Of particular focus in determining order out of the mass of human complexity was the degree to which a society mastered nature. The basic "four-stage" model of development placed societies along a continuum from hunting and foraging to pastoralism, to agriculture, and finally to commercial society. Pacific societies did not neatly fit into this model (although fishing could be seen as analogous to hunting, and gardening analogous to pastoralism or agriculture).[65] Overlaying and working alongside such models, "primitive" and "civil" societies were variously encompassed using metaphors of infancy to maturity,[66] constructions of noble savages living in a state of nature through to depraved metropolitan sophisticates,[67] or hot-climate darkness of skin and sluggishness of temperament to temperate fairness and briskness of achievement.[68] Whether the paradigm hinged on climatic determinism or the force of culture over nature, it was the human relationship to the natural environment that was central.

Assessments of Tahiti by those on the *Dolphin, Boudeuse, Étoile,* and *Endeavour* took in the type of cultivation that was in evidence. Bougainville's imagining and naming of the island as Cythère implied a landscape that was fit for a deity, of which the Tahitians were the carefree heirs.[69] Banks, too, said "benevolent nature has not only supplyd them with nescessaries but with abundance of superfluities."[70] He wrote of the ease with which Tahitians could sustain themselves simply by planting a few breadfruit trees, and, he said, "the earth almost spontaneously produces" coconuts, yams, sugar cane, and thirteen varieties of banana.[71] These were romantic conclusions, drawn from his excited and superficial experience of the place. It was part of his vision of Tahitians existing in a pure, unencumbered "state of nature."

From Cook's second voyage, observers started to recognize the effort the Tahitians expended in cultivating their land.[72] Johann Reinhold Forster and his son George, the expedition's naturalists, noted with approval the extensive plantations, terraces, and stone irrigation channels for the taro fields. Voyagers were often still torn between admiration for the richly productive landscape with its happy inhabitants and disquiet over the relatively little work the Tahitians invested in making it productive.[73] Granted, there were numerous plantations of *aute* (*Broussonetia papyrifera*) and 'ava (*Piper methysticum*), but it bothered the European eye (particularly the Protestant, work-focused eye) that they were not kept neatly weeded. There were a wide range of useful plants being cultivated near the houses, but some were left unfenced, open to pigs and chickens to forage in. While George Forster reported he had his heart filled with "rapture" at contemplating the Tahitian's peaceful, simple life and the abundance of their fruits,[74] William Bligh blamed that very abundance for the people's moral shortfalls:

> So much sloth and indolence may be attributed to the vast support that all bountifull nature has given to them in the use of the most valuable of all Fruits of the Earth, the Bread Fruit and Cocoa Nutt.[75]

These many judgments were published in voyage accounts from the 1770s and, through English, French, and German editions, provided fuel for debates about production and the state of civilization. The implications of European readings of the landscape were not just philosophical. It made a fundamental difference to the relationship between Britain and Tahiti that the British generally judged Tahitians to be making productive use of their land. The British did not attempt to colonize Tahiti nor move in to indulge in intensive "improving" of the island's "neglected" forests. The landscape was too obviously someone else's property, and the inhabitants were already working it with what most considered suitable productivity. These conclusions were the diametric opposite of the conclusions drawn about Australia. British voyagers and colonial administrators judged that because indigenous Australians did not cultivate the land, they were letting it go to waste. The indigenous inhabitants kept on the move and gathered and hunted food, rather than settling on marked-out patches of earth, so the administrators concluded that the people had no claim to the land that they need honor. They argued Britain could legitimately establish a colony there. Perceptions of landscape carried deep consequences.

Taming the Exotic

Despite Britain's growing colonial confidence across the Pacific, there were limits to the assurance with which they ventured into the new landscapes.

Voyagers may have presented their mastery triumphantly to an audience at home, through journal descriptions of proud flag planting, assigning names, inserting their nation onto places already named indigenously, and in paintings of picturesque land ripe for exploitation. These were impressive declarations, but these men were operating in an atmosphere of almost constant uncertainty. The natural environment in each new place was strange and possessed an undercurrent of danger. Ocean waters contained hidden shoals and reefs; forests could rapidly become tangled and trackless. A meal of brightly colored tropical fish could poison the eater (as J. R. Forster discovered).[76] No landscape is ever passive—each place presented difficulties and dangers that got the better of travelers. Travelers found themselves subject to the landscape and at the mercy of those who did know the environment. When Tobin and William Frankland, the surgeon on the *Assistant,* went for an excursion to try to reach Tahiti's highest peak, they took a guide, who offered to carry Tobin's pistol, handkerchief, and the single coconut they had brought along for the days' journey.[77] The guide led them through dense, steep terrain thickly covered in fallen logs and vegetation, an exhausting, thirsty scramble. He then gave them the slip, taking their possessions and the now much-wanted coconut. It took Tobin and Frankland the rest of the day, struggling through the undergrowth, finding their way cut off by cliffs, doubling back and finally rediscovering the path, to make their way back down the steep hills, in the dark, to Matavai Bay.[78]

It had been a harrowing experience. Though Tobin makes light of it and his shipmates' teasing, the two men must have at times wondered if they would make it back at all. A drawing that Tobin composed in the early part of the walk, when the guide was still with them, shows his sense of being engulfed by the landscape (fig. 2.6).

Unlike his more typical paintings, with the figures in command of their environment, central and substantial in the frame, the view of "Matavai Bay, and the Island of Tetharōa" shows Tobin and Frankland sitting wearily, passively on a rock. The guide stands over them pointing out a view, the ferns towering heavily above them, dominating them and the scene. It is at such moments that the dynamics of the relationship between the Tahitian environment, its inhabitants, and its visitors are apparent. These dynamics gave shape to their exchanges, and, as the progress of trade, gift giving, and negotiations were underpinned by relations of power, it is important to recognize that European travelers did not automatically and simply see every landscape as lying before them awaiting their guiding hand.

The effort European visitors made to "tame" threatening landscapes by naming and conceptually domesticating them was also applied to the exotic

Figure 2.6. *George Tobin, "Matāvai Bay, and the Island of Tetherōa, from the hills, South of the Bay. O'tahȳtey, 1792." Watercolor, page 13.7 x 10.2 in. (35 x 26 cm). SLNSW (PXA563 f.36).*

food species they encountered. *Uru,* a hard, green, segment-skinned fruit the size of a person's head, with a starchy white flesh, became *breadfruit.* The round *vi* fruit, with a mature diameter of about three inches (about seven centimeters) and a yellow skin became the "Tahiti apple" for the British and, for the French, "Pomme Cythère." Each new type of fruit, nut, mammal, bird, crustacean, or fish was compared to and slotted in alongside a familiar species of flora and fauna. Thus the Tahitian pig was said to be as good as could be found at Leadenhall Market; a fish described as not unlike a cod in shape; a bird said to resemble a pigeon, despite its purple and orange plumage.[79] Familiar things that were known to be good to eat were additionally useful—consciously or not—as a guide to what was likely to be edible and nontoxic in new environments that lacked otherwise readable signs.

The Europeans who visited Tahiti—especially the mariners—had a strictly regularized approach to portioning and trading the readily consumable parts of the natural world. The naval establishment arranged foodstuffs by dividing them into standardized measures, allowing ease of management and ensuring that each seaman had his allotment of carefully accounted for daily portions of meat, breads, grains, and antiscorbutics. The increasing to and fro of international commerce also demanded recognizable measures. Captains surveying exotic foods such as breadfruit, taro, and coconuts as shipboard provisions needed to find ways to standardize them. Standardization would bring them into the smooth operation of the ship and the purser's accounts. Captain Bligh kept a particularly close eye on the value of provisions he bought for the crew of the *Bounty*.[80] On making it back to England after the mutiny, Bligh approached the Victualling Office with his "Number and Content Book," seeking reimbursement for the Tahitian provisions he had purchased with his own trade goods. The Office reported Bligh had received on 25 March 1789 in Tahiti:

> 10,600 pounds of Yams, equal to 5,300 pounds of Bread. 1,060 pieces of Pork of four pounds each, and 25 live Hogs, equal to 435 pieces more; . . . The amount of which, at the credit prices allowed by this office, is £64.19.7.[81]

This piece of calculation exemplifies the rapid commodification of exotic plants and animals that accompanied Britain's push into the Pacific. Bligh and the Victualling Office were able to conveniently equate a pound of the dense, starchy taro to half a pound of the sailor's usual bread. One Tahitian pig, despite the widely variable sizes and degrees of plumpness of these animals, would (according to Bligh) yield a tidy average of seventeen standard naval "pieces" of salt pork.

Tahitians had their own ways of counting the measures that were important. There were words to convey the sense of number in a shoal of fish or flocks of birds, and there were words for individuals and small groups of things. All these terms were useful when bargaining with Europeans. The more complex Maohi conceptions and categorizations of the world were visible only in glimpses when Maohi made transactions with the spiritual entities around them. The deeper meanings were silent partners in most of the exchanges, shaping Tahitian approaches but remaining beyond the understanding of most European visitors.

Border Crossings

While Tobin was on a walk with a small party to view the *marae* near the northern coast in May 1792, he came across several palm trunks carved into tall, slim stacks of human-like figures (fig. 2.7). The women traveling with him told him this carving was called a *ti'i* (an abbreviation of *ti'i-potua-*

ra'au).[82] Tobin referred to it as a "God of Gardens" and continued on his way.[83] To a Tahitian viewer, the *ti'i-potua-ra'au* was a boundary marker and it signaled the need for caution. It indicated a restricted, sacred piece of land. A figure of this sort was carved from a single tree from a chief's *marae*. It was designed to attract and accommodate guardian ancestor spirits, providing them with an abode from which to keep watch.[84] Some observers suggested they may have also been designed to encourage the fertility of a field or a region.[85] Whether watching over a restricted plantation, a *marae,* or a burial ground, the spirits in the *ti'i* provided protection. Anyone transgressing

Figure 2.7. *George Tobin, "Figures, called Ettēē. Island of O'tahȳtey. Carved on a tree, 1792." Watercolor, page 13.7 x 10.2 in. (35 x 26 cm). SLNSW, Sydney (PXA 563 f. 50).*

the correct forms of behavior while nearby could expect to be punished by their chief or by the *ti'i*'s spirits, who would bring sickness and misfortune.[86] The area near the *ti'i* could be permanently restricted or, in the case of a plantation, the raising of the *ti'i* could mark the start of a temporary *rahui*.[87] Tahitian viewers knew they needed to change the way they moved within that portion of land (usually lowering their clothes from their shoulders) and change the way they responded to the living elements within it.

The cosmos the Maohi occupied centered on their cluster of islands in the middle of a deep, broad sea, covered by an overarching, layered canopy lit by the sun, moon, and stars. It was populated by living things: people, plants, animals, fishes, insects, all living in the *Ao*. The *Ao* was a space containing the living and light. It was a temporal space, encompassing the day. It was the source of positivity, prosperity, knowledge, insight, clarity, health, and happiness. The good reign of a chief would be referred to poetically as *Ao*.[88] Mortal humans, animals, and plants lived in the *Ao*. When a living thing died, its essence (*iho*) became a *varua*—a soul—and entered the *Po*.[89] This was the crowded realm of the dead, full of greater and lesser gods and the spirits of dead ancestors. The *Po* was the night. It was the source of darkness and illness, of hidden, incomprehensible things, bad fortune, and death.[90] Combined, these two opposing realms formed the cosmos.[91]

Ta'aroa, the Maohi's original and most powerful god, lived in the *Po*. Several gods closely associated with Ta'aroa and creation also occupied this space: Tu, Tane, 'Oro, and Atea. Below them were the *atua* with more specialized responsibilities, such as Tipa (the primary god of healing) Hina (god of the moon, once wife of Ta'aroa). Least powerful, and most populous, were the minor *atua*. They included local gods who oversaw specific districts or portions of the sea, tutelary gods of kin groups or of occupational groups such as fishermen. Members of a valley, a lineage, or a cooperating team of fishermen maintained their own small *marae*. They would make gifts and ask favors of their particular *atua*. Lower-ranking gods would also preside over risky events such as childbirth, canoe travel, and activities imbued with *mana*—such as archery, making *tapa*, and fermenting breadfruit.[92]

Gods of various ranks could slip out of the *Po* and into the *Ao* in several ways. Some entered temporarily or on a longer-term basis into an *ata*, an object or being selected by gods for manifestations.[93] Sharks, dolphins, turtles, and pigs could contain gods, and the islanders consequently treated them with care. The *ata* of the deity Tumu, who originally held the sky and the earth together, was appropriately the great spotted octopus (*fe'e*). This octopus was the "natural" embodiment of Tumu. It was accorded respect at all times, as it could at any time be possessed by the god.[94] A particularly large or distinctive rock could be the permanent residence of a localized divinity. The less divine entities that occupied the landscape—small woodland sprites, for instance—had *ata* that were much less portentous and more common, such as the gray duck *mo'ora oviri*.[95]

Negotiating with gods required careful selection of gifts of living things, killed and brought to the *marae* to allow priests to offer their essences up for consumption. According to a chant recited by two high priests of Tahiti and Mo'orea, *marae* were the "sanctity and glory of the land; they were the pride of the people." They were also a "place of dread and of great silence . . . a person's errand must be to pray in going there, but for no other purpose." It was the basis of laws, of the ruling family; "it awakened the gods; It fixed the red feather girdle of the sovereigns [high chiefs]."[96]

Dolphins, turtles, pigs, dogs, and humans were creatures possessing sufficient *mana* to fit them for sacrifice at a *marae*. Leaves from the *miro* tree (*Thespesia populnea*, rosewood) and the leaves or the entire *ti* (*Cordyline fruticosa*) plant were used to properly and safely address a god. Islanders made routine gifts of food on a more everyday basis to keep the spirits of ancestors satisfied and pacified, to avoid having them slip back into the *Ao* in search of sustenance, where they could cause trouble for their living relatives. The exchange of plants and animals was, therefore, not only occurring between Europeans and Tahitians, and not only between Society Islanders, but also taking place in the exchange of essences between the living and the dead.

Chiefly families and the priests who assisted them had a key role in managing relations between the *Ao* and *Po*. Chiefly women may not have had a regular role in ceremonies at their district's *marae*, but there were many other ways in which spiritually potent women contributed to the governance of the flows of sacred power. The chiefly woman 'Itia (1760–1814), Tu's primary wife, was a feisty figure in the exchanges of this period. Bligh described her as "one of the most intelligent persons I met with at Otaheite."[97] When the *Providence* arrived she went on board, perused the available trade goods in each officer's cabin, and shrewdly selected George Tobin as her *taio*. He was able to provide her with a wide range of treasures, including the pistols that had been high on her list of demands (she fired pistols with exceptional accuracy, and with far more aplomb than her nervous husband[98]).

In 1789, shortly after the birth of her daughter, Captain Bligh described 'Itia's using two handfuls of cracked coconut, sugar cane, and a small branch of the shrub *rauava* to hold to her own head and then to her baby's forehead to break her connection to the child's dangerous spiritual potency.[99] This *āmo'a* ("head-freeing") rite allowed 'Itia to pick up food and feed herself without consuming too much of her child's *mana*.[100] The sugar cane (*tō; Saccharum officinarum*), to take one element of this complex of active plants, was connected through its name, its form, and essence with conception. Both sugar cane and conception were called *tō*.[101] Conception, birth, and death were crossover moments between realms, points at which the relationship between the *Ao* and *Po* needed to be managed especially carefully with the support of the most appropriate and effective plants and animals.

When 'Itia's daughter died of illness in 1792 she carried out a ceremony to ensure the safe and proper passage of her daughter's *iho* to the *Po*. Her servants constructed a *tupapa'u mere*, a burial platform resting on posts about six feet high—and they ensured it was "fenced round with reeds and neatly ornamented with coloured Cloth, leaves and Flowers."[102] The leaves would have been a twist of coconut leaves or *maire* ferns (*Polypodium vitiense*), part of the protection given to help the soul avoid hostile spirits.[103] Food would be placed by the corpse as part of the preparations to distract hostile spirits, something for them to consume other than the departing soul.[104]

Cosmologies Contrasted

While in most respects Maohi and European cosmologies had few points of connection, had the Tahitians explained their cosmos to their European visitors in a way they could understand, the Europeans may have seen some parallels with their own construction of the universe. In the European basic opposition between the physical world on the one hand and the spiritual worlds of heaven and hell on the other, there was some comparison with the Maohi balance of *Ao* and *Po*. The key difference lay in the amount of travel that occurred between those worlds. As we have seen, the boundaries between the *Ao* and the *Po* were highly fluid. Europeans on the other hand, looking out onto a stretch of land, primarily saw a place that was relatively knowable and reasonably fixed in its essence. In the belief of most Europeans, one could move through a landscape, shoot its birds, cut parts of it down, burn it and reshape it with either no particular consequence or simple, positive results.

Europeans wanted to take away from the Tahitian environment whatever was practically and conceptually useful to them, and they spared little sustained concern for the offenses or damage they caused. Despite the clues they were getting, the British remained resistant to acknowledging or respecting the particularities and deeper significances of the Tahitian worldview. George Tobin, for instance, found that there was something particular about the dark gray heron (*Egretta sacra, out'u,* Pacific Reef Heron) which the Tahitians held "a superstitious reverence towards, being always displeased at our shooting them."[105] In its physical manifestation in the *Ao*, Teuira Henry records, the god Rua-nu'u (Source of armies) took the form of this heron.[106] If the heron and its divine inhabitant were offended, "People's necks got twisted round so the face looked behind."[107] Tobin did not notice any direct consequences for dispatching the bird and he must have felt little need to heed the Tahitians' anger. The Tahitians were "always" displeased, after every instance, so he had shot several, and he did not suggest he was going to curtail his hunting. Their response interested Tobin, but it only indicated to him a "superstition" and need not get in the way of his collecting birds for eating or the pursuit of natural history. His view of their landscape had been elaborated and unsettled by the Tahitians to a certain extent, but not so much that he could come close to seeing it through their eyes.

The Genesis direction to Christians to "replenish the earth and subdue it," to "have dominion" over every living thing in the creation, created in European culture a sense of responsibility for the proper employment of the natural world. This notion developed in many practical and deep ways in Europe, particularly during periods of expansion into new territories. The idea was to become especially prominent in the next phase of encounters between Europeans and Tahitians, when the missionaries arrived.

Jehovah in the Tropics

In 1795 in Britain a group of evangelically spirited Protestants from a variety of denominations established the London Missionary Society (LMS). The Pacific Ocean was their first target. Members were concerned by the populations of people described in Cook voyage narratives living without knowledge of the Christian creator and practicing a wide range of ungodly acts (such as human sacrifice, infanticide, and homosexuality).[108] Another spur to targeting the Pacific was their sense of the lost opportunity of Ma'i's recent visit to England. Ma'i had learned to play chess and ice skate, but virtually nothing of the Christian religion. He had returned to the Society Islands with guns, armor, a horse, puppets, an electrical apparatus, and apparently not a single Bible.[109] There had already been a suggestion in 1791, not pursued, that missionaries be sent out to Tahiti with Bligh on the *Providence*.[110] The Rev. Thomas Haweis, one of the founders of the LMS, spoke to congregations of the imperatives and advantages of a mission in the South Seas. He described idyllic lands, warm but fanned by breezes, bursting with fruit and never-ending food from the sea, a perfect place for a missionary, whose time would "neither be engrossed with labour, nor his attention distracted, and his anxiety exercised about his or his family's provision."[111] It was a highly attractive prospect. By 1796, after a little less than a year of raising funds, the missionary ship *Duff* was equipped, packed with provisions and livestock. A group of four ordained ministers and another twenty-five missionary brothers went aboard, six accompanied by their wives and children.[112] Many were artisans and craftsmen, variously literate. The LMS directors gave them last-minute instructions and scant preparation for the life they were embarking on.[113] They set sail for Tahiti with a plan to settle most of their number there, with smaller groups in the Marquesas Islands and Tonga. They stopped at Rio de Janeiro to take on more provisions, further livestock, and a range of seeds and plants to establish in the islands.[114] On 4 March 1797 the *Duff* reached Matavai Bay.[115]

They discovered, on talking to two Swedish men living on the island,[116] that there had been a series of earthquakes the day before the *Duff*'s arrival. They had been the first earthquakes in living memory and had caused great terror, convincing many that a serious disaster was about to strike. When the chief Tu questioned the Swedes about it one of them said it was his own (Christian) God that had caused it, "being angry with the Natives for their Wickedness; and that he could cause the Island to sink into the Sea if he pleased."[117] Tahitians attributed the quakes to the *Duff* when it arrived the next day and named the ship Te-rapu (The Stirrer).[118] For the mission, the earthquake, a "prodigy" as Brother Henry called it, was a clear sign of the divinely sanctioned upheaval they expected to bring to those "dark parts of the earth."[119]

Eleven men, four women, and four children settled at Point Venus, on the northern point of Matavai Bay. Tu gave them permission to move into "fare no Britanne," a house the Pomares had built to receive British visitors.[120] They organized themselves into an orderly society. One of the ordained ministers, a respected thirty-six-year-old, John Jefferson, was voted president of the group.[121] He maintained the daily journal until 1806 (he died, after a drawn-out illness, in September 1807).[122] His account of the mission charts the difficulties they had establishing themselves; the language was frustratingly difficult to learn, the Tahitians had little interest in their mission, and managing day-to-day affairs in the complicated political and cultural nexus they had landed in was far from the life of comfort and grace they had expected.

The Tahitians likewise found that the missionaries defied expectation. First, there was the novelty of having women and children among the group. The chiefly families were particularly pleased about this development, curious about the women and indulgent of the children.[123] Second, the missionary men were unlike the European voyagers, traders, and castaways the Tahitians had met before. These new Englishmen had different priorities. They did not have the same approach to exchanges or to the island's resources. They did not welcome offers of sexual hospitality, and although they did agree to some *taio* friendships, they did not seek them out to get trade going.[124] Unlike earlier visitors, they did not set up a marketplace where they could barter for provisions. They had a cautious, selective approach and frequently sought audiences with the Pomares, to whom they would give carefully counted portions of ironware and cloth. Despite all this, Tu recognized they would be useful go-betweens with visiting ships and as a link to British interests. He sent them regular gifts of food, lent them his protection, and early in their stay made a ceremonial presentation of the Point Venus district, at which the Swedes translated, saying the missionaries "might take what *houses, Trees, Fruits,* and *Hogs* [they] thought proper." [125]

The local owners did not view this gift with equanimity, and over the years the people of Point Venus repeatedly pointed out to the missionaries they were intruding on land they did not possess. The missionaries wrote to the LMS directors in 1813 warning that if they intended to settle more brethren on Tahiti, they needed to be aware that the district of Matavai had not been bought from Tu by the captain of the *Duff,* as the directors assumed. The regions' inhabitants did not see the missionaries as owning the land:

> not any part of it, except the small sandy spot we occupy with our dwellings and gardens: and even as to that, there are persons who claim the ground as theirs, and have, more than once, mentioned it to us.[126]

The missionaries were reliant on the Tahitians to supply them with food, especially as they had trouble establishing their own gardens and livestock. The missionary journals reflect the tensions within their exchanges as the years went by. They also recorded the mismatch of two cosmologies. The Tahitians were uninterested in the missionaries' message, and several years of learning to speak and translate Christian concepts into Tahitian did little to make the foreign faith relevant. Only occasionally did someone agree to change their "customary practices," and there was no guarantee they intended to make a permanent change. Talking to local people and traveling around Tahiti and Mo'orea to preach to gathered groups, the missionaries became increasingly despondent about their prospects. Their intended audiences either removed themselves from the vicinity, stayed but fell asleep, talked among themselves, laughed, parroted the preachers' words back at them, asked for payment for coming, or asked them why the missionaries' god left the brethren and their families so unprotected from illness and misfortune.[127]

John Jefferson and the others were consistently troubled by the Tahitians' explanations of spiritual or divine presences in the landscape. In 1798 the brothers felled a sacred breadfruit tree at a *marae* and brought it down the river to the shore. A large wave suddenly washed it against Brother Henry's leg, breaking it. The missionaries were perplexed by this "alarming providence," not knowing "what to make of" it. However, the Tahitians had an explanation, recorded by the missionaries, that "their god was angry at us for cuting down the breadfruit trees in the Morāi and told he provd it by causeing the tree to Brake our Bro. leg."[128]

The missionaries also made interpretations of divine interventions in the landscape when it suited their purposes, whether earthquakes or storms diverted, rough seas calmed, or breadfruit ripening in nearby groves. They dismissed as nonsense, however, the Tahitians' own readings of divine assistance and approval within the natural world. Rowland Hassall was, one day in 1797, trying to convince a Tahitian priest to abandon a particular ceremonial practice. After the priest had apparently agreed, Hassall reported that a bird "much like the Swoollow at home" landed near them and chirped a "Cheerful Note." The priest smiled and said:

> that God had sent that Bird to inform him that he was not angry at
> him for puting away that Costom. I asked him where his god dwelt,
> He told me that his god hid in darkness, But he always sent that Bird
> to inform him when he was pleased.[129]

Hassall remonstrated with the priest, telling him that birds were common and "his god, Worship, & Bird, were mere Vanity, &c &c," but the Tahitian was not to be shaken from "his faith in his Bird, and God."[130] There was much in the Tahitian cosmology that would not be shaken, even after Pomare II—and his people—eventually converted to Christianity. The volatile, changeable nature of the land and its inhabitants remained in place, operating alongside Christian beliefs. The care that observers noticed Tahitians taking in their environment—avoiding venturing out at night and listening for the presence of spirit beings signaled by particular animal and insect sounds[131]—has remained. The night still seems connected to the *Po* and is a more likely time to meet a dangerous spirit roaming about.[132] A woman I spoke to in 2001, an active Christian, asked me to turn off my tape recorder before telling me about the spirit presence from the forest she sensed in her house one night, and the *ti* plants she planted around her garden to ward off any further visitations.[133] The Tahitian environment was and remains a responsive one, full of presences and consequences for actions taken.

Conclusions

The varying perceptions of the landscape held by Tahitians and Europeans formed a fundamental part of their cultural divide. Despite the different conceptions of the world that both sides were operating within, the frequent misunderstandings, frustration, and tensions, both sides remained committed to working to maintain a flow of exchange. Tahitians readily bartered away their more common ecological resources to the visitors. More strikingly, both sides often managed to successfully exchange animals and plants that were loaded with high degrees of significance and potency in their own cultures. There were several factors that made it possible for the two groups to engineer a workable ecological exchange. The most fundamental was that the Maohi occupied a conceptual environment that was fundamentally mutable, transformative in essence, and responsive to change. Creating new roles for the plants and animals Europeans desired was another form of transformation. It was one that, as we will see in the chapters to come, allowed greater access to parts of the environment that had previously been restricted by sacred boundaries and property divisions. This flexibility meant that within the confrontation between conflicting visions of the island, the Maohi were able to create some common ground.

Part II

INTO TAHITI

Captain Cook and his domestic animals, engraving from Andrew Kippis,
A Narrative of the Voyages around the World performed by
Captain James Cook *(London, c.1839).*

CHAPTER 3

Getting Captain Cook's Goat
And Other Tales of Ecological Introduction

On the island of Moʻorea in October 1777, one of Captain Cook's goats went missing. Several of the animals had been taken ashore to graze, and Cook was sure a chief called Mahine or one of his followers had stolen one. Cook had already given away two goats to a local chief and had intended to keep the others. He sent messages demanding the stolen goat be returned but received no satisfactory reply. Cook told his men to start setting fire to nearby houses and break up the huge, elaborately carved war canoes on the beach. They followed their orders with some reluctance.[1]

Families fled up into the mountains and men came in procession to lay plantain branches before Cook, pleading for the largest canoes to be spared. These canoes were sacred and embodied their chief's prestige.[2] It would take years for the islanders to recoup the losses. When further messages failed to secure the goat, Cook threatened to extend the rampage of destruction throughout the island. The only result was that another goat went missing. As the smell of burning thatch and the sound of splitting canoe timbers spread, the goats were finally returned.[3]

We can but wonder what was going on. What had rendered a pair of goats so valuable to Cook that he was prepared to lash out at anyone within reach to get them back?[4] And what value did the goats hold for the chief Mahine that he was prepared to embroil himself in all of this?

When Cook explains the goat incident in his journal he says: "The loss of this Goat would have been nothing if it had not interfered with my views of Stocking other islands with these Animals."[5] The goats were part of a larger, more ambitious program. Cook brought into Tahiti, during the course of his three Pacific voyages, orange seeds and pineapple plants, vines, sheep, pigs, dogs, peacocks, geese, cats, a horse, and even cattle. Cook was not alone in his efforts. Captains Wallis, Bougainville, Boenechea, Vancouver, Bligh, members of the London Missionary Society, traders, and others brought in plants and animals ranging from peas, garlic, leeks, mangoes, figs, tamarind, apricots, and coffee to pigeons, parrots, guinea fowl, ducks, turkeys, donkeys, horses, sheep, and more (see Appendix B). These exotics entered the island through exchanges heavily burdened by European expectation.

From the mid-eighteenth century those who directed the distribution of new plants and animals across the Pacific held a range of priorities and ideals that were being increasingly pursued in Europe. They were aware of the potential for putting the lands and resources of the Pacific to use, for improving on them and bringing them into the sphere of European activity. The projects of plant and animal transfer that Pacific discoveries inspired grew partly out of a desire to extend the reach of British, French, and Spanish interests, but also to fulfill a set of practical and ideological concerns that were not as baldly linked to imperialism as some writers have supposed.

In a society like Tahiti's, where messages from the gods were found in the song and flight of specific birds, where pigs were needed to secure a marriage or discern the course of a coming battle, where groves of coconut palms were reserved for chiefly use and specific breadfruit trees were for women, any change to the availability and consumption of those ecological elements was a major change. However, as we have seen, Tahitians expected fluidity in their landscape. The importation of exotic species into the island had occurred during the early phase of Maohi settlement, continued in the trade of species between islands, and was reinforced through legends and creation histories. The introduction of foreign plants and animals by Europeans was, for the most part, actively encouraged by the islanders. But these introductions brought waves of impacts to the island no one had expected. Cats from England discovered how easy it was to catch Tahiti's flightless land birds. The guava bushes planted by Captain Bligh went wild and spread across valley floors, smothering indigenous plants. Species entered into and altered the island's ecology. With it, the texture of life in Tahiti changed. This chapter explores why Europeans went to such lengths to introduce exotic species into Tahiti, the challenges they faced, and how the islanders managed the introductions. A series of case studies reveals the impact of mingling ecologies from opposite sides of the globe.

In *The Apotheosis of Captain Cook* (1992), Gananath Obeyesekere argues that Cook proceeded around the Pacific planting English gardens and releasing livestock as part of his ceremonial acts of possession for the Crown. Cook's acts of gardening, Obeyesekere states, were "primarily symbolic," supplanting the disorderly way of savage peoples with ordered land-scapes on the English model. Pairs of domestic animals are care-fully set loose, away from the depredations of unthinking savages, to *domesticate* a savage land.[6]

There are several objections to this view, principal among which is Obeye-sekere's ignoring both the basic practicality and the rhetoric of benevolence behind Cook's introductions, reducing them to symbolic acts of control. Cook and his accompanying gentlemen of science did not automatically see Pacific landscapes as territories to be claimed and Europeanized. When Tu offered to grant Cook the use of land near Matavai Bay, the captain reflected how readily a British settlement could be set up. However, he could see "no one inducement" for doing so.[7] As we saw in chapter 2, observers in Poly-nesia were frequently impressed by the islanders' cultivation of neat fields, admirable irrigation systems, picturesque plantations, and orchards. The landscapes of Tahiti, Tonga, Hawai'i, and New Zealand's North Island did not need extensive remodeling to be seen as a basically civilized landscape. Part of the impulse to stock Pacific islands sprang from the conception that the islanders occupied a developmental stage Europeans had already passed through,[8] a stage that depended on simple agriculture and through which, by the gift of more complex animal husbandry and a wider range of useful plants, they could be helped to advance to a more advanced state and more comfortable quality of life. Despite the inherent paternalism, the relationship between the visitors and the islanders placed limits on the con-ceptual and practical application of condescension. In contrast to Obeye-sekere's statement, Cook and the other captains could rarely set animals loose "away from the depredations" of the islanders; the islanders had too much of a controlling presence to allow such sidestepping. In the majority of cases, Europeans introducing plants and animals did so in unavoidably intimate engagements with Polynesian peoples.

As Cook knew well enough by the time he was struggling to have his goats returned, islanders—particularly island chiefs—had agendas that could often be advanced by possessing European property. Chiefs and their people involved themselves enthusiastically with European visitors and their accompanying menageries. They managed relations and trade to their own ends, split up and redistributed breeding pairs, weeded out foreign fruits, and ran off with the wrong goats. Adding to the complexity of the melée was the captains' need to rely on the islanders to supply the crews with provisions. The interchange of plants and animals was two-way, and engage-ments over them were complex.

Prospects for Improvement

At the Cape of Good Hope in 1776 on the outward leg of his third Pacific journey, James Cook took on board "two young Bulls, two Heifers, two young stone Horses, two Mares, two Rams, several Ewes and Goats and some Rabbits and Poultry." All of them, he stated, were:

> intended for New Zealand, Otaheite and the neighbouring islands, or any other place we might meet, where there was a prospect that the leaving of some of them might prove usefull to posterity.[9]

This concentration on usefulness was a keynote of the age. Cook's statement was heavily loaded. Within the word "posterity" he held a sense of the future benefit of two groups of people.

When Cook settled Ma'i and a range of livestock on Huahine in 1777, completing his work in the Society Islands to his satisfaction, he was confident the animals would multiply and the islands would then "equal, if not exceed any place in the known World for provisions."[10] Ensuring the capacity of the islands to provide provisions for Royal Navy crews in the short and long term was only one of Cook's aims. The other was to be of benefit to the indigenous inhabitants. While on the northeast coast of New Zealand in the *Resolution* in 1773, Cook was disappointed to find the breeding pairs of pigs and goats Captain Furneaux of the *Adventure* had left just five months before had been divided and some of the goats killed. Cook wrote:

> thus all our endeavours for stocking this Country with usefull Animals are likely to be frusterated by the very people whom we meant to serve.[11]

Cook was presenting his project as one that was benevolent beyond national borders, designed to be of benefit to the people of the Pacific. This could be dismissed as an attractive veneer put over actions that were actually about personal and national self-interest. But there is room for a complexity of motivations, and while it can be tempting to assume that one must read between the lines, there is value in reading the lines themselves. Cook's statements fit within the discourse of improvement. If Cook's approach to the Pacific was to endeavor to do not only what he could for his country, but also what he could to improve the general condition of peoples in "less favoured" lands, he shared his approach with many of his compatriots. As we saw in chapter 2, the ideal of improvement was a keynote to the age of Enlightenment. Early impetus had been given by Newton's and Locke's calls for human energies and human rationality to be directed to better understanding and managing both the workings of society and the natural world of God's creation. Those in society's higher circles were increasingly called to their duty to work for the improvement of those less fortunate and for the betterment of humanity as a whole. People on the lower rungs of society's ladder could be expected to concentrate on self-improvement, through education, piety, and industry. These were ideals consistent with an era that was energetically concerned with progress.[12]

Throughout the eighteenth century the "culture of improvement"[13] inspired projects of charity, civil works, technology, public education, and, particularly, agricultural advance. In Britain, interested landowners secured governmental support for breeding and propagation programs to improve livestock and crops. Such experiments were appealing even to the highest levels of society: George III and Joseph Banks were particularly interested in working to improve sheep breeds.[14] Organizations such as the Society for the Improvement of Knowledge of Agriculture, the Board of Agriculture and Internal Improvement, and the Society for the Improvement of British Wool operated throughout the eighteenth century to promote research that promised to raise the nation's economic standing and quality of life.[15] Cultivation and "civilization" went hand-in-hand.

As further treasure troves of geological, botanical, and zoological wonders were uncovered around the world, there was a growing sense in Europe of the seriousness of the duty to bring these natural resources to their full potential. One way to make use of the new abundance of known species was to carry them by ship for installation in places that lacked them. James Dancer, director of the botanic gardens in Jamaica, one of Britain's Caribbean colonies, pointed out that "people of every Climate may be benefited by a Reciprocity of Products."[16] It was possible for George Forster to state, without fear of controversy, that the expense, difficulties, and risks of a voyage to the other side of the world could be justified simply by its contribution to the distribution of useful animals:

> I cannot help thinking that our late voyage would reflect immortal honour on our employers, if it had no other merit than stocking Taheitee with goats, the Friendly Isles and New Hebrides with dogs, and New Zeeland and New Caledonia with hogs.[17]

His selection of dogs for Tonga (the "Friendly Isles") and Vanuatu ("New Hebrides") underlines the extent to which the focus was the benefit of the local population; Polynesian dogs were of considerable cultural and practical significance on whichever island they inhabited, but they were not a resource needed by British mariners, even though they were considered by Cook and a handful of others as an unusual yet tasty meal. Goats for milk and meat and hogs for pork were of course the desired ecological imports for provisioning stops, including the favored Tahiti. Introducing European animals and plants would, Forster and others felt, increase the health and prosperity of humanity in general and the fortunes and reputation of their own nation. This meant that care had to be taken at every step of the process. It was important to manage how gifts of livestock and plants were made and how the gift was to be remembered by all those who would experience or witness its benefits. When Cook presented breeding pairs of cattle, horses, and goats to three chiefs in Tonga in July 1777, he asked Ma'i (who was able to translate) to point out how the animals should be cared for to ensure they would proliferate. He also wanted the Tongans to understand the "trouble and expence" that had been taken to bring the animals, and, "lastly," that "they and their Children were to remember that they had them from the Men of Britane."[18]

While gathering glory to the nation was an aim, there were limits to how far British captains were able, licensed, or interested in proceeding in promoting national interests. Captain Cook's destructive response to the stolen goats could be viewed as a brutal demonstration of colonial power. His display was not, though, directed to establishing an imperial hold on the island, but to managing relations with people he would have to rely on into the future. After days waiting on the coast of Tahiti issuing demands and threats to try to get the goats back, Cook admitted:

> I was now very sorry I had proceeded so far, as I could not retreat with any tolerable credet, and without giving incouragement to the people of the other islands we had yet to visit to rob us with impunity.[19]

There was also a sense, as many have discussed, that throughout the third voyage Cook was losing his emotional control and judgment. The crew talked of him dancing a "heeva"—a passionate, stamping Tahitian *heiva*— on the deck whenever in a fury. They grew uneasy with his behavior; they felt he had lost dignity and power in New Zealand when he befriended rather than punished the man who had previously murdered three men from the *Adventure,* and again in Tonga when he agreed to take off his shirt and untie his hair to be permitted to participate in a ceremony. In the Society Islands, officers started to intervene to halt the brutal punishments Cook proscribed for islander thieves. When the goat incident in Mo'orea flared up, Captain King of the *Discovery* wrote:

Not being able to account for Captn Cooks precipitate proceeding in this business, I cannot think it justifiable. . . . I doubt whether our Ideas of propriety in punishing so many innocent people for the crimes of a few, will be ever reconcileable to any principle one can form of justice.[20]

Some historians have pointed to Cook's not being completely recovered from the strain and illness of the second voyage.[21] Anne Salmond has suggested he was acting like an islander chief.[22] He certainly, like a chief, meted out punishment with little mercy for those who crossed him. So many things went wrong during the voyage—frequent frustrations with shepherding livestock through the long sea passage, and the concessions he felt he was making to islanders being periodically flung back in his face. His response to the theft of the goat was loaded with accumulated tension. This project, which he had begun with a sense of personal pride and generosity, was starting to drive him to distraction.

Thus we can see that the efforts of Cook and others to introduce exotic plants and animals during the eighteenth century did not simply spring from a grand, overarching project of imperialism as formulated by Obeyesekere. Their ecological importations were, rather, a disjointed series of endeavors.[23] They were instigated and funded by an assorted collection of interest groups and patrons, for a wide variety of philosophical, idealistic, economic, and political reasons. During the eighteenth century, moving into Pacific places was by no means accepted as a useful or commendable way of proceeding. There was a general uneasiness over the justice of establishing colonies, and many British authorities opposed the establishment of colonies in places already inhabited. Many shared this unwillingness. Tu might have invited Cook to establish a Tahitian settlement, but, Cook said, it was a proposal that "for the regard I have for them I hope will never happen."[24]

Indicative of this absence of a grand project of empire is the lack of any triumphalist images of captains introducing plants and animals into the Pacific during the eighteenth and early nineteenth centuries. During this period there was a reticence about showing the exchanges that were bringing change to the face of the islands. Artists and those who employed them were concerned to record Pacific islanders' social, religious, and governmental customs, their methods of production, construction, and travel, as they found them. Only the most dramatic engagements between Europeans and islanders—primarily battles—were illustrated in contemporary publications. It was not until the late 1830s, when Britain was settling into a colonial mode, that artists and engravers constructed scenes of benevolent gifts of useful plants and livestock being presented to places increasingly being seen as primitive, unsupported, and unfortunate (see part 2 fig., p. 89). It was within this changed approach that British colonizers rolled out systematized projects of species acclimatization. Before this, in the eighteenth century, installing plants and animals had not been simply an "arm of colonial power."[25]

Challenges to Success

The British pursuit of progress in the Pacific and the urgent hopes for easier provisioning were frequently brought up short by an overabundance of obstacles. The art of cross-hemisphere transplanting was no easy pastime. In 1770 the author of a book of advice for "Captains of Ships, Sea Surgeons, and other curious Persons," on how to transport seeds and plants from distant places, stated that barely one in fifty survived.[26] Certainly, Banks discovered that of all the vegetable, herb, and other "divers seeds" they brought from Mile End packed in small bottles sealed with resin, the seeds proved "so bad" that only the mustard sprouted.[27] Voyagers also transported seeds held between pages of paper, set in wax, sugar, or in tubes of peat to try to keep them from rotting, drying, or sprouting uselessly en route. These efforts often failed.[28] Plants and seeds were nonetheless more straightforward to carry than livestock, and there were many more introductions of plants into Tahiti than animals or birds (see Appendix B). By the 1790s, cuttings and tubers were being loaded onto ships in soil-filled troughs. These were fitted with canvas covers or moveable panels at the top which could be lowered to let in sun and fresh air or raised to protect the leaves from salt spray. The hoops supporting the covers also helped to keep shipboard cats from using the boxes as litter trays, and the pet dogs and monkeys from damaging the plants.[29] By the 1830s Wardian cases with panels of glass made the task of keeping plants alive less of a gamble.[30] Before this, throughout most of our period, introducing new species was a more vexed process than armchair devisers of transplantation schemes were prepared to recognize.

The hopes and projections that drove the transportation of European plants and livestock to the Pacific were held firmly despite the continual challenges this presented the transporters. By the time Cook unloaded his goats, sheep, and cattle at Tahiti and Mo'orea in 1777, he and his crew had weathered nearly a year of sharing their limited space with an unusually large herd, substantially more than the standard naval complement of one or two sheep or goats to assist with provisioning. The seamen had to keep working the ship in extremes of weather, storms and calms, crowded by the animals' bulk, smell, and noise. During the second voyage through freezing Antarctic waters, the animals that survived were moved next to J. R. Forster's cabin: "I was now beset with cattle & stench on both Sides," he wrote, "having no other but a thin deal partition full of chinks between me & them."[31]

Animals on board had to be fed and watered, detours to shorelines made along the way to cut fresh fodder, treatments given when they were sick, slings used to keep them safe in their stalls in bad weather. Feeding the livestock was a major difficulty; hay often ran out before fresh fodder could be cut from a suitable coastline and the stock sickened and died.[32] Some captains, when near land, lifted the animals onto the ships' boats and ferried them on and off shore. Livestock consumed precious water—in quantities that Captain George Vancouver, with a dozen cows, six bulls, and about thirty sheep aboard, called "vast," and which ran their supply for the crew uncomfortably low.[33]

The health of imported plants and livestock on the journey out was only the initial hurdle. The animals that survived the trip out were often too sick (commonly with scurvy) by the time they reached the middle of the Pacific to last long on shore. Some species were not well-adapted to the heat and humidity of a tropical climate. Sheep, for instance, struggled in these conditions (and the available food in tropical locations could be positively dangerous; one sheep at least died from eating too many bananas).[34] There was also stiff competition from local species.

Voyagers continued to make concerted efforts to introduce plant and animal species, efforts that were continued by the missionaries from 1797. The London Missionary Society families found their struggles to establish gardens and livestock were just as frustrating as their attempts to gather a flock of converts.

The Rev. John Jefferson instituted a monthly report of the state of their garden, noting the brothers' planting of leeks, turnips, lemons, and cabbages and working to keep their sheep, ducks, geese, and chickens alive. He grimly noted the crops and livestock that failed or were lost to the people, pigs, and goats who pushed through the fences. In 1804, a year in which the journal is particularly focused on gardening, the brothers planted citrons, apricots, sweet potatoes, figs, vines, "long pumpkins," and watermelons, as well as potatoes and peaches from New South Wales.[35] The melons, pumpkins, and pineapples proved to be consistently good crops, becoming standard produce in Tahiti and Mo'orea (and remaining so today). However, the missionaries soon recognized that the most reliable garden plants were the species of taro and *umara* (*Ipomoea batatas*, sweet potato) endemic to the Society Islands. They began importing additional strains of the Polynesian *umara* from New Zealand (called *kumera*) and had good results from a Hawaiian variety, acquired from some Hawaiians who stopped by with a trader in 1803.[36]

There were frequent problems with many of the exotic plants. Some things failed to grow; a dry season would cause vegetables to wither and young fruit to fall off the struggling fruit trees. Jefferson reported in October 1804 that of their grapes, only about a third of the bunches were edible; many were "blasted"—damaged either by parasites or heat—before they had ripened.[37] Jefferson also talked at length about attacks by small sap-sucking insects on their young citrus trees. Many of the trees died.[38]

Attacks by Tahiti's larger predators also made life difficult for the imported species. Local, untethered pigs broke through fences at night and feasted on melons, pumpkins, and pineapples; goats introduced by earlier voyagers ate up the missionaries' vines and ring-barked the fruit trees. The newly introduced farm animals were targeted too. One sheep after another was attacked by Tahitian dogs—they would be found with a torn thigh or a broken leg. Most, despite careful nursing, could not be saved.[39] The neighborhood dogs were "useless & mischievous" in the missionary's opinion, but there was nothing they could do. The islanders valued these animals, which they would "kiss and hug as much as they do their children, and call them good property and good food."[40] Twenty-seven years earlier, in 1777, Captains Cook and King had also lost their carefully imported English and Cape sheep to Spanish dogs soon after landing them. It was particularly galling to Cook to discover that not only had the Spanish preceded him in installing livestock on the island (as we will see in chapter 4), but that his efforts were further undermined by the aggressive breed of dogs they had imported. The Spanish, he said, "would have done the island a great deal more service if they had hanged them all in stead."[41] He issued orders to shoot any Spanish dogs seen near the tents. King, Forster, and James Burney all reported on the "very vexatious" event of a dog "of the Spanish breed" killing a ram that had been born on the ship and raised carefully on goat's milk.[42] Dogs were a persistent problem. In 1804 Jefferson wrote resignedly, "The society has now no more than 7 sheep though we have been upwards of 8 years in endeavouring to rear them on the island."[43]

It was probably dogs that tidied up the pair of rabbits that Brother Henry brought in from Australia in 1800 and "put away to burrow."[44] If the pair did survive long enough to breed, their offspring did not take over the island as they did elsewhere.[45] Rabbits are well known to have been devastatingly effective colonizers across a broad range of environments within Australia and New Zealand, on Hawaiian islands, and in South America. However, in Tahiti, the combination of a limited piece of terrain populated with an unusually high concentration of dogs and pigs (both enjoying an omnivorous diet) would have meant rabbits were heavily predated. In addition, Henry could have brought in either domestic or wild rabbits; domestic rabbits are less effective adapters than the wild rabbits that took over Australia.[46] Rabbits only appear fleetingly in the historic record of Tahiti's landscape. A sailor's watercolor of 1822 seems to show a few of them looking at home on a grassy slope inland (fig. 3.1), but no evidence of the animals shows up in other sources and they do not figure on the island now.[47]

The Tahitians living near the missionaries formed another set of enthusiastic consumers of the animals and plants the brethren were trying to establish. Brother Davies wrote that "between the natives, goats, and hogs little or nothing is left to us, or if we sometimes get a little of the fruit of our labour it is by a mere chance."[48] The missionaries' neighbors would typically wait for nightfall or until the missionaries were gathered at their worship before making holes in the fences and helping themselves to fruit,

Figure 3.1. *Anon., detail of "The chapel at Matavai, Jany. 14," 1822 (rabbits at left). Pen drawing on paper, 8.3 x 13.8 in. (21.3 x 35.3 cm). In "Views taken while serving on the East India Station in HM Ship* Leander *and* Dauntless *1820–1822." National Library of Australia, Canberra (nla.pic-an6820434).*

vegetables, goose eggs (including those in the process of being incubated), and animals from the pens.[49] There was good reason for the routine "depredations";[50] the missionaries were not voluntarily including themselves in the local system of sharing produce, which acted as a form of social security. They were not entering into exchanges willingly and thus, as James Morrison had observed was the standard response in such cases,[51] they were being plundered of their wealth. At the end of 1807, when Brother Davies was particularly exasperated about their losses, he acknowledged that it was a time of great scarcity in the district and many of the thefts were thought to have been committed by women. The paucity of food to be foraged was combining with the various *tapu* on consumption the women were placed under, and, according to the missionaries, some of them were "ready to starve."[52]

In conditions such as these, with persistent competition from so many quarters, the missionaries often gave way to despair about their project as a whole:

> None can easily conceive but ourselves, the discouragements we are labouring under, in almost every respect; if we view ourselves in our principal work as Christian missionaries, we see little but discouragements on every hand; if we look upon the pains we have taken for a number of years in the cultivation of the ground, gardening &c, we can see nothing but disappointments and discouragements.[53]

In an attempt to improve their food production and to lay "the foundation of a regular system of industry amongst the natives,"[54] in 1818 the missionaries employed John Gyles, a lapsed missionary and former overseer of a Jamaican sugar plantation, to come to the island to carry out "the cultivation of some of the indigenous plants of the Islands," presumably in a more "orderly" and European style than that already practiced on the island for many centuries. Sugar cane and other tropical products were tried, with limited success and without achieving the commercial scale the missionaries had hoped for.[55]

Islander Management

There were many ways in which Tahitians, from chiefs to commoners, made use of the animals Europeans introduced, making sure their presence worked to their own advantage. The Maohi had existing models for dealing with the gifts and trade of exotic plants and animals from the tall ships that arrived from 1767. They had a long history of managing the species they introduced themselves and of managing visitors to their shores.

Each island in the Societies group had previously possessed a relatively narrow ecological profile, populated by those seeds, insects, amphibians, and birds that could be borne by air, sea, or the occasional floating log. The arrival of a new predator was extremely rare. When the Maohi arrived in their voyaging canoes and settled the Society Islands, they imposed a barrage of new demands on the islands' ecology. They were hunters themselves, catching the islands' birds for food and feathers. The animals and plants they introduced had dramatic, frequently devastating effects on the endemic species. The small Pacific rats that had accompanied the canoes devoured birds' eggs and chicks. Pigs foraged and rooted up forest floors. The Maohi converted marshlands into irrigated taro fields, hillsides were cut into terraces, and groves of breadfruit, coconuts, and paper mulberry were installed in place of existing vegetation.[56] Michel Orliac's archaeological excavations in Tahiti's Papeno'o Valley have revealed a sudden drop in bird species and a marked reduction in plant diversity during the early years of Maohi occupation.[57]

Over time the process of introducing species continued between islands. Each island and atoll of the Societies gradually developed a distinctive range of endemic and introduced species. Some settlers were successful in retaining a particular dye plant; another lost theirs when their island was struck with a period of drought or cyclone. Some islands had particularly rich soils that supported a broad range of species; other islands had poor soils that supported only a narrow range. The islanders maintained a commodity trade network throughout the region.[58] Reports during the eighteenth century showed Tahitians to be traveling regularly to the drought-prone Tuamotu atoll, about 200 miles (322 km) to the northeast of Tahiti, to trade Tahitian produce for Tuamotu turtles, pearls and pearl shell, mats, and white dog fur for fringing *taumi* (visually striking warriors' breast plates). Tahitians also traded more locally with Mo'orea, Huahine, and the Leeward Islands for yams and precious parakeet feathers. Chiefs on Tahiti forbade the people of the nearby Tetiaroa atoll from growing breadfruit or other productive trees, to keep them dependent on trading their "Oil . . . a Variety of Fine Fish and a Sauce Made of Ripe Cocoa Nuts" in return for Tahitian provisions.[59] Tahitians also took *tapa* to Porapora and Taha'a to exchange for bamboo flasks of coconut oil.[60]

Whatever the ruling families around the island thought Europeans were trying to achieve by pushing seeds into Tahiti's soil, the chiefs had their own priorities and dealt with the gifts as it suited them. They either ignored or kept the strange creatures and ambiguous green shoots under their care as they saw fit. Like any chiefly possessions in Tahiti, these living gifts were vulnerable to changes of political fortune and the destructive violence of hostile rivals. The first European animals to be installed had been the poultry and pregnant cat Wallis gave Purea in 1767. Six years later, during Cook's visit in 1773, Lt. James Burney heard that of these animals:

> 1 of the Geese died—the Guinea hens were Stole from her & killed—the Turkey hen had 5 young ones but the cat killd them all. The Cat who was with kitten miscarried, was stole & carried away to another Island. . . . So unlucky has Obreea been with these presents.[61]

Such a sequence of events was not uncommon. Many newly introduced animals and plants had little noticeable impact on the island's ecology and featured only fleetingly as a presence in the social life of the place. Despite the lack of success of many introduced species, there is ample evidence to suggest that, in general, European animals were valued by chiefly families and their people. As we will see in the next chapter, horses were highly prized as mounts, and cattle were valued as symbols of status.

When the islanders—not just the chiefs but those of lower ranks—found an animal or a plant and its products valuable, the course of introduction was much more likely to proceed as the Europeans hoped. When fruits such as mangoes, pineapples, and watermelons first fruited on the island, the locals tasted them and worked to ensure they flourished. Joseph Banks was confident that the watermelon seeds he brought in would "come to perfection" because locals valued them highly:

> I have given away large quantities among the natives and planted also in the woods; they now continually ask me for seeds and have already shewd me melon plants of their raising which look perfectly well.[62]

Watermelons remain a popular garden plant in Tahiti today, and when they are in season, landowners sell them off in large numbers at roadside stands. Conversely, some introduced species failed to prosper because the islanders actively discouraged them.

Bitter Fruits

Grapevines had been brought into the Society Islands by Spanish missionaries arriving with Boenechea in 1774. Three years later, while visiting the island, Cook heard that one of the vines had just produced some grapes. He reported:

> A number [of] the Natives got together to taste the first fruit it bore, this was probably done before the fruit was half ripe, as it was unani-

mously declared that if it was suffered to grow it would poison every person in the island and was immediately troden underfoot.[63]

There was little that could be done to establish a species if there was decisive action taken against it soon after its introduction. When Bligh arrived on the *Bounty* he tried to establish the seeds of almonds and various fruits he had brought from the Cape of Good Hope, along with roses, because he had previously noticed Tahitian women enjoyed ornamenting themselves with sweet-smelling flowers.[64] The gardener David Nelson planted these, but a few days later Bligh "had the mortification to see" the garden ground "much trod over; and, what was worse, the chiefs appeared but little concerned at it."[65]

When Bligh returned to Tahiti in 1792 he was there to pot up the islanders' breadfruit seedlings for transplantation, but he also devoted considerable energy to putting foreign plants into Tahitian soil. He brought in oranges, pines, guavas, pomegranates, quinces, figs, vines, firs, "Metrocedera" (*Metrosideros,* myrtle) and "Aloes" (genus *Aloe*) from England, South Africa, and Australia.[66] Of these, he reported:

> The Natives only have a desire for the three last,—the Firs & Metrocedera because I assured them they would grow to very large Trees, & were fit for building Ships; and the Aloes on account of its being a very fine Flower. No Value is set upon any of our Garden productions, it is really taking trouble to no purpose to bring them any thing that requires care to get it to perfection. A fine Shaddock Tree [*Citrus grandis,* pomelo] I saw Yesterday, very nearly destroyed by Fire, and the Fruit of it they told me was good for nothing.[67]

Amongst the dynamics of trying to establish seeds, seedlings, and animals within Tahiti and the ecological conditions that faced them there, the desires of the islanders maintained a persistent determining presence.

Ecological conditions combined with European and islander motivations to drive the specific histories of each plant and animal introduced to the island. To investigate the implications of these particular ecological exchanges for the island's ecology and its people, we need to trace the histories of several species beyond their initial introduction, uncovering the environmental and social impacts they had.

Environmental Impacts of Introductions

The extent and nature of the environmental change caused by a particular introduced species is often too obscure to allow any clear conclusions to be drawn. The goat, however, is an animal that started its Tahitian history being mentioned routinely by Europeans. They were introduced to the Society Islands, not only by Cook on his final voyage, but by Boenechea (1772 and 1774), Cook and Furneaux in 1773 and 1774, and various introductions by the missionaries from 1797.

The Mo'orean chief Mahine made efforts to secure himself some goats because he knew a rival *ari'i* had been given a pair. They were valued status items. Cook reported in Tahiti in 1777 that goats were "in tolerable plenty, there being hardly a chief of any note that has not got some."[68] According to Bligh, Tahitians would not eat the goats; "neither," he said, "will they taste the milk."[69] He mixed some goat's milk with fruit to try to tempt 'Itia and Tu to try it, but they found the idea disgusting and jeeringly asked Bligh why he didn't go and milk a sow.[70] But exotic animals had other uses: owning them displayed one's prowess as a negotiator with foreigners and the respect one was accorded. Goats seem to have benefited from chiefly patronage. They bred well and soon became part of the landscape.

By the 1790s, captains and officers found it possible to barter for goats' meat and for live goats to take on their homeward journeys. The drawings of goats by a sailor on the *Dauntless* confirms that goats were still comfortably settled on the island in 1822 (fig. 3.2).

In fact, the Europeans found that they flourished rather too well and were interacting with the other introduced species in unexpected ways. The

Figure 3.2. *Anon., detail of "Matavai Bay, Taheite, May 15."* 1822. *Pen drawing, 7.1 x 13.6 in. (18.2 x 34.7 cm). In "Views taken while serving on the East India Station in HM Ship* Leander *&* Dauntless *1820–1822." National Library of Australia, Canberra (nla.pic-an6820444).*

missionaries wrote to William Bligh in 1808 with news that the Tahitians considered him "a Benefactor" for bringing them oranges, which were becoming widely propagated, but that:

> the mischief done by Goats is a great hindrance to this, & we c^d wish in several respects that these destructive animals were banished off this island.[71]

Cook's countrymen were finding that his goat project, backed by widespread chiefly interest, was proving rather too productive for comfort.

We can presume that goats were eating their way through indigenous plant stocks as well as the oranges. Goats are notoriously voracious and are generally acknowledged to be the "single most destructive herbivore" in island environments.[72] We do not know, however, the details of what was being eaten and whether any plant species failed to survive the onslaught of this new predator. There is evidence that from the late 1780s Tahitians had worked to curb the presence of goats. According to James Morrison (resident in the northern districts following the *Bounty* mutiny), these "distructive animals" were eating the bark of the young trees in the region's paper mulberry plantations. The animals could not be kept out by ditches or fences, and those that caused a nuisance were either kept tied up or driven up into the mountains where, said Morrison, "they run wild—as they are not esteemed of Great value."[73] Missionaries were still referring to them as destructive into the 1820s. But, interestingly, they then drop out of the written record and they appear to have had a minimal presence in the late nineteenth century and beyond.

It seems likely that the Tahitians decided to take further action against the goats in the later nineteenth century. Unlike in the Marquesas, where goats are common and an important part of hunting culture, in Tahiti today there is no talk of wild goats in the forests. No goats graze on hills or rest on the beaches. There are a few kept in paddocks here and there. After making their presence felt initially, goats receded as a force for environmental change. It was other introduced species that had significant long-term impacts.

Oranges and Lemons

Citrus fruits were among the first European plantings in the Society Islands. Wallis planted orange, lemon, and lime seeds near Matavai Bay.[74] Bougainville included oranges in the garden he planted for Reti in 1768. When the *Endeavour* stopped in Rio de Janeiro en route to the Pacific later the same year, Joseph Banks acquired a variety of seeds, including oranges, lemons, and limes. These he planted "in as many varieties of soil as I could chuse" near Matavai Bay.[75] According to later British reports, Banks' orange plant-ing (of *Citrus aurantium* or *Citrus sinensis*) did produce fruit.[76] Pomelos, a large, grapefruit-like fruit, were planted by Cook, Bligh, and others,[77] but although they grew to maturity, the Tahitians did not like their bitter taste. Only one man was known to have cared for a stand of pomelo trees, and this was because they were trees planted by his friend, Cook's gardener David Nelson.[78] Missionaries reported to Bligh, as we have seen, that his plantings of orange trees near the Pomare family's residences during both his *Bounty* and *Providence* visits had been more generally successful. In 1792 Poeno (*ari'i* of Matavai) showed one of George Vancouver's officers the *Bounty* orange trees. They were reported to be "two feet high & in a very thriving state."[79] The missionaries brought a range of citrus seeds with them. They also succeeded in propagating cuttings from one of Bligh's oranges, pro-ducing a "great number of young trees." By 1808 the missionaries reported that Tahitians, seeing the success of the plantings of orange (which they named *anani*), began to plant them too.[80]

The Tahitians continued to propagate oranges. By the mid-1800s the trees lined the beaches, filled valleys, and were featured in gardens.[81] Visi-tors to the island referred to oranges as a part of Tahiti's standard fare and standard landscape. A British captain visiting in 1846 stated:

> Whilst dinner was preparing the boats crew brought more cocoa nuts & oranges than we could consume. . . . We dined under the shade of a grove of bread fruit trees—surrounded by orange, pau, palm & ironwood.[82]

The production of oranges became so substantial that they were being used for making large exchanges within the island. In 1875 an estimated 1.9 mil-lion oranges produced by the Tautira district on Taiarapu's east coast were reported to have been exchanged for the construction of a church.[83]

It also became profitable to export oranges to the United States. For instance, in 1860, before the American orange industry had established itself, the Society Islands sent nearly five million oranges to California.[84] In the 1870s several Tahitian-owned ships were transporting passengers and oranges between the United States and Tahiti once a month.[85] The island-ers picked the fruit, rolled them in pandanus leaves, and packed them into *purau* wood crates for the journey.[86] The island presented an orange-stud-ded vista. With such an abundance of orange groves, the reliance on other cultivated fruits can be presumed to have dropped. The seeds of oranges, lemons, and limes distributed around the island by people, birds, pigs, and goats would have taken root in a multitude of habitats. Competing with the existing vegetation for light, nutrients, and water, wherever citrus trees won the indigenous plants lost ground. The populations of insects and micro-organisms that relied on the indigenous vegetation in groves and forests could not have survived in the numbers and niches they had before. Then, in the mid-twentieth century, a new microorganism found the oranges' Achilles' heel. A virus that attacked citrus trees became the latest ecological import.[87] Within a few years most of the island's citrus died. There is now only one orange grove left in a protected valley on the west side of the island in Puna'auia. The government allows only authorized visitors onto the site.

Guava/Tuava

In 1846, Captain Henry Byam Martin of the Royal Navy anchored off Pape'ete on the northern coast of Tahiti. He had been sent by the British Admiralty to observe the activities of the recently arrived French forces. He wrote in his journal on 19 October:

> a slight skirmish took place this morning, in which a French soldier was wounded. It seems the French were clearing the guava bushes in the valley, which the natives considered an act of hostility & resented.[88]

Apart from giving us a glimpse of the ongoing scuffles between the Tahitians and the French, Martin's log entry provides an additional view: the impact of guava on the island and the value the Tahitians placed on it. Guava plants were introduced to the island, probably from South Africa, by Captain Bligh in 1792. Guava from Brazil (*Psidium guajava* or *Psidium cattleanium*) was also brought in by Brother Bicknell of the London Missionary Society in 1815.[89] One observer, living on the island in the 1830s and 1840s, referred to the "missionary gentleman" who had introduced guava seeds from Norfolk Island, and "so well have they liked the soil, that the land is now overrun with them."[90]

Later travelers described guava being common in Tahitian gardens. Lady Brassey, visiting the island in 1876, mentions visiting the chief of Pape'ete's "native style" house, which was "surrounded, as usual, by breadfruit, cocoanut, banana, mango, and guava-trees."[91] Brassey also described a "thick undergrowth of guava" in the gardens of the Pomare family.[92] Having a presence in gardens suggests that Tahitians were deliberately propagating the fruit. So guava bushes had not just taken over—they had been taken over.

The fruit was popular; it appealed to the Tahitian palate. Today it is featured as a typically Tahitian flavor. Guava—either under its Tahitian name *tuava* (or *tuvava*) or the French term *goyave*—is included alongside coconut, taro, and pineapple as standard Tahitian food; in supermarkets around the island one can buy guava jam, guava yogurt, glacé de goyave, and guava pies. The guava plant has also long been a part of *raau Tahiti*—the medicinal knowledge and practice of Tahiti. Recipes for syrups using guava seeds and bark to treat digestive problems and period pain have been handed down through generations.[93]

Guava also took firm root in an environmental sense. E. Lucett, visiting the island in 1842, was concerned by the Tahitians' acquiescence to the spread of guava, explaining (in typical nineteenth-century mode) their failure to curb the bushes as a failure of energy, saying they were

> too listless to attempt exterminating them, although they see the fearful rapidity with which they spread, choking and destroying nearly every thing in their way. They have killed vast numbers of the bread-fruit and other valuable trees, and unless some means are adopted to keep them under they will prove a great curse.[94]

It is likely that Tahitians let the guava spread because they valued the fruit; it was encouraged in gardens, and a valley floor covered by them was considered worth defending from the French. By the time Lady Brassey was visiting in 1876, the fruit composed "the greater part of the woodlands and bush in the lower lands," and, she said, "now overruns the whole island, and cannot be got rid of."[95] Beyond a certain point, it takes a project on a massive scale, centrally organized and centrally funded, to eradicate a well-entrenched plant from an island. The ability of guava to insinuate itself into any tropical environment has had serious consequences. Indigenous plants in the Society Islands, Marquesas, and Hawaiian islands have been increasingly losing habitat to this dominant species. Some native birds, such as the *u'upa*, the green fruit dove (*Ptilinopus purpuratus*), were able to adapt to guava as one of their food sources.[96] On the whole, however, the spread of guava has narrowed the range of food sources and habitat for native species. Recently, the Ministère chargé de l'Environnement in French Polynesia has classified *Psidium cattleanium* as a noxious weed.[97] International environmental agencies now rank guava (both *Psidium guajava* and *Psidium cattleanium*) as one of the most invasive plant species in Polynesia.[98] The consequences of Bligh and the missionaries' ecological "donations" have spread unsettlingly far.

Cat among the Pigeons

Tahiti used to have several species of ground-dwelling birds called rails. One of them, the *meho*,[99] was reported to have been the *ata* (material animal form) of the god 'Tū-o-te-ra'i-marama (Stability-of-the-moonlit-sky). However, as the missionary J. M. Orsmond learned from a Society Island elder in the mid-1800s, it came under threat soon after the Europeans arrived. Teuira Henry, working at the turn of the century from Orsmond's 1849 manuscript, wrote:

> This bird, almost extinct now, shouts "Ho!" at intervals in a high tone like a person. . . . Formerly at Paofa'i, just back of the site where now stands the Tahitian Protestant church, was a swamp inhabited by many *meho*. On the border of the swamp stood a *marae* called Tū-marama (Stability-of-the-moon), which was sacred to the rails.[100]

This was a bird of significance. Orsmond described other rails and the gods that occupied them from time to time. One species used to live near marshes in burrows but, Orsmond reported, "as they fell easy prey to cats, they are now extinct."[101] Some of Tahiti's birds were seen, described, or collected by naturalists only once, before the species disappeared. Only one drawing was ever made of *Rallus pacificus* (*Tevea*, Tahiti rail), by George Forster during his stay on the island with Cook's second voyage.[102] One specimen of the Tahitian sandpiper (*Torome* or *Tete*)[103] exists in Leiden, Germany, along with a 1773 painting by George Forster. The species was eradicated soon after the introduction of European cats and rats. The last known example of the black-fronted parakeet (*Kuku peti*) was collected on Tahiti in 1844.[104]

Europeans had offered cats as gifts to high-status Tahitians—particularly high-status women—from Wallis' visit onwards. Cook reported having "furnished" the islanders with a "Stock of Catts" in 1774, "no less than twenty" for the Tahitians. Others were left at Huahine and Ra'iatea, all in all a tribute to how well cats could multiply on long-distance voyages.[105] Cats were work animals on board a ship, catching mice and rats, and they continued to be good hunters on shore. However, when European visitors presented them as gifts—given exclusively, it seems, to chiefly women—the animals took on a new role as pets. Cats had a long association in the European mind with women (and had long been linked to women in popular culture as either pets or witches' familiars).[106] There were also connotations of sexual license associated with cats that could have entertained the crew witnessing the gifts of a cat to a Tahitian woman, enjoying the frisson of a

neatly hidden joke.[107] For Tahitian women, cats would have stood instead
as rare and status-rich possessions as well as appealing objects of curiosity.
Purea was delighted to receive those she was given and tried to keep them
safe from rivals. While she lost Wallis' cat to her enemies, the one from
Cook fared better. When Purea visited the *Bounty* in 1784 she carried her
"favourite cat," a descendant of Cook's gift.[108] Keeping animals as pets was
not a new Tahitian practice; as we saw earlier, dogs were given the role,
being treated affectionately, carried about and fed special food, and being
kept near houses. Dogs were, nevertheless, primarily a person's property
and a meat animal. Purea does not seem to have hesitated in offering her
plump pet dog to Cook and Banks to eat; it was strangled and roasted for
them.[109] They declared it delicious. Eels were reported to have been "great
favourites" (perhaps as food animals as well as pets—it is not clear) and
were kept in specially dug water holes where they grew large and, when
whistled to, would emerge from their dens to be hand-fed.[110] As pets, cats
were protected and given value, and they continued to thrive on the island.
One instance of Tahitians carrying "Pigs, Dogs and Cats" on board as gifts to
complete a *taio* friendship ceremony indicates that cats were firmly entered
into the ranks of valued animals.

Cats were noted by later voyagers to be feeding well on the small,
brown Polynesian rats (*Rattus exulans*) that had formerly swarmed around
the houses, seemingly in the "thousands." Bligh on the *Endeavour* visit had
reported rats being very tame, flocking around the people at mealtimes,
waiting "for the offals, which were commonly thrown to them."[111] When
Bligh revisited the island in 1789 he said that "at this time, we scarce ever
saw a rat, which must be attributed to the industry of a breed of cats left
here by European ships."[112]

Rats also had been added to the ranks of bird predators. The diet of
the Polynesian rat comprises fruits, seeds, and vegetables,[113] but from 1767
the larger, European black ship rat (*Rattus rattus*) arrived.[114] The black rat
preyed on birds' eggs and small birds. Larger birds such as rails, sandpipers,
and green pigeons had few defenses against European rats and even fewer
against cats. Today only a small number of indigenous birds survive in Tahiti.
Cats remain active predators in Tahiti's forests and urban environments.

Conclusions

By the end of the voyaging era, those who had designed the projects of
Pacific plant and animal introductions could look back on a difficult period
with some sense of vindication. Some of their original Enlightenment ideals

had been met; the islanders did find fruits such as oranges and guava useful. The captains' efforts to ensure better provisions did have some success; over the last decades of the eighteenth century they were able to obtain goat's meat, melons, pumpkins, and other familiar foods. The projects of plant and animal transfer were perhaps not the tributes to the scientific and naval majesty of their empires some of them had hoped, but in European eyes they had succeeded in distributing some of the "natural advantages" of the world's regions more evenly.

The people of Tahiti had been managing the new arrivals in ways that sprung from well-established traditions of propagating useful food species and trading with other regions. From the mid-eighteenth to the early nineteenth century, many chiefs had been able to secure a range of animals and plants as status-enhancing European possessions. The composition of a typical garden and grove of trees had changed, bearing new kinds of fruits and crops. The range of birds and animals present on the island had altered. New animals, without any connection to the world of the gods and with a tendency to be voracious, were increasingly making themselves at home. Birds that had once been common could no longer be found. Some of these birds had provided the voice of gods, and those gods were now silent. The effects of this could not help but touch the relations between Maohi and the inhabitants of the *Po*. Perhaps new ways of discerning the messages of gods were found. Perhaps those gods were seen to have lost some of their power in the *Ao*, proof that their *mana* had ebbed away if they could not protect even their own *ata* from harm. There were also more people dying of diseases, another proof for the Maohi of disrupted relationships between the *Ao* and *Po*. The viruses and bacteria Europeans imported in their bodies and on the insects, rodents, and other animals that accompanied them had introduced a range of diseases: syphilis, gonorrhea, and others, where they acted on the islanders' unprepared immune systems with debilitating and often deadly effect.[115] As Anne Salmond has noted, Bougainville's ships may have imported rats with fleas carrying the plague: Tahiti's Hiti'a district suffered a crippling epidemic. It fortunately did not succeed in spreading across the island as a whole. The sudden prevalence of sickness after the Europeans entered the island would have been convincing evidence for the islanders of the consequences of their visitors' transgressing many sacred restrictions. The island's population plummeted from a figure variously estimated from between 35,000 to 120,000 in the early decades of European contact to around 6,000 by 1802.[116] The Maohi would have found it hard to avoid the conclusion that the support of the gods had been lost. The land and its occupants had changed irreparably.

As ever, bringing new plants and animals into the dense complexity that makes up the combined ecology of humans and their environment had effects that could not be adequately predicted. Whether bringing in goats in eighteenth-century Polynesia, introducing cane toads into Australia as agents of biological control in the twentieth, or beginning the cultivation of genetically modified crops in the twenty-first, the environmental and social results of these well-intentioned disruptions tend to surprise—and dismay—an ecology's human inhabitants.

CHAPTER 4

Chiefly Cattle

The danger [lies in believing] . . . that history is the result of great generalities, instead of the sum of millions of small particulars, like bad drainage and sexual obsession and the anopheles mosquito.
—Morris West, *The Shoes of the Fisherman*

It is the path taken by specific historical actors and the effects of specific dynamics coming together in particular places that provide us with the surest views through the dark density of the past. While we need to establish a more overarching synthesis than Morris West's "millions of small particulars," it is by starting the process of questioning at the level of particulars that the changes undergone in any historical environment become readable. There are no easy generalizations to be made when every introduced species responds to its new environment in unique ways, no "great generalities" to explain the varied reactions of people meeting those new species within the complexities of their cultural environment. We have already seen that even brief investigations of the changes that foreign fruits and animals can bring to an island's cultural, economic, and physical landscapes are instructive. But it is through a more extensive study of the path taken by a specific species that we can start to properly grasp the broad social, political, and conceptual parameters that determine the effects an introduced species can have on its new physical and cultural environment.

One of the key parameters that has persistently surfaced during my investigation of ecological exchange in Tahiti is the central role of relationships of power. While looking for clues to why the history of an introduced animal or plant unfolded as it did, the voices and gestures of chiefs have surfaced repeatedly. The relationships between island chiefs, their people, and the Europeans who negotiated with them have persistently proved crucial to determining the fate of the living cargo that reached Tahiti's shores. The play of power was inextricable from the operation of ecological exchange.

When investigating power relations in the Pacific and their environmental impact (to adopt Gísli Pálsson's approach), cattle are "better to think with" than other animals.[1] The arrival of cattle on islands was highly visible; their presence could not be ignored. The locals dealt with the cattle more deliberately and with more discussion than with the smaller, less useful creatures being introduced at the same time. Cattle were considerable property in both Europe and the Pacific. They belonged to people with some social and economic standing. The size and rarity of cattle meant they were clear and impressive statements of the connection between a gift giver and receiver. The actions and discussions over cattle were noted in voyaging journals more often than the minor arrivals. Cats, mice, and fleas rated a mention in journals only in passing, usually in the context of the benefit or nuisance they were on shore. There were no systematic assessments of their progress. European voyagers were more likely to pester islanders for news on large, introduced livestock and to note their breeding success or failure on paper. Because of all they stood for in both Pacific and European contexts, the management of cattle was significant.

Commandante Boenechea, James Cook, George Vancouver, the London Missionary Society, and traders from New South Wales all transported cattle into Polynesia. They brought in breeding pairs of cows and bulls to Tahiti and gave them as gifts to the local chiefs. They did the same in Hawai'i. In Hawai'i, European cattle made themselves very much at home. They grazed on native vegetation, compacted the soil they walked upon, and multiplied rapidly. They still maintain a destructive presence in Hawaiian forests today, where few indigenous trees survive. Cattle have had a huge environmental impact on the Hawaiian archipelago. The breeding pairs introduced to Tahiti could easily have had the same effect. Cattle could have sustained themselves just as readily in Tahiti's climate, within the island's equally suitable forests and grasslands. But they did not. Despite all the efforts of captains and missionaries, cattle did not flourish in Tahiti. The question, of course, is why not?

The first cattle to reach Tahiti were brought across from South America on Commandante Boenechea's *Aguila* and *Júpiter* expedition in 1774. Several of the animals had survived the journey. On reaching Taiarapu (Tahiti's peninsula), in December, Boenechea unloaded a bull and a cow as gifts for the local chief, Vehiatua (along with "the most useful seeds and plants the Realm of Peru produces" and tools to cultivate them).[2]

The gift of the two animals was not a straightforward affair. During the presentation Vehiatua met the two Franciscan padres who, "as a mark of friendly confidence," would be staying on the island.[3] Two of the witnesses to this exchange were Society Islanders Pautu and Tetuanui, who had traveled with the Spanish in 1772 to Lima to be taught Catholicism and who were now returning to the island.[4] They had developed a poor opinion of their hosts. According to Don José Varela, one of the members of the expedition, on seeing the cattle being led over to Vehiatua, Pautu rushed up and warned him not to trust the gifts or the padres. Pautu reportedly called out to his fellow islanders that "all these things were for the purpose of deceiving them," for making the Spanish "masters of the island and reducing them to slavery."[5] The ari'i, although taken aback, heard the Spanish side of the story through an interpreter and, "struck with the kindly attitude of the Comandante"[6] (and probably the further material advantages he foresaw), agreed to accept the presence of both the Franciscans and the cattle. Vehiatua was clearly confident enough in his own position, sufficiently trusting of the Spanish motives, and sufficiently swayed by the advantages of the alliance and the gifts to take the risk that his new allies could turn out to be conquerors. Vehiatua's confidence was well placed; unlike earlier Spanish ventures on the extremities of the Pacific rim, this project of Catholic colonization did not succeed.

The Franciscan padres, Geronimo Clota and Narciso Gonzalez, established themselves in an imported house around which they built a tall reed screen. They were joined by Máximo Rodríguez, a Peruvian-Spanish marine who had become fluent in Tahitian in the course of the previous Spanish visit and from conversations with Pautu, Tetuanui, and the third Tahitian to make the journey to Lima, Heiao (who died there of smallpox). Acting as an interpreter on this return journey, Rodríguez stayed with the friars and compiled a report on the country and its people, involving himself (with persistent high-handedness) in his adopted community. The Franciscans, on the other hand, remained isolated, maintaining as much of a protective barrier between themselves and their strange new environment as possible. Their unwillingness to enter into the sharing of possessions, except to a limited degree with Vehiatua, soon lost them the respect of the local people. The islanders would call taunts through the screen (calling them thieves, fools, and poreho: shellfish, a double insult as it was also a word for genitals), and make raids on the garden and chicken pen.[7] Conflicts between Rodríguez, Clota, and Gonzalez were constantly and increasingly flaring up. When the Aguila came past to deliver extra provisions a year later, the missionaries, increasingly alarmed with their situation, beseeched the captain to give them passage.[8] The captain agreed, and recommended their remaining livestock also be loaded on board to contribute to ship's rations, ensuring the animals could not become the means by which rival nations could provision.[9]

While the negotiations over cattle and friars were taking place in Tai-arapu, Cook and the crew of the *Resolution* were traveling eastward across the Pacific toward the southernmost tip of South America. It was the home-ward leg of Cook's second Pacific voyage, with two visits to Tahiti behind them. There had been no cattle on the island when they left. The *Resolution* reached England in July 1775 and within a year Cook and the Admiralty were preparing another Pacific venture. This expedition was primarily to look for the theorized northwest passage for shipping through the high reaches of North America. The expedition also presented another oppor-tunity to distribute useful animals to Pacific provisioning stops. Before embarking Cook took on sheep, a bull, two cows, and their calves on "His Majestys Command and expence."[10] The intention was "stocking Otahiete and the Neighbouring Islands with these usefull animals," and there were other "attentions" paid the islands through the "many other useful articles" provided by the Admiralty, plus "Iron tools, trinquets &c" for cultivating friendships and alliances.[11] After a detour to Teneriffe to pick up feed for the livestock, they reached the Cape of Good Hope, shipped the animals ashore to graze, then gathered in more cattle and other creatures (includ-ing peacocks and guinea fowl) for the onward journey.[12] The *Resolution* must have looked and felt like a small, vividly alive ark.

On reaching New Zealand, two chiefs in Queen Charlotte Sound "begd of me some Goats & Hogs," said Cook, to which he agreed, exacting a prom-ise from them not to kill the animals.[13] He considered leaving a bull and two young cows, but decided against it, for a reason that revealed his expe-riences and motivation in introducing animals to Polynesia. He was not prepared to entrust his precious cargo to this place because he was unable to find "a chief powerfull enough to protect them from harm."[14]

Tahiti was the next anchorage and the place Cook felt most confident about leaving his livestock. On reaching Taiarapu's Vaitepiha Bay on 24 August 1777, they received some unpleasant news. Since Cook's last visit, the Spanish had been to Tahiti twice. The Spanish were rivals with the British not only for territory and resources, but also for supremacy of their respec-tive religions. The Spaniards had started to muscle in on the island Brit-ish voyagers had considered their particular preserve. Cook was affronted to find that the close and useful ties he and his compatriots had carefully nurtured had been undermined by Spanish slander. Boenechea's men had been broadcasting that the British were an "idle, piratical people," with no place of abode, "who lived entirely by plunder."[15] The people of Taiar-apu offered Cook only a lukewarm welcome.[16] It got worse: Cook invited a group of islanders onto the *Resolution* and waited for their amazed response to the impressive animals on deck. But they simply stated that the Spanish had already given them cattle like those.[17] James King reported glumly:

> We saw that our Act of benevolence from its being too long deferrd, had lost its hour, & its reward; We saw . . . an immence deal of trouble all thrown away to no purpose.[18]

As Nicholas Thomas has pointed out, Cook would have found this a heavy blow.[19] The captain and his nation were not the first to bring cattle to the Societies. In an era of firsts, this one had been resoundingly won by the Spanish. To cap it all, King and the others heard the Spanish cattle were:

> much finer than ours; the disappointment & vexation on this last information was visible on all our Countenances.[20]

There was some consolation in realizing that the Spanish introduction, while claiming the glory of first place, would not be the act to permanently establish cattle on the island. After the friars left with apparently most of the livestock, there was only one bull remaining. They heard it was kept at the northern end of the island, near Tu's chiefly residence at Pare.[21] The *Resolution* continued on to Matavai Bay. Cook went shore on 18 September 1777 with a small party, including Ma'i, who had returned with them to the Society Islands after his two-year visit to England.[22] They went ashore in the northern district of Pare with a small flock of three ewes and a ram from the Cape of Good Hope, plus a ewe and ram from England, all of which Cook gave to his old ally Tu.[23]

Cook could console himself that his imports compared well with those of the Spanish. Along with the three cows and bull, he brought in the first pair of horses to be seen in the Societies, along with the soon-to-be-con-tested goats, European pigs, sheep, turkeys, geese, and a pair of peacocks (a present from by "my Lord Besborough," a Lord of the Admiralty).[24] If Cook's were not the first cattle he was at least installing a more useful num-ber. After presenting the livestock, Cook wrote of his relief at feeling him-self "lightened of a very heavy burden." The "trouble and vexation that attended the bringing these Animals thus far" was, he said, "hardly to be conceived."[25]

Cook assumed that Tu possessed a role analogous to a king, and with the additional prop of a decade of politically supportive English goods and weapons including muskets and ammunition, he judged that Tu would easily be a sufficiently powerful chief to protect imported livestock. The situation was not, however, that straightforward. As we will see, the possession of these status-enhancing creatures was always going to be buffeted by internal struggles for power.

Cook's plans for the cattle encompassed not just Tahiti but other Society Islands—he also wanted to ensure that Ra'iatea, a few days' sail to the west, was stocked. Negotiations began between Cook, Pomare, and a priest from Porapora called Etari (who was so sacred he was conveyed around in a small cart to keep him from rendering the ground *tapu* to common people).[26] Etari owned the Spanish bull, having apparently acquired it from the Spanish in exchange for a mat. He wanted to transport the animal from Tahiti to Porapora. Cook tried to convince him to leave it in Tahiti, offering to give him instead an English bull and cow, which Cook would take to Ra'iatea. With some encouragement from Ma'i, Etari eventually agreed to this, but just as the English cattle were being loaded onto a boat, one of Etari's followers opposed the deal.[27] Cook decided it was safest to leave Etari to his own devices, forget about stocking Ra'iatea, and install all his own cattle in Tahiti with Tu. This he did,

> with a strict injunction never to suffer them to go from Oparre [Pare] not even the Spanish bull, nor none of the Sheep, till he should get a stock of young one[s] which only he was to dispose of to his friends and to send to the Neighbouring islands. This being settled, we left Etary and his party to ruminate on their folly.[28]

Holding confidence in Tu's authority and ability to keep the cattle safe, Cook departed in good spirits. But not having observed the normal operation of island politics and not realizing the contribution he had made to the unsettling of power, Cook had overestimated Tu's position.

After five years, the cows had bred eight calves, resulting in about thirteen cattle in Pare.[29] This was a large enough group to allow a strong population to develop. But their fortunes were about to take a downturn. Tu's relations with the chiefs of Mo'orea and Atehuru were becoming increasingly strained. The Pomare clan, with their allies, were preparing to wage war against Mahine, the childless *ari'i* of the island of Mo'orea, in what would become a long-lasting struggle over succession.[30]

The islanders were, during the late 1770s and 1780s, embroiled in a difficult period of unease and devastating battles. Over this period no European ships stopped by until, after eleven years, the *Bounty* arrived in 1788. On disembarking, Bligh took his first walk around the Matavai district and pronounced himself pleased. He could see a good range of the vegetables, fruit, and goats that he had witnessed being installed when he was master of the *Resolution,* on Cook's last visit. However, there were no cattle in evidence. He made enquiries. Back in his cabin he wrote that the reports he received were "very unfavourable, and so various, that, for the present, I shall forbear speaking of them."[31] The news did not improve. For some reason, the animals had failed to become established. They had not been held back by environmental factors—both Tahiti and Mo'orea were fundamentally amenable environments for cattle. Particularly hot days would have caused stress to the animals, but shade and fresh water were readily available and between the high, cool mountain forests and the open lowlands, the island provided suitable grazing land for cattle.[32] The answer did not lie in the island's ecology. Tu filled out the picture for Bligh. He told the captain that "five years and three Months" after the *Resolution* and *Discovery* had sailed, in 1783, an alliance of the western district of Atehuru and the island of Mo'orea had attacked Pare. Tu's warriors fought back but many were killed and the chiefly family made their escape to the mountains. The victors, now the masters of Pare property, destroyed:

> every thing they could get hold of, among which were the Cattle, Sheep, Ducks, Geese, Turkeys and Peacocks left by Captain Cook in 1777.[33]

Bligh bemoaned the destruction of the animals and the accompanying destruction of his "fond hopes" for Cook's introduction of "so many valuable things." He had himself been a part of the cattle project, as master of the *Resolution.* He had assumed that by now the trouble they had taken would have been "productive of every good" on the island.[34]

On questioning people further he found the warriors of Mo'orea had killed and eaten some of the cattle, but others had been taken back alive on canoes to Mo'orea.[35] He heard there were at least eight there. There was also a cow and a bull kept by two of the victorious *ari'i* on Tahiti. They were kept "25 or 30 miles from each other,"[36] the bull at Hiti'a on the east side of the island, the cow at Fa'a'a on the west.[37] This might have been a fair way to split up the spoils of war, but it was counterproductive for the British breeding plan. Bligh set about negotiating to purchase and reunite the pair.

The trouble Bligh took sent a clear message to Tu. The cattle were obviously, as ever, things of consequence to the English. They held potential as bargaining chips to mobilize European forces in Tu's favor. The British, for their part, were also strategizing. In a bid to keep their alliance with the Tahitians on a secure footing, they decided not to let word get out to the Tahitians that their esteemed *taio* Cook had been killed in Hawai'i in 1779.

Bligh told Tu that Cook was alive and growing old in England. Tu therefore asked him to tell Cook about the attack so that he "might come out in a great Ship to revenge his cause."[38] This annoyed Bligh. In his journal he complained to his readers that Tu had not recognized that Bligh had "shared with Captain Cook in the trouble of this business, and had been equally anxious for the success," and that he, too, "could be affected by the destruction of them."[39] He took pains to explain this to Tu. This was an even better situation than the *ari'i* could have hoped for, and he immediately suggested Bligh help him "take vengeance on the people who had deprived him of them." Bligh was far from mollified. Over the "loss of the cattle," he stated, Tu "appeared so unconcerned and indifferent, that I was very angry with him."[40]

The two men had divergent expectations over the value of the animals. They both saw political advantages residing in owning or controlling the cattle, but the means by which these advantages were to be activated ran at odds. Bligh's rhetoric placed the emphasis on long-lasting benefits as a direct result of the presence of cattle; Tu's purposes were more immediate, and he employed the cattle as a tool rather than as an end in themselves. Tu's efforts to get military support from his foreign ally were unsuccessful. But Bligh did at least coordinate a major negotiation effort between the various opposing *ari'i* possessing the scattered cattle and reunited them back at Matavai, under the care of Poeno. Poeno was now one of Tu's allies and Bligh could see that as one of the "principal men" of the district, it was in Bligh's "interest to be on good terms" with him.[41]

There were no corresponding attempts by the *ari'i* to keep the cattle carefully together to increase their numbers. The animals were not sufficiently valuable, it seems, to warrant going to great lengths over their care or asking English captains to bring in more. There is no evidence that European livestock in the Society Islands had become enmeshed in the cycles and flows of sacred power. There is no indication that they were rendered *tapu* or accorded any role that came close to approaching sacredness. Far from being sacred cows, they were primarily valued as politically useful novelties. James Morrison recorded that the chiefs spared little concern for breeding cattle because they were primarily seen as "curiosities."[42] Bulls and cattle were showy and exotic, but there was not enough mileage in their possession—they were not useful enough—to make them worth the effort of protecting. The careful husbandry that was given to pigs of either Polynesian or European breeds was not carried across to cattle, and it was left to Bligh and other Europeans to keep breeding pairs together. As with goats, cattle were not in demand as a meat animal or for their milk. Maohi did not value the livestock in the terms the Europeans had expected.[43] Consequently, while cattle were taken on as chiefly property in Tahiti, they were not, on balance, considered anywhere near as important as a commodity like muskets.

There was another animal of similar stature to cattle which chiefs did accord significant value. Horses were impressive and graceful enough to be suitable mounts for those of high standing. When, in Matavai Bay in 1777, Cook and Clerke landed and then rode horses in Tahiti for the first time, they were met by the "Very great surprise and astonishment of a great train of people."[44] Ma'i rode one of the horses (after initial difficulties staying on), and he later made an impressive attack on his enemies in Huahine, mounted on a horse and wearing his British suit of armor.[45] Whenever rivals saw him approaching in armor on horseback, they "thought it impossible to hurt him, and for that reason never attempted it. . . .Victory always attended him and his Party."[46] At Matavai in 1777 Cook's officers went riding each day, and Cook said the locals:

> were exceedingly delighted with these Animals after they had seen the use that was made of them. And I think they gave them a better idea of the greatness of other Nations than all the other things put together that had been carried amongst them.[47]

Cattle could not compete. When Cook was preparing to depart Tahiti in September 1777, Tu gave his "commands" to Cook, instructing him to request the *"Earee rahie no Pretane"* (*ari'i rahi,* the paramount chief, of Britain):

> to send him by the next Ships, red feathers and the birds that produce them, axes, half a dozen muskets with powder and shot, and by no means to forget horses.[48]

Wrestling for Power

In Tahiti, far from being protected by chiefly power, cattle became the victims of struggles over it. They were mobilized for demonstrations of secular power rather than sacred purposes. There was no one chief who could effectively protect his property from the clutches of other chiefs.

The Europeans visiting the Pare-'Arue region had initially regarded Tu as the paramount chief of the island. They held on to this assumption for some time; it was not until the late 1780s that Bligh and others gradually recognized the error of this view. The British still focused their dealings on Tu and his son Pomare II as the *ari'i* presiding over Tahiti's best anchorage. These two were also the *ari'i* who had the most experience of how the Europeans liked to be treated, and were thus the most useful to be kept on side. With all the riches, weapons, and ammunition the British bestowed upon the Pare-'Arue *ari'i*, captains would have expected an ever-increasing power over the island to develop in these most convenient of hands. In his pursuit of the remaining cow, Bligh decided to sail over with Tu, his brother Ari'ipaea, and Poeno to make inquiries in the neighboring district of Tetaha (now known as Fa'a'a) a little way to the west.[49] While Bligh went ashore and asked where Te Pau, the district's *ari'i rahi*, could be found, he noticed that Tu:

> had remained all this time in the boat. I observed that no respect was shewn to him at this place, nor was he able to procure a cocoa-nut, or a bread-fruit, otherwise than by purchasing it. The heifer being here, is a proof of this district not having been friendly to the people of Matavai and Oparre.[50]

Tu held little if any authority out of his district. His attempts to become a dominant force on the island had brought the alliance of previously independent chiefs together to quash his ambitions, and he was still watched with simmering hostility. His own people obeyed him, within traditionally defined limits, but he inspired no real fear in his opponents. Even with his new firearms, Tu could not extend enough of his chiefly reach of power over his possessions to keep them safe—and this included cattle.

Te Pau asked Bligh if he had come to simply see the cow or if he intended to take it by force. Bligh and the chiefs sent reassurances and arranged a meeting. Once the cow was brought in, the captain's relief at seeing her was palpable; he described her as "the most beautiful brown heifer that ever trod the Earth."[51] Negotiations got under way, a deal was struck, and the *ari'i* agreed to bring the heifer to Matavai. By the end of his stay, Bligh was able to describe with satisfaction a walk to Matavai in which he saw the bull and cow grazing in "a very fine pasture" and was told they had already mated. "So," said Bligh, "if no untoward accident happens, there is a fair chance of the breed being established."[52]

Bligh's description of the lengths he went to and repeated statements he made about being personally affected by the loss of the cattle had specific motivations. He could have been working to reunite the cattle for all the benevolent aims other voyagers expressed regarding the benefit of future sailors and the general good of the islanders, but unlike Cook, Bligh makes no overt statements about these goals. His more personal set of concerns—

having "shared in the trouble" of introducing the cattle, is more likely to have driven his efforts to bring the project to a successful conclusion. His logs, letters, and journal attest to his being persistently concerned about his own reputation. Whether fretting over the English public's assumptions of his role in prompting the mutiny, or being offended by the Tahitians not appearing to be upset at the prospect of his departure, his anxiety over how much respect and admiration he could command was never far from the surface.[53] Demonstrating that he was working to ensure the success of a project that Cook had worked toward could have acted as another prop in the edifice he was constructing; his dedication to Cook's honored memory and noble aims could be expected to impress his readers at home. A healthy breed of beef and dairy cattle in the South Seas would bring kudos to whoever had made it possible.

By 1788, fourteen years after the first introductions, there were only two cows on Tahiti and a small herd of about eight in Mo'orea. Although cattle had proved useful in the struggles for various chiefs' personal and political positions, they were still not being put to use as beef or dairy resources. By the time George Vancouver visited from December 1791 to January 1792, there were a total of four cows and one bull on Mo'orea. The bull had received an "injury in his loins" and without new introductions the herd would expand no more.[54] When Bligh returned to the island again on the *Providence,* shortly after Vancouver's visit, he kept an eye out for livestock but only noticed goats.[55] Later in his stay he noted in a single, unelaborated line that he had heard from Purea's nephew that there were six cattle on Mo'orea.[56] This time Bligh did not expend his energies discussing or chasing around after cattle. He had other fronts on which he had to fight to rescue his public face. His priorities were now the more pressing ones of managing a new shipment of breadfruit plants, keeping his crew in check, and juggling relations with local chiefs.

Cattle had achieved none of the ease in the Tahitian landscape that European goats and cats found or that the new breeds of pigs and dogs possessed. Those animals were more suitable for integrating into the cultural and ecological life of the island. Pigs and dogs interbred with the local Polynesian breeds, assimilating not only physically but also fitting with only a few aberrations (caused by their more aggressive natures) into virtually the same cultural role held by the existing animals. Goats appear to have been more robust than cattle, better equipped to fend for themselves, more nimble, and, being smaller, perhaps less of a target for marauders. Cats, being taken on as pets, were integrated more intimately within the house-hold of a chiefly family and were given a greater degree of protection than other introduced animals.

The Mission for Cattle

The arrival of the missionaries would have seemed to promise more success for the cattle project. For the first time since the two Spanish friars had tried to maintain a settlement, there would be a body of Europeans in Tahiti who would be intent on providing ongoing care. A settled group could establish a herd and, being on the spot, could exert some influence to keep it safe from the political storms that kept engulfing the *ari'i*. These were surely the ideal conditions for properly raising English livestock on the island.

As we saw in the previous chapter, there were considerable environmental challenges to the establishment of European species. The missionaries faced an additional challenge. They were highly reliant on the generosity of the chiefs and the "generality of Tahitians." The relationships they formed with the Pomares and the people turned out to be the primary factor shaping the fortunes of the animals the missionaries tried to introduce.

The occupants of the Pare-'Arue district saw their new neighbors as a much less imposing set of Europeans than any they had met before. This perception had substantial consequences. The missionaries had no cannons to fire into crowds on beaches, no swivel guns to turn on retreating thieves, and only a few muskets in their storehouse, which they kept for trade with the chief rather than for use. Their whole demeanor was different. The missionaries knew that being "men of Peace" made them an easy target. "Otoo's people were exceedingly daring," wrote Brother Jefferson in 1799, "frequently making attempts to take things out in the middle of the day before our faces, & only laughed at us when spoken to."[57] Tu and his family made some efforts to safeguard the missionaries and their goods, but they did not feel obliged to go to great lengths. Brother Jefferson wrote in 1803 that since the recent departure of a visiting trading ship the islanders had stolen the two hundred pigs the brothers had bought from surrounding districts for salting. They had also lost "by theft . . . ducks and fowls and things from the gardens."[58]

The missionaries' project of establishing a wholesome, productive farmyard on the island had met obstacles before they even arrived. On the way out to the Pacific on the *Duff* they had been concerned about their milk cow after she suffered repeated falls during gales.[59] When the feed ran out three months from Tahiti, they resigned themselves to killing "the poor lean animal," and much regretted her loss, especially when they realized she was pregnant.[60] Some other livestock, tethered on deck, died "either by the cold or the spray of the sea," and William Ellis was worried that they might lose them all.[61] They did manage to keep some animals alive and, once on the island, purchased more from passing ships and bartered for pigs from the Tahitians. By 1804 the missionaries were referring to having sheep, goats, and pigs in their care.[62] Brother Henry owned a cow ("a fine beast") and that year arranged with Captain Campbell, a visiting trader from New South Wales, to bring them a bull calf.[63] Although they initially balked at the considerable price of £29 the traders placed on the bull, they paid it in the end.[64] The resulting calves did not fare well. In September 1808, while the herd was "rambling," untended, on the plains, one young bull broke its jaw fighting with its father and was eventually found almost too weak to walk and had to be killed. The cattle were not being kept enclosed; trying to keep fences up against broaching by pigs, goats, and people was a continual trial for the missionaries, and in the middle of considerable political strife, it appears there was little time spare to watch the cattle. As the likelihood of another war rose in November 1808, the missionary group split, half of them retreating with 'Itia and Tu to calmer conditions on the island of Huahine, the others retreating from Matavai to the Pare district to be closer to the remainder of the Pomare family. Soon afterwards two of the brothers returned to Matavai to try to round up the cattle to bring them to the new settlement:

> where we will be able to attend to them better . . . though, should we be obliged to quit the island we consider it of small consequence where they are, as in that case they will be sure to fall into the hands of the natives.[65]

They were able to find most of them (a group that appears to have numbered at least five), but one of the calves was found to have already been speared and was very weak.[66] Like Tu losing his herd in the 1770s, the missionaries lacked sufficient authority on the island to keep their cattle safe.

The missionaries were able to get themselves more securely established after 1811, when Pomare II decided to start making political headway out of them and their religion. As we will see in chapter 6, on 18 July 1812 Pomare asked to be baptized. In his wranglings for power over the people of Tahiti and Mo'orea he gave the missionaries a new position of security and influence. The brethren were able to start building up their resources—and their herds—again.

Meanwhile, the British colony in New South Wales had been growing in importance. The London Missionary Society had established a base there under the direction of the Rev. Samuel Marsden. Traders from Sydney, increasingly extending out to the Pacific Islands, provided the missionaries in Tahiti with a connection to a much more ready source of material support than had been possible before. Provisions, presents for the Pomares, and livestock were now much more accessible. Cows and bulls were shipped in from New South Wales at various times—in 1817 and possibly earlier—at the missionaries' request.[67] Other imports increased as cross-Pacific trade routes grew busier.[68] The missionaries had started to experiment with producing their own commodities to barter with the Sydney traders, preparing coconut oil and some salted pork, through which they were able to arrange for more effective gifts for the Pomare family. The traders were careful to bring in suitable gifts on their own account. When the ship carrying the missionaries' cattle arrived in 1817 from New South Wales, Pomare II went out to the ship to see the animals. He was most interested, though, in seeing the horse that "the owners of the ship had sent him as a present."[69]

Tahitians remained unsupportive of any project to get cattle established on the island. There were still few by the 1820s and 1830s. A visitor to the island in 1832 described what he saw as the islanders' laziness over cultivation and animal husbandry. They would not, he said, "trouble themselves with the care of horned cattle, sheep, or goats."[70] They still remained without value or significance in the Maohi world. R. G. Crocombe has suggested (1972) that cattle were not taken up in most parts of the Pacific because they required large areas of land and fencing, and to fence was to cause offense to neighbors and kin who had rights of access.[71] However, cattle were bred successfully on other islands without fences, and chiefs could make use of large swathes of land when they possessed sufficient authority. These are unlikely to be reasons for Tahitians' declining to pursue cattle husbandry. Having a protector who valued the animals sufficiently and who extended protection over them against those who might seek to harm them was a far more decisive factor.

In 1847 Captain Henry Martin, during his survey of the Society Islands, reported on the political and physical landscape of Ra'iatea. He mentioned that a "few bullocks run wild in the mountains and are very fierce."[72] No other cattle appear in his report. The British attempt, over forty years, to stock these islands in the middle of the Pacific with readily accessible fresh beef and milk had not succeeded. It was later, under French direction, that substantial herds were established by colonists with large tracts of land, protected and managed without reference to the land's former owners.

The French in Tahiti: Ecological Impacts

When Tahiti's political structures underwent a complete reshaping in the 1830s and 1840s, the position of cattle on the island took a major turn. The French emerged from their period of internal uncertainty and the 1830 Revolution wanting to extend their sights across the Pacific. The prevalence of British, and specifically Protestant, footholds caused unease in many circles. Roman Catholic missionaries landed in the Gambiers in 1834 and on the eastern coast of Tahiti in 1836. They attempted to settle in Tahiti, but the Protestant missionaries who had been acting as religious, political, and legal advisors to the Pomares for the previous thirteen years pointed out the necessity of obtaining permission to take up residence. They needed to apply to Pomare II's daughter, Aimata, who had become "Queen Pomare" of Tahiti in 1827.[73] The two Catholics requested an audience with Aimata and offered her money to secure residency, which she declined.[74] Aimata and her advisors were no doubt unwilling to have another faith promoted on the island. There was already substantial discord being sown within Tahiti by the Mamaia religious group, which pursued a blend of traditional Maohi and Christian beliefs. When some disaffected chiefs decided to align themselves with the two Catholics, Aimata quickly arranged for the Frenchmen to be taken back to the Gambiers.[75]

It was not long before this insult was being reported to the French authorities stationed on the coast of South America. In 1838 Commodore Abel Dupetit-Thouars of the armed frigate *Venus* was sent to Tahiti. On 30 August, three days after arriving, he demanded a letter of apology from Queen Aimata, 125 ounces of gold (equivalent to two thousand Spanish dollars), and a twenty-one-gun salute to the French flag, flown at the queen's residence, all by ten o'clock the following morning.[76] Failure to comply would result in war being declared on the Societies, the destruction to begin at ten. George Pritchard, the resident British consul (since 1837) rallied his friends, supplied the money, and organized enough powder and guns for the salute, with a few minutes to spare.[77] Aimata was pressed to sign a treaty of friendship, allowing French rights of trade and residence and free practice of religion in the islands. She sent repeated letters to Britain asking for help to defend her islands against the French, but no ships were ever sent in her support. French ships stopping by at the island were reported to have already started taking liberties, forcing local women to be "wives" to the sailors and cutting down quantities of trees without negotiating or providing compensation to the owners.[78] By 1842 Dupetit-Thouars was back, without the knowledge of his superiors in France, troubled by British expansion and wanting to secure a base for French whaling and commerce. Redeploying his 1838 tactic, he used the excuse of some "evils" against resident Frenchmen to demand compensation of either $10,000 or provisional occupation of the island, to be granted in forty-eight hours to avoid an attack.[79] A group of chiefs arranged a declaration requesting French protection in return for a guarantee of Aimata and her government's retaining their authority, for the people to keep their lands, and to have free will in religious adherence. Aimata signed before the deadline expired, and, as Colin Newbury has said, this "novel piece of imperial constitution-making," creating a distinction between external French sovereignty and Tahitian "possession of the soil," was delivered to the French ship.[80] It was not long before the French were annexing the island and the other Society Islands.

The installment of the French protectorate over the Society Island group in 1842 were carried out under martial law and in the face of active rebellion.[81] Tahitian communities, refusing to accept the French pennant, were shot at, plundered, forced into camps at the ends of valleys, cut off from the life-giving sea and fertile coastal lands. The Tahitians battled against the French until 1847, attacking the soldiers and making ambushes. In the end, Aimata was ousted from independent leadership and reduced to a figurehead, ending the reign of the Pomares.[82] European settlers moved in and established plantations and large, fenced pastures. Martial law remained in place, the Tahitian death rate escalated, and the landscape was rendered increasingly foreign.

A very different environment for introductions was established. Colonial administrators, missionaries, and the suite of economically minded settlers, with control of the crucial coastal flats, were reshaping the island's economy. Although cotton, copra, and vanilla became the key commodities, cattle had an important role to play. Conway Shipley, visiting Tahiti in 1848, reported that an English settler on Moʻorea, Mr. Bell, had recently established a "large sugar factory and a vast number of cattle."[83] Those who were taking over the land were farming it in ways they knew from home. It was by no means a straightforward proposition, however, and plantation owners remained reliant on the land's former occupants. Mr. Bell's workforce deserted him to join in the ongoing fighting against the French, and with no one to cut the canes, boil up the sugar, or tend to the cattle, he had to sell and leave the island.[84]

Increasingly, those who possessed a growing hold on power ensured that their farms were able to supply their daily wants. In the late nineteenth century a passing traveler reported that the missionaries on the island pos-

Figure 4.1. *Conway Shipley, "Queen Pomare's house, Papeite." 1851. Lithograph, 8 x 10.8 in. (20.5 x 27.6 cm). In Shipley,* Sketches in the Pacific: The South Sea Islands *(London, T. McLean, 1851). National Library of Australia, Canberra (nla.pic-an9947724).*

sessed "a few hundred head of cattle."[85] Charles Blin, an aide-commisaire de la marine visiting Tahiti in 1881, noted the operation of a market in the growing town of Pape'ete, which included two butchers. They sometimes sold mutton, but beef and pork were available every day.[86] Holding a tight grip on authority meant, in Tahiti and across Oceania, control over ecological resources like cattle.

Cattle across the Pacific

The history of cattle on other islands took courses that differed substantially from Tahiti's. In the 1600s Jesuit missionaries and troops from Spain had installed themselves aggressively on a range of islands in the northern Marianas in Micronesia. The indigenous Chamorros people rebelled against their presence for decades until the Spanish forcibly removed them to Guam. In the mid-1700s the Spanish were looking for ways to expand local food production. They selected the small island of Tinian as a cattle station. The station was so successful it reportedly supported around ten thousand cattle by 1767. The once verdant island was soon reduced to an uninhabit-able, trampled wasteland, thick with flies.[87] In another part of Micronesia in 1780, the Ibedul (chief) of Koror in Palau was given cattle by the East India Company. They were reported to be thriving, and apparently not causing difficulties by overrunning the island, more than sixty years later.[88]

The case of Hawai'i is particularly distinctive. The first cattle intro-duced to Hawai'i were given to Kamehameha by Captain Vancouver when he arrived in Kealakekua Bay in 1792.[89] Kamehameha, paramount chief (ali'i) of the region, came on board and was captivated by the animals there: several cows, a bull, two ewes, and a ram. It was apparently the first time Hawaiians had seen such large and ominous-looking animals, and they had no basis for knowing what to expect from them.[90] Thomas Manby wrote that the cattle fascinated Kamehameha, but he was nervous of their bite and "he called them large Hogs."[91] Vancouver presented the livestock to the chief and was pleased to see "the particular attention" the chief paid to moving the animals into the canoes.[92]

The cattle did not manage well at first; the bull had grown weak and ill during the voyage, and a few days after it had landed Kamehameha with visible regret reported its death to Vancouver.[93] Vancouver said he would try to bring more on his return journey. While surveying on the west coast of America, Vancouver purchased some black cattle and in January 1794 returned to Hawai'i with a young bull, two cows, and "two very fine bull calves, all in high condition."[94] In total Vancouver had introduced ten head of cattle to the "big island" of Hawai'i.[95] It was a few more than had been landed by the Spanish and Cook in Tahiti, and it had been done in a more concentrated time period. This would have helped the Hawaiian cattle in the process of establishing a population, but it is not sufficient in itself to explain the stark difference between the long-term history of cattle in the two island groups. The small group of cattle in Matavai had managed to multiply well over a short period, and in the right political conditions, this trend could have continued.

It could be that the differences in the success of cattle on Tahiti and Hawai'i can be explained by the ecological differences between islands themselves. Hawai'i, the Hawaiian archipelago's largest island (and the one that received the most cattle), is just over ten times the size of Tahiti and therefore provided a more extensive environmental arena for cattle to range over and find food. However, only a thin portion of the island of Hawai'i is useful cattle-grazing area. The island is dominated by two peaks with elevations above 13,000 feet (3,900 meters). Three-quarters of the island's area has an elevation of 2,000 feet (about 600 meters) or higher.[96] The extreme steepness of much of the land, scree slopes, unregenerated lava flows, and the drop in temperature as the altitude increases—to the extent that the peaks are often capped with snow—renders a substantial portion of Hawai'i unsuitable for cattle.[97] Both Hawai'i and Tahiti possess regions containing vegetation suitable for fodder, few competitors for food, and, at the end of the eighteenth century, few parasites.[98] The ecological distinctions between the two islands are not substantial enough to be the key factor determining their different cattle histories. We need to look to other causes.

The crucial difference lies, I argue, in the degree of power residing in the chief who received the cattle. Kamehameha was an exceptional chief. From 1782, there was a succession of battles on the island of Hawai'i for control of lands and people. By the end of the year the island was divided between three powerful *ali'i*: Kamehameha, Keoua Kuahuula, and Keawemauhili. The battles were hard and bloody, but by 1791 Kamehameha had won the upper hand with his well-consolidated fighting forces and his skills in diplomacy. His warriors were supplemented by the warriors of lesser chiefs, who had aligned themselves with this persuasive and prestigious leader. Kamehameha's fortunes were on the rise. He possessed the right claims on sacred power; his descent line endowed him unquestionably with sufficient rights and sufficient *mana* to claim secular leadership. His skills in collecting European goods, above other chiefs, also served to underline his *mana*, highlighting his ability to ensure the prosperity of the island and its people. It is likely the majority of the populace would have conceived of his maneuvering for the reins of power as justifiable. He managed his relations with rival chiefs well, working to gain their alliance by distributing local and European objects of prestige. His canny negotiations stand in contrast to the awkward struggles for supremacy made by the Pomares in Tahiti in the face of growing opposition and popular unease. Kamehameha was also sufficiently ruthless. By 1791 the only obstacle to his possessing dominion over the whole island was the chief Keoua Kuahuula. In the summer Keoua came to Kamehameha with a proposal for peace. Kamehameha had him speared to death.[99] Vancouver, arriving the year after, had no trouble identifying the island's most powerful leader with whom he should leave his cargo.

The other, recently surpassed *ali'i* did not make any overt attacks on Kamehameha's position of the sort that Tu suffered in Tahiti. During Vancouver's visit, *ali'i* from other islands—and quite possibly some of the recently conquered *ali'i* of the big island—did make attempts to undercut Kamehameha's monopoly on English valuables. Vancouver noted that

"Kahowmotoo" (possibly Keeaumoku, c.1736–1804, a chief of Kona)[100] "appeared much rejoiced" at the arrival of some sheep and cattle, but "could not refrain from observing, that he considered it a very unequal distribution, to give all the large cattle to *Tamaahmaah*, and none to himself . . . or the other principal chiefs."[101] To this Vancouver replied that he had already done Kamehameha an "injustice" by giving "Kahowmotoo" the sheep that had been "designed for the king," and that he would endeavor to bring further cattle on his return.[102] Despite the talk, there were few effective rivals to Kamehameha.

Kamehameha was able to command respect among Hawai'i's people for his person and his possessions, livestock included. When one of the cows gave birth while the great chief was visiting an eastern district, some of the men in charge of the cattle were so delighted and so anxious that their *ali'i* should see it that they carried the calf on their backs for several days to Hilo, sustaining the animal, surprisingly, on water and fish.[103] It is hard to imagine Tu or Pomare's people extending a similar degree of attention to their chiefs' cattle.

Histories of Hawai'i that mention cattle refer to Kamehameha's making cattle *kapu* (taboo), rendering them sacred and beyond the reach of ordinary people. According to Captain Vancouver, he himself inspired Kamehameha to take this course of action. In February 1794, just before leaving Hawai'i, Vancouver met with the great *ali'i* and pointed out the "difficulty, trouble, and concern" he had gone through to introduce the livestock. He then "demanded, that they should be *tabooed* for ten years, with a discretionary power in the king alone to appropriate a certain number of the males of each species . . . to the use of his own table."[104] He further stipulated that traditional restrictions on women eating meat be dropped, allowing them to consume both lamb and beef, because "the intention of their being brought to the island was for the general use and benefit of every inhabitant of both sexes, as soon as their numbers should be sufficiently increased to allow of a general distribution amongst the people."[105]

Whether Kamehameha did actually make the animals *kapu* is unclear. He may have placed a temporary restriction equivalent to a *rahui* or ignored Vancouver's insistence outright. It is fairly certain the restriction on women eating meat was not relaxed—as we will see it was through a later, deliberate breaking of food *kapu* in 1819 that Hawai'i's ancient belief system started to collapse. Whatever Kamehameha's final decision regarding the cattle, the animals did seem to have been protected. If he did make the cattle *kapu*, he was taking a step that appears not to have been taken on other Polynesian islands. The *ali'i* would have been rendering these foreign creatures analogous to chiefly groves and chiefly turtles. They would have been included in local affairs in a way that identified them not just as property, like other European commodities, but as valid participants within the complexes of negotiations between realms of the living and dead, seen and unseen. By marking cattle as *kapu* the *ali'i* would have been marking the animals as an aristocratic resource, connected to the flow of *mana* the *ali'i* managed, encompassed within his supervision of living resources, at the beck and call of not just himself but also the gods with whom he maintained a relationship.

An object included in this system of *kapu* was marked as beyond the reach of commoners. It would take a brave rival to challenge this and risk the retribution of the powerful gods who were so clearly supporting and endowing their potency in this *ali'i*. There were no raids on the cattle, no attacks on the *ali'i*'s property in this period. Whatever the mechanism, the cattle were closely enough allied with Kamehameha for them to be protected. The cattle had become more than European cattle; they were chiefly cattle.

These protected animals bred in sufficient numbers to establish a sustainable population. They then started to impact negatively on their well-vegetated, safe surroundings. Those not kept alongside the chief's residence with his other possessions roamed loose in the forests. By the early

Figure 4.2. *Cattle and other livestock near the chiefly residences, Hawai'i. Victor-Jean Adam, "Port d'hanarourou." 1822. Hand-colored lithograph after Louis Choris, 6.3 × 12.9 in. (16.5 × 33 cm). In L. Choris,* Voyage *Pittoresque autour du monde (Paris: Imprimerie de Firmin Didot, 1821–22). National Library of Australia, Canberra (nla.pic-an10460625).*

decades of the nineteenth century cattle had become common in the forests of Hawai'i, Maui, and Kauai'i.[106] Cattle have a particularly destructive grazing method, tearing off the bulk of a plant or pulling it roots and all from the ground.[107] In the gaps created by overgrazing, vigorous and fast-growing introduced plants took root, causing a cascading chain of threats to the survival of native species. With fewer native plants available, there were fewer habitats and food sources for the islands' associated insects, bird, and reptiles. Particular Hawaiian woods became rare, including the *koa,* a wood with specific sacred qualities that had been used for carvings of god figures for *heiau* (sacred grounds), food bowls, and furniture for the *ali'i.* Specific plants used for medicines and familiar food plants became harder to find or disappeared altogether.[108]

After Kamehameha's death in 1819, his favorite wife, Kaahumanu, ensured that their son retained Kamehameha's position, while she managed the actual power. As she rose in influence, she began overriding the old system of restrictions, breaking the *kapu* on eating sacred food, and eating in the company of men, which were deeply demoralizing acts for the population.[109] Alongside the breakdown of *kapu,* diseases (many of foreign origin) continued to take their toll, and Hawai'i's people lost confidence in the efficacy of their gods and sacred practices.[110] It was at this point that restrictions on using chiefly cattle dissolved. Individuals began to gather, fence, and brand the free-range cattle. Specialist *paniolo* ("cowboys") from California and South America were hired by both local chiefs and the new white settlers to whom the chiefs were leasing their land.[111] By 1846 there were about 35,000 head of cattle in the islands, 10,000 of them on ranches.[112] Three years later the *Honolulu Mercury* was reporting the first beef export to America.[113]

The head count by 1866 was 60,000 cattle, a large proportion still undomesticated, grazing loose in the forests,[114] gradually reducing the forests to open grassland.[115] Today, cattle continue to compete with the reproductive cycle of *Acacia koa* trees in the remaining forests and in the parkland on the peak of Manua Kea. The suckers are routinely eaten, and rarely grow above four inches (ten centimeters).[116] Periodic culls help to keep the number of wild cattle down, but fencing stands of *koa* appears to be the only way to preserve the tree and the species that depend on it.

Conclusion

In 2001 there were an estimated 10,000 head of cattle on farms in French Polynesia.[117] The number is rising. While most meat sold on the island is imported from New Zealand and France, the protectorate's government is supporting the importation of additional livestock from Australia, New Zealand, and Europe to bolster local production.[118] The introduction of European animals to Tahiti is a process that is likely to continue.

The case of cattle in eighteenth-century Polynesia demonstrates how intersections of environment, society, and power can operate. The contrasting cattle histories of the Hawaiian archipelago and the Society Islands provide a clear corrective to Moorehead's simple "fatal impact" theory. The result of introducing exotic species is not predetermined to end in ecological disaster. The complexities and "small particulars" of each ecological and cultural situation mean the equation is much more complex. As it turned out, the chiefly protection of cattle in late eighteenth-century Hawai'i has been one of the most influential factors determining the shape of Hawai'i's landscape. It has also had implications for Hawaiian cultural practices. In both places, with societies intimately integrated on so many levels with the specifics of particular timbers, medicinal plants, food plants, and associated species, the chiefly relationship to cattle and the ability of one *ari'i* to protect his possessions had deep consequences. With a different set of circumstances, particularly a contrasting set of power relations, the establishment of cattle in Tahiti foundered and the Maohi relationship to the land was unaffected.

These histories of ecological exchanges in contrasting contexts add evidence for the ways island chiefs managed the Europeans who visited their islands and those who settled there. Stories of cattle have shown how chiefs in Tahiti and Hawai'i managed their authority, and also—something that is usually harder to discern—the workings and negotiations of power between island chiefs and their people. In assessing the eighteenth-century histories of both places, cattle have been particularly good to think with.

Part III

OUT OF TAHITI

*George Tobin, "West side of Port Morant, Jamaica, Blue Mountains &c. 1793."
Watercolor, page 13.7 x 10.2 in. (35 x 26 cm). SLNSW (PXA 563 f.83).*

CHAPTER 5

Breadfruit Connections

In February 1793, two ships arrived in Port Royal, Jamaica. The deck of the larger ship was crowded with greenery. There were broad-leaved trees more than seven feet tall on the quarterdeck, and ranks of smaller trees in pots. A mass of leaves was visible through the windows of the great cabin, the tops of hundreds of plants stretching back out of view. Locals paddled out in their canoes to investigate "the ship that has the bush."[1] On board were a tired, sun-browned crew and a captain jubilant in his successful arrival at this island. There were also two Tahitian men on deck. On first approaching the Caribbean islands, and sighting the lush peak of St Vincent, these two had joyously called out "O Tahiti, O Tahiti [it is Tahiti]!"[2] But they were six months' sail from home. It was because of breadfruit that they and the ship were there. Of all the exotic and valuable plants being moved around the globe—cinnamon, nutmeg, saffron, tea, sugar, cocoa, coffee, quinine—it was plain, starchy breadfruit that attracted the particular attention of the British at the end of the eighteenth century and provided the strongest links between England, the Pacific, and the Caribbean.

Breadfruit is a large, hard, pock-skinned fruit with a flavor reminiscent of artichoke. It is really only palatable when roasted, fermented, or pickled. It grows in many places across Southeast Asia and the Pacific. It is a basic food, a tropical staple. It was hardly likely to be a candidate for the dining tables of Europe. It could not be expected to revolutionize eating nor drinking habits there. It could not cure ill health, soothe nerves, help to preserve other foods, or even add spice to a dish. Yet the British government, prompted by a wide range of interested and influential people, had decided by the mid-eighteenth century that it was as worthwhile sailing around the world to collect breadfruit as any of those valuable spices. The British did not expect breadfruit to take off as a commodity at home. It was valued only in terms of its local importance for a small group of British plantation owners in the Caribbean. Despite the limited scope of the return it promised, the government, navy, and Royal Society had been gradually convinced of the importance of bringing breadfruit from the Pacific to

Figure 5.1. *George Tobin, "The Bread Fruit of O'tahȳtey, 1792 . . . about the size of a Shaddock." Watercolor, page 13.7 x 10.2 in. (35 x 26 cm). SLNSW (PXA 563 f.2).*

the Atlantic. Interest groups clamored for its transportation. Letters and petitions were written. Medals were offered. It was an extraordinary venture. Even if the plants could be gathered up successfully in Tahiti—if the Tahitians could be convinced to enter into exchanges for the plant—there was still no guarantee the seedlings would survive the long voyage through extreme changes of temperature and humidity, at risk from salt, the nibbling of ships' rats and mice, and rationed fresh water. Yet the British persevered. In the end two separate expeditions were sent out, the second two years after the first had failed. The expeditions employed a total of three ships, 190 seamen and officers, four gardeners, and two captains. Thousands of pounds were spent fitting the ships as floating plant nurseries, and thirty-three months of voyaging was borne,[3] all in an attempt to pot and transport Tahitian breadfruit trees.

Surprisingly, the British pursued this costly, risky project of ecological exchange believing that breadfruit had already been established in the Caribbean by the French. Some simple negotiations could surely have been entered into to allow a more straightforward transplantation from a neighboring island, rather than from across the globe. There was more going on here than the simple economic advantage of some plantation owners. One historian has pondered whether, on the subject of breadfruit, the British were gripped by a kind of "collective national madness."[4]

A Role for Breadfruit

> *Where all partake the earth without dispute,*
> *and bread itself is gathered as a fruit;*
> *Where none contest the fields, the woods, the streams:*
> *The Goldless Age, where Gold disturbs no dreams.*
> —Lord Byron, *The Island*[5]

Finding ways to explain the ideas and expectations that gave rise to the British breadfruit project requires uncovering what the fruit had come to represent in minds of those involved: plantation owners, men of science, commentators, policymakers, lords and officers of the Admiralty, and government officials. Further, by exploring the way the saga unfolded, we can understand more of what breadfruit meant to the Tahitians and to the people of the Caribbean. British and Tahitian approaches to this plant reveal many of the underlying approaches to the natural world, in both cultures, particularly the moral, economic, sentimental, and pragmatic attachments made to particular elements within their landscapes. It is a story that neatly demonstrates the typically unpredictable range of effects that results from entering into ecological exchanges. This project of ecological exchange was an especially sustained one, and the *Bounty* and *Providence* voyages brought Tahitians the most extensive engagements with Europeans experienced to that date. All these outcomes were the result of conceptions of breadfruit that directed decisions and actions on both sides. This chapter is a *mentalités* history of breadfruit, unraveling the perceptions that explain why this plain fruit captivated so many for so long.

In the Society Islands, breadfruit—*uru*—had always held a prominent place in the Maohi consciousness. The *Artocarpus* (Moraceae) species was a key part of Pacific islanders' colonizing equipment. Carried from Southeast

Asia, where it was being cultivated by 2500 BC,[6] *Artocarpus* was first propagated in the western Pacific, then the central islands of Samoa and Tonga, and from there it was taken on voyaging canoes into the eastern islands of the Societies, the Marquesas, and beyond.[7] Early colonizing voyagers set off from their home islands with cuttings from the roots or young shoots of a variety of *uru* cultivars. The travelers sustained themselves during the voyage with food that included balls of *mahi* paste made of fermented breadfruit.[8] On reaching a new shore, the *uru* cuttings were planted and in time would form the core of their food production. During the five or six years until the first fruits were produced, fishing and gathering of whatever vegetable foods already existed on the island were the main means of support.[9] These staples were supplemented by the pigs, chickens, dogs, root crops, and other food sources the settlers had brought with them.

The simplicity and basic reliability of breadfruit as a food source were exactly the qualities that appealed to the British. The original Maohi role given to *uru* as a savior in times of famine was also the role the British bestowed upon it. In addition, they, like the Tahitians, had in mind a broader range of purposes for this fruit to fulfill.

The first Europeans to see breadfruit would have been Portuguese and Dutch voyagers arriving in Indonesia and Malaysia in the early sixteenth century.[10] If so, they appear to have been unimpressed, as they made no written record of the plant, concentrating instead on the more exciting spice discoveries. Ferdinand de Quiros, the Portuguese pilot of Mendana's fleet, wrote the first identifiable account in 1595 when they came across the islands they named the Marquesas. De Quiros decided that the pineapple-sized fruit was so good and sweet, and was so efficient (leaving only a bit of shell as waste), that there was "no superior fruit." [11]

A description of a fruit that could act as a substitute for bread was published in England in 1697. William Dampier's compendium of his voyages had an appendix of the plants and creatures he had seen, which included "The Bread-fruit (as we call it)," from Guam.[12] Dampier described a spreading tree as big as the largest of English apple trees, with fruit:

> as big as a Penny-loaf, when Wheat is at five Shillings the Bushel. It
> is of a round shape, and has a thick tough Rind. When the Fruit is
> ripe, it is yellow and soft, and the taste is sweet and pleasant.[13]

He noted the fruit stayed in season for eight months of the year and that people in Guam ate "no other sort of bread" while it was available. The only problem with it was that needed to be eaten within twenty-four hours. Otherwise it became "dry and eats harsh and chokey," a quality that, in their minds, would have disqualified it for use as a sea provision. Fifty years later, George Anson reported in the same vein on the breadfruit he and his crew ate "constantly" in Guam, it being "so universally preferred . . . that no ship's bread was expended" throughout their stay.[14]

When Wallis and his men returned from Tahiti they brought news that the breadfruit was cultivated there and the islanders were prepared to barter it away. James Cook had access to all these accounts when he set off for his first voyage in 1769. Joseph Banks, seeing the Tahitians' reliance on the fruit, was impressed by the ease by which they could sustain themselves. As he and Cook both wrote (they referred to each others' journals along the way), they felt it could hardly be said that the Tahitians earned their bread "with the sweat of their brow," when their "cheifest sustenance Bread fruit is procurd with no more trouble than that of climbing a tree and pulling it down."[15] All a man need to do in his lifetime to provide for his family and future generations, Banks judged optimistically, was to plant ten breadfruit trees—about an hour's work.[16] It was a flawed perception but a potent image to present back to a work-focused Britain.

John Hawkesworth included this attractive prospect in his bestselling *Account of the Voyages Undertaken for Making Discoveries in the Southern Hemisphere* (1773), based on the journals of the four most recent British Pacific voyagers.[17] The reading public had been waiting anxiously for the full story of the Cook discoveries, and the Admiralty-commissioned *Account* sold out rapidly. Hawkesworth's literary rendering of the voyages, including the more sensual scenes from the Tahitian journals and his own controversial musings on the workings of Christian Providence, fueled a controversy that no doubt assisted sales.[18] It went through many more editions over the next few years, was serialized and pirated, and translated into French, German, and Italian. Anyone who read the *Account* read of the usefulness of breadfruit. Breadfruit was rapidly taking conceptual shape as a labor-saving tropical staple. It was not notably delicious, but a good solid food, versatile and reliable. As Lord Byron would later express in *The Island,* it was being seen as a fruit that helped to construct a utopia, an idyllic and simple life far from the corruptions of civilized, materialistic Europe.

Eroding the Caribbean

Meanwhile, in the Atlantic, slaves on sugar plantations were dying of starvation. Tens of thousands of African slaves on British plantations in the Caribbean were weathering increasingly difficult conditions, and the history of hardship in the region already stretched back more than a hundred years.

British colonists had begun moving into Barbados in the mid-1600s during the disruptions of wars and food shortages at home. They sectioned Barbados up and cleared forests to make way for sugar. Small amounts of sugar from the tropics had been imported into Europe for some time, sweetening the other newly imported luxuries—coffee, tea, and chocolate. It commanded an impressive price. There was as yet no British-owned sugar source, and, as Portuguese plantations on Madeira had been demonstrating since the 1420s, the climate in the Caribbean was ideal for this enterprise. By 1643 there were in Barbados sixteen thousand English owners of properties of more than one hundred acres.[19] Within twenty years they had exhausted the soil. They imported cattle in the hopes of replenishing the nutrient content with manure, and they tried smaller, more varied plantings of cinnamon and other spices, with no success.[20] There were so few trees left they had to import wood from England for the fires to boil down sugar. The island was completely deforested by 1665.[21] It was far simpler to start again on another island.

The British moved into Jamaica, with help from Cromwell's military. The Spanish had already eradicated much of the indigenous Arawak and Carib population and, from the 1530s, imported African slave laborers to work the plantations.[22] On the huge, sprawling estates that did not need to be run as carefully or efficiently as on small Barbados, British planters brought in an increasing number of slaves to wrest a profit. An average Jamaican estate had five hundred working slaves, whereas the average in Barbados had been twenty.

In 1763, at the end of the Seven Years' War, Grenada, the Grenadines, St Vincent, Tobago, and several other Caribbean islands were ceded officially to Britain under the Treaty of Paris. William Pitt's government endeavored to bring some legislative order to its new acquisitions.[23] The plans for St Vincent granted annexation rights to any settler who could clear and cultivate land. However, the past history of devastation of Atlantic islands through deforestation was not going unnoticed in Britain. Some commentators were advocating the maintenance of forest reserves.[24] Following debates it was decided that local governors would select reserves of timbered land. Governors such as William Young, chief settlement commissioner at St Vincent, had firm ideas about the role of forests in their colonies' plans. With fewer forests, Young proclaimed in 1765, rains would be less frequent and the airs more salutary.[25] The reserve areas, he decided, should be those least fertile and least needed for plantations, and in places most convenient for processing and transporting timber.[26] The inhabitants would have applauded his decision, not only for the priority he gave to plantations but for his efforts to reduce the illness that was assumed to accompany tropical forests. The "miasmas" and warm, moist airs of these "hot and reeking" forests were thought to breed diseases that were carried on the wind.[27] It wasn't long before large portions of the islands were denuded. A 1790s watercolor depicting an estate in St Vincent shows steeply rising hills, crowned with a few sparse trees on the summits, each hill covered with patchwork quilts of cultivation, the square fields rising so steeply they approach vertical.[28] In these conditions, water runoff increased, as did soil erosion and nutrient leaching. The local climatic system started to shift, and with fewer trees to process ground water, fewer roots to bind the soil, and few effective windbreaks, the cycle of transpiration was disrupted. It is possible the increase in humidity that accompanied the higher incidence of irrigation fed thunderstorms—serious storms became increasingly common.[29] It became harder to safeguard the sugar cane and food crops.[30]

In August 1764 a planter, Simon Taylor, wrote to his brother in desperation that for the past three months the island of St Vincent had become the victim of "some Evill Genious." Severe storms had destroyed crops and there was not enough timber; everyone was doomed to ruin.[31] The planters sent a memorial to their governor requesting he lift an embargo on American colonists' ships, so they could buy food while they waited for sufficient provisions to be brought from England. The governor vacillated. Taylor allowed himself at this point to give vent to despair:

> if the importation is not allowed we must inevitably Perish or bring in Provision without Permission and indeed if some Intercourse is not opened with America we must throw up the Sugar Estates into Provision Grounds and Penns or Migrate with our Negroes to the French Islands.[32]

Without access to imported food or better cultivation of provisions, periodic famine was all that could be expected. The planters and absentee landlords with an "interest" in the Caribbean grew more alarmed and more desperate for a solution. A writer in the 1790s estimated that fifteen thousand Africans had died in Jamaica on account of the trade restrictions following American independence. This may have been overstating the case, but, as historian David Mackay has stated, it provides an indication of the high degree of distress in the islands during the period.[33] With the slave families struggling with starvation and disease in addition to overwork and typically brutal punishments, their productivity plummeted and the planters faced bankruptcy. From the late 1760s, during the height of the crisis, accounts of Wallis' and Cook's discoveries of an accommodating group of islanders in the Pacific and their labor-free, staple fruit were circulating widely enough to have reached the Caribbean.

Seeking Solutions

On the eve of Joseph Banks' expected departure for a second Pacific journey in April 1772, a letter arrived from Valentine Morris, captain general of the West Indies. He wondered "whether there was no possibility of procuring the bread tree, either in seed or plant so as to introduce that most valuable tree into our American Islands." [34] Such a possession, he assured Banks, would be "one of the greatest blessings" the islands could receive. Morris' interest in the issue was his "humane benevolent desire of benefitting so considerable body of people"—and, he admitted, his own "considerable property" there. [35]

Morris may not have been the first plantation owner to suggest a project of plant transfer as a solution to their problems. Banks had been corresponding with residents of Jamaica and St Vincent since his return from the Pacific the previous year. Banks' position, his focus on arranging plant transplantations, and his recent observations in Tahiti meant he presented the planters' best hope for a patron. The initial suggestion of breadfruit to address the planters' difficulties appears to have originated with Prime Minister Pitt, in conversation with Banks. [36] While Banks decided not to return to the Pacific, [37] he maintained a long-term interest in Tahitian breadfruit. He also took to sending seeds and encouragement to the government-run botanic gardens in Jamaica and St Vincent, and to private gardeners, such as Hinton East on his Jamaican estate. [38] In return, estate owners and the gardens' superintendents shipped back interesting seeds, fruits, and plant cuttings for Banks to cultivate in his garden and the king's garden at Kew. [39] Several well-placed gentlemen with botanical interests, such as Sir George Yonge, secretary of war, joined Banks in doing their reciprocal duty, shipping seeds out to the Caribbean. [40]

The suggestion of a grand, transglobal plant transfer was, to a large extent, a product of this climate of botanical exchanges. As we have seen, there was a growing sense amongst the British at home and in the new colonies that efforts should be made to share the benefits of plants of different regions, and a growing sense that such attempts were likely to succeed. There was a general mood of optimism in Britain by the mid-eighteenth century. Victory in the Spanish War of Succession (1701–1714) and defeating France in the Seven Years' War (1756–1763) bolstered British confidence enormously. The spoils from captured ships had enriched the state's coffers. The Royal Navy was claiming increasing mastery over seas and oceans. Expanding trade routes were bringing greater wealth and material well-being to the nation, enabling further growth. As the important annual directory *The Present State of Britain* stated in 1718, "we are the most considerable of any nation in the world for the vastness and extensiveness of our trade."[41] Success in trade was also proof to Britons, as Linda Colley has shown, of their being the "freest and most distinctively Protestant of nations."[42] The reach of Britain's scientific exploits was likewise growing, joining and contributing to the development of continental ideas about the ordering of the universe. The number of British circumnavigations, the extraordinary distances spanned, new peoples, flora and fauna observed and classified, new wonders experienced and described for the rest of the world; there was seemingly no limit to the reaches the British could encompass. In a world that graded almost every facet of life—divinity, royalty, society, family, economy, natural history—into hierarchies, the mounting evidence that Britain could be counted in so many important respects the greatest of nations was highly satisfying.[43] Such a position needed to be maintained.

There was a positive assuredness within the discussions over this period that the breadfruit could be transplanted if only the time and outlay for a ship could be lent. The practical hurdles of such a venture were acknowledged, yet a blithe confidence maintained that the venture would succeed. There were now the resources to fund it, the shipping power and navigational acumen, the voyaging experience, the scientific know-how, and the local relationships to make an attempt worthwhile. As Lord Auckland said to Joseph Banks a few years later, it was an auspicious time for undertaking a project of breadfruit transfer, an undertaking which reflected:

> that fair sentiment of just pride which every good Englishman feels at present respecting his Country. We certainly are at the height of foreign pre-eminence & of internal prosperity.[44]

To arrange for the transportation of the breadfruit to the Caribbean was considered a benevolent and economically useful act, the sort of enterprise responsible gentlemen should support. The fruit was associated inextricably with the interests of the British colonists in the Caribbean. When naturalist John Ellis published an account in 1772 of the mangosteen and the breadfruit, his title proclaimed mangosteens to be "the most delicious" and breadfruit to be "the most useful of all the fruits in the East-Indies" (Indonesia). His book included instructions to voyagers for transporting these plants, "which would be extremely beneficial to the inhabitants of our West India [Caribbean] Islands." [45]

During preparations for Cook's third voyage in December 1775, a London publisher, Daniel Wray, stated he had heard the expedition's purpose was to take Ma'i and "such provisions of plants, and of animals, as may be useful to our *tropical allies.*" On the return journey they would apparently bring "the bread-tree for our *West Indies,* and *St. Helena.*" [46] The Admiralty had included no such plan in Cook's instructions. However, with Banks' continued engagement in the issue and his encouragement of George III's interest in experimenting with new economic roles for plant and animal species, it is likely that such a proposal had been mooted. It was instead the taking of cattle and other livestock to Tahiti that won out, as we have seen, as the *Resolution* and *Discovery*'s main project of ecological economy. With still no firm proposal from the Admiralty for securing breadfruit, in 1777 the Royal Society for the Encouragement of Arts, Manufactures and Commerce offered a prize for the first half-dozen breadfruit trees to be introduced to the West Indies. [47] During the 1780s the several botanical gardens in the Caribbean prepared themselves as centers for the landing, nurturing, and distribution of plants they hoped to introduce. In 1786 Yonge reported to Banks that Alexander Anderson, superintendent of the botanic garden at St Vincent, had grown three mature cinnamon trees from the seeds Banks had sent from Indonesia and was expecting a "good Encrease of them." [48] Planters and botanists were still, in the 1780s, sending requests to Britain for the breadfruit to be transported, to afford "a wholesome and pleasant Food to our Negroes." [49]

Judging Plants

The breadfruit was not the only plant that could have been selected as a staple food for African slaves. Other contenders from similar climates, known from visits to Indonesia, the Pacific, and the Cape of Good Hope, were the mango, pineapple, sweet potato, yam, many varieties of banana and plantain, custard apples, and the "Tahiti apple," *vi,* which was larger than an English apple, similar in flavor, and, conveniently, fruited often.

But the breadfruit had come to stand for simple, wholesome food. It was thought to be reasonably nutritious (although it is not especially so relative to other fruit). [50] It was, importantly, perceived as "wholesome and pleasant" rather than exotic and delicious. Sharing associations with bread, it carried connotations of a staple, plain and virtuous food, the food that sustained the poor. Breadfruit carried additional conceptual weight; as Greg Dening has said, the breadfruit tree was "the very symbol of a free and unencumbered life, from the island of freedom, Tahiti."[51] The paradox that no one seems to have commented on was that this fruit was being transported from this island of freedom to "the islands of bondage."[52] The slaves in the Caribbean were, nevertheless, seen to be worthy of a basic food, the bare minimum a humble man or woman should be sure of. The fruit of an unencumbered life could yet have a role in an enslaved society.

The moral overtones of plants were of considerable interest in Georgian England. Flowers and plants carried a host of associations from their use as biblical, classical, and cultural symbols; the "Annunciation Lily" stood inviolably for the Virgin Mary's purity. An oak was always "noble," "venerable," "reliable," an ancient symbol of strength and a mainstay of shipbuilding, making the oak a favored emblem of the British people.[53] The way plants were considered in Britain received a jolt in the 1730s when Carl Linnaeus' *Systema Naturae* and *Species Plantarum* began circulation. As we saw in chapter 2, Linnaeus' classificatory system was based on plants' sexual structures and created an uneasy frisson in Britain. Some condemned the system for its unseemliness and strove to find a way of marshaling the plant kingdom in a way that anyone, even a young woman, could be introduced to. Others embraced Linnaeus' personification of a flower's parts—in which the stamen became "husbands" and the stigma and other female organs were "wives." Linnaeus referred to the calyx as the marriage bed and each plant was classified by the relationship the wife took with one, two, three, or more husbands, or of husbands with concubines.[54] Erasmus Darwin presented the public with accounts of each of Linnaeus' taxonomic groupings according to their sexual lives in poetic verse. Despite the critics, his *Loves of the Plants* (1789) was a huge success. Janet Browne has shown that popular botanical texts over the following fifty years were "rampaged through" by "suggestiveness and downright explicitness."[55]

Among all the luscious, tempting fruits being discovered in the furthest reaches of the world, the breadfruit was the plain maiden aunt. The fact that most breadfruit varieties were seedless, relying on chaste, asexual, human-directed reproduction through the taking and laying of cuttings, could have had some influence on popular judgments of the fruit. More noticeably, it was not a blushing red, soft, succulent fruit but a hard-skinned pale one with a starchy middle. These associations are unlikely to have gone unregistered in the search for an appropriate food for a workforce.

The practical advantages of breadfruit, however, were what contributed the most to its appeal. It was well known to require little labor to cultivate and harvest, and it would produce fruit several times a year. The Caribbean planters continued their campaign for a solution for their slaves. The French, too, were concerned to find reliable food sources for their colonies as well as at home, where the acclimatization of food plants was being sought to lessen the country's periodic famines. Bougainville's report of utopian Tahiti in the late 1760s had created breadfruit as an ideal of physical and (as some argued) moral sustenance.[56] The French minister of the marine and colonies heard news in 1787 that the British were about to introduce breadfruit to the Caribbean. He made plans with André Thouin, head gardener of the Parisian Jardin du Roi, for naturalizing the plant.[57] Thouin duly instructed the gardener being sent on d'Entrecasteaux's 1791 Pacific expedition to gather as many breadfruit saplings as possible to transport to the Europe and the French colonies. He stated:

> If [the gardener] succeeds in enriching us with this tree, he will make the most useful of all presents to his fatherland, and by himself will have done more for the happiness of mankind than all the savants of the world.[58]

British plantation owners continued to complain that their government would not rally to assist them, a particularly frustrating situation when the "Attention of the French to their Colonies" was so often before them.[59] The rivalry between the two nations seems to have been the most effective goad to action. In an entertaining piece of circularity, Sir George Yonge heard a report in early 1787 of France's breadfruit endeavor in their Caribbean colonies, which, although incorrect, proved to be the starting gun that finally got the British breadfruit project up and running.[60] Yonge wrote to Banks on 3 February:

> It seems past a Doubt that the Rima or Bread Fruit Tree, Is arrived in the French West Indes. . . . It must therefore be acknowledged the French are beforehand with us.[61]

Yonge railed that it threw the differences between France and Britain into sharp relief: "while from our Forms, & the Coldness of our Tempers, we are deliberating," he said, the French with their vivacity "act unencumberd."[62] It was at this point, when suddenly it seemed there was more at stake than just the welfare of slaves or plantation owners, that the leaders of the British government and maritime enterprises decided to act.

Bounty

Joseph Banks had been discussing with the Pitt government the possibility that the ships about to transport the first convicts to Botany Bay could transport breadfruit from Tahiti on the return journey. On 13 February 1787 Prime Minister Pitt wrote to the treasurer of the West India Committee instructing the equipping of an expedition.[63] The First Fleet proposal had to be abandoned, however, when the logistics of constructing suitable plant boxes in the embryonic colony proved too difficult.[64] Banks gained support from Lord Hawkesbury (president of the Board of Trade), Lord Mulgrave (member of the Board of Trade), and Lord Sydney (secretary for home affairs) to win government agreement in 1788 to commission a new ship dedicated to the project.

A vessel was to be prepared for the task and the command given to "some able and discreet Officer," no doubt to try to keep the attempt from French eyes until it was successfully completed. The commander should sail to the Society Islands, where the fruit was to be "found in the most luxuriant State."[65] Banks proposed William Bligh, who accepted. He was already familiar with the ways of the Pacific and with Tahiti through his role as master of Cook's *Resolution*. More recently, Bligh had been running merchant vessels between England and the Caribbean. Of the two botanists recommended by Banks, one was David Nelson, whom Banks had already sent to Tahiti on Cook's third voyage[66] and therefore had rare experience in the "art of taking care of Plants at Sea."[67] Nelson had also:

> made an acquaintance with inhabitants of the South Sea Islands & their Language which will in all probability Facilitate his Obtaining the number of Plants wanted.[68]

Banks recognized that this was important. The plants needed to be acquired through negotiation, a proper exchange established. Banks pointed out that the islanders had "never been accustomed to sell" the plants. It was an untried type of exchange and he recognized the threat to the project if any "difficulties" arose.[69] Bligh made no overt statements regarding the forthcoming negotiations until he reached the island, only that he had arranged to be "furnished with a quantity of iron-work and trinkets, to serve in our intercourse with the natives in the South Seas."[70]

When the *Bounty* arrived at Matavai Bay in 1788, Bligh made it appear as if they were like any other ship stopping for provisions. He had decided to keep his mission secret and ordered his crew to be silent on the subject.

He needed to ensure that the price settled on would be covered by the goods he had with him. He was nervous that the Tahitians would place a high cost on breadfruit seedlings if they discovered the plants were in demand. Instead, soon after landing at Matavai, Bligh met with Tu (then "chief-regent" for Pomare II, who was still a boy) and asked if there was anything he wished to send to King George. Tu assented and began to "enumerate the different articles in his power, among which he mentioned the bread-fruit." This, said Bligh:

> was the exact point to which I wished to bring the conversation; and, seizing an opportunity, which had every appearance of being undesigned and accidental, I told him the bread-fruit-trees were what King George would like; upon which he promised me a great many should be put on board, and seemed much delighted to find it so easily in his power to send any thing that would be well received by King George.[71]

For Tu, the returns he expected from supplying breadfruit trees to Europeans were a continuation of the already established practices of consolidating links with the head of a foreign power by sending gifts via British ships. Breadfruit plants were a much easier gift to provide than other presents he had sent previously. Complete, painstakingly constructed chief mourner's costumes (*parae*) had headdresses made of an array of tropical bird tail feathers, each pair of feathers plucked by men climbing vines down cliff faces to reach the nests. The shimmering chest-covering of hundreds of tiny, rectangular-carved shell beads, the apron of coconut shell plaques carved in spine and tortoise patterns, the decorated *tapa*, the hand-plaited cord wrapped in bicolored tapa strips—all these things were time-consuming and laden with potency and spiritual danger. The Tahitians had already traded more than ten of these away to former voyagers.[72] It was far easier for a chief to give away a common, rapidly renewing plant that made no appreciable impact on food resources of his own people. Young breadfruit plants could be easily dug up and replanted. It was no trouble for Tu to have his people fill the English carpenters' tubs.

Bligh ordered the tents to be set up to shade the plants and cordoned the area off to keep them safe once they had been potted. He had the chiefs of the region tell their people not to "trespass."[73] A few of the other chiefs may have entered into the arrangement as well—when Bligh gloatingly records the way the project was proceeding, he refers to chiefs in the plural: "I had now, instead of appearing to receive a favour, brought the chiefs to believe that I was doing them a kindness in carrying the plants, as a present from them to the *Earee Rahie no Britannee* [paramount chief of Britain]."[74]

Bligh *was* doing them a kindness. He was presenting them—Tu particularly—with a new way to not only consolidate links with Britain but also visibly demonstrate to their people and to rivals their prestigious connections with a source of material and conceptual power. Tu was able to maintain a visible connection to the British visitors throughout the ship's stay and ensure that Bligh would not decamp and favor another chief instead. Potting up shoots and waiting for them to take root was a slow process. Bligh ended up staying more than five months, much longer than the usual visitors' few weeks. No rival chief would be prepared to threaten Tu while the *Bounty* was there. Tu, his son, and their supporters were confident that the more they could demonstrate and build upon the allegiance with the British, the stronger their position. Tu and his family also expected a return gift from Britain's *ari'i rahi*. Bligh reported that Tu:

> did not forget to remind me, that when the next ship came out he
> hoped King George would send him large axes, files, saws, cloth of
> all kinds, hats, chairs, and bedsteads, with arms, ammunition, and
> in short every thing he could think of mentioning.[75]

All these actual and predicted benefits Tu secured for little personal cost.

The first day's work of gathering the breadfruit plants from the "delightful breadfruit flats" of Pare was 5 November 1788.[76] Bligh later wrote that "we had much pleasure in collecting them, for the natives offered their assistance, and perfectly understood the method of taking them up and pruning them."[77] The Tahitians who helped with digging up the young shoots, potting, pruning, and loading them onto the ship may have been assisting under instruction from their chief, but they would have nonetheless expected some type of material return from the Europeans. As with any other provision of service or goods, it is likely the visitors would have given the Tahitians beads, combs, and other small-scale items of trade at regular intervals.

Bligh was fortunate the exchange had worked out so smoothly. Joseph Banks had been right to be concerned about the potential for difficulties. The exchange with the Tahitians was of a new type, commodifying an element of the Tahitian physical and conceptual landscape that Europeans had not formerly tried to commandeer. The chiefs could have refused Bligh's request. Breadfruit did have a carefully regulated code of access and use.

Luckily for Bligh, this code was primarily attached to the preparation and consumption of the fruit rather than the plants that produced them.

There were some limitations on who could cultivate breadfruit trees. For instance, as we saw earlier, the Pomares forbade the people of the coral atoll Tetiaroa, to the immediate north, from planting any. This was to ensure the residents were kept in subjugated reliance on food imported from Tahiti.[78] For the most part, though, the decision about how many young breadfruit a Tahitian would cultivate depended only on how much land he or she had to plant on. Little of the Maohi system of values attached to *uru* was apparent to Bligh, but later Tahitian writers, as well as early European observers, described practices and ways of living with breadfruit.

Being a staple food, *uru* was treated with care. The trees grew primarily on the coastal flats, but some were planted on the low hills where they tended to provide a later fruiting. Groves belonged to family groups and acted as one measure of a family's standing and prosperity. For poorer families, though, there were ways of ensuring that breadfruit resources were shared. For instance, one tree could be owned by two families.[79] A family without enough trees to keep them fully supplied throughout the year could, when the fruits of the district were ripening, present a garland of the "piripiri" shrub to their neighbors.[80] This indicated a breadfruit baking day was being planned and those neighbors who were able would bring gifts of breadfruit for the family on the specified day.[81] The Maohi identified around fifty named varieties of breadfruit tree, which produced at staggered intervals from December to early or mid-May.[82] There was then a smaller crop in August to September.[83] During these ripenings *ari'i* and *ra'atira* (landowners) could send around a coconut leaf to call for breadfruit to be brought in for baking from the trees of their subjects or tenants.

In these coordinated bakings on behalf of leaders or among neighboring families, a group would dig a pit about ten feet in diameter. They would lay wood and stones in the pit and light a fire and load in their breadfruit whole. These were covered up with large breadfruit leaves, then layered with grass and earth. After three or four days the oven was opened up, the breadfruit was lifted out, the blackened skin was scraped off, and the brown-baked flesh was eaten. Any breadfruit not eaten immediately were kept covered until used.[84] During the nonfruiting seasons, taro, plantains, and arrowroot came into greater use and people turned to the fermented breadfruit paste, *mahi*. The reliance on *mahi* meant the preparation of the paste was carefully managed to ensure that no spoilage from physical or spiritual sources could occur.

Women prepared their own *mahi*, away from the dangerous contamination of men's spiritual power. When the fruit was ripe they would place the skinned pulp into a pile and allow it to ferment for several days. It was then placed in pits lined with leaves, covered with stones and earth. The fruit continued to ferment and soften in the pit, and months later the paste could be taken out and baked as needed.[85] The *mahi* would be rendered inedible if a man touched a women's fruit in preparation, as Banks did in 1769[86] (an event significant enough for the mutineer James Morrison, in Tahiti twenty years later, to have heard about it[87]). Neither could the place of preparation ever be used again by a woman. Men could eat *mahi* prepared by a woman, but not the *mahi* for women.

Other uses for the breadfruit tree included the wood for canoes and other hard-wearing carvings. The sap was used as a gum. The leaves, bark, and particular parts of the fruit were used for infusions to treat respiratory problems, and the fruit was externally applied as a poultice for wounds.[88] *Uru* trees were propagated throughout the Society Islands. There could well have been as much care surrounding the spiritual and physical act of propagation as there was surrounding the preservation of *mahi*, but there is no recorded evidence to suggest this. What is clear is that Bligh's suggestion of breadfruit shoots or cuttings being taken out of the island to establish them elsewhere was not a new one. In the legend of the *uru*'s creation, after the compassionate father Rua-ta'ata had transformed himself into a breadfruit tree, the chief of Ra'iatea heard of the new fruit. He ordered the tree brought to him and planted at Opoa, where first fruits were inaugurated.[89] Rua-ta'ata's family, at first distraught at their loss, were soon delighted to see shoots grow quickly up from the roots left behind. At Opoa, too, a woman "begged for a bunch of roots, which she planted in a valley . . . and there they grew."[90] Another woman took a root to Porapora and it became the first *uru* in that island.[91]

For the Tahitians, conversant with the legend and many of them practitioners of *uru* transplanting themselves, Bligh's request to take up small *uru* plants by their roots and take them to another place was perfectly comprehensible.

Fruits of Mutiny

With permission for transplanting in hand, Bligh busied himself overseeing a group of nine Tahitian and British gardeners at the post, checking their progress and counting the number of pots they produced each day. By November 1788 they had a hundred plants at the tent, all looking healthy.[92] Bligh worked on tracking down the whereabouts of animals and plants Cook had left on the island in previous years and tried to keep the forty-six *Bounty* seamen and officers under some sort of control. As the weeks went by, this became increasingly difficult. Because of the long stay, they were forging firm friendships with the Tahitians, and, rather than having fleeting sexual encounters with the women, many had Tahitian girlfriends. Their captain was constantly curbing their activities.

Finally, by 24 April 1789, with 1,015 breadfruit plants loaded onto the ship along with a range of other plants useful for various botanic gardens, Bligh was ready to leave.[93] He rounded up the deserters and, after emotional farewells from all the Tahitians who had been enjoying the benefits of the visit, set sail. On board, the difficulties spawned by modifications to accommodate the plants added to the tensions between the captain and his disgruntled men. Greg Dening has shown how from the start of the voyage, the conversion of the great cabin into storage for pots of breadfruit meant Bligh's quarters had been squeezed into a space like that of an officer's, making it difficult for Bligh to clearly "perform" his power.[94] The drama was heightened by the personalities involved and the increasingly sore point of ownership of the provisions obtained at Tahiti. Fletcher Christian, appointed to the ship as a favor to his well-connected family, felt belittled by Bligh; the captain's accusation over some missing ship's coconuts was one insult too many. He found sympathy from others, bitter over a recent disciplinary reduction of their rations.[95] On 28 April Christian and his supporters mutinied. They dumped Bligh and some crew into a longboat and the plants into the sea.

The tensions that had led to that point had been exacerbated by the breadfruit. The ranks of green leafy stems had meant something quite different for the seamen. The plants had taken them away from Tahiti, had been cramping the ship and soaking up the fresh water that should have formed their own, full water rations. The plants were seen to have been lavished with more care and concern by their captain than the crew had received themselves.[96] Small wonder the men threw them overboard so promptly.

The *Bounty* and the twenty-five remaining on board headed back to Tahiti. They were to make a substantial impact on the island, being the first group of Europeans to settle there as residents. It was one of the more unusual repercussions of the breadfruit project, and, though incidental to it, it remains relevant here as it was primarily the desire to engage in further ecological exchange that brought Christian back to the island. The cross-cultural engagements that arose between Tahitians and these British men were exceptional and, for a considerable number of Tahitians, life-changing. Back at Tahiti, the mutineers explained their reappearance by saying they had met up with Cook, who was starting a new settlement nearby (the secret of Cook's death had been maintained). Bligh and the plants had been taken aboard Cook's ship, they said, while they had been sent back in the *Bounty* to collect pigs and the cattle Cook had left previously. It was a useful fiction for Christian, who needed stocks for the settlement he planned to establish in a remote spot, away from Tahiti's conspicuous harbors. The Tahitians around Matavai agreed to this and provided great numbers of animals. With these boarded, the mutineers set sail and settled on Tubuai, one of the Austral islands, south of Tahiti. They ferried to shore more than two hundred pigs, the sight of which apparently terrified the islanders.[97] While setting up a settlement, Christian managed to offend one of the chiefs and, as tensions rose, increasingly violent attacks broke out.[98] Failing to maintain order among the mutineers, Christian mustered both them and the stock and returned to Tahiti.

The *Bounty* crew then divided up. Those who had been actively mutinous were focused on evading a hanging back in Britain. They resolved to leave to find a more obscure hiding place as soon as some fresh livestock could be loaded on board. The men and various islander companions were staying on board while preparations were being completed when on 23 September, unannounced, Christian slipped the cable in the middle of the night. As dawn broke the six Tahitian men and eighteen women were shocked to find themselves at sea. Mo'orea was still quite close by; one woman dove overboard to try to reach it.[99] When a canoe came alongside, Christian offloaded the six older women into it. The brutal history of the eventual settlement the mutineers founded on Pitcairn Island is well known. Few of the Tahitians managed to escape.

The other crewmen, those who had been supportive of Bligh but not permitted to go on the longboat, felt relatively safe and remained ashore, waiting for the next ship and allying themselves in the meantime to the Pomares. They donated a musket and their manpower to an attack by the Pare-'Arue–Atahuru alliance on Mo'orea, which resulted in the death of Mo'orea's powerful *ari'i*, Mahine. Four of the crewmen made alliances with chiefs on the more discreet southern side of the island. There they helped with battles and became involved in intrigues that resulted in the murder of several high-ranking men of the Vehiatua lineage and one of their own number.[100] James Morrison wrote a detailed account of Maohi practices, with observations on the subtleties of their economic, political, social, and spiritual life. His text reveals how integrated within Tahitian society he (and most probably the others) had become. Knowledge passed both ways. As

Morrison became fluent in the Maohi language, the Tahitians were gradually offered insights into the British approach to the world. The fallout from the *Bounty*'s ecological exchanges were unusually wide-ranging.

Providence

A few months after Bligh made it back to England in March 1790, plans were being formulated to send him out to Tahiti again. He had survived the extraordinary ordeal of navigating the *Bounty*'s longboat, open to the elements, from near Tonga across 3,600 miles (5,800 km) of sea to Timor with nineteen crewmen, a sextant, compass, some nautical tables, and a daily ration of a few ounces of food each to keep themselves alive.[101] He furiously wrote up the account of the mutineer's deeds on his way back to England on Dutch ships.[102] The news caused a thrill of alarm—this antiauthoritarian coup on a British ship had occurred at the same time the people of Paris were storming the Bastille.

The Admiralty sent Captain Edwards and the *Pandora* in October 1790 to track down Fletcher Christian and his supporters to bring them to England to stand trial.[103] An example had to be made of the mutineers if the authorities were to quash further ideas of absconding with a ship in the merry, warm waters of the South Seas. There was too much at stake for Britain's reputation to let the breadfruit mission sink along with the plants. George III was anxious to make a second attempt at transplanting the breadfruit, no doubt spurred by the unwillingness to have the project scuttled by a bunch of mutineers as well as the still salient motivations that had set the *Bounty* on its original course. Sir George Yonge wrote to Banks in September 1790 reporting with pleasure:

> the King spoke to me this week, of resuming the Idea of the bread fruit Ship, & bid me talk to you & Lord Chatham about it . . . and I have only to add that the *sooner the better*.[104]

The Admiralty had "ships of all sorts to spare" and Lord Chatham was happy to support the project.[105] Bligh had been cleared of blame for the mutiny at a court martial in October 1790, and in March 1791, his health probably not completely recovered from the six weeks of exposure and near starvation while painfully navigating to Timor, he received orders for a renewed breadfruit expedition.[106] It was an escalated project, with two ships: a new West Indiaman, *Providence*, accompanied by the *Assistant*, a small armed tender captained by Lt. Portlock and filled with marines for security. They left England on 5 August 1791.

On reaching Tahiti nearly eight months later, Bligh set about establishing a trade in the plants as effective as the one he had secured before. Unfortunately, there was a conflict in progress between the people of Matavai, under the *ari'i* Poeno, and the Pomare family in the neighboring district. An English ship, the *Matilda,* had been wrecked on a reef nearby and the Matavai people had managed to secure most of the ship's weapons and property before the Pomares could get to them. Fighting over the spoils was devastating the region. Bligh looked on nervously, but he judged that despite the rival warriors ring-barking mature trees and destroying houses, doing the "Country irreparable injury," it would not, he said, "affect my plan, as the Plants are numerous."[107] Tu's brother, Ari'ipaea, told Bligh he would need to wait for Tu's return before approval could be given. The captain watched for several days as tensions between the districts continued to simmer, then announced to Ari'ipaea he "would wait no longer":

> in the Morning I should go on Shore to prepare a Place for my Plants in which it was his interest to assist me, but that he might do as he liked; for I would have no more fighting.[108]

Bligh was applying the high-handedness that characterized his dealings with his crew to Tahitian chiefs. His anxiety to succeed and the apparent ease with which he had secured the chiefs' compliance on the *Bounty* trip now inspired him to give, with a bald arrogance, ultimatums over the use of their resources and land. Luckily for Bligh and the breadfruit project, the Pomares were mindful enough of the advantages to not heed the insult. Bligh stated in his log that his ultimatum "brought [Ari'ipaea] about" and the chief agreed to help.[109] With Ari'ipaea's organizational assistance, Bligh selected a site, arranged for lines to be marked out, a fence erected, and a shade set up about one hundred feet (thirty meters) long and twenty feet (six meters) wide.[110]

The first day of work they pulled up sixty-four young breadfruit shoots, leaving the roots and a surrounding clump of earth intact. These were potted up, with some pieces of shell or rock in the base of each pot to assist drainage, two shoots in each pot.[111] The gardeners gained pace. On 21 April Bligh was able to count more than 1,140 plants potted in six days. By 30 April they had potted 2,388 plants plus four "tubs" made by the cooper. The plants were being carefully guarded and assessed daily. Those that failed to "flourish" or had insect damage—nearly five hundred—were thrown out and new plants repotted.[112]

News of the gathering of breadfruit had reached around the island. Bligh was told of a "vastly superior" variety that grew in Taiarapu and he sent some of his crew to acquire a sample for potting.[113] At the end of May Bligh recorded with pleasure that all the plants were "now in charming order, spreading their leaves delightfully."[114] The gardeners estimated that all the plants would be properly established in another six weeks. The carpenters got to work making a large greenhouse frame to allow some plant accommodation on the quarterdeck. This was fitted with canvas coverings to keep the salt spray off.[115] Railings and netting were placed over the ship's skylights to prevent anything falling on the plants stored in the great cabin.[116] Some larger trees, about seven feet high, would go unprotected on deck.

As we have seen in earlier chapters, Lt. George Tobin and the other officers were not immediately caught up in the work of the gardening or the ship's renovations and had time for indulging in conversations and entertainments with the Tahitians, collecting items of "natural and artificial curiosity," exploring the island's landscape, flora, and fauna, and, in Tobin's case, taking tours and making observations of Tahitian cultural practices. In the meantime, Bligh supervised the breadfruit work and paid attention to his diplomatic duties. He also planted gardens in various locations with fruits, vegetables, and timber trees he had brought from England and the Cape of Good Hope. It was the most botanical of expeditions the Tahitians had witnessed.

Encounters over the plants were not entirely benign. Bligh's anxiety and possessiveness over the developing seedlings had some painful consequences. He was nervous about thieves and troublemakers: "One viscious fellow may destroy all our Plants, or cut our Ships adrift."[117] Put on the alert about trespassers at night, one of the marines shot a Tahitian man through the shoulder. Bligh issued warnings via the chiefs that anyone else coming close at night would be fired upon.[118] Some of the Pomare family moved their quarters close to the post to help, they said, with protection. No vicious fellows attempted to damage the plants and, with no serious setbacks, by the end of June 1792 Bligh was able to write in his journal for the benefit of his navy superiors, his patrons, and other readers:

> It gives me peculiar satisfaction to see my Plants thriving. I have now once more with unwearied Zeal and attention procured that great and valuable object, and hope God will grant my endeavours may be crowned with success.[119]

He was concerned, as ever, about the effects the breadfruit project would have on his personal reputation. Preparing for departure, barrels were emptied of their old water and fresh water was taken on board from the

Matavai River (see fig. 2.4), with every care to make sure "not a particle" of salt was splashed in, as the plants would be relying on this water across the expanse of the Pacific until they reached Timor.

Tu grew uneasy as the British made their preparations for departure. The people of Matavai had held off attacking him while his well-armed allies were there, but he knew they were likely to weigh in again once his protectors had sailed away. Bligh and his officers had made some attempts at retrieving the *Matilda*'s property from Tu's enemies but had not been very successful. Poeno was still rumored to be keeping one of the muskets under his sleeping mat. Tu pressured Bligh to make his parting gift a musket.

Tu also pressed to accompany them to England. He was sure that King George, having sent him so many gifts, must be wanting to see him. Bligh refused. Tu countered that if their friendship was to continue, Bligh would have to agree to at least take Tu's loyal *teuteu* (his retainer or servant), Maititi. The young man would be able to learn about England and return to Tahiti to inform his chief. Tu was sure "King George would not refuse him if he had been here" [120] and pointed out the many ways he had been of service to Bligh and to Edwards of the *Pandora* a few months earlier. Bligh, weighing Maititi's character and the cost of his upkeep, "could not help thinking this was the least thing we could do" for Tu, and "whether the Man returned or no it was no great burthen to our Country." [121] Although Bligh rarely admitted such things in writing, he knew he still needed Tu's cooperation.

By July Bligh noticed an unusual decline in the Tahitians' interest in their visitors. Few people came out in canoes with provisions. There were often only about twenty people about the ship and by the post to see the marines exercised in the evening. They were also starting to be "suspicious"—or perhaps just weary—of answering Bligh's questions about their "customs and the country." [122] The stay had been a long one. As the plants started to be loaded, however, interest revived. Maititi prepared to depart and Tobin reported that "there was, I believe, scarcely an individual that would not, with a little perswasion have embarked with us." [123] Tahitians helped to carry the many hundreds of pots, tubs, and boxes to the boats.[124] By leaving only narrow gangways between the pots for the crew, they were able to fit in 756 more plants than predicted.[125] The total came to 2,126 breadfruit plants (more than twice the number on the *Bounty*), with 472 pots containing other fruits and 36 containing "curiosity plants" that Bligh had obtained for the king's garden at Kew. The total number of plants on board was 2,634, and the ship now sat nine inches lower in the water.[126]

Both the *Providence* and *Assistant* were also stocked with bunches of plantains, coconuts, fruits, and vegetables for feeding themselves and the noisy collection of live pigs, chickens, and parrots.[127] After visiting the ship to make farewells, Tu and 'Itia were taken back to shore on the cutter with a swathe of gifts, including a musket and arms for Tu and a pistol with ammunition for 'Itia. Tobin later captured the scene on paper, showing himself waving his hat as he returned to the "floating forest," *Providence.*[128]

Gardeners at Sea

Maititi was accommodated on board, and as the ships left Tahitian waters, another of his countrymen suddenly appeared on deck. He had been helping the gardeners and had decided to stow away. He was referred to variously in the journals as "Bāubo" and "Pappo"—Paupo is probably a fair approximation. Tobin said he had "ever attached himself to the botanists Messieurs Wiles and Smith; to the latter in an affectionate degree, and was determined to follow his fortunes across the oceans."[129] The wind was too strong for Bligh to tack back into the bay, and because the gardeners argued convincingly for his future usefulness in getting the plants established in Jamaica, he was not made to jump and swim for shore. Bligh reasoned that as he was, like Maititi, a *teuteu* of the Pomares, the family would not mind his going; they could expect to "benefit by it in the end."[130] Paupo may have been particularly attached to Smith, who was probably his *taio*, but he was also attached to voyaging in general. It was not the first time Paupo had taken the opportunity to travel with Europeans. He had accompanied Fletcher Christian to Tubuai and back. Tobin said that Paupo "ever recounted their exploits at that island with wonderful satisfaction."[131] For this Tahitian, and for Maititi, the potted breadfruit plants meant a ticket to foreign adventure.

The ten-week trip to Timor and across the Atlantic brought another, significant range of cross-cultural encounters, all integral to the breadfruit project. The islanders met along the way would have each made specific conclusions out of the arrival of a ship carrying Europeans, Tahitians, and a multitude of plants, most of which have gone unrecorded. We do have some insights, from Tobin's journal, into the conclusions Maititi and Paupo drew about the Cook Islanders, Fijians, Torres Strait islanders, Indonesians, and the inhabitants of the Atlantic. They made attempts to communicate with these new people and, like European travelers in new territory, did not hesitate to make quick, frequently unflattering judgments about them. On 5 August, for instance, the ships reached the easternmost islands of Fiji. There, some men from Mothe canoed out to meet them, and Maititi and

Paupo expressed "great disgust" that they did not trim their beards or pluck the hair from "various parts of the body," as was the custom in Tahiti.[132] They were able to recognize some words in common; "tattoo" drew an instant response from the Fijians and a display of their own tattoos.[133]

Maititi and Paupo were joining the ranks of unusually far-reaching Society Island travelers, including Tupaia, Ahutoru, Hitihiti, and Ma'i.[134] Those who had returned—Hitihiti and Ma'i—did so with riches, a blaze of fame, and long-term possession of authority. Paupo and Maititi, knowing the considerable dangers, decided that traveling across the world with the breadfruit was a risk worth taking.

After picking their way slowly through the Torres Strait and surviving several violent skirmishes with islanders,[135] the ships reached Timor on 2 October. Maititi and Paupo enjoyed the sight of European houses and various Europeans in the port of Kupang.[136] Traveling on across the Indian Ocean, the gardeners would have been increasingly anxious for the plants. Many had already been lost through the straits, and as they approached the much colder latitudes of the Cape of Good Hope, 272 died off. The gardeners are likely to have been following the precautions Joseph Banks had recommended, wrapping up the exposed trees in old sails or whatever was to hand and taking as many of the quarterdeck pots as possible below deck. It would have been hard to forget Banks' warning that meeting with "one night's frost" could cause the whole voyage to fail.[137]

They reached St Helena, the first place due to receive some plants, in December 1792. They unloaded a selection for the English colonists there, including some of the breadfruit, then continued on to St Vincent, to leave breadfruit and other exotic plants with the superintendent, Alexander Anderson.[138]

The people of Jamaica had heard of the expedition's approach and had been excitedly looking out for its arrival. The reception at Port Royal was warm.[139] The total number of plants delivered to the botanic gardens in St Helena, St Vincent, and Jamaica was 1,217.[140] After a wait of twenty-one years from the time of the first requests, the Caribbean colonists had finally received the breadfruit tree.

Paupo and Maititi were by this stage not well, and both moved off the ship to residences on Jamaica in the hopes that a "change of air" might help.[141] Paupo helped look after the plants at the gardens and seemed to improve. He became "a favourite with all the neighbourhood," Tobin said, through his "great good humour."[142] Maititi learned to ride horses confidently and traveled about in carriages, and he did get better for a while.

The crews were now anxious to return home but were frustrated by being commandeered to assist the colonies with a foray into a battle that had broken out afresh with the French. After five months they were finally given word they could leave, and Maititi rejoined the ship. A range of 686 useful and unusual plants collected in Tahiti—and some from the Atlantic—were loaded on for King George's garden and, after a few weeks' sailing, the *Providence* and *Assistant* reached the Thames in August 1793. The pots were taken up the river to be settled into Kew Gardens.[143] Maititi did not get a chance to settle. He had been increasingly ill since leaving the Caribbean. No one described his symptoms, so what he had caught is unknown, but it was the most common result of any overseas trip that islanders undertook: contracting a foreign virus. He died as the boat was being cleared of its stores and was buried in Deptford.[144] Tu was not to have the benefit of his *teuteu*'s explorations in England after all. Paupo stayed in Jamaica with Wiles, but like Maititi his involvement with the breadfruit project had brought him little joy. By October 1793 Wiles was writing to Banks in concern, saying Paupo had been severely ill for some time and was complaining that the climate did not agree with him.[145] Wiles tried for a while to find a sponsor to help get him to England, believing it would help him recover, but Paupo died in Jamaica on 27 October 1793.[146]

Aligning himself to the breadfruit project had brought Bligh a happier realization of ambitions. On returning to England he received most of the approval of his peers he had anticipated. There was still a degree of reserve surrounding him as the *Bounty* inquiry, continued in his absence, had thrown his qualities as a commander into question. With opinion still divided, the Admiralty received Bligh's junior, Lt. Portlock, soon after the expedition returned but humiliatingly delayed granting Bligh an audience, and he had to wait two and a half years before securing his next post.[147] He was, however, officially thanked and presented with a gold plate by the Jamaican House of Assembly Botanic Gardens Committee for bringing the task "to so happy a conclusion." [148] He was awarded the prize of the Society for the Improvement of the Arts, and, especially flattering, George Keate wrote an eight-verse poem in his honor. Keate was a literary gentleman with an interest in the Pacific, having befriended and written the story of Li Buu, the son of a Palauan chief who accompanied Captain Wilson to England in 1783.[149] He proclaimed:

> *Yes, my respected friend, this trophy's thine;*
> *Where with their weight of fruit thy Bread-Trees bend,*
> *Afric's dark sons shall in their shade recline,*

And to the skies thy well-earn'd praises send,
Their comforts share; and, conscious whence they came,
Teach children yet unborn to venerate thy name.[150]

The success of the project was met with general interest; it was reported in the press, discussed by botanists, celebrated as a victory for Enlightened endeavor and, with a degree of blinkered reasoning, an example of British beneficence toward the colony's slaves. Keate's sentiments and a comment by Tobin, for instance, were typical:

> we have reason to believe . . . in the course of a few years, [bread-fruit] will become the chief sustenance of a large proportion of our fellow creatures, whose lot in life loudly calls on our sympathy and consideration.[151]

Banks and his circle were pleased with the result, and it was gratifying to be able to distribute accounts and specimens of Tahitian plants to appreciative colleagues. Banks sent some "rarities" to the German naturalist Johann Freidrich Blumenbach in 1794. Blumenbach found these "highly instructive" and:

> Their arrival (particularly the Bread fruit) excited the universal curiosity of our little Town. . . . I may say there was in the first fortnight a kind of pilgrimage to my house, to see them, & above all that fruit so famous since your voyage round the world & so inestimable for the benefit of mankind.[152]

However, the tide of public opinion was shifting. From the 1790s a rising campaign called for the abolition of slavery, rather than just providing slaves with better provisions.[153] It was becoming less clear that supporting the sugar planters in the colonies was a triumph to be trumpeted. However, Bligh, Banks, and others in the naval and scientific establishment continued to watch the progress of the breadfruit and to bask in the project's success. The efforts of so many years could still be cast in terms of glorious humanitarianism. When Bligh had neared the Caribbean on the *Providence* in December 1792 he had written to his patron, Banks, lending what gilding he could to the breadfruit project, a gleam that would reflect well on both of them:

> I most sincerely pray you may live to hear they flourish, and to know Thousands are fed with their Fruit. Posterity will ever remember

you for being the means of transmitting to them such an inesti-
mable Jewel.[154]

Setting the "Jewel" in Place

The breadfruit plants did well in the Caribbean colonies. Gardener J. Wiles
reported regularly to Banks on their progress; in October 1793 they were
"thriving with astonishing vigor" on the eastern side of the island.[155] The
fruit, he said, was "much liked."[156] It was not one of those foods that had
appealed to everyone who tasted it, but it was apparently proving useful
to some degree. Alexander Anderson said the fruit made a "very good
pudding" and when toasted was like ordinary bread. He found "everyone
exceeding anxious to get plants of it," although some "old conceited &
prejudiced creoles" said they preferred plantains and yams.[157] Plantation
owners were anxious to secure the trees and some, out of the loop in St
Vincent and Jamaica, resorted to asking Banks to intercede with the nurseries to ensure they would not miss out.[158] The French did succeed in introducing a variety of seeded breadfruit to the islands while the British were
busy sending ships to Tahiti. This cultivar was producing fruit by the time
the *Providence* arrived. In 1796 Anderson said this variety was doing well,
and baked or boiled, "Negroes are passionately fond of them." Boiling the
seeds with some salt beef or fish was "a substantial & nutritive mess for a
Negroe."[159] By 1801 Wiles was stating that "the Breadfruit Tree is now perfectly naturalized in Jamaica," along with all the "South-Sea Plants" (except
for the *vi*).[160] Banks was delighted that the project had exceeded his "most
sanguine hopes."[161]

Breadfruit was not, though, the saving stroke for the plantations' economies or workforces that had been imagined. The diversification of crops
in the Caribbean and the resumption of imports from the fledgling United
States into the region had already relieved the cycle of famine. Then, in
1807, the act to abolish slavery was passed in Britain.

In 1838 some visitors to the islands had breakfast with a seventy-year-
old coffee planter, the *Providence* botanist Wiles. He told them the breadfruit tree he had worked so hard to install forty-four years before never
reached the "luxuriant growth of its native climate."[162] The most valuable
introduced tree was rather the mango, "a few plants of which were taken
out of a French prize, captured about half a century ago." Mangoes had
spread rapidly, produced abundantly, and served as "dessert for the whites
and food for the negros, as well as for cattle, horses, and hogs."[163]

Breadfruit were included in the productions of Jamaica at the Paris

Universal Exhibition in 1855,[164] and by the end of the century the Jamaican Agricultural Society was stipulating breadfruit as one of the fruit trees, along with pears, oranges, cocoa, and kola, that should be planted on their model farms.[165] Back in Britain, breadfruit had fallen out of botanical and political interest.

Conclusions

Breadfruit still has a presence in the Caribbean. It forms a part of the national cuisine, possessing distinctive styles of preparation. Austin Clarke wrote in 1899 in his deliberately Caribbean voice about the history of the

Figure 5.2. *Veronika Lafon with one of her* tifaifai—*an appliquéd quilt—featuring an* uru *design. Village des Artisans Tipaerui, Tahiti. March 2009. Photo: author.*

breadfruit voyage and how a botany-loving, slave-trading Bligh brought the fruit in. "But," he says, "Cap'n Bligh really did the Wessindies a favour."[166] From the "green and large harvest of breadfruits," people make breadfruit cou-cou, steamed, roast, or pickled breadfruit, and all these "have come in good-good, many a day, to put food in the belly of a lot o' poor people."[167]

In both the Caribbean and the Society Islands, breadfruit is used as a symbol of what is distinctive about their countries. It is part of the islands' identities, a vibrant part of their histories. The role is of course more integral to Tahiti's cultural landscape. There is still at least one breadfruit tree in every Tahitian garden. In addition to using the fruit as a staple food and the timber for carving, Tahitians surround themselves with breadfruit imagery. The large, deep-lobed leaf, often with the round fruit, make a frequent appearance on fabric prints, *tifaifai* appliquéd quilts, print media, and Tahiti-themed merchandise in souvenir shops.

Breadfruit leaves, fruits, roots, and bark still have a prominent role in *raau Tahiti*, the traditional medicine of the island. Some of the few things people outside the Pacific can identify about Tahiti, apart from its association with Gauguin, is its connection to the British captain Bligh, the mutiny, and breadfruit. Breadfruit has a substantial place in national imagery both within and without the island.

Throughout its history, the qualities of the breadfruit brought people into new contacts with each other, assisting migrations and interisland visits across Polynesia, bringing British to the island ambitious for the glory of their nation and their own reputations, and indirectly bringing Tahiti's first long-term residents to the island. The mutineers started the tipping of political scales in one *ari'i*'s favor, and finally, the breadfruit project brought two Tahitians to the other side of the world, making the first contact between the two island groups. The breadfruit took and has retained a firm hold of imaginations in Tahiti, Britain, and the Caribbean, creating surprising connections between them.

CHAPTER 6

Pigs, Muskets, and a New Order

O n Sunday morning, 12 November 1815, Pomare II assembled together some one thousand of his supporters, most of them Christian converts, at his place of exile in Mo'orea. They had been gathered from Tahiti, Ra'iatea, and Huahine by some pork traders from Sydney who were willing to lend a hand to support their primary pork supplier.[1] On this Sabbath morning they made the provocative step of paddling to a Christian chapel at Pape'ete on Tahiti's northern shore to conduct worship. Opuhara, *ari'i* of Papara, a chief deeply embittered against Pomare and his Christians, heard news of their arrival. In the excitement a *taura* (priest/oracle) went into a trance and had a vision of Opuhara's triumph against the Christians. Opuhara rushed to gather his warriors, his allies, and their muskets and descended on Pape'ete. Pomare heard the gunfire of their approach but kept his people at their devotions until the service was concluded. They then rose and turned to face Opuhara's men, forming battle lines. Pomare's people raised muskets and the cannon mounted on boats were readied. Opuhara did not waver and gave the signal to start firing. The combat was vicious and drawn-out, but Pomare's warriors held the strength of arms, the bounty of fourteen years of intensive bartering of their pigs for guns from Sydney. Opuhara was shot. As he died, his warriors fled. Through this, the battle of Fe'i Pi, Pomare secured the island.[2]

Pigs (*pua'a*) were once one of the most important animals in the Maohi world. They were "good food for gods and men." They were a means by which value, requests, alliances, and even insights were transferred between people and between realms. Pigs were necessary for securing marriages, appeasing chiefs, and asking favors of gods. They formed the backbone of a household's prosperity and they could provide a conduit between the worlds of the *Ao* and the *Po*.

In the last few decades of the eighteenth century and into the early nineteenth, the role of pigs in Tahitian society changed dramatically. The political ends the Pomare chiefs strove to meet through the trade of pigs were to have wide consequences for the Pomare lineage, for foreign interests, and the island's people.

This chapter traces the economic, environmental, political, and cultural changes set in motion by a strikingly new kind of ecological exchange that began in Tahiti in 1801: the salt pork trade between the island and Port Jackson, Australia. Engaging in this trade brought profound changes to the roles pigs held in Maohi communities. There were certainly continuities of meaning, some of which are still active in contemporary Tahiti. For the most part, however, the Polynesian breed of the species *Sus scrofa* was transformed both culturally and biologically through its contact with European trade. Once ubiquitous, domestic pigs are no longer a significant part of life on the island and the *pua'a* in its original, lean, dark, long-legged form is gone.

A new kind of ship arrived in Matavai Bay on 26 June 1801. Captain Scott, of the *Porpoise,* was carrying a letter for Tu from Governor King of New South Wales, discussing arrangements for a shipment of Tahitian pork. Scott had on board more than 11,000 nails, 280 axes, 180 pairs of scissors, 50 hoes, 72 cooking plates, 356 yards of red and yellow bunting, 100 white shirts, 287 combs, and 6 stand of arms, all ready to barter. With Tu's assistance, he spent the next month collecting pigs. As the Tahitians brought their pigs into the camp on shore, the crew butchered the animals, rubbed the resulting pieces of pork thoroughly with salt, laid them on a rack, placed boards on top, and loaded them with weights. The following day the pieces were wiped and checked for signs of rot; anything dubious was discarded and the rest was placed in casks of strong brine. Another check the next day caught any pieces that had not taken up the salt.[3] Just over three weeks later the *Porpoise*'s crew had successfully salted nearly 350 pigs.[4] They probably secured more before leaving Tahiti after a further three weeks, but whatever the number of pigs they butchered, the figure that mattered to Captain Scott was the saleable result: 31,000 pounds of pork. The casks were loaded onto the *Porpoise* for the 3,230-mile (5,200 km) journey to Australia.

This was a significant visit for many reasons. It was the first truly commercial expedition Europeans had sent to the Society Islands. It was also the first successful trading venture of the young colony in New South Wales. It brought the islands and the colony together despite their geographic distance. The relationship would soon draw Tahiti into a cash economy, decades before other Pacific islands.

In the months and years that followed the *Porpoise*'s stay, a stream of ships went to the Society Islands to buy pigs. Many of the ships were run by private traders, operating independently or on behalf of the colonial government. Whether state-financed or privately financed, the trade was substantial. At a moderate calculation, most ships bartered for and salted down between 400 and 500 pigs. The larger ships secured from 1,000 to 1,500.

On the surface, the arrival of a ship to gather great quantities of one of the islands' natural resources for the use of a British colony seems to continue the impetus of the breadfruit project. Both enterprises were carried out with the assistance of Tahitians, and both benefited British colonies. But the transplanting of breadfruit and the trade of salt pork differed in fundamental respects. Breadfruit had been sought by the British for symbolic, economic, and scientific reasons. Exporting the trees had significant but limited consequences for the Tahitians. It had little impact on their political structures, their social relations, economy, spiritual life, or health of their environment. Certainly, the lives of the *teuteu* Maititi and Paupo were profoundly affected by their involvement in the project, and the consequences of having the *Bounty* mutineers on the island were considerable. But the actual act of supplying breadfruit seedlings had very little lasting impact in Tahiti.

The pork trade did not provide the British with the scope to highlight their nation's (or their colony's) achievements in commerce, science, or benevolence that breadfruit had offered. Instead, pork had practical purposes: feeding convicts and settlers, and it was a trade that encouraged the economy. In the Society Islands, the implications of the pork trade were enormous. After fifteen years of dealing in salt pork, Tahiti's political economy and its surrounding society had shifted fundamentally.

Small Beginnings

The trade for pigs in Tahiti had started on a limited scale during the eighteenth century. As discussed in chapter 1, Tahitians were from the start prepared to barter pigs. Mariners were consistently anxious to obtain them. George Tobin wrote that on arriving in Tahiti, one of the first words a sailor learned (along with *vahine,* woman) was *pua'a,* hog.[5] George Forster reported that the "squeaking of pigs" heard when the *Resolution* finally anchored off the coast of Tahiti in August 1773 was "a more welcome sound to us, than the music of the most brilliant performer."[6] Nevertheless, the first visitors were moderate in their enthusiasm for the local pigs as a meat animal. In 1767, George Robertson described them as a small Chinese breed. He said the average was between forty and sixty pounds (18–27 kg), none above eighty pounds (36 kg).[7] Don José de Andía y Varela, on Boenechea's 1774 expedition, described Tahitian pigs as "a very small breed," although "plump and well flavoured."[8]

Early written sources suggest that the Polynesian breed of pig differed little from the typical Southeast Asian and Melanesian breed of the world's primary pig species, *Sus scrofa*. The breed typical to Southeast Asia and Oceania has a distinctive, steeply sloping skull (giving a long nose and a high cranium), tusks, a round body with dark hair, narrow legs, and a straight-hanging tail. They are relatively easily tamed and tend to stay near their owner's residence, grazing in grasses, under fruit trees, and along shorelines.

The human domestication of *Sus scrofa* appears to have occurred in Thailand from as early as 10,000 BC, and in China from 4,900 BC. This original species gave rise to all domestic and wild pigs around the world, distributed with human settlement, across Asia to Europe, Africa, and the Americas, as well as across the Pacific. Reconstructions of Austronesian vocabularies have provided evidence for *Sus scrofa*'s being present in island Southeast Asia from 2,500 BC.[9] The domesticated *Sus scrofa*, with a possible genetic contribution from the Celebes wild boar, *Sus celebensis*,[10] contributed to the viability of human migrations eastward from Melanesia. The species usefully produces several litters throughout the year (with five to ten young at a time), is omnivorous, and can be supported on a household's scraps. The pig has always been a highly valuable part of a settlers' stock. Yoshiko Sinoto's archaeological digs in Huahine, one of the Leeward Islands, uncovered pig bones with radiocarbon dates ranging from AD 850 to 1,200.[11] Pigs are likely to have been present on the Leeward Islands earlier than this, accompanying the first migrants arriving around AD 100 to 300.

A new breed of *Sus scrofa* was brought into the Society Islands in the eighteenth century. Don Domingo Boenechea with Don José Varela (commanders of the *Aguila* and the storeship *Júpiter*, respectively) were the first to bring in European pigs, during their visit to Tahiti in December 1774. The five pigs Varela released at Taiarapu were of course the same species as the Polynesian pigs, but they were much larger, paler, and stockier than the Polynesian breed.[12] They appeared to enjoy their new habitat and successfully interbred with the local pigs. Crucially, the Tahitians supported the new breed, enabling the pale animals to inhabit their districts and cohabit with their existing pigs. By 1777 Cook was noting that the Spanish pigs had "already greatly improved the breed originally on the island, and were at the time of our arrival very numerous."[13] He left English pigs with Ma'i in Huahine, adding to the several Ma'i had already in his possession, and at Ra'iatea he introduced "an English Boar and Sow . . . so that not only Otahiete but all the neighbouring islands" would, in a few years, have their "breed of hogs considerably improved."[14] Bligh reported in 1788 that the islanders preferred European pigs to their own because of their larger size, and that the "Otaheite breed of Hogs is effectually destroyed." [15] By the time Captain Vancouver stopped by in 1792, no one was referring to Tahitian pigs as small. Vancouver's Lieutenant Edward Bell declared:

> The Breed of Hogs here is far superior to anything I ever saw of the kind, both in size and quality, we got many that weigh'd when dead and clean'd upwards of two hundred weight . . . the meat is delicious. [16]

Between 1774 and 1792, a mere eighteen years, the standard Tahitian pig had more than doubled in size. [17] The Rev. William Ellis reported, after his residence on the island between 1817 and 1823, that from time to time people saw a type of pig that used to be the only variety in Tahiti. He described its long legs, long nose, erect ears, and "curly or almost wooly hair," and noted with approval that this variety was, unusually for the species, "almost totally averse to the mire." [18] The "generality" of pigs on the island were, though, a "mixture of English and Spanish." [19]

The new, more common breed was not only twice as big as the island's original pig. It also had a more aggressive nature. Tahitians needed to put yokes on them, break off the points of their tusks, and build increasingly strong fences to keep them out of gardens. Even then, some owners needed to run a stick across the top of a troublesome pig's head and through holes pierced in its ears to restrain it from pushing between the fence posts. [20] The missionaries recorded skirmishes between households over a rampant pig ravaging a neighbor's garden. It was becoming harder to sustain the familiar, more straightforward role pigs used to hold within the domestic sphere.

Pigs in Tahitian Society

It had been a long-established practice in the Society Islands for pigs to be hand-reared by women, children, and elderly members of the *manahune*. George Forster reported in 1777 that in the Society Islands pigs were "allowed to run about, but received regular portions of food, which were commonly distributed by old women." [21] It was a type of domestication common across the Pacific, still practiced in many western and central Pacific islands, which includes hand-feeding as a way to foster the pigs' attachment to a household as they mature. This process, when a pig takes to it, makes it possible for the animals to roam untethered, foraging roots, fallen nuts, and fruits for themselves yet staying close by for an evening feed and remaining the property of their owners.

Pigs were an ever-present part of the domestic and local environment. Pigs could be used as payments to secure the labor of canoe makers, help from neighbors in preparing a piece of land for cultivating paper mulberry trees or taro, or arranging a long-term supply of other food. The value of a single pig was substantial within this system. James Morrison described a type of property exchange called *ho'o* or *taui* (the latter having the additional meaning of "compensation") in which, for instance, a man could take a pig to a fisherman and arrange for him to supply daily fish for one or more months, depending on the size of the pig.[22]

Social bonds were strengthened through gifts of pigs. William Anderson noted in 1774 that if a young man and woman wanted to marry, the man would present her father with "such things as are necessary in common life; as hogs, cloth, or canoes."[23] Such gifts were crucial; both Anderson and later observers pointed out that if a man did not possess enough of these valuables he would be rejected as a suitor.[24] A wedding of high-born men and women, called a *fa'aipoipora'a*, required fatted pigs for a feast that would last several days.[25] Gifts of cloth, pigs, and other livestock were made by both families. The ceremony for a *manahune* couple was of a smaller scale but still involved the presentation and consumption of pigs.[26]

A gift of pigs was symbolically valuable enough to maintain and, at times of tension, restore good relations between commoners and their *ari'i*. In 1801, for instance, one of the Pare divisions was slow in constructing the roof of a *fale* (house) for a visiting chief and his retinue. Fearing the Pomares' anger, they made a hasty procession to Tu's residence, headed by their *ra'atira* and a priest, with an offering of a pig, a chicken, and a young plantain tree.[27]

But pigs were not just peaceable, useful domestic animals to be moved about as gifts and trade items. The boar was the chosen *ata* (embodiment or "shadow") of the god 'Oro when in his daunting, man-slaying form, 'Oro-tauà (Warrior-at-war).[28] The boar carried messages that were of particular importance to *ari'i*, and the Pomares and their priests were attentive to their actions. When a normally quiet, domesticated boar became suddenly aggressive, it was "known that 'Oro was dwelling in him." This violent pig was an indication of danger for the region; its aggression was a "sign that the mouth of 'Oro was open ready to consume the chief and his clans."[29] In the late eighteenth century 'Oro had become the paramount god worshipped in Ra'iatea and Tahiti. It can be guessed that pigs, as well as turtles and other creatures associated with the god, would have had a parallel increase in their potency.

'Oro's intentions and insights could be conveyed through boars, and it was therefore important for *ariʻi* to watch and use them as part of their rule. For instance, to determine when it would be prudent to take action against enemies and discern the will of 'Oro, a *tahua* (priest) would prepare the wrapped, tapering form of the *toʻo* into which 'Oro would be called and place it in the *fare atua*, a small, protective house for the god. A *fare atua* the missionary George Bennet later sent to London was nearly three feet (87 cm) long, of a rounded, cylindrical form reminiscent of a pig's body, with four short pig-like legs, topped with a carved roof resembling a *fale*.[30] Once the *toʻo* was in place at 'Oro's *marae*, the *tahua* would strangle a pig. Its body would be stuffed with miro leaves and smeared with blood. It was placed over a fire several times, then settled on the altar in a crouching position, facing the *fare atua*. Then:

> while the high priest prayed for the success of the warriors, an adept
> from among the priests scanned the pig. If its eyes were well closed
> or partially open, if both eyes looked alike or one eye was more
> open than the other, if the head and one eye had a tendency to turn
> from the land or towards the land (interpreted to mean they were
> to invade), and if the mouth was closed or showing the teeth and
> tongue—all these signs conveyed special meanings.[31]

The intestines, which had been laid aside on the paving of the *marae,* were stirred slightly with a stick and read for further omens. They were then burnt and, with the rest of the pig, offered to 'Oro as food.[32]

Offended *atua* could cause illness and misfortune, but they could be contacted and appeased through pigs. If a doctor was unable to cure a patient, a priest was called on to make a prayer at the family's *marae*. He would hold a young pig by the leg to make it squeal and attract the god's attention. Requesting that the *atua* remove the sickness, the priest would present the pig, live, as an offering. It was marked with a coconut fiber cord in its ear and released to join the sacred pigs of the *marae*.[33] Teho, *ariʻi* of Hitiaʻa, was able to make a powerful offering in early 1801, filling "3 altars with dead pigs in sacrifice" when he fell ill.[34] The smell of pigs, roasted or rotting, would captivate the gods' interest. Commoners did not always have access to pigs and in some instances an afflicted person's parents could stand in at the *marae* ceremonies as "human pigs."[35] Though the parents were only offered symbolically, when a chief decided to have one of his people killed for a sacrifice, the limbs of the corpse were typically tied and the body taken to the *marae* slung from a pole like a pig. John Webber, artist on

Figure 6.1. *Pigs and dogs on a* marae *offering platform, Atehuru, with Cook, Ma'i, and a few officers observing.* William Woollett, "A Human Sacrifice, in a Morai, in Otaheite," etching after John Webber, in A Voyage to the Pacific Ocean . . . in the Years 1776–1780 *(London, 1784).* © The Trustees of the British Museum (Department of Prints and Drawings 1868,0808.3152).

Cook's third voyage, recorded one of these sacrifices, along with pigs and dogs, when Tu invited Cook, some officers, and Ma'i to attend a ceremony at the Taputapuatea *marae* in Atehuru in 1777.

Tu, Pomare II, and the Trade of Pigs

From their first meeting, when the *Dolphin*'s sailors grunted and pointed to shore to show what they wanted, the Tahitians understood that pigs were valued by Europeans as a food. Chiefly families, with pigs at their disposal, capitalized on the Europeans' desire, routinely bringing pigs to meetings with ship's captains and specifying the gift they wanted in return, such as Purea's making Cook "sencible" that he "must give her a hetchet & then she would give me a Pig," to which he complied.[36] Tu, Pomare II, and 'Itia regularly used pigs to strengthen diplomatic relations with the British as well as with other *ari'i.* This role was to expand after 1800, taking priority over a more traditional range of uses.

The trade was generous; in their enthusiasm to cement relations with Europeans the chiefly families would sometimes offer more pigs than a ship could manage. George Tobin reported in July 1792 that as they prepared to leave, "Hogs were so numerous that many could not be received for want of room to accommodate them."[37] Unlike the later traders from Australia, the Europeans initially wanted pigs only for immediate consumption or for shipboard provisions, so the quantities being exported were substantial but not excessive.

When Cook visited Taiarapu and Pare in August-September 1773, the regions were recovering from a recent war between Tu and Vehiatua. There was a serious shortage of pigs and Cook lamented that "hardly any thing will induce the owners to part with them."[38] Despite the enticements of European goods and the fear of offending or angering their guests, the people were not to be cajoled into trading away their pigs. However, eight months later, when Cook returned to Matavai, the region was again prosperous. People had rebuilt their houses and there were "several large hogs near every house and every other Sign of a riseing state."[39] At this stage, with enough owners managing to maintain the trade in pigs at a sustainable level, the animals had time to breed again in sufficient numbers in between ships' visits. But engaging in this particular ecological exchange was about to become a major disruptive force.

The New Pork Economy

On the far side of the Pacific in 1800, the young British colony of New South Wales was struggling to feed itself. Farming Australian land was not as straightforward as the planners had expected. The population of around two thousand convicts and military personnel, landed in successive shiploads since 1788, still relied on imported rations. An important but little-known point is that over this early period, the shipping of salt pork from England was the colony's greatest expense.[40] Of the £16 the British government paid for each individual's annual rations, £10 was spent on pork.[41] Governor Phillip Gidley King, responsible for the colony after September 1800, knew a cheaper alternative had to be found.[42] He was also anxious for the settlement to establish some form of independent commercial enterprise. Trading ports within reach of the colony in Southeast Asia and China were caught up with East India Company's monopolies, but New Zealand and the Pacific islands were still unregulated and open for trading.

Under King's former governorship on Norfolk Island (in the Tasman Sea), British settlers had, by 1792, started producing a surplus of pigs. Hundreds of these were shipped to New Zealand to breed in the expectation of future provisions. Others were shipped to Sydney.[43] King also arranged for cattle to be brought in from India. But further supplies were needed. King had heard from voyagers and missionaries about the availability and plump-

Figure 6.2. *John Williams* [*Maori bargaining with a* pakeha], *1845 or 1846. Sepia, ink and wash, 10.2 x 14.1 in. (26 x 36 cm), Alexander Turnbull Library, Wellington. N.Z. (A-079-017).*

ness of the pigs in Tahiti, and the willingness of Tahitians to trade. Tahiti retained its reputation as the safest and easiest provisioning stop in the Pacific. Further, King's governorship of New South Wales had been described to him as encompassing not just the colony but the "islands adjacent in the Pacific Ocean," without specifying an eastern limit. He interpreted his area of responsibility as extending all the way to the Society Islands.[44] He knew he had to negotiate with local titleholders there, but he felt justified in appointing the missionary John Jefferson as a justice of the peace in Tahiti, and, until the situation was clarified by a 1817 statute, he and then governor Macquarie presumed Tahiti to be within British dominion.[45]

The small settlement of Sydney was an outward-looking, ocean-minded community. Perched uneasily on the eastern Australian coast, its citizens negotiated their presence and managed a fraught relationship with the Gadigal, Wangal, Gamaragal, and other tribes of the region, without the local knowledge or sufficient tools to farm the land, and with a workforce largely unused to farming.[46] The colonists kept their eyes on the harbor for ships arriving from the more populous island ports, bringing news of the broader world and bringing the food and raw materials they could not produce themselves. Port Jackson enticed traders and explorers from around the world, sealers and whalers from America, visiting Maori, Tahitians, Hawaiians, and others. It would not last, but the early 1800s was the period of Australia's most active engagement and, in many respects, reliance upon the Pacific.

Captain Vancouver had been told of the governor's search for a source of pork. When Vancouver's storeship was due to return in 1793 from the northwest coast of America to Sydney, he directed his lieutenant to stop in the Marquesas and Tahiti to trade for some livestock: "hogs, goats, fowls, &c" for the benefit of the colony. The Marquesans were not interested in trading, but the Tahitians were willing to provide, during the stay from 13 February to March 1793, about one hundred live pigs. Eighty of them survived the trip to Sydney, arriving on 20 April.[47] The breed was praised, but it appears not to have made much impact; salt pork continued to be imported from Britain at a crippling cost.[48] The colony was "suffering greatly both from the want of animal food, and all other sorts of provisions."[49] With no established local source of pork, King decided to take action. In October 1800 he sent an initial proposal and gift to Tu with the *Albion* whaler.[50]

Tu welcomed Governor King's offer of an alliance. He wrote to King, stating that he would gladly offer protection to subjects of King George, but that he currently stood "in fear of the commonality, many of them being disaffected towards me." This was due, he said, to their being encouraged by some European sailors who had deserted their ships and were living on the island. He wished King "to present me with a few fire-arms, whereby my authority may be maintained, and the peace of my kingdom preserved."[51] King was unwilling to risk the venture by refusing Tu's request, so he gathered what the colony could spare: a stand of six arms, some powder, and ammunition. He also obtained a large quantity of salt from a whaler, arranged for gifts such as red feathers and sumptuous clothes emblazoned with "O.R." ("Otoo Rex"),[52] and prepared a ship, the *Porpoise*, to sail. He was uneasy about the implications of arming this chief and told Captain Scott to consult the missionaries on the "propriety" of the guns being given.[53] King was apparently unaware that through the assistance of missionaries, the Pomare family had by this stage already managed to secure some impressive pieces of ordnance. The missionaries had allowed the Pomares, their protectors, to make use of the iron in the missionary storeroom to make ammunition, acted as go-betweens in the acquisition of firearms from passing traders, attached two swivel guns onto carriages for use on the Pomare fleet,[54] and set up an "18 pounder Cannonade."[55] As K. R. Howe has said, the Pomares and missionaries had a relationship of "mutual exploitation" that lasted for decades.[56]

A few years later the missionaries would complain that their already "precarious situation" was being heightened by the uncontrolled importation of muskets.[57] In June 1801, however, when the *Porpoise* arrived, the ship and its gifts were seen by the mission as well as the Pomares as a "very providential interference":

> for the affairs of this country were brought to such a crisis, that a few days, if not hours, would have either dethroned Otoo, or established him in his authority.[58]

The people in the Pare-'Arue district were becoming discontented with their chiefs, particularly with the increasing claims Pomare II, now just over twenty, was making. Pomare did not follow the conventional subtleties and indirect methods of gaining influence with his own people. He had for years been demanding heavy tribute payments, making frequent human sacrifices, attempting to redistribute land, and making blatant efforts to manipulate kin relations to bolster his position. His attempts to stretch the privileges of sacred rank and secure wide-ranging secular power were resented.[59] The missionaries reported on 21 May 1800:

> there are commotions among the lower classes of natives against Pomerre, chiefly on account of his tyrannical conduct (it is said) in frequently plundering them of their little property.[60]

The people wanted a return to the old system in which every district was ruled independently by its own chief, without having to defer to a higher, dictatorial authority.[61] In October, with the threat of war still looming, some of the Pomare clan went to Point Venus to speak to the missionaries. Tu fretted, unable to determine which of the districts' chiefs "were his friends, or who his foes."[62] One of the brothers suggested to him that perhaps "the arbitrary proceedings" of his son were the cause of the discontent. Tu did not deny it. He said he "wished much for a ship of war to arrive, which he supposed, by an interference in his favour, would restore tranquility, and confirm his, and his son's authority."[63] Having some more Englishmen to live on the island, he said, would also be a way of avoiding a war.

The Pomares wasted no time in making the most of the *Porpoise*'s "providential" arrival. Tu told Captain Scott he would be "diligent in procuring" pigs for the traders. On 29 June, Scott planned to formally present Tu and 'Itia the gifts from Governor King, but he had to wait: they were "absent in quest of hogs."[64] As the *Porpoise* neared the end of its stay, Tu made an important decision. He announced:

> when the ship departed, he would lay a prohibition on hogs, that there may be a greater supply ready for the next vessel that shall be sent.[65]

Tu's prohibition on pork is probably the first recorded instance of a *rahui* being used to build up stocks of an animal or plant not for ceremonial purposes, feasting, or conservation, but in order to trade them away to Europeans. Tu was taking a risk. Instituting a wide-scale *rahui* was a bold political move. Just after Wallis had left in 1767 Purea had made a similar broadranging *rahui* as part of her maneuvers to establish a new, potent *marae* at Mahaiatea at Papara (on the southern coast of Tahiti) and have her young son's claim to dominance recognized. An alliance of chiefs, incensed by Purea's actions, invaded in a rampage of killing and desecration, destroying her *marae* and forcing Purea and her family into exile. Tu's *rahui* was not as clearly a statement of intent to dominate as Purea's had been. His rivals did not challenge him, and his people seem to have borne the restriction. His son's actions and the scale of *rahui* would get bolder in years to come.

While Tu was giving his people orders to halt consumption of pork, the *Porpoise* was sailing back to Port Jackson with a hold full of salted meat. The round trip had only taken five months and had been cost-effective.[66] Governor King was satisfied, and there followed a succession of ships pulling into Matavai Bay (see Appendix A). The *Royal Admiral* dropped off a new contingent of missionaries and gathered four to five hundred pigs for salting in June and July 1801. Some private merchants with larger ships, the *Norfolk* and *Venus,* arrived with only a few days between them in January 1802. The *Norfolk* had started well, managing to get pigs in return for axes, knives, and shirts. Then the *Venus,* captained by the merchant-venturers George Bass and Charles Bishop, trumped the trade by bringing in pistols.[67] They could get five pigs per gun. The *Norfolk*'s men suddenly had to struggle to find anyone who was prepared to exchange their pigs for checked shirts or lengths of cloth. Although the *Venus* traders soon ran out of pistols and had to pay two cartridges of powder and two large axes for a single pig, they nevertheless collected 123,000 pounds (55,000 kg) of pork, mostly from Tahiti but also some from Hawai'i, where Bass had previously gone to purchase salt.[68]

To gain some sense of the material impact the trade was having on the islanders, an estimate can be made of the numbers of pigs given to each ship. If the *Porpoise* had shipped 31,000 pounds (14,000 kg) of salt pork from the (at least) 350 pigs the missionaries mentioned, it can be said that a (conservative) average of 88 pounds (40 kg) of pork was yielded from each pig.[69] The *Venus,* then, with its 123,000 pounds (55,000 kg) had managed to acquire nearly 1,400 pigs in total. This is a staggering number, and another six ships were yet to come that year.

Over the course of 1802 eight ships came for pork and there were only four months that year when there were no salting parties on shore. In September there were three ships in Matavai Bay at the same time, all wanting pigs. There were additional pressures on the pig population that year. Pomare had removed the six-foot-long *to'o*, for 'Oro, from the *marae* at Atehuru to his own *marae*.[70] The *ari'i* Rua launched an attack on the Pomares, devastated the region of Pare, secured the *to'o*, and took or killed any pigs and other livestock he could find. The Pomare family fled to Matavai Bay, where they were given protection by the crews of the *Norfolk* and *Venus*.[71] The supply of pigs faltered just as the pork traders were becoming important to the island economy.

Back in Port Jackson in March 1803 the first issue of the *Sydney Gazette* declared:

> The abundance of animal food throughout the Colony, is an undoubted testimony of the solid advantages that have accrued from a correspondence with the native inhabitants of Otaheite.[72]

In the previous year a total of 266,000 pounds of pork had been imported into Sydney, amounting to at least 3,000 pigs.[73] Although some of these were from other islands, the vast majority—around 2,850—had been provided by Tahitians. And that had been during a year that saw frequent civil wars on the island. The 2,850 pigs were taken from the depleted stocks that remained, primarily from the Matavai district. Securing this quantity had not been easy, and the *Norfolk* traders, competing with the *Venus* crew, had fanned out over six miles from Matavai Bay to find pigs for sale.[74] On an island that five years previously had been estimated to support 16,000 people, the number of pigs each household supplied to the ships each year must have been significant, as many as 5.6 per household if the demand had been evenly spread across the island.[75] The concentration of the demand around the northern districts meant a heavier reliance on those stocks, so each household was probably being pressured to give up nine or ten each year. This would not have left many, or any, for their own use.

With so many pigs leaving the island, mature breeding pairs were lost. A female pig is usually able to produce her first litter at about eighteen months and the gestation period is four months. There would then have been a lapse before the young pigs could be used for exchanges. In any case, householders would not have been able to put these pigs to any of the usual purposes with a *rahui* in place. The only type of exchange the pig owners of Pare-'Arue could engage in was for their chief's trade and the only return was the hope of escaping their chief's anger. The process of commodification was transforming pigs into gifts and trade items for outsiders on a scale that had not been attempted before. Despite all they were giving up to Pomare, despite the guns and other European goods he was amassing, the communities were receiving little material benefit. The young chief was still unable to protect them from frequent attacks by rival districts. The pigs that used to be tribute, "good food for gods and men," tradable for services, status, and allies, had become a currency. A significant step was taken in 1804: "Two of the principal chiefs," the missionaries complained, had prevailed on their people "not to barter, but to reserve their hogs for musquets."[76] This was a new kind of restriction, and it made the pig's commodification as a trade item for weaponry explicit. It was a tense situation for those who owned pigs. In many regions, when a pig owner decided to go out on a limb and take some cloth or ironware from the missionaries in exchange for a pig, they would often then change their minds, give back the goods, and "demand back their hogs."[77] Pomare continued to display the symbols of traditional power, the *maro 'ura* feathered loincloth and the potent *to'o,* but through the pig trade he was consolidating a new, less negotiable type of authority.

In 1802, after Pomare had run to the pork ships in Matavai Bay for safety, twenty or thirty of the crew of two of the ships, all armed, descended on Atehuru. The defending army sensibly fled.[78] But the Pomare family could not rely on continuous or even regular support from the Port Jackson crews. The traders did not visit for a year after the bumper cargoes of 1802 and early 1803. They knew the pig population had been overtaxed and that supplies, and thus profits, were less certain. Despite the *rahui,* there were not enough pigs to sustain the trade. Some of the traders tried nearby islands in 1803. One ship purchased more than 660 pigs in Porapora and Ra'iatea. The people of Porapora, inspired by the goods and trading prospects presented by the pork ship, tried to capture the next ship to stop, the *Margaret.* However, the crew managed to escape and warned the other traders against the place.[79] The *Margaret* found more congenial, if limited, trading in Me'etia. The inhabitants of this small island had been sufficiently beyond the sphere of direct European trade to still value scissors, knives, paper, mirrors, and small hatchets in exchange for the twenty pigs they could spare.[80] Meanwhile, in Tahiti, Pomare managed to get a mounted swivel gun from the captain of a commercial ship in return for ten pigs. In June 1804 the *Harrington* arrived and found Pomare ruling the region singlehandedly, his father having died nine months earlier.[81] In the coming years Pomare continued to strive for ascendancy. Disruption, dissatisfaction, and discord rose.

Pork Traders in Tu's Navy

A series of battles in 1808 sent the missionaries on the run to Huahine and Pomare to Moʻorea. One of the missionaries, Henry Nott, accompanied Pomare, and they spent the next five years on the island. They were not isolated in Moʻorea. The Port Jackson traders soon shifted their trade to Moʻorea's Opunohu Bay after the chiefs reigning around Matavai (eager for European goods since the removal of Pomare's monopoly) made the tactical error in 1808 of capturing the first ship to turn up.[82]

Pomare was not going to give up his ambition to obtain full power over Tahiti. He planned a counterattack against the alliance of chiefs on the island, looking for support, as he always had, from both local and foreign communities. H. E. Maude has argued that Pomare's power was "ultimately dependent" on recognition by visiting ships and the arms he could get from them.[83] But local support was also necessary to his maintenance of power. It suited him to allow the missionaries to believe he fully relied on British support and that he was necessary for their own safety, but the situation was more complex. In 1809 he called on his familial and diplomatic ties with *ariʻi* in the Leeward Islands and further strengthened his alliance with Raʻiatea by marrying Terito, daughter of the *ariʻi* Tamatoa IV, in 1810.[84] As tensions rose in the years leading to the battle of Feʻi Pi, the chiefs of these islands agreed to send warriors to Moʻorea to support him. Several pork traders, salting in Moʻorea and heading to the Leeward Islands for pigs, agreed to ship the men from Raʻiatea and Huahine on the return journey. It was a difficult time, with not just political unrest but large numbers of people dying from a range of diseases brought by the visiting ships.[85] It is at such times of despair that a people can start to abandon existing gods and look for new sources of hope and protection.

Pomare appears to have decided at this point that there were fresh avenues for support via the missionaries. In 1812 he asked to be baptized. Brother Nott did not accede to his request, being too uncertain of the chief's motivations and commitment.[86] But Pomare had stated a definite intention, and it was the first indication the missionaries had received, after fifteen years of trying, that they might succeed in their endeavor. By 1813 they were feeling triumphant, writing to their directors in London of his continued and apparently sincere conversion, framing it as one of the world's "greatest miracles of grace" and giving thanks for "so great and wonderful a change in so exceedingly great and wonderful a sinner!"[87] The rejection of one god for another had not occurred on the island for about a hundred years, when the creator god Taʻaroa had been replaced by ʻOro.

Under New Authority

Pomare may have been genuinely convinced of the efficacy of the Christian god, but his conversion was also politically astute. If he could step away from 'Oro he would not need to rely on the much-contested marks of 'Oro's status and potency—the *maro 'ura* and *to'o*. He could create his own terms of governance rather than adhere to traditional forms. Pomare continued to gather supporters. A growing number of islanders were converging on the missionaries' settlement, still at Mo'orea, for religious instruction. By 1814 Brother Davies could count ninety-four students, not including "irregular stragglers."[88] Further, some incidents in 1814 were apparently interpreted as proof of divine support from the Christian god and a failure of the old gods. One of these centered on a Tahitian woman who was enduring a lengthy labor, making no progress. A local priest was sent for and tried to intercede with the appropriate deity, with no result. Then, by the missionaries' account, a "native man, a worshipper of the true God," knelt down and prayed on her behalf. She was suddenly delivered, to everyone's surprise. The missionary chronicle records:

> The people were so struck by this event, that they went immediately to the Morai, which they completely demolished, broke down the altars, brought forth their gods, and burnt them in the fire as false.[89]

A great change was under way. Chiefs in Tahiti, still loyal to 'Oro, made plans to attack Pomare and his growing band of supporters, most of whom were Christian converts, many of them refugees from Tahiti where life was increasingly difficult for followers of the new religion. After the battle of Fe'i Pi, Pomare and the missionaries installed themselves back on Tahiti and settled again into their houses at Point Venus. With Pomare's approval they built a church, the focal point of the religion that the island's new *ari'i rahi* supported. Pomare was finally baptized in 1819 and the whole island became formally Christian. Regardless of beliefs still held in private, there would be no more sacrifices of *pua'a* at the *marae*, no more public reference to the actions and characteristics of pigs for signs of 'Oro's will.

Pomare II used the missionaries to draw up laws and help with the management of the island as well as directing religious observance. The missionaries were also trying to manage some salt pork production to their own ends. By 1817 the Rev. J. M. Orsmond was referring to the salting of pork as their "daily employ."[90] Whenever a ship came past, the pork was used to purchase spare ships' stores—cloth, tea, flour, needles, and buttons. They sent casks of pork with ships that had space to the Rev. Samuel Marsden or Rowland Hassall, leaders of the church in Sydney. Marsden and Hassall arranged for the sale of the pork and sent the profits back as provisions whenever a ship was heading to the island. It was an erratic arrangement and the brothers informed the LMS directors in London, not for the first time, that what they really needed was a small ship of their own.[91] The costs of running it would be, they argued, covered by trading the pork they would take to Port Jackson. Following a continued lack of response from the LMS, the brothers (many of whom had backgrounds in carpentry and other trades) built a ship themselves. It was to belong to Pomare officially, and he arranged timber, assistance, and food for the builders. The *Haweis* was ready to launch in December 1817. It took several cargoes of salt pork, coconut oil for lamps and soap-making, coconut fiber, and arrowroot from Mo'orea to Port Jackson.[92] It was almost certainly the first island-owned ship to trade at the Australian port.

In the colony of New South Wales, public opinion was not unanimous in supporting the outwardgoing trade to the "South Seas." In a continuation of the late eighteenth-century British disquiet over the degrading effects of European alcohol, arms, and trade, in 1817 J. T. Campbell (secretary to Macquarie, then governor of New South Wales), sent an anonymous letter to the *Sydney Gazette* complaining about the colony's taxes going to support the missionary society's "gospel venders and bacon-curers"[93] and satirizing the missionaries' activities in the Pacific:

> An ardent thirst for the influence of the Spirit at this time pervades
> the Inhabitants of the Pacific, with which we have any Intercourse,
> and pigs, and pine trees, *New Zealand* flax, &c. are the returns made
> in full tale for the comforts of spirit, instilled into them, and by
> which they are inspired.[94]

Campbell went on to talk of the missionaries bolstering the honor of the Christian Church and the "pecuniary advantage of the chosen few" through propagating the Gospel and delivering "Muskets and Cutlasses."[95] He was fined for libel, but such observations already had a broad currency.

Shifting Trade

With an increasing range of islands being settled by the English, traders were discovering the advantages of New Zealand, Fiji, and Tonga as effective sources of commodities.[96] The convenience of these closer islands, plus the growing success of the Australian settlers' own agricultural enterprise, meant that shipments from Tahiti became uneconomic.[97] In addition, sandalwood had been found in the Marquesas and pearls in the Tuamotus, drawing the interest of the Port Jackson traders.

This mattered less to Pomare in the 1820s than it would have earlier. He was welcoming ships from a growing range of nations and arranging to enter the trade more actively. He started to rely less on the missionaries, not trusting them to put his interests above their own in matters of trading. He ordered his people to build storehouses to contain the growing quantities of commodities he was gathering for trade. The missionaries commented crossly that Pomare had ordered every one of his people to "bring him a hog or they are to be banished from the land and go upon the reef."[98] Members of their congregations, even the sick, were absent, as "all are employed getting pigs for the King or making his oil or building his store houses &c."[99] In June 1820 he entrusted Samuel Henry, the Tahitian-born son of Rev. Brother Henry, with buying a ship on his behalf in Port Jackson, giving him instructions to "seek out Polynesians in Port Jackson" for advice.[100] Henry

Figure 6.3. *Ivan P. Fridrits [Pomare II receives the Russian Captain F. F. Bellingshausen and his officers at Point Venus], 1820. Engraving after Pavel Mikhailov, in the album of the voyage of Bellingshausen to Antarctic Seas, 1819–1821 (Sanktpeterburg: Tip. I. Glazunova, 1831). National Library of Australia, Canberra (Map RA 288).*

bought the *Governor Macquarie* in January 1821, and Pomare gave him the captaincy.[101] The new laws Pomare inaugurated for the island with missionary advice a few years earlier in 1819, the Code of Pomare, took the place of ancient regulations and included a set of rules dealing with pigs. Rather than letting missionaries, passing traders, or the agents and merchants who had started settling on the island gather profits as go-betweens, he made it illegal for anyone but himself to buy pork from local producers. Supplying pigs to anyone but himself was another offense to be punished by banishment.[102] He told Samuel Henry in 1820 that he had put all the pigs in Tahiti and Mo'orea in reserve, and:

> we will not sell pigs to those preachers, and the people will not roast pigs. We have set aside the pigs for ship sale, and for trade goods to be shipped to Botany Bay. Do not tell just anybody about this.[103]

But Pomare did not live long enough to benefit from these strictures; he died on 7 December 1821. He was succeeded by his one-year-old son, Pomare III, under the regency of his aunt, Ari'ipaea Vahine.

From the 1820s whalers started stopping by, and the most active trade in Matavai Bay returned to general provisioning.[104] Developing a range of foods that would meet the growing European market within the Pacific became the new priority. The missionaries planted coffee seeds from Rio de Janeiro in 1817, and from 1818 they employed John Gyles to develop sugar cane plantations and a small mill in Mo'orea, negotiating with Pomare over ownership of the resulting sugar.[105] The ruling elites of Tahiti—Pomare's high-born supporters—were committed to joining as full participants the greater network of British commerce they had formerly participated in only within the bounds of the island. Pomare had asked the missionaries to set up schools in each of the island's districts from 1816, and the first printing press arrived with a missionary from Sydney in 1817. After years of assistance with reading, writing, and translation, the island's leaders could communicate more readily with international governments. In 1822 Tahiti's "Prince Regent" Hitoi[106] wrote in Tahitian, with a translation by a missionary to Britain's principal secretary for foreign affairs:

> we have commenced our little mercantile concerns by the purchase of a Brig, which we intend sending to Port Jackson with Pork, Cocoanut Oil and Arrow root, to which we hope soon to add Coffee, Cotton, Tobacco and Sugar.[107]

With Pomare firmly established in power, affairs quieted into a begrudging peace. The islanders were no longer asking for arms. To the traders' surprise, the items of real value were once again clothes and cloth. The last significant export of pork was in 1826. There were no pork exports at all in 1827, which was the year that the infant Pomare III died and was succeeded by his fourteen-year-old sister, Aimata, Pomare IV. In that year the only ships that stopped by were owned by the Pacific Pearl Fishery. Traders still called at Tahiti, and the Pomares continued to send a few shipments of mixed goods to Port Jackson in 1828, but pork was a minor commodity. A more balanced supply of commodities, without the skewed reliance on pork, had been achieved.

Records of the 1830s are slight, making it difficult to determine what happened to pig populations after the salt pork trade diminished. After the French invaded in 1842, the management of exchange—including ecological exchange—was removed from the island's elites.

The surrender of power did not occur quickly or easily. Because Tahitian chiefs had commodified their local resources, making a prize pig into the currency that could purchase a gun, they had a fighting chance against the French. Resistance fighters came close to defeating Commodore Dupetit-Thouars, Captain Armand Bruat, and their marines. But the French soon controlled trade and local production, determining which crops and plantations would be introduced and which export commodities would be produced. Pigs did not figure. Regulations were drawn up controlling the uses of pigs and placing restrictions on keeping them near households. Fines were payable on damages caused by pigs.[108] Many of the residual roles *pua'a* had retained in Tahitians' daily lives ended.

A degree of domestic familiarity with pigs persevered, although in a very altered form. When Lady Brassey visited the island in 1876, she said, "Pigs are great pets here." She often saw women walking in Pape'ete,

> with their little favourites carefully brushed and combed, with dainty blue or red rosettes and bows on their necks and tails, and led by a long ribbon like the pug dogs in some of the old Dutch pictures.[109]

Much had altered in the way pigs intersected with Tahitian lives. The island was now a very different place.

Conclusions

If you look for pigs in Tahiti today, you will be hard pressed to locate any. While there in 2001 I peered surreptitiously into gardens, trudged along quiet tracks, and checked around the beachfront houses. There were no pigs. I asked around and the general reply was that Chinese market gar-

Figure 6.4. *Max Radiguet, "Tahitians coming from Church," lithograph from an original drawing, 1843. Reproduced from Colin Newbury,* Tahiti Nui *(Honolulu, 1980). National Library of Australia, Canberra (996.211 N535).*

deners were the ones who now kept pigs. Finally, over the concrete wall of a piggery on the southern side of the island, I found a hundred or more roundly fat, pale, floppy-eared, thoroughly European pigs. This was part of a small pork industry, but it is an imported industry, working to foreign models, with no relationship to earlier practices. I looked in souvenir shops and the regional handicrafts stalls for the sorts of images you can find on other Polynesian islands: pig carvings, boar-printed T-shirts; perhaps there would be pig-print motifs on cloth or painted on *pareu*. I looked in vain for any sign that pigs held creative significance in Tahiti, whether it was being associated with Maohi tradition or a general Pacific identity. There were dolphins, turtles, sharks, *tiare* flowers, hibiscus—all recognizable island motifs—but no pigs. I did see postcards showing *"Ma'a Tahiti"* (traditional Tahitian food), featuring a baked pig, appearing little different from the descriptions of pigs baked for feasts in the time of the Pomares. People I spoke to confirmed that whole, butchered pigs for social occasions could be bought easily at the market. Robert Koenig, president of the Société des Etudes Océaniennes, pointed out that in his home valley on the west side

Figure 6.5. Pua'a *in Robert and Denise Koenig's garden. Te Maru a Po, Tahiti. Photo courtesy of Denise Koenig, 2003.*

of the island, he had seen some self-sufficient pigs of the old sort.[110] They spent most of their time in the forest, but they had started coming down to the houses to forage. People are fencing their gardens again.

There remains little of the *pua'a*'s former role. The animal that once created connections between people and gods has been transformed, altered physically during the period of exotic introductions, then transformed conceptually in the great, energetic exchanges that dominated Matavai Bay for twenty-five years after 1801. What had been a sacred animal of use to all within Maohi society was turned into a commodity the Pomares used to buy themselves power. The island's political, economic, spiritual, social, and physical landscapes had changed profoundly, spurred by engagements with ecological exchange.

Conclusion

Ecological exchange is a common accompaniment to cross-cultural engagement. Bringing together plants and animals from diverse ecologies creates dramatic waves of impact on physical and cultural landscapes. Within and between cultural groups, the many-layered processes of gift giving, barter, haggling, taking, and trade moves around the plants and animals that form the substance of everyday existence, sacred conversation, metaphor, and allegiance. Using plants and animals as the currency of gift and trade creates roles for those species that are especially susceptible to change, because the role and form of exchanges between groups are themselves always in flux.

Selecting Tahiti as a focus, a place where ecological exchanges were particularly well documented, has rendered visible the processes by which ecologies and cultures alter each other. Tahitians engaged with Europeans more fully and from earlier in the eighteenth century than did other Pacific islanders. Tahiti's exchanges were complex. Starting with European mariners and Tahitians meeting from 1767 over the supply of provisions, bringing together their mutually opaque conceptions of the world, exchanges continued with European captains' endeavors to establish stock and seeds, the bargaining of *ari'i* over cattle and pigs, the missionaries' gardens, and the breadfruit project. These transactions challenged all the actors involved.

Bright Expectations

One of the factors this study has traced is the frustration periodically experienced by European visitors in trying to ensure that the exchanges proceeded as they desired. They frequently failed to establish a species on the island or make a good bargain. Ship captains and officers were often confounded in their efforts to secure sufficient quantities of Tahitian pigs, fruit, or wild parrots. A perplexing, delicate, often unobservable set of conditions were at work every time a pair of rabbits was let loose from their hutch or some oilskin-wrapped seeds were opened up and raked into warm soil. The Tahitians, their environment, and the interactions between them had much more of a controlling hand than the voyagers found comfortable.

Other types of exchanges ran more smoothly. A gift of a hat, a sexual encounter, a trade of scissors for a piece of barkcloth, learning the various words for seawater, all these things could be complicated and contrary, but in the eighteenth century, Europeans in the Pacific generally found that it was ecological exchanges that were the most difficult to predict. There were more variables governing ecological exchanges. The visitors had high expectations for the outcomes of their imports and relied heavily on negotiations with islanders for the health and survival of their crews. These transactions over plants and animals were often the most difficult to control.

When things failed to turn to their advantage, European visitors and settlers only occasionally decided to move their exchanges elsewhere. After decades of experiencing the island and writing and reading about it, the British had established relationships with the Tahitians that, of all the locations they visited in the Pacific, were the most consistently workable and lucrative. Setting up a market at Point Venus could generally be expected to bring in local suppliers to trade, and some bargaining with the Pomare family could be expected to bring about an agreement to supply provisions, pigs, or breadfruit seedlings. It remained one of the easiest places to trade.

For the Tahitians, ecological exchange often worked to their advantage, but at times it had uncomfortable consequences. The new commodities traded into the island in return for natural resources lessened the reliance on traditional forms of production, created political imbalances, and stirred up tensions. When too many plants and animals were traded or given away there was less produce available for local consumption, particularly for the *manahune*, who possessed the least power to command resources. Environmental changes often led to other losses. The ability to communicate with gods was eroded when particular plant and animal species which had embodied or carried messages disappeared from the landscape.

Explanations

When British captains and officers looked in vain for signs of cattle or geese on a return journey to the island, they usually assumed human error or intervention. The chief had not looked after the breeding pair or guarded the garden perimeter sufficiently, or a neighboring group had stolen the stock. If there were still some seeds or a pair of animals on board that could be spared, or another set sent out on the next voyage, another attempt could be made, this time with more emphatic instructions to the chief.

The voyagers were not from a culture that perceived the natural world as possessing much active power. If an earthquake, storm, or tide impacted on human affairs, it was seen by most as an act of God. The agency of (what we now think of as) ecology—the complexity and active role of a landscape—did not usually figure in their calculations. There was little overt assessment of the likelihood of a receiving environment being receptive to the species being introduced. Any environment was worth a try, with any species. The British did not consider, in the Pacific, the combination of cultural and ecological factors that governed species success. The stories I have traced here have demonstrated the active role played by the Tahitian environment and the Tahitians themselves in determining this process.

It is possible for us to identify a range of key factors that shaped the course of ecological exchange and the ecological fallout from contact with European people and their "portmanteau biota." First, the Tahitians already had finely tuned, clear, centralized structures in place for managing the transaction and consumption of plants and animals, and they adapted these in their interactions with Europeans. There were power structures in place that ensured that the head of the community commanded a high degree of obedience from his or her people. There were social structures—*taio* friendships in particular—by which exchanges with Europeans were managed.

Second, there was significant Tahitian enthusiasm for engaging in ecological exchange. While introduced manufactured commodities were usually more enthusiastically pursued than the plants and animals a ship brought in, Tahitians did actively seek horses, cats, European pigs, and other animals. Sweet oranges and guava were popular with the people of the Matavai region and were propagated and protected until they became a common part of the island's landscape. Without *ari'i, tahua, 'arioi, ra'atira,* and *manahune* working to nourish and protect cattle and sheep, pomelos and grapes, the likelihood of these species becoming established was greatly reduced. No matter how anxious Cook, Bligh, and the missionary families might have been to ensure that these plants and animals flourished, there was little they could achieve through their repeated requests to the Tahitians for compliance. These projects of species introduction had mixed success. Exporting species from the island, on the other hand, was taken up by many Tahitians with vigor, as it provided an excellent route to acquiring manufactured European goods. The *manahune* might not have always had sufficient stock, or been given permission by their *ari'i* to trade their produce, but in contrast to many places in the western Pacific, Society Islanders were keen and the trade was often brisk.

Third, there is the agency of the environment to consider; there were a host of ecological factors that did much to shape the operation and results of ecological exchange. The Tahitian environment contained predators, competitors for light, soil, and water resources, climatic patterns, and other hindrances to the continuance of introduced species. Some introductions—goats, cats, guava, miconia—found that their new environment entirely suited their needs and presented few restraining factors. Many others could not compete with local challenges. Sheep, for instance, were too prone to stomach upsets, often becoming weak and ill in the humidity and high temperatures, and were too vulnerable to dog attacks. They did not succeed on the island despite repeated attempts over thirty years.

There were also environmental contingencies—severe storms, floods, or droughts—which contributed to the success or failure of a newly introduced species. One change could trigger a cascade of others, a chain of reactions enacted over scales of time and geography beyond the sight of the human eye. There were too many variables in operation to permit a human group to exactly govern a flow of exchanges or predict a set of outcomes.

Changing Ecologies

The sort of ecological exchange that was carried out on Tahiti's shores from the mid-eighteenth to the early nineteenth century was, and continues to be, carried out wherever routes of travel and trade were established. Islands that are subject to transactions involving plants and animals from other ecologies frequently fare badly. On some islands the introduction of livestock has resulted in the complete collapse of a forest system (as in Barbados in the seventeenth century), the loss of culturally important species (as in Hawai'i in the eighteenth century), or, after the accidental introduction of snakes, the loss of every bird on an island (as happened in Guam in the late twentieth). Tahiti escaped this degree of devastation.

When cattle and goats began destroying the forests on Hawai'i, causing a wide range of ecological and economic difficulties, there were fleeting statements of concern in the colonial presses. When the sandalwood forests across the Pacific were almost exhausted by intensive logging for trade with China, alarms were raised about the end of a lucrative export. Yet species continued to be imported and exported with little discussion of potential longer-term consequences. It has taken many losses and disappointments to establish, recently, a habit of ecological foresight. Around the world, environmental learning is slow.

The lack of immediately noticeable detrimental results has often been identified as a key reason for the consistent failure of humans to learn from their environmental mistakes.[1] Clearing the trees from a hill will quickly create productive pasture. But it is also likely to increase water runoff and halt the transpiration cycle. The raised water table and the salts the water often bears can render the soil barren within decades. Who, before such effects were recorded and circulated, could predict that chain of events without a concerted effort of shared information and imagination?

Writing histories of the longer-term interactions between species, cultural groups, and environments is important for raising our ability to not only understand the specifics of environmental impact, but to also recognize the likelihood of unexpected consequences flowing from our own acts of transplantation and extensive consumption.

The eighteenth-century naval officers, men of science, and missionaries who carried out ecological exchanges in the Pacific did know of the potential for environmental devastation. When Madeira and St Helena in the Atlantic were stripped bare by introduced goats and rabbits, it could have been seen—and was seen by some—as a clear instance of serious environmental damage caused by a chain of human actions, rather than as an unfortunate but random event. Within Enlightenment concerns to maintain stewardship over the natural world, Madeira could have become a symbol of warning. But the example of those islands failed to embed in European memory.

What was more important within the chambers of Parliament, the Palace, the Admiralty, and the Royal Society was the incorporation of new Pacific discoveries into British endeavor. The aim was to make use of the plant and animal resources of Pacific islands, as well as improving the range of useful produce upon them. This was understood as good economic sense and, further, these ecological imports and exports were a moral obligation, designed to make the most of the creator's productions and to highlight the glory and benevolence of Britain.

The approach to ecological change on these islands reflects the common pattern of human attention to environmental evidence. Even when there is a clear indication of how damage can be inflicted on an ecology, when the detrimental results of that damage for all its living inhabitants is made obvious, there are few who take notice. Many of us know and care too little to learn effectively from these ongoing mistakes.

New Niches

In the early meetings between Tahitians and the crews from Europe, the transfer of species was mutual. There were live plants and animals introduced that brought changes Tahitians did welcome. They considered oranges, pineapples and melons, guava, cats, and horses appealing additions to the island. New foods, new medicines, new plantation crops, and new status symbols were incorporated into daily life.

Coconuts, breadfruit, taro, pigs, and fish had always been provided for visitors from other islands; after the British became the new type of inter-island visitor, a wider range of fruits and vegetables were added to this list. Goat meat could also be supplied for a visitor's mess table. As food and as symbols, old and new plants and animals were a means of communication that allowed practical requests and friendly gestures. These were old roles that did not noticeably alter with the addition of new species.

Not all impacts were welcome. Ground birds and other bird species did not survive the predation of cats and the more voracious species of rats that disembarked from European ships. Polynesian pigs altered after cross-breeding with the larger Spanish and British pigs, becoming more effective as meat animals but possessing much more troublesome temperaments. However, the Tahitian enthusiasm for engaging in ecological exchange did not diminish. For all those engaged in the trade, particularly those in positions of power, there were too many personal material advantages and boosts to political and social prestige to be gained from these transactions of fish, fruit, vegetables, and livestock to turn them away. The exchanges also provided some new opportunities. Maohi men (particularly) traveled with the ships that came to provision, gaining perspectives that, in some instances, they had opportunity to share on their return.

The pace of exchanges increased throughout the eighteenth century and into the nineteenth. The range and number of introduced animals and plants grew from the voyagers' cargos to the frequently refreshed stocks the missionaries imported in an effort to support themselves. As the nineteenth century began, an increasing number of visitors and traders requested more food supplies and trade commodities. *Ari'i* demanded more from the *mana-hune,* and the flow of food species out of the island increased. Other alterations spread across society more broadly and deeply. Political machinations spurred by the salt pork trade in some respects helped to lead changes in religious observance. By the end of the 1820s the texture and detail of everyday life in Tahiti, and to some extent the Tahitians' construction of themselves, had altered.

Despite the changing face of the landscape, despite the accompanying shifts in local political and economic structures, there were aspects of Maohi life that did not fundamentally alter. There was continuity in many relationships with the world around them. To varying degrees around the island, Tahitians continued to manage aspects of their marine resources, groves, and crops as they always had. Many maintained their sense of active spiritual presences within the landscape. And there was a continuance of the daily reliance on breadfruit, taro, fish, and chicken that had sustained the Maohi from their beginnings on the island. Many of these relationships

Figure C.1. Marché, *Pape'ete, Tahiti. 2003. Photo: author.*

continue today. In Tahiti now, the strappy leaves of the shoulder-high *ti* plants growing in most gardens are used to provide protection from misfortune or spirits, to make costumes for dance performances, and to mobilize the protective power required for fire walking. When asking Tahitians now whether any plants are still used in ceremonial ways as in previous eras, it is *ti* that people point to.

Currently in Tahiti, exchanges of plants and animals—living and dead—take place in the urban market, small streetside stands, supermarkets, on shipping wharves, and in airports. The trade today is affected by more complex global economies and heavier regulations, but the processes are essentially the same as in earlier centuries. The drains on and additions to the local populations of flora and fauna have the same types of consequences.

The *marché* in Pape'ete focuses and exemplifies today's networks of ecological exchange. The *marché* is now held in a building two stories high, the internal space a tall central space flanked by a ring of shops. On the ground floor, long trestle tables are piled high with produce. It is here that fisherpeople bring their daily catch. It is here that the fruit, vegetable, and

Figure C.2. *Offloading goods in Pape'ete harbor, 2001. Photo: author.*

vanilla growers trade their produce, where a woman can set up a stall to sell a few dozen breadfruit from her trees. Early morning is best, when all the fresh produce arrives. The buyers come from all parts of the island. Prepared fruit, pounded with coconut cream to form a paste called *poe,* is sold wrapped in banana leaves. Shellfish hauled from reefs around Tahiti and other, less polluted islands is on sale, plus large spears of exotic orchids, alongside bunches of the island's floral emblem, the delicate native gardenia, *tiare.*

The port lies across from the *marché.* Cruise ships pull in regularly and the *marché* is the one guaranteed destination of the tourist in Pape'ete. The provisions for their ship will be bought in bulk, but the tourists—like George Tobin tracking down curiosities and trying out delicacies—will buy plaited pandanus hats, fresh mangoes, and gift-packaged vanilla pods. Cargo ships also come to port three times a week. The *Ono-ono* travels to Ra'iatea and Huahine with passengers on deck and supplies for the islands below. A regular cargo ship stops in Mo'orea to load up copra and pineapple juice to take to Tahiti and beyond.

These ships move large quantities of plant and animal products in and out of the island on a regular, relentless schedule. Like the trade in provisions of the eighteenth century and the pig trade of the nineteenth, this export arrangement provides a way for producers to acquire the desired merchandise of Europe.

There are more transactions between ecologies in Tahiti than there have ever been. Ecological exchange continues to bring change to the island. The motivations behind the exchanges are as varied as ever and continue with nearly as little interest in the consequences as when, in 1767, Captain Wallis left his geese and cats on shore.

APPENDIX A

Timeline of Tahiti: Events, Ships, and Chiefs

Year	Event	Visitors - Captain (ship)	Reigning chiefs, Pomare lineage	Reigning chiefs, other selected lineages
AD 300	• First migrants arrive in Leeward Islands from Western Polynesia.			
1600s	• Rise of 'Oro cult throughout Soc. Islands.			
Mid-1700s			Tutaha (Pare-'Arue district) in power	Purea and Amo (Papara district) in power
c.1728	• Teu born, son of Ta'aroa and Tetuaehuri, nephew of Tutaha.		Teu born	
c.1750	• Tu born, son of Teu and Tetupaia-i-Hauviri (of a Ra'iatean chiefly lineage).		Tu, "Pomare I" (Teu's son) born	
1758	• Ari'ipaea, Tu's brother, born.			
c.1760	• 'Itia born. Sister of Mo'orean chief, niece of Purea.			
1760	≠War between Puni (of Porapora) against alliance of Ra'iatea & Huahine.			
1767	• Purea and Amo attempt to install their son as *ari'i rahi*.	Wallis (*Dolphin*) 19 June–27 July, Matavai		
1768	• Ahutoru departs with Bougainville, becomes first Pacific islander to visit Europe.	Bougainville (*Boudeuse* & *Étoile*) 6–15 April, Hitia'a, Tahiti		

Appendix A (*continued*)

Year	Event	Visitors - Captain (ship)	Reigning chiefs, Pomare lineage	Reigning chiefs, other selected lineages
	≠Battle of Papara: Pare, Oropaʻa, Taiarapu defeat Purea and Amo.			
1769	• Tupaia, high-ranking ʻOro priest, accompanies *Endeavour* to New Zealand, Australia, and Batavia (Jakarta), acting as translator and guide.	Cook (*Endeavour*, 1st voyage) 13 April–13 July, Matavai		
1770	• First epidemics of European diseases in Tahiti. • Tupaia dies of illness in Jakarta, 20 Dec.			
1771	≠Naval battle of Taiarapu. • Ahutoru dies of smallpox during return voyage from France to Tahiti.			
1772	Four Tahitian men depart with Boenechea for Lima.	Boenechea (*Aguila*) 12 Nov.–20 Dec. Taiarapu		
1773	≠Battle of Taiarapu, Vehiatua victor. Tutaha dies (March); Vehiatua dies (Sept.). Tu acknowledged as having highest rank-status in Tahiti and Moʻorea. Has rights to wear *maro ʻura*.	Cook (*Resolution* and *Adventure*, 2nd voyage) Matavai, Tahiti (17 Aug.–1 Sept.); then Huahine, Raʻiatea	Death of Tutaha (March). Tu takes on active authority over Pare-ʻArue district.	Death of Vehiatua. Vehiatua II succeeds
1774	• Maʻi (ʻOmai') departs with Cook, becomes first Pacific islander to visit England. ≠Battle of Athuru: Tahiti vs Aimeo (Moʻorea).	Cook (*Resolution* and *Adventure*, 2nd voyage). Returns to Matavai, April–May.		

Appendix A (*continued*)

Year	Event	Visitors - Captain (ship)	Reigning chiefs, Pomare lineage	Reigning chiefs, other selected lineages
1774–1775	✳Return of the two surviving Tahitians. Installation of two Catholic missionaries. • Death of Boenechea from illness, 26 Jan.	Boenechea (*Aguila* and *Jupiter*) 27 Nov.–28 Jan. 1775, Taiarapu		
1775	✳*Aguila* gives passage to missionaries, 12 Nov.	Langara (*Aguila*) Returns 3 Nov., Taiarapu	Marriage of Tu and 'Itia	Death of Vehiatua II
1777	• Ma'i settles in Huahine on returning from England.	Cook (*Resolution* and *Adventure*, 3rd voyage). 24 Aug.–30 Sept.; then Mo'orea, Huahine, Ra'iatea, and Porapora.		Death of Purea; Death of Puni (Porapora)
1779	*Death of Cook. Kealakekua Bay, Hawaii, 14 Feb.*			
1782	• Birth of Pomare II, son of Tu and 'Itia.		Pomare II (son of Tu) born	
1783	≠Pare district laid to waste in battle against alliance of Atehuru and Aimeo (Mo'orea).			
1788	*Creation of British colony in Port Jackson, New South Wales, Australia.*	Sever (*Lady Penrhyn*), convict transport. 10–23 July, Matavai.		
1788–1789	• First breadfruit voyage.	Bligh (*Bounty*). 26 Oct. 1788–4 April 1789, Matavai.		Poeno (headman, Matavai district) in power
1789	• Mutiny of the *Bounty*, at sea, west of Tahiti, near Tonga, 28 April. • Mutineers return to Tahiti, gather livestock, leave for Austral Islands, then Pitcairn.	Christian (*Bounty*). 6–23 June, Matavai.		

Appendix A (*continued*)

Year	Event	Visitors - Captain (ship)	Reigning chiefs, Pomare lineage	Reigning chiefs, other selected lineages
	Six stay behind on Tahiti, including James Morrison.	22–23 Sept.		
	• Vehiatua III killed by mutineer, Taiarapu.			Death of Vehiatua III. Vehiatua IV succeeds.
1790	• British/Swiss expedition.	Cox (*Mercury*). 13 Aug.–2 Sept.		
	• *Maro 'ura* transferred to Pare.			
1791	≠Submission of Taiarapu by Tu			
	• Capt. Edwards removes the remaining *Bounty* men from island.	Edwards (*Pandora*). 23 Mar.–8 May.	Pomare II invested as *ari'i* with *maro 'ura* (13 Feb.)	
		Vancouver (*Discovery* & *Chatham*). 30 Dec.–24 Jan., Matavai.		
1792	• Second breadfruit voyage.	Bligh, Portlock (*Providence, Assistant*). 9 April–19 July, Matavai.		
	• British and American whalers in Matavai Bay.	4 whalers (*Matilda, Mary Ann, Prince Wm. Henry, Jenny*). Feb.–Mar., Matavai.		
	≠Battles of Papeno'o and Atahuru, Aug., Sept.			Death of Amo
1793	≠Tu dominates Tahiti.	New (*Daedalus*). Feb.–Mar., Matavai.		
1794	≠Tu defeats Mo'orean chiefs.			
1795		Broughton (*Providence*). 29 Nov.–11 Dec., Matavai.		

Appendix A (*continued*)

Year	Event	Visitors - Captain (ship)	Reigning chiefs, Pomare lineage	Reigning chiefs, other selected lineages
1797	• Population of Tahiti estimated at 16,050.			
	✳ Wilson disembarks 18 LMS missionaries.	Wilson (*Duff*) 5 Mar.–4 Aug., Matavai.		
1798	• Alliance of Pomare II & priest Haʻamanemane vs Tu.	Bishop (*Nautilus*). 6 Mar. Two Port Jackson Whalers		
	≠ Matavai devastated in conflict between Tu & Pomare II, 23 Nov.	(*Cornwall & Sally*) 24–27 Aug., Matavai.		
	• Reconciliation. Haʻamanemane killed.			
1799		Clerke (*Betsy*) 30 Dec.–22 Jan. 1800, Matavai.		
1800	✳ Construction of first church, Matavai	Swain (*Eliza*) and Bunker (*Albion*). British whalers. 5–14 Jan. 1800; 27 Dec. 1800–3 Jan. 1801, Matavai.		
1801	• Assembly of chiefs at Pare forms strategy to keep Pomare II's power in check. Jan. 12.			
	• First ship from Port Jackson at Matavai to negotiate for pork.	Scott (*Porpoise*). 26 Jun.–15 Aug., Matavai.		
	✳ 2nd contingent of LMS missionaries arrive with Capt. Wilson. Wilson trading for pork.	Wilson (*Royal Admiral*) 10–31 July, Matavai.		
	✳ First sermon in Tahitian, 16 Aug.			
1802	• Assembly of chiefs at Atehuru. Refuse to return *toʻo* of ʻOro to Pomares.	Buyers/Turnbull (*Margaret*), House		
	• Pomare II secretly takes *toʻo* and installs at Taputapuatea *marae,* Tautira in Taiarapu. March.	(*Norfolk*); Bass/Bishop (*Venus*) all pork traders, Jan.–Mar.		

Appendix A (*continued*)

Year	Event	Visitors - Captain (ship)	Reigning chiefs, Pomare lineage	Reigning chiefs, other selected lineages
	≠Destruction of Pare, attack on Tautira, *to'o* reclaimed. Pomares under protection of *Norfolk* and *Venus* crews.	Simpson (*Nautilus*); Scott (*Porpoise*); Buyers/Turnbull (*Margaret*); June–Nov.		
	≠Armed attack on Atehuru by Pomares with 20–30 sailors of the *Bishop,* 3 July	Simpson (*Nautilus*) 5 Nov. 1802– Feb. 1803, Matavai.		
1803	≠Capture of ship attempted by people of Porapora.	Buyers/Turnbull (*Margaret*); Mar–27 May, Matavai, Porapora and Me'etia.		
	≠Submission of Atehuru by Pomares, reclaim *to'o.*	Porter (*Unicorn*); (*Hope*); McLennan (*Dart*), pork trader, 4 Apr.–4 Sept., Matavai		
	• Death of Tu, father of Pomare II, 3 Sep.		Tu dies (3 Sept.)	
1804		Campbell (*Harrington*), pork trader, 26 June–29 Dec., Papetoai, Mo'orea.		
1805		4 whalers (American, British), Matavai.		
1806	✱Rev. Samuel Marsden arrives.	Ferguson (*Lucy of London*), Edwards (*Hawkesbury*), Port Jackson, pork traders, Mar; Nov.–Dec., Matavai.		

Appendix A (*continued*)

Year	Event	Visitors - Captain (ship)	Reigning chiefs, Pomare lineage	Reigning chiefs, other selected lineages
1807	≠Surprise attack by Pomare II against Atehuru & Papara.	6 British traders and 1 whaler, Matavai. 5 pork traders.		
1808	≠General uprising, Hitoi, Pa'ofa'i defeat Pomare II. Pomare escapes to Mo'orea. ✳Missionaries flee to Huahine.	5 British and American whalers and traders, Jan.– Dec., Matavai.	Pomare II defeated and in exile.	
1809	≠Near-famine conditions in Mo'orea. War affecting all of Society Islands. ≠Ship captured by enemies of Pomare, mate killed, crew held captive. • Campbell releases *Venus*'s crew. Then collects missionaries in Huahine, takes all but Br. Nott to Port Jackson. • Leeward Island warriors (c. 700) arrive in Mo'orea to help Pomare II.	Berbeck (*Venus*) Sept., Matavai. Cambell (*Hibernia*) Oct., Matavai.		
1810	• Pomare II marries Teri'itaria, daughter of Tamatoa, *ari'i* of Ra'iatea.	Bishop (*Venus*), Walker (*Mercury*) Aug., Sept., Mo'orea.	Pomare II marries Teri'itaria.	
1811	✳Pomare II starts to abandon traditional beliefs. Requests missionaries rejoin him. Several return on ships, Oct. and Dec.	Kable (*Endeavour*), Burnett (*Mercury*)		
1812	✳18 July. Pomare II asks to be baptized.	Fiske (*Favourite*), Burnett (*Mercury*), Walker (*Macquarie*)		
1813	≠Pomare II achieves submission of Matavai.		Pomare II regains power in Matavai.	

Appendix A (*continued*)

Year	Event	Visitors - Captain (ship)	Reigning chiefs, Pomare lineage	Reigning chiefs, other selected lineages
	• Ships anchoring in Mo'orea throughout year.	Fodger (*Daphne*). Powell (*Queen Charlotte*), Walker (*Endeavour*), Walker (*Gov. Macquarie*), Campbell (*James Hay*), pork traders.	Aimata, future Pomare IV, born (28 Feb.)	
	＊Protestant church established. at Papetoai, Mo'orea.			
1814	• Pomare II returns to Mo'orea.		'Itia dies (16 Jan.)	
	• 6 British ships through-out year, 1 Portuguese ship (*Minerva*). Most anchoring in Mo'orea.	Campbell (*Macquarie*), Thomas (*Minerva*), and others.		
1815	＊Public burning of *to'o* and other "idols," Mo'orea. Start of Christianization of Tahitians.			
	＊Tahitian *ari'i* meet, under Opuhara, to expel Christians.			
	• Pomare II's army, under Mahine, chief of Huahine, to Tahiti (October).			
	≠Battle of Fe'i Pi 12 Nov.			
	• Base of shipping returns to Matavai. 3 ships May–Nov.	Martin (*Queen Charlotte*), Rutherford (*Agnés*), (*Active*), Matavai.		
1816	＊Churches and schools built, Tahiti & Mo'orea.	Eight trading ships		
1817	＊Rev. Ellis arrives with printing press.	Five trading ships		
	＊Construction of LMS ship *Haweis* begins, Mo'orea.			

Appendix A (*continued*)

Year	Event	Visitors - Captain (ship)	Reigning chiefs, Pomare lineage	Reigning chiefs, other selected lineages
1818	*Pasteur Crook founds parish of Pape'ete. • Arrival of Gyles, planter sent by LMS.	Four trading ships		
1819	• Code of laws (Code Pomare), 13 May. • Pomare II orders Gyles' work on sugar cane be stopped, 14 May. *Baptism of Pomare II, 16 May. • Death sentence pronounced for rebels. • Population of Tahiti: 12,019.	Lewis (*Arab*), American	Pomare II baptized (16 May)	
1820	• Severe epidemic in Leeward isles (and Australs). • Pomare II buys *Queen Charlotte* ship (ex-Powell). *Pomare II visits Ra'ivavae. Introduction of Christianity there.	Bellingshausen (*Vostok & Mirni*) 21–28 July	Pomare III born (25 June)	
1821	• Pomare II buys ship *Macquarie* for trade to Port Jackson (Jan.). Captain Henry.	(Three ships at Uturoa)	Pomare II dies (7 Dec.)	
1822	•Tahitian ship *Endeavour*, under Captain Ellis, operating from 1822.	Six visiting ships, including one from Peru		
1823	*Some popular resistance to missionaries begins in Huahine • Captain Henry, *Queen Charlotte*, Tahitian ship, operating out of Matavai.	Duperry (*Coquille*) expedition, May. Also four traders, whalers.		
1824	• *Haweis* and *Endeavour*, Tahitian/Mission-owned ships, operating out of Matavai.	Kotzebue (*Predpriatie*) expedition, March. Another three ships.	Pomare III crowned (21 April)	

Appendix A (*continued*)

Year	Event	Visitors - Captain (ship)	Reigning chiefs, Pomare lineage	Reigning chiefs, other selected lineages
1825	• Pomares' request for England's protection refused.	Four ships visit Matavai.		
1826	• *Minerva,* Tahitian-owned ship operating out of Matavai.	Six British and American ships.		
	• Emergence of *Mamaia* religion.			
1827	• Regency assumed by Aimata's aunt.		Pomare III dies (8 Jan).	
	• *Haweis,* under Capt. James, operating out of Matavai.		His sister, Aimata (age 14), invested as Pomare IV (1827–1877).	
1829	• Population of Tahiti: 8,568.	Three British and American trading ships		
1830	• Tahitian Parliament convened	Two French trading ships		
1836	• Expulsion of Catholic missionaries			
1838	• Dupetit Thouars delivers ultimatum to Aimata (August).	Dupetit-Thouars (*Venus*) 29 Aug.–17 Sept. Port of Pape'ete.		
	• Aimata requests help from Britain. None sent.			
		D'Urville & Jacquinot (*Astrolabe & Zélée*) (Aug.–Sept.).		
1842	• Dupetit-Thouars delivers ultimatum to Aimata (September).	Dupetit-Thouars (*Reine Blanche*).		
	• French protectorate declared over Society Islands.			

Sources: Douglas Oliver, *Ancient Tahitian Society,* 1974; Louise Peltzer, *Chronologie des Événements Politiques, Sociaux et Culturels de Tahiti,* 2002.

≠ Battles

✶ Activities of missions, churches

APPENDIX B

A Survey of Species Introduced to the Society Islands 1767–1820s

Animals

Species	Location	Origin	Date	Introd. by	For*	Source
Cat (pregnant)	Matavai	England	1767	Wallis	Purea	Hawkesworth, 469.
Cats (20 in Tahiti and some left on other islands)	Tahiti, Huahine, and Rai'iatea	England?	May 1774	Cook	Society Islanders, to "stock" the islands.	Beaglehole, ed., *1772–75*, 412.
Cats	Tahiti	Various	1789	European visitors	Tahitians	Bligh, *Bounty*, 121.
Cats	Tahiti	NSW, Australia	1817	Ellis	Not presented as a gift: let to "run wild"	Ellis, *Polynesian Researches*, 1829.
Cattle (pair)	Taiarapu	Peru?	Dec. 1774	Boenechea	Tahitians	Corney, ed., 298–299.
Cattle (bull, 3 cows)	Matavai	England &/or Cape of GH	Sept. 1777	Cook	Tu	Beaglehole, ed., *1776–80*, 194.
Bull	Matavai	NSW, Australia	1804	Mission-aries	Purchased from a trader, for Mission	Davies, Journal 1807–1808, 13 Sept.
Cattle	Matavai	NSW	1817	Mission-aries	Missionaries	Ellis, *Polynesian Researches*, 1829, 147.
Dog (spaniel)	Matavai	England?	Aug. 1773	J. R. Forster	Given to Tu after he expressed a desire to own it	Thomas & Berghof, eds., *Voyage*, 183.
Donkeys (pair)	Taiarapu	Peru?	Dec. 1774	Boenechea	for Spanish use	Corney, ed., 298–299.
Ewe (3)	Tahiti, Pare	Cape	Sept. 1777	Cook, Ma'i, Anderson	Given to Tu	Beaglehole, ed., *1776–80*, vol. 3, 23.

Appendix B (*continued*)

Animals

Species	Location	Origin	Date	Introd. by	For*	Source
Ewe	Porapora	Cape	1777	Cook	Given to Puni, Chief of Porapora	Thomas, *Discoveries*, 351.
Goat (1, pregnant)	Huahine	Table Bay, Cape of GH	1777	Cook	Gift for Maʻi	Beaglehole, ed., *1776–80*, 238–239.
Goats (pair)		Matavai	Aug. 1773	Furneaux	Given to Tu	Thomas & Berghof, eds., *Voyage*, 183.
Goats (2)		Taiarapu	Dec. 1774	Boenechea	Tahitians	Corney, ed., 298–299.
Goats (male, 2 females)		Taiarapu	Dec. 1774	Boenechea	Given to chiefly families, and the people	Corney, ed., 309.
Goats (pair with 2 kids)		Tahiti	April 1774	Furneaux	Tahitians	Thomas and Berghof, eds., *Voyage*, 352.
Goats (2)	Raʻiatea	England or Cape of GH	Sept. 1777	Cook	Given to Orio, *ariʻi* of Raʻiatea	Beaglehole, ed., *1776–80*; Thomas, *Discoveries*, 351.
Guinea pigs	Taiarapu	Peru?	Dec. 1774	Boenechea	For Spanish provisions?	Corney, ed., 309.
Horse	Matavai	Table Bay, Cape of GH	Sept. 1777	Cook	Given to Tu/ a mount	Beaglehole, ed., *1776–80*, 194.
Horse (mare)	Matavai	Table Bay, Cape of GH	Sept. 1777	Cook	Given to Tu/ a mount	Beaglehole, ed., *1776–80*, 194.
Horses (pair)	Huahine	Table Bay, Cape of GH	Oct. 1777	Cook	Gift for Maʻi	Beaglehole, ed., *1776–80*, 238–239.
"Livestock"	Taiarapu	Peru	Dec. 1774	Boenechea	Tahitians	Corney, ed., 298–299.
"Livestock"	Taiarapu	Peru	Jan. 1775	Boenechea	Tahitians	Corney, ed., 174.
Pigs (5)	Taiarapu	Peru?	Dec. 1774	Boenechea	Tahitians	Corney, ed., 298–299.
Pigs (boar, 2 sows)	Huahine	England	1777	Cook	Gift for Maʻi	Beaglehole, ed., *1776–80*, 238–239.
Pigs (1 or 2 sows)	Huahine	England	1777	Maʻi	Gift for Maʻi	Beaglehole, ed., *1776–80*, 238–239.
Pigs (pair)	Raʻiatea	England	Sept. 1777	Cook	Gift for Orʻio	Beaglehole, ed., *1776–80*; Thomas, *Discoveries*, 351.

Appendix B (*continued*)

Animals

Species	Location	Origin	Date	Introd. by	For*	Source
Rabbits (pair)	Tahiti	NSW, Australia	1800	Brother Henry	Put out to "burrow," / for game?	Jefferson, Journal 1800, 4.
Sheep (ewe, 2 rams)	Taiarapu	Peru?	Dec. 1774	Boenechea	Tahitians	Corney, ed., 298–299.
Sheep (3)	Matavai	Cape of GH	Aug. 1773	Cook	Gift for Tu, for peace-making	Thomas & Berghof, eds., *Voyage*, 194–195.
Sheep	Matavai	England?	Sept. 1777	Cook	Given to Tu	Beaglehole, ed., *1776–80*, 194.
Sheep (pair)	Tahiti, Pare	England	Sept. 1777	Cook, Ma'i, Anderson	Given to Tu	Beaglehole, ed., *1776–80*, 23, 211. But note that ram was killed by a dog, 5 Sept., 207.
Sheep (2 pairs)	Tahiti	NSW, Australia	1800	Brother Henry	Given to Tu/ for Missionaries	Jefferson, Journal 1800, 4.

Birds

Species	Location	Origin	Date	Introd. by	For*	Source
Australian parrots (possibly crimson rosellas)	Matavai	Port Jackson	1800	Brother Henry	Given to Pomare II, I'tea, and other *ari'i*, presumably valued for red feathers	Jefferson, Journal 1800, 4.
Ducks (drake, 4 ducks)	Pare		1777	Cook	Given to Tu	Beaglehole, ed., *1772–75*, 193–194.
Geese (pair)	Matavai	England	July 1767	Wallis	Gift for Purea	Warner, ed., *Account*, 102.
Geese (gander, 3 geese)	Pare		1777	Cook	Given to Tu	Beaglehole, ed., *1772–75*, 193–194.
Geese (gander, 2 geese)	Near Poeno's House, Matavai	Cape	1792	Vancouver	Given to Pomare	Lamb, ed., *Voyage*, 411n., 440.
Geese (4)	Matavai	Australia	1800	Brother Henry	Missionaries	Jefferson, Journal 1800, 4.
Guinea hens (3)	Matavai	England	July 1767	Wallis	Gift for Purea	Francis Wilkinson, His Book 1766–1767, 553.

Appendix B (*continued*)

Birds

Species	Location	Origin	Date	Introd. by	For*	Source
Muscovy ducks (4)	Matavai	Australia	1800	Brother Henry	Missionaries	Jefferson, Journal 1800, 4.
Peacock and hen	Pare	England	1777	Cook and Lord Bessborough	Gift for Tu	Beaglehole, ed., *1772–75*, 193–194.
Pigeons (4)	Taiarapu	Spain? Peru?	1774	Boenechea	Tahitians	Corney, ed., 1:309.
Pigeons (2 pairs)	Matavai	Australia	1800	Brother Henry	Missionaries	Jefferson, Journal 1800, 4.
Rooster and hen	Taiarapu	Spain? Peru?	1774	Boenechea	Tahitians	Corney, ed., 1:309.
Turkeys (pair)	Tahiti, Hitia'a	France?	April 1768	Bougainville	Tahitians	Dunmore, ed., 299.
Turkey cock	Matavai	Australia	1800	Brother Henry	Tahitians	Jefferson, Journal 1800, 4.
Turkey cock and hen	Matavai	England	1767	Wallis	Gift for Purea	Francis Wilkinson, His Book 1766–67, 553.
Turkeys (pair)	Pare		1777	Cook	Given to Tu	Beaglehole, ed., *1772–75*, 193–194.

Plants

Species	Location	Origin	Date	Introd. by	For*	Source
Almonds	Matavai		1788	Bligh	Distributed among chiefs for planting	Bligh, *Bounty*, 86.
Aloes	Matavai	England/ Cape of GH/or Holland	1792	Bligh		Bligh, *Providence*, 19 April 1792.
Apricot plants	Matavai		1804	Missionaries	Missionaries	Jefferson, Journal 1804, 6.
Barley	Tahiti, Hitia'a	France?	April 1768	Bougainville	Sowed in a small square for Reti	Dunmore, ed., 299.
Beans	Tahiti, Hitia'a,	France?	1768	Bougainville	For Reti	Dunmore, ed., 70.
Beans	Taiarapu	Peru?	1774	Boenechea	Tahitians	Corney, ed., 1:390.
Beans	Matavai	Possibly stores from England	July 1801	Br. Scott	Missionaries	Jefferson, Journal 1801, 40.

Appendix B (*continued*)

Plants

Species	Location	Origin	Date	Introd. by	For*	Source
Cabbages	Tahiti, Hitia'a	France?	April 1768	Bougain-ville	For Reti	Dunmore, ed., 299.
Cabbages	Matavai	Port Jackson, Australia	July 1801	Br. Scott	Missionaries	Jefferson, Journal 1801, 35.
"Calicoo green" [uniden-tified]	Point Venus	Jamaica?	1789	Bligh	Pomares?	Bligh, *Bounty*, 121.
Carrots	Matavai	Port Jackson, Australia	July 1801	Br. Scott	Missionaries	Jefferson Journal 1801, 35.
Cauli-flowers	Matavai	Port Jackson, Australia	July 1801	Br. Scott	Missionaries	Jefferson, Journal 1801, 36.
Cherry (seeds)	Tahiti, inland	West Indies?	1767	Wallis	Tahitians	Hawkesworth, 476.
Chervil	Tahiti, Hitia'a	France?	1768	Bougainville	For Reti	Dunmore, ed., Commerson, 299.
Chick peas	Taiarapu	Peru?	1774	Boenechea	Tahitians	Corney, ed., 1:390.
Citrons (large bed)	Matavai	Garden	1804	Missionaries	Missionaries	Jefferson, Journal, 1804, 6.
Coffee	Mo'orea	Rio de Janeiro	April 1817	Wm Ellis	Missionaries' use and commerce	Davies & Crook, Journal 1817, 1.
Cucumber	Parae?		1789	Bligh	For Poeno	Bligh, *Bounty*, 68.
Cucumbers	Matavai	Mile End, England	May 1769	Cook	Tahitians	Beaglehole, ed., *1768–71,* 274.
Fig layers	Matavai		1804	Missionaries	Missionaries	Jefferson, Journal, 1804, 6.
Fig tree	Matavai		1788	Bligh	For Poeno	Bligh, *Bounty*, 86.
Fig trees	Matavai	Port Jackson, Australia	July 1801	Br. Scott	Missionaries	Jefferson, Journal 1801, 35.
Figs	Matavai	England/ Cape of GH/ or Holland	April 1792	Bligh	Tahitians	Bligh, *Providence,* 19 April 1792.
Firs	Matavai region	As above	April 1792	Bligh	For ship's timber	Bligh, *Providence,* 19 April 1792.

Appendix B (*continued*)

Plants

Species	Location	Origin	Date	Introd. by	For*	Source
Fir trees (8, young)	Pare	England	May 1792	Bligh	For timber	Bligh, *Providence,* 29 May 1792.
Fruit seeds	Matavai		1788	Bligh	Tahitians	Bligh, *Bounty,* 86.
Fruit trees	Matavai	Australia?	Jan. 1800	Br. Henry	Missionaries	Jefferson, Journal 1800, 4.
Garlic	Taiarapu	Peru?	1774	Boenechea	Tahitians	Corney, ed., 1:390.
Grape vines (several slips)	Huahine	Cut from the Spanish vine	1777	Ma'i	Planted by Ma'i	Beaglehole, ed., *1776–80,* 195.
Guava	Matavai	South Africa	1792	Bligh	Tahitians	Bligh, *Providence,* 19 April 1792.
Haricot beans	Tahiti, Hitia'a	France?	April 1768	Bougainville	For Reti	Dunmore, ed., 299.
Kidney beans (white)	Matavai		July 1767	Wallis	Garden planted for Purea	Hawkesworth, 469.
Indian corn	Matavai	Cape?	Jan. 1789	Bligh	Planted for Poeno	Bligh, *Bounty,* 121.
Indian corn	Matavai	England?	July 1801	Br. Scott	Missionaries	Jefferson, Journal 1801, 40.
Leeks	Matavai	Port Jackson, Australia	July 1801	Br. Scott	Missionaries	Jefferson Journal 1801, 35.
Lemons	Parae?		1789	Vancouver	Tahitians/ Probably planted as an antiscorbutic	Lamb, ed., *Voyage,* 440.
Lemon seed	Tahiti, Hitia'a	France?	April 1768	Bougainville	as above	Dunmore, ed., 299.
Lemon seed	Tahiti, inland	West Indies?	1767	Wallis	as above	Hawkesworth, 476.
Lemons (large quantity)	Matavai	Rio de Janeiro	July 1769	Banks	Planted around fort, Point Venus and in woods	Beaglehole, ed., *Banks,* 308–309.
Lentils	Tahiti, Hitia'a	France?	1768	Bougainville	For Reti	Dunmore, ed., 70.
Lettuce	Tahiti, Hitia'a	France?	1768	Bougainville	For Reti	Dunmore, ed., 299.
Lettuce	Matavai	Port Jackson, Australia	July 1801	Br. Scott	Missionaries	Jefferson, Journal 1801, 36.

Appendix B (*continued*)

Plants

Species	Location	Origin	Date	Introd. by	For*	Source
Lime (large quantity)	Matavai	Rio de Janeiro	July 1769	Banks	Planted round fort, Point Venus and in woods	Beaglehole, ed., *Banks*, 308–309.
Lime seeds	Tahiti, inland	West Indies?	1767	Wallis	Tahitians (antiscorbutic)	Hawkesworth, 476.
Maize	Tahiti, Hitia'a	France?	April 1768	Bougain-ville	For Reti	Dunmore, ed., 70.
Maize	Taiarapu	Peru?	1774	Boenechea	For Tahitians	Corney, ed., 1:390.
Melons	Parae?		1789	Bligh	For Poeno and "Moannah"	Bligh, *Bounty*, 68.
Melons	Matavai	Mile End, England	May 1769	Cook	Tahitians	Beaglehole, ed., 1769–71, 274.
Melons	Taiarapu	Peru?	1774	Boenechea	Tahitians	Corney, ed., 1:390.
Metro-cedera	Matavai	England/ Cape of GH/ or Holland	April 1792	Bligh	For timber	Bligh, *Providence*, 19 April 1792.
"Millions"	Matavai point	England?	Aug. 1777	Cook	Tahitians	Beaglehole, ed., *1776–80*, 195.
"Millions"	Huahine, near Ma'i's House		1777	Cook	Gift for Ma'i	Beaglehole, ed., *1776–80*, 235.
Norfolk Island Pines	Matavai	Norfolk Island/ Australia likely	1800	Brother Henry	Missionaries	Jefferson, Journal 1800, 4.
Okra	Point Venus	Jamaica	1789	Bligh	Planted for Pomares?	Bligh, *Bounty*, 121.
Onions	Taiarapu	Peru?	1774	Boenechea	For Tahitians	Corney, ed., 1:390.
Onions	Matavai	Port Jackson, Australia	July 1801	Br. Scott	Missionaries	Jefferson Journal 1801, 35.
Oranges	Pare?		1789	Vancouver	Tahitians	Lamb, ed., *Voyage*, 440.
Orange seed	Tahiti, Hitia'a	France?	April 1768	Bougain-ville	Reti	Dunmore, ed., 299.
Orange seedlings	Near Poeno's house, Matavai	Raised in frames since Cape of Good Hope	Jan. 1792	Vancouver	Poeno?	Menzies, Journal, 131.

Appendix B (*continued*)

Plants

Species	Location	Origin	Date	Introd. by	For*	Source
Oranges (9 young trees and a few pips)	Matavai	Port Jackson, Australia	1800	Rev. Johnson	Missionaries	Rev. Johnson to Br. Henry, 23 Aug 1800.
Orange seeds	Tahiti, inland	West Indies?	1767	Wallis	Tahitians	Hawkesworth, 476.
Oranges (large quantity)	Matavai	Rio de Janeiro	July 1769	Banks	Around fort, Point Venus, and in woods	Beaglehole, ed., *Banks,* 308–309.
Orange (2)	Matavai		1788	Bligh	Poeno	Bligh, *Bounty,* 86.
Oranges	Matavai	England/ Cape of GH/ or Holland	April 1792	Bligh	Tahitians	Bligh, *Providence,* 19 April 1792.
Oranges (several plants of "consider-able size")	Pare/ Matavai	From Bligh's trees	1808	Missionaries	Missionaries	Davies, Journal 1808, 11.
Oranges & Citrons (59)	Pare		May 1792	Bligh	Tahitians	Bligh, *Providence,* 29 May 1792.
Pallares (*Phaseolus pallar*)— white bean	Taiarapu	Peru or Chile	1774	Boenechea	Tahitians	Corney, ed., 1:390.
Parsley	Tahiti, Hitia‘a	France?	April 1768	Bougain-ville	Reti	Dunmore, ed., 299.
Peach trees (16 young trees)	Matavai	Port Jackson, Australia	July, Oct. 1801	Br. Scott	Missionaries	Shelley, Journal on Porpoise 1801, 9; also Jefferson, Journal 1801, 35.
Peach seeds	Tahiti, inland	West Indies?	1767	Wallis	Tahitians	Hawkesworth, 476.
Peas	Matavai	West Indies?	1767	Wallis	Purea	Hawkesworth, 469.
Peas	Tahiti, Hitia‘a	France?	1768	Bougain-ville	Reti	Dunmore, ed., 70.
Peas	Matavai	Possibly stores from England	July 1801	Br. Scott	Missionaries	Jefferson, Journal 1801, 40.
Pineapples (2 plants)	Matavai	Cape of GH	1788	Bligh	Gave to Poeno	Bligh, *Bounty,* 86.

Appendix B (*continued*)

Plants

Species	Location	Origin	Date	Introd. by	For*	Source
Pineapples (12 plants)	Pare	Cape	1792	Bligh	Tahitians	Bligh, *Providence*, 29 May 1792.
Pineapples (2 plants)	Matavai point	Cape of Good Hope?	Aug 1777	Cook	Tahitians	Beaglehole, ed., *1776–80*, 195.
Pineapples	Huahine, near Ma'i's House		Oct. 1777	Cook	Ma'i	Beaglehole, ed., *1776–80*, 235.
Pineapples (reported to be in blossom)	Matavai		1804	Missionaries	Missionaries	Jefferson, Journal, 1804, 6.
Pines	Matavai region	England/ Cape of GH/ or Holland	April 1792	Bligh	Tahitians, and for ship timber	Bligh, *Providence*, 19 April 1792.
Plants	Society Islands	Hawai'i	1824	Wm Ellis	LMS	Ellis, *Researches*, 1:378.
Plum seeds	Tahiti, inland	West Indies?	1767	Wallis	Tahitians	Hawkesworth, 476.
Pomegranates	Matavai	England/ Cape of GH/ or Holland	April 1792	Bligh	Tahitians	Bligh, *Providence*, 19 April 1792.
Pomelo ("Shaddock")	Matavai point	Tonga	Aug. 1777	Cook (David Nelson, gardener)	Tahitians	Beaglehole, ed., *1776–80*, 195, 235.
Pomelo slips ("shaddock")	Matavai		1789	Bligh	Poeno	Bligh, *Bounty*, 121.
Pomelo ("Shaddocks")	Huahine, near Ma'i's House		1777	Cook	Ma'i	Beaglehole, ed., *1776–80*, 235.
Potatoes	Taiarapu	Peru?	1774	Boenechea	Tahitians	Corney, ed., 1:390.
Potatoes	Matavai point	England?	Aug. 1777	Cook	Tahitians	Beaglehole, ed., *1776–80*, 195.
Potatoes	Matavai	Port Jackson, Australia	July 1801	Br. Scott	Missionaries	Jefferson Journal 1801, 35.
Pumpkins ("Long pumpkins")	Matavai		Sept. 1804	Missionaries	Missionaries	Jefferson, Journal 1804, 6, 29.

Appendix B (*continued*)

Plants

Species	Location	Origin	Date	Introd. by	For*	Source
Pumpkins	Matavai		Sept. 1804	Missionaries	Missionaries	Jefferson, Journal 1804, 29.
Quinces	Matavai	England/ Cape of GH/ or Holland	April 1792	Bligh	Tahitians	Bligh, *Providence,* 19 April 1792.
Radishes	Matavai	Port Jackson, Australia	July 1801	Br. Scott	Missionaries	Jefferson, Journal 1801, 36.
Rape (Canola)	Tahiti, Hitia'a	France?	April 1768	Bougainville	For Reti	Dunmore, ed., 299.
Rose seed	Matavai	Cape of GH?	1788	Bligh	Gave to women as they "delight to ornament themselves in sweet-smelling flowers."	Bligh, *Bounty,* 86.
Scarlet beans	Matavai	Port Jackson, Australia	July 1801	Br. Scott	Missionaries	Jefferson, Journal 1801, 36.
Seeds (16 sorts of garden seeds; great quantity)	Matavai and inland		1767	Wallis	For Purea	Hawkesworth, 469.
Seeds (garden seeds)	Pare?		1789	Vancouver	Tahitians	Lamb, ed., *Voyage,* 440.
Seeds (garden seeds) and plants	Taiarapu	Peru	Jan. 1775	Boenechea	Tahitians	Corney, ed., 1:174.
Seeds (salad)	Tahiti, Hitia'a	France?	April 1768	Bougain-ville	For Reti	Dunmore, ed., 299.
Seeds (replace-ment set of garden seeds)	Tahiti, Hitia'a	France?	April 1768	Bougain-ville	For Reti	Dunmore, ed., 299.
Seeds	Matavai	Rio de Janeiro	July 1769	Banks	Planted around fort, Point Venus and in woods	Beaglehole, ed., *Banks,* 308–309.
Seeds	Matavai	Mile End, England	May 1769	Cook	Planted	Beaglehole, ed., *1769–71,* 274.

Appendix B (*continued*)

Plants

Species	Location	Origin	Date	Introd. by	For*	Source
Seeds (salad)	Pare?		1789	Bligh	For Poeno	Bligh, *Bounty,* 68.
Seeds	Pare	Cape	1792	Bligh	Tahitians	Bligh, *Providence,* 29 May 1792.
Seeds of different kinds	Matavai, near tents	Cape of Good Hope	Nov. 1788	Bligh	Tahitians	Bligh, *Bounty,* 86.
Seeds	Matavai	Australia?	1800	Brother Henry	Missionaries	Jefferson, Journal 1800, 4.
Squashes	Taiarapu	Peru?	1774	Boenechea	Tahitians	Corney, ed., 1:390.
Sweet potatoes	Taiarapu	Peru?	1774	Boenechea	Tahitians	Corney, ed., 1:390.
Sweet potatoes	Matavai	Pacific?	1804	Missionaries	Missionaries	Jefferson, Journal 1804, 6.
Tamarind	Matavai		1789?	Bligh?	Tahitians	Bligh? See entry below.
Tamarind (raised from seed)	Matavai	Seeds from Bligh's trees	1808	Missionaries	Missionaries	Davies, Journal 1808, 11.
Turnips	Matavai	Port Jackson, Australia	July 1801	Br. Scott	Missionaries	Jefferson, Journal 1801, 35.
Underground peas	Point Venus		1789	Bligh	Pomares?	Bligh, *Bounty,* 121.
Vine cuttings	Pare?		1789	Vancouver	Tahitians	Lamb, ed., *Voyage,* 440
Vines (probably grape vines)	Huahine, near Ma'i's House		Oct. 1777	Cook	Ma'i	Beaglehole, ed., *1776–80,* 235.
Vines	Matavai		1788	Bligh	For Poeno	Bligh, *Bounty,* 86.
Vines	Matavai	England, Cape of GH, or Holland	April 1792	Bligh	Tahitians	Bligh, *Providence,* 19 April 1792.
Vines	Matavai	Port Jackson, Australia	July 1801	Br. Scott	Missionaries	Jefferson, Journal 1801, 35.
Watermelons	Matavai	Rio de Janeiro	July 1769	Banks	Around fort, Point Venus, and in woods	Beaglehole, ed., *Banks,* 308–309.

Appendix B (*continued*)

Plants

Species	Location	Origin	Date	Introd. by	For*	Source
Water-melons	Taiarapu	Peru?	1774	Boenechea	Tahitians	Corney, ed., 1:390.
Water-melons	Matavai	Local source?	1804	Missionaries	Missionaries	Jefferson, Journal 1804, 6.
Water-melons	Matavai		Sept. 1804	Missionaries	Missionaries	Jefferson, Journal 1804, 29.
Water-melons	Matavai		Oct. 1804	Missionaries	Missionaries	Jefferson, Journal 1804, 29.
Wheat	Tahiti, Hitia'a	France?	April 1768	Bougain-ville	Sowed in presence of Reti	Dunmore, ed., 70, 299.
Wheat	Taiarapu	Peru?	1774	Boenechea	Tahitians	Corney, ed., 1:390.
Wheat	Matavai	Possibly stores from England	July 1801	Br. Scott	Missionaries	Jefferson, Journal 1801, 40.

* The introductions listed were for the purpose of general "improvement" of the islands and provisioning of ships, unless otherwise specified.

NOTES

Introduction

1. Discussion with Celestine Hitiura Vaite, "Pacific Voices," December 2000, Research School of Pacific and Asian Studies, ANU, Canberra.

2. Geoff Park, *Ngā Uruora, The Groves of Life: Ecology and History in a New Zealand Landscape* (Wellington: Victoria University Press, 1995), 16.

3. William Cronon, *Uncommon Ground: Toward Reinventing Nature* (New York: W. W. Norton & Co., 1996), 458–459.

4. I use "ecology" as a term to describe the relationships between an environment and its inhabitants. I also use it as a noun, encompassing the whole system of a natural environment and its dynamics. The eighteenth-century people I refer to here would not have recognized the term "ecology," since it was not current until the nineteenth century, but the concept of a system of relationships between organisms and their environment has a much longer genesis.

5. For place names and personal names I primarily follow the orthography employed by Louise Peltzer (linguist, professor of Polynesian languages at the Université de la Polynésie française and member of the Académie tahitienne). Louise Peltzer, *Chronologie des Événements Politiques, Sociaux et Culturels de Tahiti et des Archipels de la Polynésie Française* (Pirae, Tahiti: Au vent des îles, 2002).

6. Tom Griffiths, in *Forests of Ash: An Environmental History* (Cambridge and Melbourne: Cambridge University Press, 2001), 194, discusses the importance of storytelling as a (rigorous, demanding) method for scholars in the humanities, pointing to William Cronon's statement that stories remain "our chief moral compass," changing the way we act in the world. William Cronon, "A Place for Stories: Nature, History and Narrative," *Journal of American History* 78 (1992): 1375.

7. Robin Torrence and Anne Clarke argue usefully for the term "engagement" as a closer reflection of cross-cultural relationships in the Pacific rather than persisting with the confrontational overtones of "encounters." Encounters suggests brief, unexpected, and "arms-length" meetings, suitable enough when describing first meetings between islanders and Europeans but not an adequate description of ongoing relationships. Robin Torrence and Anne Clarke, eds., *The Archaeology of Difference: Negotiating Cross-Cultural Engagements in Oceania* (London: Routledge, 2000).

8. Alfred W. Crosby, *Ecological Imperialism: The Biological Expansion of Europe 900–1900* (Cambridge: Canto, 1986).

9. K. R. Howe, *Nature, Culture and History: The "Knowing" of Oceania* (Honolulu: University of Hawai'i Press, 2000), 14.

10. B. H. Farrell, "The Alien and the Land of Oceania," in *Man in the Pacific Islands*, ed. R. Gerard Ward, 34–73 (Oxford: Clarendon, 1972); Andrew Mitchell, *The Fragile South Pacific: An Ecological Odyssey* (Austin: University of Texas Press, 1989). See also Douglas Oliver's *Pacific Islands* (Honolulu: University of Hawai'i Press, 1989).

11. For a discussion of the development of the ANU school of Pacific History from 1950, see Robert Borofsky, ed., *Remembrance of Pacific Pasts* (Honolulu: University of Hawai'i Press, 2000), 23–24; K. R. Howe, *Where the Waves Fall: A New South Sea Islands History from First Settlement to Colonial Rule*, Pacific Islands Monograph Series (Honolulu: University of Hawai'i Press, 1984).

12. On recovering uncertainty and finding metaphors, see especially Greg Dening, *Islands and Beaches: Discourse on a Silent Land. Marquesas 1774–1880* (Honolulu: University of Hawai'i Press, 1980). On eighteenth-century Europeans and islanders possessing the other through the "cargo" obtained from each other, see Greg Dening, "Possessing Tahiti," in *Performances* (Chicago: University of Chicago Press, 1996), 128–167.

13. See for instance Albert Wendt, "Novelists and Historians and the Art of Remembering," in *Class and Culture in the South Pacific*, ed. Antony Hooper (Suva: Centre for Pacific Studies, University of Auckland and Institute of Pacific Studies, University of the South Pacific, 1987). Hau'ofa published *Tales of the Tikongs* (Honolulu: University of Hawai'i Press) in 1994, in the same year as his influential essay "Our Sea of Islands," *Contemporary Pacific* 6 (1994). This essay and others are brought together in Epeli Hau'ofa, *We Are the Ocean: Selected Works* (Honolulu: University of Hawai'i Press, 2008). A pertinent example of Katerina Teaiwa's work is "Our Sea of Phosphate: The Diaspora of Ocean Island," in *Indigenous Diasporas and Dislocations*, ed. G. Harvey and C. Thompson (Aldershot, Hampshire: Ashgate, 2005), and of Teresia K. Teaiwa's work is "Mānoa Rain," in *Pacific Places, Pacific Histories: Essays in Honour of Robert Kiste*, ed. Brij V. Lal (Honolulu: University of Hawai'i Press, 2004). Vilsoni Hereniko, a playwright and academic, has produced Fiji's first feature film, centering on Rotuma's founding ancestor: *The Land Has Eyes (Pear ta ma 'on maf)* (Honolulu: Te Maka Productions, 2004).

14. Hau'ofa, "Our Sea of Islands," 160.

15. Ibid., 153–154.

16. The crews were male. The only woman known to have traveled to the Pacific then was Jeanne Barré on Bougainville's *Étoile,* disguised as a manservant to naturalist Philibert Commerçon. The Tahitians saw through her disguise immediately. Jeanne Monnier, et al., *Philibert Commerson: Le découvreur du Bougainvillier* (Châtillon-sur-Chalaronne: Association Saint-Guignefort, 1993),

93–97; Gavan Daws, *A Dream of Islands: Voyages of Self-Discovery in the South Seas: John Williams, Herman Melville, Walter Murray Gibson, Robert Louis Stevenson, Paul Gauguin* (Milton, Qld.: Jacaranda Press, 1980), 9.

17. For more about islanders traveling with Europeans, see Jennifer Newell, "Pacific Travelers: The Islanders Who Voyaged with Cook." *Common-place* (web journal) 5 no. 2 (2005): www.common-place.org.

18. Francis Wilkinson, Log of Francis Wilkinson on HMS Dolphin, 1767. Public Record Office, Kew (ADM 51/4541/96), book 2, 553.

19. Robert Darnton, *The Great Cat Massacre: And Other Episodes in French Cultural History* (New York: Vintage Books, 1985), 13.

20. The exchange of a piece of Tahitian *tapa* cloth for a pair of English scissors, on the other hand, cannot be readily classified as ecological. Though *tapa* is made of the inner bark of the branches of breadfruit or mulberry trees, collecting the bark does not kill the trees nor impair their reproductive capacities (to any noticeable degree), so the trees remain unchanged within the ecosystem.

21. Recorded in logs of the *Endeavour* (1769) and the *Providence* (1792). J. C. Beaglehole, ed., *The Endeavour Journal of Joseph Banks 1768–1771*, 2 vols. (Sydney: Public Library of NSW and Angus & Robertson, 1963), 275; George Tobin, Journal on *HMS Providence* 1791–1793 (1797). Mitchell Library (State Library of New South Wales), Sydney (MLA 562), 149.

22. Nicholas Thomas, *Discoveries: The Voyages of Captain Cook* (London: Allen Lane/Penguin Books, 2003).

23. Peter Bellwood, *The Polynesians: Prehistory of an Island People* (London: Thames & Hudson, 1987), 6, 56; Geoffrey Irwin, "Voyaging and Settlement," in *Vaka Moana: Voyages of the Ancestors*, ed. K. R. Howe, 77 (Auckland: Auckland War Memorial Museum and David Bateman, 2008).

24. Shane Wright and Annette Lees, "Biodiversity Conservation in the Island Pacific," in *The Origin and Evolution of Pacific Island Biotas, New Guinea to Eastern Polynesia: Patterns and Processes*, ed. Allen Keast and Scott Miller, 443 (Amsterdam: SPB Academic Publishing, 1996).

25. Patrick V. Kirch and Terry L. Hunt, eds., *Historical Ecology in the Pacific Islands: Prehistoric Environmental and Landscape Change* (New Haven, Conn., and London: Yale University Press, 1997), 1, and Patrick V. Kirch, "Epilogue: Islands as Microcosms of Global Change?" in the same volume, 284–286.

26. Richard Grove, *Green Imperialism: Colonial Expansion, Tropical Island Edens and the Origins of Environmentalism 1600–1800* (Cambridge: Cambridge University Press, 1995); J. R. McNeill, ed., *Environmental History in the Pacific World*, The Pacific World: Lands, People and History of the Pacific 1500–1900, vol. 2 (Aldershot: Ashgate, 2001); Patrick D. Nunn, Pacific Islands Landscapes (Suva: Institute of Pacific Studies, University of the South Pacific, 1998).

27. The ships' logs and journals that mariners submitted to the Admiralty are kept at the Public Records Office, Kew, and the daily journals that LMS mis-

sionaries sent back to the LMS directors are kept in the Manuscripts Room of the School of Oriental and African Studies (SOAS), University College London (UCL).

28. Nicholas Thomas, *Entangled Objects: Exchange, Material Culture, and Colonialism in the Pacific* (Cambridge, Mass: Harvard University Press, 1991), 7.

29. Douglas Oliver, *Ancient Tahitian Society*, 3 vols. (Canberra: ANU Press, 1975), 1086.

30. Ibid., 1087–1088.

31. Owen Rutter, ed., *The Journal of James Morrison, Boatswain's Mate of the Bounty Describing the Mutiny & Subsequent Misfortunes of the Mutineers Together with an Account of the Island of Tahiti* (London: The Golden Cockerel Press, 1935), 192.

32. Jonathan Lamb, "The Place of Property in the South Seas Narrative," paper given at the Exploring Text and Travel Conference, National Maritime Museum, Greenwich (London), 12 March 2005.

33. Ibid.

34. Rowland Hassall, Account of the Tahitian Mission, 1796–1799. SSJ, LMS/CWM Archives, SOAS (box 1 folio 2), 7 Feb. 1798, 6; Anne Salmond, *The Trial of the Cannibal Dog: Captain Cook in the South Seas* (London: Penguin Books, 2004), 78.

35. William Monkhouse, surgeon, was the man in question. J. C. Beaglehole, ed. *The Endeavour Journal of Joseph Banks 1768–1771*, 2 vols. (Sydney: Public Library of NSW and Angus & Robertson, 1963), 290. See also Salmond, *Trial*, 81.

36. Tom Griffiths, "Introduction: Ecology and Empire: Towards an Australian History of the World," in *Ecology and Empire: Environmental History of Settler Societies*, ed. Tom Griffiths and Libby Robin (Edinburgh: Keele University Press, 1997), 3.

37. Park, *Ngā Uruora*.

38. The cultural-geographic classifications of Polynesia, Melanesia, and Micronesia have been used, initially by outsiders, since the nineteenth century. Polynesia refers to the group of islands and the common cultural base stretching from a central hub of Samoa, the Society Islands, and the Marquesas in the central Pacific, out to form a triangle from Hawai'i in the northern Pacific, down to Easter Island in the eastern Pacific and across to New Zealand in the southwest. Melanesia refers to the islands in the western Pacific. Another system uses "Remote Oceania," referring to the relative proximity of islands across most of the Pacific, as opposed to "Near Oceania," referring to the closely spaced, tightly knit islands and communities in the western Pacific, roughly covering "Melanesia." Epeli Hau'ofa proposes straightforwardly geographic distinctions instead, such as "central Oceania," "western Oceania." This classification, though it is vaguer, is probably the most accessible and least loaded with racial and political history. While it is sometimes still useful to refer to Polynesia

and Polynesians, a geographic classification is the one I have usually employed here.

39. Paul D'Arcy, *The People of the Sea: Environment, Identity and History in Oceania* (Honolulu: University of Hawai'i Press, 2006), 7.

40. Epeli Hau'ofa, "Pasts to Remember," in *Remembrance of Pacific Pasts*, ed. R. Borofsky (Honolulu: University of Hawai'i Press, 2000).

41. For more on *to'o*, see Oliver, *Ancient Tahitian Society*, and examples illustrated in Steven Hooper, *Pacific Encounters: Art and Divinity in Polynesia, 1760–1860* (London: British Museum Press, 2006), cat. 130–133.

42. Colin Newbury, *Tahiti Nui: Change and Survival in French Polynesia 1767–1945* (Honolulu: University of Hawai'i Press, 1980), 23.

43. Cook and others also met Tutaha, Tu's great uncle. Tutaha died around 1773.

44. His formal kin title meant "Great Tu, begotten of a god." Oliver, *Ancient Tahitian Society*, 1183–1185.

45. The details of Pomare II's birth are hazy. Peltzer gives "1782?" as his birth year. Peltzer, *Chronologie*, 21. See also Oliver, *Ancient Tahitian Society*, 1187, 1253, where he suggests 1783. It is also possible that Pomare II was the son not of Tu's first wife 'Itia, but his second wife, according to the genealogy given by Teuira Henry, *Ancient Tahiti, by Teuira Henry Based on Material Recorded by J.M. Orsmond, Bernice P. Bishop Museum Bulletin* 48 (1928), 249. Henry states Pomare II was born around 1774, but this does not accord with voyagers' accounts of his age.

46. Oliver, *Ancient Tahitian Society*, 1253.

47. Jacques Florence, *Flore de la Polynésie française* (Paris: Éditions de l'Orstom, 1997), vol. 1, 13.

48. Personal communication with (among others) Christopher and Turia Vaite, Mahina, Tahiti, July 2001.

49. Institut d'Emission d'Outre-Mer. *La Polynésie Française En 2000*. Pape'ete: l'agence IEOM/Imprimeries réunies de Nouméa, 2000.

50. *La Dépêche,* Dec. 2004. Text by Miriama Bono, chef de cabinet, Ministère de l'Environnement, Pape'ete, 2 Dec. 2003.

51. *Pycnonotus cafer.*

52. Personal communication, Miriama Bono, Ministère de l'Environnement, Pape'ete, 2 Dec. 2003.

Chapter 1: "No Country More Capable"

Epigraph. Arthur Bowes, Journal of Arthur Bowes, Surgeon of the Convict Transport *Lady Penrhyn* on a Voyage from Portsmouth to Botany Bay, 1787–1789. BL (Add. Ms 47966), 24 July 1788, 111.

1. Robert Langdon (1924–2003) published widely on Pacific topics, but of particular relevance to this project were his investigations of the movement of plant and animal species across the Pacific as evidence for pathways of human

migration. See, for instance, "When the Blue-Egg Chickens Come Home to Roost," *JPH* 24 (1989); and "The Banana as a Key to Early American and Polynesian History," *JPH* 28 no. 1 (1993).

2. Howe, *Where the Waves Fall*, 71–72; Glyndwr Williams, *The Great South Sea: English Voyages and Encounters 1570–1750* (New Haven, Conn., and London: Yale University Press, 1997), 2. Of the 235 original crew members, 35 returned to Seville. Nineteen died during the Pacific passage.

3. Peter Puget of the *Chatham* wrote on Sunday, 27 Feb. 1791: "shipped several heavy Seas on Deck which being much lumbered with Casks & other Stores we lost Overboard 3 Hencoops one Barrel of pitch & 4 Water barrels which were wash'd from their lashing." P. Puget, Log Book of the *Chatham* Tender, Lt. W. R. Broughton Commander, Jan.–Sept. 1791, BL (Add. Ms 17,542), 3.

4. This statement and those that follow are based on reading the officers' logs of a range of ships and the records of the Admiralty's Victualling Board and Provisioning Committee, at the Public Record Office, Kew. See ADM111 and ADM/D series, for instance: Admiralty, In-Letters from the Victualling Board Jan. 1793–June 1794. PRO (ADM/D/38).

5. Many ship's officers kept records of provisioning; George Tobin on the Providence voyage was particularly punctilious and the examples of provisioning provided here are taken from his log. G. Tobin, Log of H.M. Ship *Providence* Wm Bligh Esq Comr . . . 1791. PRO (ADM 55/94).

6. J. C. Beaglehole, ed., *The Journals of Captain James Cook*, vol. 1, *Journal of the Voyage of the Endeavour 1768–1771* (Cambridge: Cambridge University Press and the Hakluyt Society, 1955), 1 September 1768, 5.

7. John Hawkesworth, *An Account of the Voyages Undertaken by the Order of His Present Majesty, for Making Discoveries in the Southern Hemisphere, and Successively Performed by Commodore Byron, Captain Wallis, Captain Carteret, and Captain Cook* (London: W. Strahan and T. Cadell, 1773), 363.

8. Ibid.

9. Admiralty's Secret Orders to Wallis, quoted in Hugh Carrington, ed., *The Discovery of Tahiti: A Journal of the Second Voyage of HMS* Dolphin *Round the World . . . in the Years 1766, 1767 and 1768, Written by Her Master, George Robertson* (London: Hakluyt Society, 1948), xxii.

10. Hawkesworth, *Account*, 422.

11. In the later stages of the disease the victim's bones and flesh blackened and disintegrated. Jonathan Lamb, *Preserving the Self in the South Seas 1680–1840* (Chicago and London: University of Chicago Press, 2001), 117–118, 121.

12. Oliver Warner, ed., *An Account of the Discovery of Tahiti: From the Journal of George Robertson Master of HMS* Dolphin (London: Folio Press, J. M. Dent, 1973), 19.

13. Anne Salmond has written an excellent account of the early encounters between Europeans and Tahitians—for additional information on the events described below, particularly for insights into how the Tahitians saw and expe-

rienced them, see *Aphrodite's Island: The European Discovery of Tahiti* (Auckland: Penguin Books, 2009).

14. Salmond, *Trial,* 39–40.

15. Hank Driessen, "Outriggerless Canoes and Glorious Beings: Pre-contact Prophecies in the Society Islands," *JPH* 17 (1982): 8–9; Tahitian text in Henry, "Ancient Tahiti," 5. For variant versions of this story, see Oliver, 4–6, 910.

16. Salmond, *Trial,* 40.

17. Warner, ed., *Discovery,* 20.

18. Ibid., 20–21.

19. Oliver, *Ancient Tahitian Society,* 105–106.

20. Warner, ed., *Discovery,* 21.

21. Robertson argued with exasperation that a stop was essential. Ibid., 27.

22. Ibid.

23. Ibid., 23.

24. Ibid., 28.

25. See Salmond, *Aphrodite's Island,* 51, for more detail on this series of encounters.

26. Salmond, *Trial,* 39, 42.

27. Ibid., 42.

28. Greg Dening, *Mr Bligh's Bad Language* (Cambridge: Cambridge University Press, 1992), 197–198.

29. Interestingly, the same practice can be seen in Naples, where, over Christmas, some Catholics try to increase the chances of their prayers being heard by throwing pebbles at the plaster figures of saints in the *presceppi* nativity scenes. Personal communication, Marco Vitigliano Stendardo (anthropologist, Étnoria), Naples, 2003.

30. Warner, ed., *Discovery,* 32.

31. Hawkesworth, *Account,* 443–444.

32. Carrington, ed., *Discovery of Tahiti,* 154.

33. As reported by George Forster, 1774. The war boats' carved prow ornaments projected upwards over twenty feet (six meters). Nicholas Thomas and Oliver Berghof, eds., *A Voyage Round the World by George Forster* (Honolulu: Hawai'i University Press, 2000), April 1774, 355; and Oliver, *Ancient Tahitian Society,* 30.

34. There are many instances of muskets failing at crucial moments during British voyages in the Pacific. Cook's musket, for instance, "failed to perform" in Vanuatu and thereby, he said, spared a local chief. The fatal incident on the beach in Hawai'i's Kealakekua Bay was the end not only for Cook but also several marines, who when rushed by the islanders could not reload quickly enough. See Thomas, *Discoveries,* 240, 392.

35. Hawkesworth, *Account,* 446.

36. Warner, ed., *Discovery,* 49.

37. See Anne D'Alleva, "Shaping the Body Politic: Gender, Status and Power

in the Art of Eighteenth Century Tahiti and the Society Islands" (PhD diss., Columbia University, 1996); Dening, *Performances,* chapter "Possessing Tahiti," 128–167; Salmond, *Aphrodite's Island,* passim.

38. Warner, ed., *Discovery,* 52.

39. Ibid., 52–53.

40. Ibid., 56.

41. Ibid., 60, 78; Salmond, *Aphrodite's Island,* 64.

42. Hawkesworth, *Account,* 463; Warner, ed., *Discovery,* 108–111.

43. Oliver, *Ancient Tahitian Society,* 842–850.

44. Warner, ed., *Discovery,* 103.

45. Hawkesworth, *Account,* 469.

46. Ibid.

47. Ibid., 476.

48. "Copy of the Act taking possession of the Island of Cythera," enacted on 12 April with the burying of an oak plank and bottle. Act made and signed on the *Boudeuse,* 15 April 1768. John Dunmore, ed., *The Pacific Journal of Louis-Antoine De Bougainville 1767–1768* (London: Hakluyt Society, 2002), 74–75.

49. Bougainville was experienced in this kind of work. He had undertaken colonial expeditions in the Atlantic for France in the early 1760s and had assisted with establishing the Falkland Islands as a base for involvement in the new South American trade routes.

50. Across Polynesia, wrapping people and objects was practiced as a way to contain *mana* (sacred, ancestral power); unwrapping released this power.

51. L. Davis Hammond, ed., *News from New Cythera: A Report of Bougainville's Voyage 1766–1769* (Minneapolis: University of Minnesota Press, 1970), 26.

52. Ibid.

53. Ibid., 25.

54. Ibid., 28.

55. Ibid., 28.

56. Dunmore, ed., *Journal of Bougainville,* 66.

57. Ibid., 70.

58. Commerçon, in ibid., 299.

59. Ibid.

60. Bougainville, in ibid., 74.

61. Ahutoru enjoyed a year of celebrity before accepting a passage back to the Pacific with Marion du Fresne in 1770. He died of smallpox en route, in Mauritius in 1771. John Dunmore, *Visions and Realities: France in the Pacific 1695–1995* (Waikane, Hawai'i: Heritage Press, 1997), 56, 78.

62. With some exceptions, including the ongoing public fascination with the mystery of La Pérouse's disappearance. D'Entrecasteaux and Kermadec were sent out in search of him in 1791. Ibid., 101, 107.

63. Helen Rosenman, ed., *Voyage Au Pole Sud et dans l'Oceanie sur les Corvettes l'Astrolabe et la Zélée, by Jules Sébastien César Dumont d'Urville,* English ed.

(Honolulu: University of Hawai'i Press, 1988). Dumont d'Urville returned to the island in 1838.

64. The more widely dispersed the observers were, the greater the chance of an effective, cloud-free range of measurements being made, and a repeat of the embarrassing British failure on the planet's previous passage in 1761 would be avoided. If the scientific community lost the 1769 opportunity, there would not be another for 105 years. For a general survey of early Pacific voyages and collecting, see Jennifer Newell, "Irresistible Objects: Collecting in the Pacific and Australia in the Reign of George III," in *Enlightenment: Discovering the World in the Eighteenth Century*, ed. Kim Sloan (London: British Museum Press, 2003).

65. Bowes, Journal, 104–105.

66. Oliver, *Ancient Tahitian Society*, 147–148.

67. A good example of this is the *tipairua* (tunic) at the British Museum made of *tapa*, in the new, *hapa'a* style (see fig. 1.2), with designs scissor-cut from dark-brown dyed *tapa* pasted on a tumeric-dyed, fern-printed ground (British Museum object Oc,Tah.102, 228 x 117.5 cm). See Anne D'Alleva, "Continuity and Change in Decorated Barkcloth from Bligh's Second Breadfruit Voyage, 1791–1793," *Pacific Arts* 11–12 (1995): 33.

68. Mai, *ari'i rahi* of Porapora [Bora Bora], 1824, recorded by J. R. Orsman. Quoted in Oliver, *Ancient Tahitian Society*, 364.

69. Advice from a chief of Porapora [Bora Bora], 1824. Oliver, *Ancient Tahitian Society*, 364.

70. Anne D'Alleva, "Framing the 'Ahu Fara: Clothing, Gift-Giving and Painting in Tahiti," paper presented on 23 June 2003 at the "Translating Things: Clothing and Innovation in the Pacific" conference, UCL, 23–25 June 2003.

71. Tobin, Journal, 147–148, 156.

72. Ibid., 162.

73. For more on this subject, see Jennifer Newell, "Exotic Possessions: Polynesians and Their Eighteenth-Century Collecting." *Journal of Museum Ethnography* 17 (2005): 75–88.

74. Thomas, *Entangled Objects*, 103f.

75. See Thomas, *Discoveries*, 66.

76. For more on these engagements, see Maria Nugent, *Botany Bay: Where Histories Meet* (Crows Nest, N.S.W.: Allen & Unwin, 2005), and Maria Nugent, *Captain Cook Was Here* (Melbourne: Cambridge University Press, 2009).

77. Thomas, *Discoveries*, 317–318.

78. Thomas and Berghof, eds., *Voyage*, 156–157.

79. Oliver, *Ancient Tahitian Society*, 265–267.

80. Beaglehole, ed., *Cook Journals 1769–1771*, 13 July 1769, 118.

81. Ibid.

82. D'Arcy, *People of the Sea*, 34.

83. So, for instance, in Stimson's listing of Maohi "Nights of the Moon" (1928), during the moon phase called *Hamiamu-mua,* "The fish make their

appearance in wide curves, they swim in separate schools, this (is) a most favourable night for finding fish; the method of fishing is by torchlight, moving along from within the reef outward (and) fishing by torchlight from the canoe; the torch is then a coconut leaf." Quoted in Oliver, *Ancient Tahitian Society*, 305.

84. Ibid., 297.

85. Ibid., 287.

86. Basalt figure (possibly a *puna*), British Museum object Oc,LMS.122, 44.2 x 12.1 cm. *Puna honu:* Maupiti, Society Islands, Musée de Tahiti object MTI D2007.2.1, 38 x 27.5 x 14 cm. See Musée de Tahiti et ses Îles/Te fare Manaha, *Nōhea mai mātau?: Destins d'objets polynésiens*, STP Multipress, Tahiti, 2007, 47.

87. William Ellis, *Polynesian Researches, During a Residence of Nearly Six Years in the South Sea Islands*, 2 vols. (London: Fisher, Son & Jackson, 1829), 2:286.

88. Oliver, *Ancient Tahitian Society*, 652–653.

89. Ibid., 492.

90. Rutter, ed., *Journal of James Morrison*, 196.

91. Warner, ed., *Discovery*, 80.

92. Ibid., 80–81; Salmond, *Aphrodite's Island*, 71–72.

93. The man had suddenly dropped dead while on a canoe with his chief (and several missionaries) in 1800. John Jefferson, Journal of the Missionaries Proceedings on Otaheite, 1800. SSJ, LMS/CWM Archive, SOAS (box 1 folio 7), 4 Feb., 25.

94. Rutter, ed., *Journal of James Morrison*, 28.

95. Warner, ed., *Discovery*, 78.

96. Ibid., 104.

97. Tobin, Journal, 160–161.

98. Beaglehole, ed., *Banks Journal*, 1:252.

99. Wilkinson, Log, 51.

100. J. C. Beaglehole, ed., *The Journals of Captain James Cook*, vol. 3 parts I and II: *The Voyage of the Resolution and Discovery 1776–1780* (Cambridge: Cambridge University Press and Hakluyt Society, 1967), I:187.

101. Rutter, ed., *Journal of James Morrison*, 29.

102. Ibid.

103. Lord George Byron, *The Island: Or, Christian and His Comrades* (London: John Hunt, 1823), canto 1, verse X.

104. For instance, William Bligh, *The Log of H.M.S.* Providence *1791–1793*, facsimile ed. (Surrey: Genesis Publications Limited, 1976), 11 April 1792, 24 April 1792 (unpaginated). For discussion of the general European anxiety over their physical and moral contamination of Pacific islanders, see P. J. Marshall and Glyndwr Williams, *The Great Map of Mankind: British Perceptions of the World in the Age of Enlightenment* (London, Melbourne, Toronto: J. M. Dent and Sons, 1982), 282–284.

105. Bligh, *Log of Providence*, 11 and 24 April 1792.

106. Tobin, Journal, 149–150.

107. Ibid., 150.

108. W. Kaye Lamb, *A Voyage of Discovery to the North Pacific Ocean and Round the World, 1791–1795* [by George Vancouver], 4 vols. (London: Hakluyt Society, 1984), 436.

109. Thomas, *Discoveries,* 233.

110. Beverley Hooper, ed., *With Captain James Cook in the Antarctic and Pacific: The Private Journal of James Burney Second Lieutenant of the Adventure on Cook's Second Voyage 1772–1773* (Canberra: National Library of Australia, 1975), 17 Aug. 1773, 62.

111. Ibid.

112. For instance, the missionaries complained in 1801 of a group "passing their time for the most part in revelling. They have almost cleared the district of breadfruit already. When they will remove from this is uncertain." John Jefferson, Journal of the Missionaries Proceedings on Otaheite, 1 Jan.–30 July 1801. SSJ, LMS/CWM Archive, SOAS (box 1 folio 10), 15–16.

113. Beaglehole, ed., *Banks Journal,* 1:252.

114. These were the *Discovery* and *Chatham,* the whalers *Matilda* and *Mary Ann,* the American sealer *Jenny,* the whaler *Prince William Henry,* HMS *Providence* and *Assistant,* and the convict vessel *Daedalus.*

115. George Vancouver, for instance, noted in January 1792 that his "original intention in calling" at Tahiti "was for the sole purpose of recruiting our water, and obtaining a temporary supply of fresh provisions." He decided that they were unlikely to find any place better for wintering and making a range of repairs to their ships and boats. Nowhere else could the work be "executed with so much ease and convenience." Lamb, ed., *Voyage of Discovery,* 396.

116. "At every other island," King continued, "some address and much circumspection is necessary in having any communication with the natives, which the momentary error either of a native or seaman might destroy." King to Portland, 1 March 1802, *Historical Records of Australia,* series I, 3, 432–433.

117. Dorothy Shineberg. *They Came for Sandalwood: A Study of the Sandalwood Trade in the South-West Pacific, 1830–1865* (Melbourne: Melbourne University Press, 1967), 12.

118. J. C. Beaglehole, ed. *The Journals of Captain James Cook,* vol. 2, *Journal of the Resolution and the Adventure 1772–1775* (Cambridge: Cambridge University Press and the Hakluyt Society, 1961), Aug. 1774, 486 n. 2.

119. "It is indeed the staple commodity on the Island, and what I verily believe these good people think, brings us among them." Tobin, Journal, 164.

120. James Elder and Charles Wilson, Journal Round Tyerrabboo [Taiarapu], 28 June–1 August, 1803, SSJ, LMS/CWM Archive, SOAS (box 1 folio 14), 30 July 1803, 14.

121. Personal communication, Miriama Bono, Ministère de l'Environnement, Pape'ete, 2 Dec. 2003.

Chapter 2: Conceptual Landscapes

1. This kind of marker was described and illustrated by Captain Henry Byam Martin, *The Polynesian Journal of Captain Henry Byam Martin, R.N., in Command of HMS Grampus, 50 Guns, at Hawaii and on Station in Tahiti and the Society Islands August 1846 to August 1847* (Salem, Mass.: Peabody Museum of Salem, 1981), 80.

2. Archibald Menzies, Journal of Vancouver's Voyage, 1792. BL (Add. Ms 32641). 8 Jan., 129–130.

3. Oliver, *Ancient Tahitian Society,* 71, 639.

4. Ti'i was one of the original creation gods, the first man in the world, a "fetcher" and a propagator of plants. Ancestral spirits could be called upon through the medium of an anthropomorphic *ti'i* ("fetcher") figure, but Anne D'Alleva suggests the term could also be used to describe an ancestral spirit itself. D'Alleva, "Shaping the Body Politic"; Oliver, *Ancient Tahitian Society,* 50–51, 71–74.

5. "Gentlemen of science" was the term employed at the time; "scientists" was a nineteenth-century construct.

6. Schama, *Landscape and Memory,* 6–7.

7. Ibid.; Keith Thomas, *Man and the Natural World: Changing Attitudes in England 1500–1800* (Harmondsworth, Middlesex: Penguin, 1984).

8. Thomas, *Man and the Natural World,* 243.

9. David Coffin, *The English Garden: Meditation and Memorial* (Princeton, N.J.: Princeton University Press, 1994), 71–72.

10. Thomas, *Man and the Natural World,* 243.

11. Ibid., 247–249.

12. Iain McCalman, "Introduction," in *An Oxford Companion to the Romantic Age: British Culture 1776–1832,* ed. Iain McCalman, 1–2 (London: Oxford University Press, 1999).

13. William Gilpin, *Three Essays: On Picturesque Beauty; on Picturesque Travel; and on Sketching Landscape* (London: R. Blamire, 1792).

14. On ha-has and other boundaries (conceptual and actual) that the British were installing in landscapes they created and encountered, see Lamb, *Preserving the Self,* 225, 238, 241, 247.

15. Thomas, *Man and the Natural World,* 257.

16. John Gascoigne, *Joseph Banks and the English Enlightenment: Useful Knowledge and Polite Culture* (Melbourne: Cambridge University Press, 1994), 7, 8.

17. Ibid., 7.

18. Ibid., 8, 101, 105.

19. Banks reporting, after the fact, to Johan Alströmer, 16 Nov. 1784, in Neil Chambers, ed. *The Letters of Sir Joseph Banks: A Selection, 1768–1820* (London: Imperial College Press, 2000), 78.

20. Beaglehole, ed., *Banks Journal,* 23 July 1769, 1:321.

21. "These goblins went into the forest, and also climbed up the hill to our pa (fort) at Whitianga (Mercury Bay). They collected grasses from the cliffs, and kept knocking at the stones on the beach, and we said, 'Why are these acts done by these goblins?' We and the women gathered stones and grass of all sorts, and gave to these goblins. Some of the stones they liked, and put them into their bags, the rest they threw away; and when we gave them the grass and branches of trees they stood and talked to us, or uttered the words of their language." Anne Salmond, *Two Worlds: First Meetings between Maori and Europeans 1642–1772* (Honolulu: University of Hawai'i Press, 1992), 87–88.

22. Beaglehole, ed., *Banks Journal,* 1:291.

23. Joseph Banks to Louis L. F. Comte de Lauraguais, London, 6 Dec. 1771, in Chambers, ed., *Letters of Banks,* 20.

24. Ibid.

25. Ibid.

26. While it is difficult to trace the early history of specific introductions to Kew, by 1814 the only listed plants from Tahiti in Kew Gardens were some survivors of those introduced by Bligh in 1793: *Artocarpus incisa* (breadfruit), *Spondias dulcis* (Otaheite apple), *Aleurites triloba* (candle-nut), *Securinega nitida* (Otaheite myrtle), *Ficus tinctoria* (fig). W. T. Aiton assigned in 1814 the *Lepidium oleraceum* ("scurvy-grass") introduced in 1779 to Tahiti, but it is a native of New Zealand and written records of its being collected on Cook voyages all cite New Zealand as the source. W. T. Aiton, *An Epitome of the Second Edition of Hortus Kewensis, for the Use of Practical Gardeners, to Which is Added, a Selection of Esculent Vegetables and Fruits Cultivated in the Royal Gardens at Kew* (London: Longman, Hurst, Rees, Orme and Brown, 1814), 134, 189, 287, 302, 309, 323. An earlier catalogue of 1798 does not include any Tahitian plant references; only *Ilex vomitoria,* "South-Sea Tea." There is a "Jamaican Bread Fruit Tree" listed, but it is *Brosimum alicastrum,* not the *Artocarpus incisa* of Tahiti. John Willmott, *An Alphabetical Enumeration of the Plants Contained in the Hortus Kewensis* (London: Plummer, 1798), 30, 93.

27. For more on Banks and the British Museum, see Jennifer Newell, "Revisiting Cook at the British Museum," in *Journal of the History of Collections* (forthcoming). Among the objects identifiable as coming from Banks' donation are the Tahitian *fau* headdress (Oc,Tah. 9) and quite likely the adze (Oc,Tah. 88) featured in the Benjamin West portrait of Banks. The museum's natural history specimens, including those from Banks, were moved to the British Museum's Natural History Museum in Kensington in 1827. David Wilson, *The British Museum: A History* (London: British Museum Press, 2002), 42–45.

28. Gascoigne, *Joseph Banks,* 117.

29. Andrew Kippis, *A Narrative of Voyages Round the World, performed by Captain James Cook, with an Account of His Life, During the Previous and Intervening Periods* (London: Carpenter & Son, 1814 [1st ed. 1788]).

30. T. Rodenhurst, *A Description of Hawkstone the seat of Sir Richard Hill,* 6th ed. (London: John Stockdale, 1799), 76.

31. D'Alleva, "Shaping the Body Politic," 52. Prince Leopold Anhalt-Dessau's Wörlitz's garden also featured a mechanized volcano. Schama, *Landscape and Memory,* 541.

32. Thomas, *Man and the Natural World,* 53.

33. G. L. Le Clerc, *Barr's Buffon. Buffon's Natural History, Containing a Theory of the Earth, a General History of Man, of the Brute Creation, and of Vegetables, Minerals, &c.* English ed. (London: H. D. Symonds, 1797); Thomas, *Man and the Natural World,* 53.

34. Hawkesworth, *Account,* 469.

35. T. Haweis to J. Banks, Spitalfields, 7th May 1799. NHM (DTC 11.213–214).

36. Sarah Stone, "Parokets of Oteheate," undated. Watercolor. Alexander Turnbull Library, Wellington (E-327-f.002).

37. Presumably Joseph Banks' wife Dorothea rather than Sarah Banks, Joseph's sister, whom Tobin would have referred to as "Miss" or "Mrs" Banks. Tobin prefaces his statement about Lady Banks with "if I remember right..." Tobin, Journal, 190.

38. For a discussion of the rising interest in natural history in Britain during the late eighteenth century, see Gascoigne, *Joseph Banks,* 107–110.

39. Haweis, Letter to J. Banks, from Spitalfields, 7th May 1799. NHM (DTC 11.213–214).

40. Tobin, Journal, 173–174.

41. Ibid., 140.

42. C. F. Russell, *A History of King Edward VI School Southampton* (Cambridge: Cambridge University Press, 1940), 279; Hugh Moffat, "George Tobin, RN." *Sea Breezes* 39 (1965): 562.

43. Tobin, Journal, 1.

44. Ibid., 117.

45. Kim Sloan, *"A Noble Art": Amateur Artists and Drawing Masters c.1600–1800* (London: British Museum Press, 2000). Tobin would have learnt these skills during his midshipman's training at King Edward VI School, Southampton. Russell, *King Ed. VI School,* 279.

46. Tobin, Journal, 114; on the grand tour: Chloe Chard and Helen Langdon, eds., *Transports: Travel, Pleasure and Imaginative Geography 1600–1830* (New Haven, Conn., and London: Yale University Press, 1996).

47. A note in Tobin's hand at the start of the account reads, "Copied 1819, 20 some notes having been added, and more probably will" (Tobin, Journal, 1). The journal has now been published: Roy Schreiber, ed., *Captain Bligh's Second Chance: An Eyewitness Account of his Return to the South Seas by Lt George Tobin* (Sydney: University of New South Wales Press, 2007).

48. Tobin, Journal, 173.

49. Michael E. Hoare, ed. *The Resolution Journal of Johann Reinhold Forster: 1772–1775.* 4 vols. London: Hakluyt Society, 1982, 4: 555, 557.

50. Bernard Smith, *European Vision and the South Pacific,* 2nd ed. (Melbourne: Oxford University Press, 1989), 4.

51. For instance, strolling by the fortified post they had built at Point Venus early on in their stay, Tobin found the "*Matavāi* river came suddenly on my view, on the banks of which clear and beautiful stream, the bread fruit, Cocoa nut, and *avēē* were growing in the most luxuriant state." Tobin, Journal, 132.

52. Rüdiger Joppien and Bernard Smith, *The Art of Captain Cook's Voyages* (New Haven, Conn., and London: Paul Mellon Centre for Studies in British Art and Yale University Press, 1985–1988), 1:60.

53. Harold Carter, "Note on the Drawings by an Unknown Artist from the Voyage of HMS *Endeavour*," in *Science and Exploration in the Pacific: European Voyages to the Southern Oceans in the Eighteenth Century,* ed. Margarette Lincoln, 132–134 (Woodbridge, Suffolk: Boydell Press with the National Maritime Museum, 1998).

54. For more on Tupaia, see Salmond, "Tupaia's Ship," in *Aphrodite's Island;* and Glyndwr Williams, "Tupaia: Polynesian Warrior, Navigator, High Priest—and Artist," in *The Global Eighteenth Century,* ed. Felicity A. Nussbaum (Baltimore and London: Johns Hopkins University Press, 2003).

55. Thomas, *Discoveries,* 75–77.

56. Ibid., 76.

57. Ibid.

58. The figures on the canoes are also typically Polynesian in form, in a way that does not appear to have been realistically captured by eighteenth-century European artists. The proportions of the limbs, the slightly squatting stance, the short thigh length, large, ovoid heads with pointed chins, arms bent at elbows—all these elements are seen in Society Island stone and wood carvings and are likewise represented in this drawing.

59. Thomas and Berghof, eds., *Voyage,* 26 April 1773, 105.

60. Ibid.

61. Ibid., 106.

62. Mark Adams and Nicholas Thomas, *Cook's Sites: Revisiting History* (Dunedin: University of Otago Press with Centre for Cross-Cultural Research, ANU, 1999), 22–27; Thomas, *Discoveries,* 179–180.

63. Peter Hulme and Ludmilla Jordanova, eds., *The Enlightenment and Its Shadows* (London: Routledge, 1990), 7.

64. J. G. A. Pocock, "Nature and History, Self and Other: European Perceptions of World History in the World of Encounter," in *Voyages and Beaches: Pacific Encounters, 1769–1840,* ed. Alex Calder, Jonathan Lamb, and Bridget Orr, 39 (Honolulu: University of Hawai'i Press, 1999).

65. Nicholas Thomas, "Exploration," in *An Oxford Companion to the Romantic*

Age: British Culture 1776–1832, ed. Iain McCalman, 345–346 (Oxford: Oxford University Press, 1999).

66. This was a common paradigm, and it provided many Pacific voyagers with a clear rationale for their endeavors. George Vancouver, for example, described his own explorations as contributing to "that expansive arch over which the arts and sciences should pass to the furthermost corners of the earth, for the instruction and happiness of the most lowly children of nature . . . the untutored parts of the human race." Quoted in Marshall and Williams, *Great Map of Mankind,* 301.

67. Diderot was one of the most prominent adherents of this hierarchy.

68. Johann Reinhold Forster developed several theories for explaining the differences in physical form, temperament, and habits he discerned in Pacific societies. He decided (insightfully) they were all descended from common Asian ancestry and went on to posit that many of the differences between them were due to differences of each island's temperature, air, sun, and general fertility. See particularly his essay "On the Causes of the Difference in the Races of Men in the South Seas, their Origin and Migrations," in *Observations Made During a Voyage Round the World by J. R. Forster,* ed. Nicholas Thomas, Harriet Guest, and Michael Dettelbach, 172–190 (Honolulu: University of Hawai'i Press, 1996).

69. Patrick V. Kirch, "Introduction," in *Historical Ecology in the Pacific Islands: Prehistoric Environmental and Landscape Change,* ed. Patrick V. Kirch and Terry L. Hunt (New Haven, Conn., and London: Yale University Press, 1997), 4.

70. Beaglehole, ed., *Banks Journal,* 1:342.

71. Ibid., 1:341–343.

72. Kirch, "Introduction," 4.

73. George Vancouver described a chief's house in the Pare district neatly planted with bananas, sugar cane, the narcotic *'ava,* and "a small shrubbery, of native ornamental plants." The whole planting was "surrounded by a well constructed fence of bamboo, neatly intersected with clean paths, that led in different directions, produced an effect that was extremely pleasing, and redounded much to the credit and ingenuity of the proprietor." Soon afterwards he was critiquing their inability to grow European vegetables, because they were strangers to cultivating the soil by manual labor. Lamb, ed., *Voyage of Discovery,* 411, 440.

74. "The calm contented state of the natives; their simple way of life; the beauty of the landscape; the excellence of the climate; the abundance, salubrity and delicious taste of its fruits, were altogether enchanting, and filled the heart with rapture." Thomas and Berghof, eds., *Voyage,* 359.

75. Oliver, *Return to Tahiti,* 174.

76. Thomas et al., eds., *Observations,* 373–375.

77. Tobin, Journal, 155–157.

78. Ibid., 158.

79. See, for instance, Warner, ed., *Discovery,* 86.

80. He had taken on the role of purser, so it was his own investment he was

protecting (having used his own funds to buy goods to trade for provisions). Many of the tensions on board stemmed from his anxiety over losing money on provisions, keeping watch over who was using communal stores, and his readiness to accuse individuals of stealing from him. Dening, *Bligh's Bad Language*, 22–23.

81. Victualling Office to Philip Stephens, 27 April 1791. Victualling Board letters, Caird Library, NMM (ADM D/37).

82. *Ti'i-potua-ra'au* (literally "back-to-back-wood-fetcher") indicates this stacked variety of *ti'i*. Other *ti'i* were single, portable figures used at the *marae* for containing spirits. Oliver, *Ancient Tahitian Society*, 71–74. Henry, *Ancient Tahiti*, 209.

83. Tobin, Journal, 177.

84. Oliver, *Ancient Tahitian Society*, 71–74.

85. See E. S. Craighill Handy, *History and Culture in the Society Islands, Bernice P. Bishop Museum Bulletin* 79 (1971): 31.

86. Douglas Oliver, *Return to Tahiti: Bligh's Second Breadfruit Voyage* (Melbourne: Melbourne University Press, 1988), 166.

87. Alain Babadzan, *Les Dépouilles des Dieux: Essai sur le religion tahitienne à l'époque de la découverte* (Paris: Fondation de la Maison des sciences de l'homme, 1993), 77; Henry, *Ancient Tahiti*, 209.

88. Hank Driessen, "From Ta'aroa to 'Oro: an Exploration of Themes in the Traditional Culture and History of the Leeward Society Islands" (PhD thesis, Australian National University, 1991), 41.

89. Ibid., 44.

90. Ibid., 41f. Driessen draws on Henry, *Ancient Tahiti*, and the missionary records of John Davies. See Colin Newbury, ed., *The History of the Tahitian Mission, 1799–1830. Written by John Davies, Missionary to the South Seas Islands* (London: Cambridge University Press, 1961), and Ellis, *Polynesian Researches* 1829.

91. Henry, *Ancient Tahiti*, 412.

92. Ibid., 377–378.

93. Henry, *Ancient Tahiti*, 384ff; also Oliver, *Ancient Tahitian Society*, 58–62.

94. Oliver, *Ancient Tahitian Society*, 61–66.

95. *Mo'ora oviri*, the gray duck *Anas peocilorhyncha*, Henry, *Ancient Tahiti*, 384; Société d'ornithologie de Polynésie française website: www.manu.pf/OSB.html.

96. Chant of Marae, recited by the priests Tamatera and Pati'i, the high priests of Tahiti and Mo'orea, in Henry, *Ancient Tahiti*, 150–151.

97. William Bligh, *A Voyage to the South Sea, Undertaken by Command of His Majesty, for the Purpose of Conveying the Breadfruit Tree to the West Indies, in His Majesty's Ship the* Bounty (London: G. Nicol, 1792), 31 Jan. 1789, 121.

98. Lt. George Mortimer, of the Swedish brig *Mercury* (visited Aug.–Sept. 1789), quoted in Oliver, *Ancient Tahitian Society*, 1256.

99. Bligh, *Log of the Bounty*, 24 Feb. 1789, 217.

100. Oliver, *Ancient Tahitian Society*, 444–445.

101. Ibid., 445.

102. William Bligh, Log of H.M.S. *Providence*, 1791–1793. PRO (ADM 55/151), 35.

103. Oliver, *Ancient Tahitian Society*, 488.

104. Ibid.

105. Tobin, Journal, 189–190. Tobin also painted one of these herons—see SLNSW (PXA 563 f.56). Similarly, George Forster, curious on seeing how upset and "grieved" the wife and daughters of the Ra'iatean chief Orio were when he shot some kingfishers (which they called their *atua*), tried to touch one of the daughters with the dead birds. Thomas and Berghof, eds., *Voyage*, 9 Sept. 1773, 213.

106. Henry, *Ancient Tahiti*, 385. Société d'ornithologie, *Manu*, 31.

107. Henry, *Ancient Tahiti*, 385

108. Michael Cathcart et al., *Mission to the South Seas: The Voyage of the Duff, 1796–1799. Melbourne University History Monographs* 11 (1990), 14.

109. There was no mention of a Bible among the things given to Ma'i. Decades later, during his ten years in Polynesia (from 1816), the Rev. William Ellis described an illustrated Bible being among the possessions of a chief in Huahine which had belonged to "Paari or Mai." In any case, the important point is while the LMS was forming, the perception was that Ma'i had been left without any religious instruction. Ellis, *Polynesian Researches* 1829, 2: 96–97; E. H. McCormick, *Omai: Pacific Envoy* (Auckland: Auckland University Press, Oxford University Press, 1977), see chapter 6, 254–256, and 293.

110. Tobin, Journal, 227.

111. Michael Cathcart, "Foundation of the Mission," in Cathcart et al., eds., *Mission,* 11–29: 14.

112. Tom Griffiths, "The Voyage," in Cathcart et al., eds. *Mission,* 33.

113. Cathcart, "Foundation of the Mission," 16–17.

114. Griffiths, "The Voyage," 34.

115. London Missionary Society, *Narrative of the Mission at Otaheite and Other Islands in the South Seas; Commenced by the London Missionary Society in the Year 1797* (London: J. Dennett, 1818), 3.

116. Andrew Lind, resident of the island since the shipwreck of the *Matilda* in 1792, and Peter Haggerstein, deserter from the *Daedalus*, February 1793. Henry Adams, *Memoirs of Arii Taimai e Marama of Eimeo, Teriirere of Tooarai, Terrinui of Tahiti, Tauraatua I Amo* (Paris: H. Adams, 1901), 115.

117. Rev. William Henry, Early Days on Tahiti, 1797. SSJ, LMS/CWM Archives, SOAS (box 1 folio 3), 21.

118. Henry, *Ancient Tahiti*, 31–32.

119. London Missionary Society, *Transactions of the Missionary Society to the End of the Year 1817* (London: Directors of the Missionary Society, 1818), 143.

120. Bligh had said he would come and live in the house if Tu built it. Jefferson, Journal 1801, 17 June, 22.

121. Lee Watts, "Tahiti," in Cathcart, et al., eds., *Mission*, 55–70: 56.

122. Newbury, *History of the Mission*, 36, 104.

123. 'Itia and Tu doted on Brother and Sister Henry's newborn daughter, for instance, and the Henrys were "visited almost daily by Strange Natives who come designedly to see her," and were "exceedingly well pleased when we allow them to call her, Mydidde no Otaheite, which signifies, a Child of Otaheite." Henry, Early Days on Tahiti, 5–6. See 25 verso for the hospitality extended to the missionary women.

124. Watts, "Tahiti," 56; "Several chiefs came with presents of Otaheitian Cloth, and hogs, impressing their friendship, and requesting the Brethren to exchange names with them, which was done as far as was thought prudent." Henry, Early Days on Tahiti, 24.

125. Henry, *Early Days on Tahiti*, 26 verso–27.

126. London Missionary Society, *Transactions . . . to the end of the year 1812* (London: J. Dennett, 1813), 3:39.

127. Complaints of these responses to preaching recur throughout the journals of the mission in Tahiti (South Sea Journals, LMS/CWM Archives, SOAS).

128. Hassall, Account of the Mission, 7 Feb. 1798, 6.

129. Ibid, 28 Jan. 1798, 5.

130. Ibid.

131. Tobin, Journal, 179.

132. The anthropologist Robert Levy reported in the 1970s that Tahitians avoided the forest from twilight from an anxiety over the spirits there. Robert Levy, *Tahitians: Mind and Experience in the Society Islands* (Chicago: University of Chicago Press, 1973).

133. My informant was a Catholic. French Catholic missionaries established themselves on the island since the 1840s, in competition with the English Protestants. Discussion (name withheld), Pape'ete, 5 July 2001.

Chapter 3: Getting Captain Cook's Goat

1. A number of the officers recorded their concerns and their perplexity at Cook's motivations. Several expressed sympathy for the islanders. Beaglehole, ed., *Cook Journals 1776–1780*, see 231n, 232n for the officers' comments.

2. As Nicholas Thomas has pointed out, "their loss denuded people." Thomas, *Discoveries*, 345. William Harvey noted at the time that the people's losses "would affect them for years to come." Beaglehole, ed., *Cook Journals 1776–1780*, 232n.

3. Ibid., 228–232.

4. Creating, as Jonathan Lamb has said, "super-goats," their value multiplied, rendering them equal to a swathe of houses and canoes. J. Lamb, "The

Place of Property in the South Seas Narrative," paper given at the Exploring Text and Travel Conference, National Maritime Museum, Greenwich, 12 March 2005.

5. Beaglehole, ed., *Cook Journals 1776–1780*, 228.

6. Gananath Obeyesekere, *The Apotheosis of Captain Cook: European Mythmaking in the Pacific* (Princeton, N.J.: Princeton University Press, 1992), 12 (italics in original).

7. Beaglehole, ed., *Cook Journals 1776–1780*, 28 Sept. 1777, 224.

8. Thomas, *Discoveries*, xxiii.

9. Beaglehole, ed., *Cook Journals 1776–1780*, 23.

10. Ibid., 241.

11. Beaglehole, ed., *Cook Journals 1772–1775*, 287.

12. Peter Borsay, "The Culture of Improvement," in *The Eighteenth Century 1688–1815*, ed. Paul Langford (Oxford: Oxford University Press, 2002).

13. Ibid., 186.

14. Gascoigne, *Joseph Banks*, 185–188, 196, 236.

15. Borsay, "Culture of Improvement," 186; Gascoigne, *Joseph Banks*, 187–190.

16. James Dancer, Abstract of an Oration . . . respecting the Bath & the Botanic Garden in Jamaica by J. Dancer M.D. Island Botanist, 1 March 1790. BL (Add. Mss 22678).

17. Thomas and Berghof, eds., *Voyage*, 12.

18. Beaglehole, ed., *Cook Journals 1776–1780*, 133.

19. Ibid., 229.

20. Ibid., 1383.

21. Such as ibid., xxxi, and Bernard Smith, "Constructing 'Pacific' Peoples," in *Remembrance of Pacific Pasts*, ed. R. Borofsky, 161 (Honolulu: University of Hawai'i Press, 2000), where he suggests illness may have been one factor, along with a growing cynicism, accounting for Cook's changed behavior. On the medical issue he refers the reader to Sir James Watt, "Medical Aspects and Consequences of Cook's Voyages," in Robin Fisher and Hugh Johnston, *Captain Cook and His Times* (Canberra: Australian National University Press, 1979).

22. Salmond, *Aphrodite's Island*, 444.

23. Nigel Rigby, "The Politics and Pragmatics of Seaborne Plant Transportation, 1769–1805," in *Science and Exploration in the Pacific: European Voyages to the Southern Oceans in the Eighteenth Century*, ed. Margarette Lincoln (Woodbridge, Suffolk: Boydell Press with the National Maritime Museum, 1998).

24. Beaglehole, ed., *Cook Journals 1776–1780*, 224.

25. Rigby, "Seaborne Plant Transportation," 84.

26. John Ellis, *Directions for Bringing over Seeds and Plants, from the East Indies and Other Distant Countries in a State of Vegetation: Together with a Catalogue of Such Foreign Plants as Are Worthy of Being Encouraged in Our American Colonies, for the Purposes of Medicine, Agriculture, and Commerce* (London: L. Davis, 1770), 1.

27. Beaglehole, ed., *Banks Journal,* 1:274, 308–309.

28. Rigby, "Seaborne Plant Transportation," 84.

29. John Fothergill's covered tubs were described in a 1796 publication, John Fothergill, *Directions for Taking up Plants and Shrubs and Conveying them by Sea* (London, 1796), quoted in Rigby, "Seaborne Plant Transportation," 88. See Rigby also for seed transportation and the dangers to plants en route, ibid., 89.

30. Lisbet Koerner, "Nature and Nation in Linnean Travel," in *Visions of Empire: Voyages, Botany, and Representations of Nature,* ed. David Miller and Peter Reill, 131 (Cambridge: Cambridge University Press, 1996).

31. J. R. Forster, in M. E. Hoare, ed. *The Resolution Journal of Johann Reinhold Forster: 1772–1775.* 4 vols. (London: Hakluyt Society, 1982), 15 Mar. 1773, 2:233.

32. For example, all but a couple of Vancouver's stock for New South Wales died from lack of fodder. Quote from A. Menzies' Journal, 18 Dec. 1792, in Lamb, *Voyage of Discovery,* 735 n.1.

33. Ibid., 828.

34. "Two Days since the only surviving Sheep brought at Ryde in y'e Isle of Wight, died by eating too freely of Banana's &c. to the regrett of all of us." Bowes, Journal, 112.

35. From John Jefferson, "State of the Garden from May 1st to August 1st," in Journal of the Missionaries proceedings on Otaheite, 1804. SSJ. LMS/CWM Archive, SOAS (box 2 folio 22), 1 Aug., 5–6; and Jefferson, Journal 1801, 35.

36. Jefferson, Journal 1804, 1 Aug., 6.

37. Ibid., 31 Oct., 30.

38. Ibid., 29.

39. Dealing with the loss of their animals was clearly difficult emotionally. A sheep that was attacked in June 1800 and after two days of nursing judged to be "past recovery & almost dead," was taken out to sea a little way "with a stone tied round its neck cast over board," rather than consigning it to the dinner table. Later, the editor of the journals back in London deleted this and similar passages. Jefferson, Journal 1800, 6 June, 10.

40. Ibid., 4 March, 7.

41. Beaglehole, ed., *Cook Journals 1776–1780,* 223.

42. James Cook, 29 Sept. 1777, quoted in ibid.; James Burney, 27 Sept. 1777, quoted in ibid, 207; and "King's Journal," Appendix II, 18 Sept. 1777, ibid, 1376.

43. Jefferson, Journal 1804, 28.

44. Jefferson, Journal 1800, 15 Jan., 4.

45. Rabbits denuded several Hawaiian islands of their vegetation; on Lisianski they did it so quickly they starved themselves into extinction. Domestic rabbits were introduced in 1903. An expedition in 1923 found only a desert-like

surface and bleached rabbit skeletons. J. S. Watson, "Feral Rabbit Populations on Pacific Islands," *Pacific Science* 15 (1961): 591.

46. Escaped domestic rabbits were a nuisance around Sydney, but it was the wild rabbit that was hardy enough to cover the rest of the continent. J. Owen, "Rabbit Production in Tropical Developing Countries: A Review," *Tropical Science* 18 no. 4 (1976).

47. Interestingly, some church missions are today carrying out development projects in Africa based on rabbit production for small-scale farmers. One website features a question-and-answer section on the topic, including: "Q. How do you penetrate the villages with the practical helps of rabbits and the gospel?" Martin L. Price and Fremont Regier, *Rabbit Production in the Tropics,* web publication (North Ft. Myers, Florida: ECHO, 1982). http://echotech.org/mambo/images/DocMan/RabitPro.PDF.

48. John Davies, A Journal of the Missionaries Proceedings on Tahiti, 1807–1808. SSJ, LMS/CWM Archive, SOAS (box 3 folio 31), 26 Dec. 1807 (n.p.).

49. For instance: "Within these few days and night the natives have repeatedly robbed our gardens of a great number of pine apples, they continue their old custom of committing their depredations generally at the time the brethren are assembled for worship." Ibid., 14 Nov. and 26 Dec. 1807. Jefferson reported nearly two hundred pigs being stolen over a period of eighteen months (from 31 July 1801 to 5 Feb. 1803). J. Jefferson, Journal of the Missionaries Proceedings 1802–1803, SSJ, LMS/CWM Archive, SOAS (box 1 folio 13), 17.

50. Jefferson, Journal 1807, 14 Nov.

51. As we saw in the introduction. Rutter, ed. *Journal of James Morrison,* 192.

52. Davies, Journal 1807–1808, 14 Nov. 1807 (unpaginated; f.26).

53. Ibid., 25 Dec. 1807 (unpaginated; f.33).

54. From Rev. S. Marsden to the Directors, Parramatta, NSW, 31 Oct 1816, London Missionary Society, *Transactions of the Missionary Society to the End of the Year 1817* (London: Directors of the Society, 1818), 42.

55. See Niel Gunson, "Gyles, John (–1827)," in *Australian Dictionary of Biography,* 1:495–496 (Carlton: Melbourne University Press, 1966).

56. Patrick V. Kirch, *The Wet and the Dry: Irrigation and Agricultural Intensification in Polynesia* (Chicago and London: University of Chicago Press, 1994); Dana Sue Lepofsky, "Prehistoric Agricultural Intensification in the Society Islands, French Polynesia" (PhD diss., University of California at Los Angeles, 1995).

57. Michel Orliac, "Human Occupation and Environmental Modifications in the Papeno'o Valley, Tahiti," in *Historical Ecology in the Pacific Islands: Prehistoric Environmental and Landscape Change,* ed. Patrick V. Kirch and Terry L. Hunt, 200–229 (New Haven, Conn., and London: Yale University Press, 1997).

58. See Oliver, *Ancient Tahitian Society,* 20, 212–214; Donald Denoon, Stewart Firth, and Jocelyn Linnekin, eds., *The Cambridge History of the Pacific Islanders* (Cambridge: Cambridge University Press, 1997), 75.

59. Rutter, ed., *Journal of James Morrison,* 202.

60. D'Arcy, *People of the Sea*, 52–53.

61. Hooper, ed., *Journal of James Burney*, 69.

62. Beaglehole, ed., *Banks Journal*, 1:308.

63. Beaglehole, ed., *Cook Journals 1776–1780*, 195.

64. Bligh had accompanied Cook on his third voyage. Bligh, *Voyage in the Bounty*, 86

65. Ibid., 86.

66. Several of these species are present in Tahiti today; various pine species (including Norfolk pine), several fig (*ficus*) species, and Metrosideros. It is not possible to trace whether it was Bligh's introduction that established any of these on the island. Guava is discussed below.

67. Bligh, *Log of the Providence*, 19 April 1792.

68. Beaglehole, ed., *Cook Journals 1776–1780*, 223.

69. Bligh, *Bounty*, 2 March 1789, 133.

70. Ibid.

71. LMS, Journal of the Missionaries Proceedings at Tahiti, 1808. SSJ, LMS/ CWM Archives, SOAS (box 3 folio 33), 11.

72. ISSG, *Global Invasive Species Database*, web database (accessed 2008). http:// www.issg.org/database/.

73. Rutter, ed., *Journal of James Morrison*, 149.

74. Hawkesworth, *Account*, 25 July 1767, 476.

75. Beaglehole, ed., *Banks Journal*, 1:308.

76. H. Jacquier, "Enumérarion des Plantes Introduites à Tahiti Depuis le Découverte Jusqu'en 1885," *Bulletin de la Société des études océaniennes* 1 no. 5 (1960), 124; P. Pétard, *Plantes Utiles De Polynésie Raau Tahiti* (Pape'ete: éditions Haere po no Tahiti, 1986).

77. David Nelson, gardener on Cook's third voyage, planted at Matavai Point on 28 August 1777 several "shaddock" trees, which he stated he had brought from Tonga, presumably from an earlier British planting. He felt they "could hardly fail of succeeding." Beaglehole, ed., *Cook Journals 1776–1780*, 195.

78. Tobin was touched by the devotion of the man: "These trees were planted in 1777 by the late Mr Nelson, who was with Captain Cook in his last voyage. An old man whose habitation received shade from them spoke with affection and the warmest gratitude of our countryman, and with unfeigned sorrow lamented his death when informed of it. *Here* we sufficiently understood one anothers language; little indeed was there to explain." Tobin, Journal, 137–138.

79. Menzies, Journal, 131.

80. LMS, Journal 1808, 11.

81. Gilbert Cuzent, *Îles De La Société: Considérations Géologiques, Météorologiques Et Botaniques Sur l'Île*, (Pape'ete: éditions Haere Po No Tahiti, 1983 [orig. ed. 1860]), 200.

82. Martin, *Polynesian Journal*, 50.

83. "Pour donne une idée de la quantité d'orangers que produit Tahiti, un

seul district, celui de Tautira'a, en 1875, payé en une récolte la construction de son temple, estimé à 40,000 fr., au moyen de 1,900,000 oranges." Charles Blin, *Voyage en Océanie* (Le Mans: Leguicheux-Gallienne, 1881), 204–205.

84. L. et F. Chabouis, *Petite Histoire Naturelle Des Établissements Français De L'océanie: Zoologie,* 2 vols. (Cher: Imprimerie Bussière, 1954), 2:34.

85. Lady Brassey and Col. Stuart-Wortley, *Tahiti: A Series of Photographs Taken by Colonel Stuart-Wortley with Letterpress by Lady Brassey* (London: Sampson Low, Marston, Searle and Rivington, 1882), 51.

86. Samuel Russell, *Tahiti and French Oceania: A Book of Reliable Information for the Traveller, the Sportsman, the Yachtsman, and the Resident in the South Seas* (Sydney: Pacific Publications Ltd, 1935), 80. *Purau: Hibiscus tiliacus.*

87. Bernard Salvat, ed., *Flore et Faune Terrestres,* vol. 2, *Encyclopédie De La Polynésie,* ed. Christian Gleizal (Pape'ete: Multipress, 1986), 62.

88. Martin, *Polynesian Journal,* 52.

89. Chabouis, *Petite Histoire Naturelle,* 60.

90. [E. Lucett], *Rovings in the Pacific from 1837 to 1849; With a Glance at California, By a Merchant Long Resident at Tahiti* (London: Longman, Brown, Green and Longmans, 1851), 1:221.

91. Brassey and Stuart-Wortley, *Tahiti,* 20.

92. Ibid., 21.

93. Pétard, *Plantes Utiles,* 245–247; personal communication, M. Tessier Fortuné, Musée de Tahiti et des Îles, Puna'auia, July 2001.

94. Lucett, *Rovings,* 1:221–222.

95. Brassey and Stuart-Wortley, *Tahiti,* 4, 21.

96. Phillip L. Bruner, *Field Guide to the Birds of French Polynesia* (Honolulu: Pacific Scientific Information Center, Bernice Bishop Museum, 1972), 71.

97. Ministère chargé de l'Environnement, *Les Plantes Envahissantes en Polynésie Française,* brochure (Pape'ete: Delegation à l'Environnement, c. 2003).

98. See for instance the Global Invasive Species Database www.issg.org/database/welcome.

99. *Porzana tabuensis,* "spotless crake" (rail).

100. Henry, *Ancient Tahiti,* 385–386. Paofa'i is on the western outskirts of Pape'ete.

101. Ibid., 386.

102. *Rallus pacificus* (Gmelin, 1789). Details of this and the following species provided by Manu (Société d'Ornithologie de Polynésie) www.manu.pf.

103. *Prosobonia leucaptera* (Gmelin, 1789).

104. *Cyranoramphus zelandicus* (Latham, 1790).

105. Beaglehole, ed., *Cook Journals 1772–1775,* 412.

106. Darnton, *Cat Massacre,* 88, 93.

107. The men working in the eighteenth-century French printery investigated by Robert Darnton certainly found the joke of killing, "accidentally-on-purpose," the cat of their master's wife hugely hilarious, a risqué yet safe way

of making a stab at the authority they labored under. Darnton, *Cat Massacre*, 79–104, especially 94–95.

108. Bligh, *Bounty*, 98.

109. Beaglehole, ed., *Cook Journals 1769–1771*, 103.

110. Ellis, *Polynesian Researches* 1829, 285.

111. Beaglehole, ed., *Cook Journals 1769–1771*, 559, quoting R. Molyneaux's "It is Easy to Kill 1000 [rats] in a day as the ground swarms & the Inhabitants never disturb them"; and Bligh, *Bounty Journal*, 121.

112. Bligh, *Bounty Journal*, 121.

113. Henry, *Ancient Tahiti*, 383.

114. The Norway rat, *Rattus norvegicus*, may have also arrived on ships at this period. Both species are found throughout French Polynesia today.

115. Salmond, *Trial*, 53.

116. Estimates of the island's population by voyagers of the 1760s and 1770s tended to settle around 100,000 to 120,000, based on extrapolations from the numbers who flocked to see the visitors in Matavai Bay, the warriors assembled in the war fleets and groups calculated in other districts (Cook was particularly generous with his guess of 200,000). Douglas Oliver is much more circumspect; his figure is based on a survey of the various early reports, primarily working from records of the numbers of warriors in each district. He has calculated an approximate total over the 1767–1774 period of 35,000. Imported diseases became increasingly widespread by the late 1790s. Estimates by missionaries after taking tours around the island placed the population at 20,000 to 50,000. By 1802, the population of Tahiti was down to between 5,500 and 7,000. Oliver, *Ancient Tahitian Society*, 29, 33–34.

Chapter 4: Chiefly Cattle

Epigraph: Morris West, *The Shoes of the Fisherman* (London: Heinemann, 1963), 21.

1. Gísli Pálsson, "The Idea of Fish: Land and Sea in the Icelandic World-View," in *Signifying Animals: Human Meaning in the Natural World*, ed. Roy Willis, 119 (London: Unwin Hyman, 1990). "I take the theoretical position, following Douglas (1966), Leach (1976) and some others, that some animals, because of their anomalous position, are better to think with than others."

2. Don Thomas Gayangos, from his *Aguila* journal, in Bolton Glanville Corney, ed., *The Quest and Occupation of Tahiti by Emissaries of Spain During the Years 1772–1776, Told in Dispatches and Other Contemporary Documents*, 3 vols. (London: Hakluyt Society, 1913–1919), 2:174.

3. Ibid., 2:299.

4. For more on the Spanish involvement in Tahiti, see Salmond, *Aphrodite's Island*, particularly chapters 11, 15–17.

5. Corney, ed. *Quest and Occupation*, 2:299.

6. Ibid.

7. Ibid., 2:xvii, 216. On the word *poreho,* see also Salmond, *Aphrodite's Island,* 352–353.

8. Padres Clota and Gonzalez to the Commander of the *Aguila,* Don Cayetona de Langara, 4 Nov. 1775. Corney, ed., *Quest and Occupation,* 2:376–379.

9. "Bearing in mind the best interests of our Sovereign and the good of the State, it appears to me that if we leave the livestock behind, both greater and lesser kinds, serious mischances might result. For, being well fed, and but little used up by the natives of the Island, foreigners might some day supply themselves from this source, and refresh their needs incident to so extended a voyage. They would, at least, favour the opportunity for some privateering craft or merchantman to attempt to land goods on the South [American] coast, or harass the navigation of those Seas . . . as a precaution against it, all the stock should be sent on board to be expended in rationing the crew." Cayetano de Langara to the Padres, *Aguila,* 7 Nov. 1775. Corney, ed. *Quest and Occupation,* 2:383.

10. Beaglehole, ed., *Cook Journals 1776–1780,* 10 July 1776, 4.

11. Ibid.

12. Ibid., 1 Aug. 1776, 9.

13. "I accordingly gave to Matahouah two Goats male & female the latter with kid, and to Tomatongeauooranue two Pigs a boar & a sow." Ibid., 24 Feb. 1777, 66.

14. Ibid., 67.

15. William Ellis, *An Authentic Narrative of a Voyage Performed by Captain Cook and Captain Clerke,* 2 vols. (London: Robinson et al., 1782), 1:131.

16. According to William Ellis, surgeon's mate on the *Discovery.* Ibid.

17. Beaglehole, ed., *Cook Journals 1776–1780,* 12 Aug. 1777, 186.

18. Ibid., 13 Aug. 1777, 1369.

19. Thomas, *Discoveries,* 334.

20. Beaglehole, ed., *Cook Journals 1776–1780,* 13 Aug. 1777, 1369.

21. Ellis, *Authentic Narrative,* 482.

22. For more on Ma'i's time in England, see McCormick, *Omai: Pacific Envoy;* Francesca Rendle-Short, ed. *Cook and Omai: The Cult of the South Seas* (Canberra: National Library of Australia, 2001).

23. Beaglehole, ed., *Cook Journals 1772–1775,* 18 Sept. 1777, 211.

24. Cook wrote of taking on shore "a Peacock and Hen which my Lord Bessborough was so kind as to send me a few days before I left London." (William Ponsonby, 2nd Earl of Bessborough 1704–1793, Lord of the Admiralty since 1746). Beaglehole, ed., *Cook Journals 1772–1775,* 24 Aug. 1777, 193–194; Gerard O'Brien, "Ponsonby, William, second earl of Bessborough (1704–1793)," in *Oxford Dictionary of National Biography* (Oxford: Oxford University Press, 2004).

25. Beaglehole, ed., *Cook Journals 1772–1775,* 25 Aug. 1777, 194.

26. Oliver, *Ancient Tahitian Society,* 79; and Salmond, *Aphrodite's Island,* 422.

27. Beaglehole, ed., *Cook Journals 1772–1775,* 18 Sept. 1777, 211.

28. Ibid.

29. Tu's account to Bligh. Bligh, *Bounty*, 31 Oct. 1788, 72. There were no accounts of deaths among the cattle originally introduced, other than the Spanish cow, so the surviving Boenechea and Cook introductions can be presumed to amount to five, plus the eight calves.

30. Howe, *Where the Waves Fall*, 130–131.

31. Bligh, *Voyage in the Bounty*, 27 Oct. 1788, 63.

32. J. Barrau, *Useful Plants of Tahiti* (Paris: Société des Océanistes, 1971), 2.

33. Owen Rutter, ed., *The Log of the Bounty: Being Lieutenant William Bligh's Log of . . . a Voyage to the South Seas, to Take the Breadfruit from the Society Islands to the West Indies* (London: Golden Cockerel Press, 1937), 1 Nov. 1788, 1:378.

34. Ibid.

35. Bligh, *Voyage in the Bounty*, 13 Nov. 1788, 72, 91: "I was likewise informed, that there was a bull and a cow alive at Otaheite, but on different parts of the island; the former at a place called Itteah, the latter at the district of Tettaha. All the rest were taken away or destroyed by the people of Eimeo [Mo'orea]."

36. Rutter, ed., *Journal of James Morrison*, 31.

37. Bligh recorded they were at "Itteah" and "Tettaha"—Douglas Oliver identifies these regions as Hiti'a and Fa'a'a.

38. Rutter, ed., *Log of the Bounty*, 1:379.

39. Bligh, *Voyage in the Bounty*, 14 Nov. 1788, 94.

40. Ibid., 31 Oct. 1788, 72.

41. Ibid., 29 Oct. 1788, 68.

42. Rutter, ed., *Journal of James Morrison*, 238–239.

43. As Bernard Salvat has said, despite the repeated gifts of cattle from the Europeans, the Tahitians *"ne s'empressent pas autour de ces cadeaux"* (were not at all impressed by these gifts). Salvat, ed., *Flore et Faune*, 2:102.

44. Beaglehole, ed., *Cook Journals 1776–1780*, 14 Sept. 1777, 209.

45. For a dramatic, imagined, image of this scene, see "Omai's public entry on his first landing at Otaheite," an engraving in John Rickman, *Journal of Captain Cook's Last Voyage to the Pacific Ocean on Discovery* (London: E. Newbery, 1781). It presents Ma'i in full armor riding almost into a crowd of people, who are running away in fright. He holds the horse's reins in one hand and fires a pistol above the heads of the crowd with the other.

46. Rutter, ed., *Journal of James Morrison*, 113.

47. Beaglehole, ed., *Cook Journals 1776–1780*, 14 Sept. 1777, 209.

48. Ibid., 29 Sept. 1777, 221.

49. Bligh, *Voyage in the Bounty*, 14 Nov. 1788, 93.

50. Ibid., 94.

51. Rutter, *Log of the Bounty*, 396.

52. Bligh, *Voyage in the Bounty*, 31 Jan. 1789, 121.

53. Bligh, *Log of Providence*, 13 July 1792.

54. Lamb, *Voyage of Discovery*, 429.

55. Bligh, *Log of Providence*, 18 April 1792.

56. Rather than the five Vancouver had counted. Ibid., 4 May 1792.

57. John Jefferson, A Journal of the Missionaries Proceedings on Otaheite, 1 Jan.–31 Dec. 1799. SSJ, LMS/CWM Archive, SOAS, London (box 1 folio 6), 16.

58. Jefferson, Journal 1802–1803, 17.

59. Irmgard Moschner, ed., *A Missionary Voyage to the Southern Pacific Ocean 1796–1798* (Graz: Akademische Druck, u. Verlagsanstalt, 1966), 1 Dec. 1796, 41.

60. Her milk had been "very serviceable to the women and children." They had apparently been unable to get grass for the livestock in Rio de Janeiro because of the rainy season. Ibid.

61. Ibid.

62. Jefferson, Journal 1804, 29 Nov., 38.

63. Ibid., 8 Aug., 12.

64. Ibid., 23 Nov., 25; plus the journal of 1808 refers back to 1804 and the bull they ended up acquiring from Campbell. Davies, Journal 1807–1808, 13 Sept.

65. James Hayward et al., A Journal of the Proceedings at Taheite after the Departure of the Perseverance Nov 10 1808 to Jan 7 1809. SSJ, LMS/CWM Archive, SOAS, UCL (box 3 folio 34), 17 Dec. 1808.

66. Ibid.

67. Ellis, *Polynesian Researches* 1829, 147–148.

68. B. F. Leach, M. Intoh, and I. W. G. Smith, "Fishing, Turtle Hunting, and Mammal Exploitation at Fa'ahia, Huahine, French Polynesia," *Journal de la Société des Océanistes* 40 no. 79 (1984): 941.

69. Ellis, *Polynesian Researches* 1829, 1:147.

70. Glynn Barratt, *The Tuamotu Islands and Tahiti*, vol. 4 of *Russia and the South Pacific, 1696–1840* (Vancouver: UBC Press, 1992), 179.

71. R. G. Crocombe, "Land Tenure in the South Pacific," in *Man in the Pacific Islands: Essays on Geographical Change in the Pacific Islands*, ed. R. Gerard Ward, 230 (Oxford: Clarendon Press, 1972).

72. Martin, *Polynesian Journal*, 57.

73. Peltzer, *Chronologie*, 39.

74. George Pritchard, "The Aggressions of the French at Tahiti and other Islands in the Pacific," photocopied typescript (University of Auckland Library, New Zealand and Pacific collection, Auckland, n.d. [post-1843]), 8.

75. Ibid., 9.

76. The flag was to be raised at Moto Uta, a small island off the coast of Tahiti, where the queen was convalescing following the birth of her child. Letter from A. Dupetit-Thouars, *Venus* frigate, to the Queen of Otaheiti, 30 August 1838, quoted in ibid., 9–10. See also Newbury, *Tahiti Nui*, 95.

77. He had been appointed consul for the Society Islands, Tuamotus, and Tonga. Pritchard, "Aggressions of the French," 17.

78. These instances were quoted about Captain Laplace of the *Artemis*. He had paid someone, unspecified, for the timber but no negotiation or payment was offered to the individuals who lost their trees. Ibid., 25.

79. Reporting the words of Tati, one of the chiefs who received the demand from Dupetit-Thouars. Ibid., 9. See also Newbury, *Tahiti Nui*, 104–106.

80. Newbury, *Tahiti Nui*, 109.

81. For a more detailed discussion of this phase, see Newbury, "Occupation and Resistance," in *Tahiti Nui*, 99–128.

82. There is a portrait of Aimata by Charles Giraud (official painter of the French protectorate), "Aimata, Reine Pomare," painted between 1842 and 1848 (oil on cardboard, 23 x 18 cm). It is held by the Musée des arts d'Afrique et Océania, Paris (AF15295). For more on Aimata, see Patrick O'Reilly, *La vie à Tahiti au temps de la Reine Pomare* (Paris: Société des Océanistes, 1975).

83. Conway Shipley, *Sketches in the Pacific: The South Sea Islands* (London: T. McLean, 1851), 14.

84. Ibid.

85. These could have been either Catholic or Protestant missionaries, as both were then resident on the island. Brassey and Stuart-Wortley, *Tahiti*, 4.

86. Blin, *Voyage en Océanie*, 204. "il y a deux boucheries où l'on trouve tous les jours de la viande de boeuf et de porc et quelquefois du mouton" (there are two butchers where you find, each day, beef, pork and sometimes lamb).

87. "A midshipman," Anson's voyage, 1767, quoted in Farrell, "The Alien and the Land," 129, 132.

88. Farrell, "The Alien and the Land," 53.

89. Lamb, ed., *Voyage of Discovery*, 734.

90. Vancouver had presented goats to the *ali'i* Keeaumoku of Kawaihae Bay, Hawai'i, on his earlier visit. Ibid., Feb. 1793, 799.

91. Being persuaded to approach one of the animals, says Manby, Kamehameha got a fright when it suddenly tossed its head, and "his Majesty . . . made a speedy retreat, and run over half his retinue." Cited in ibid., 812 n. 2.

92. Ibid., 812.

93. Ibid., 829.

94. Ibid., 1145.

95. Including the five cows landed in 1792.

96. County of Hawaii Department of Research and Development, *County of Hawaii Data Book. Section 6: Land Use*, web publication (2001, updated 2008); available from www.hawaii-county.com/databook_current/dbooktoc.htm.

97. J. Yanney Ewusie, *Elements of Tropical Ecology: With Reference to the African, Asian, Pacific and New World Tropics* (London: Heinemann, 1980), 155.

98. Ticks were not reported in Tahiti until 1907. Salvat, ed., *Flore Et Faune*, 102.

99. A. Grove Day, *History Makers of Hawaii: A Biographical Dictionary* (Honolulu: Mutual, 1984), 77.

100. Ibid., 73.

101. Lamb, ed., *Voyage of Discovery*, 813.

102. Ibid.

103. Reported by A. Menzies, 14 Jan. 1794, quoted in Lamb., ed. *Voyage of Discovery*, 1145–1146 n. 6.

104. Ibid., 1180.

105. Ibid.

106. E. H. Bryan, *The Hawaiian Chain* (Honolulu: Bishop Museum Press, 1954), 20.

107. Ewusie, *Tropical Ecology*, 64.

108. C. S. Lobban and M. Schefter, *Tropical Pacific Island Environments* (Mangilao, Guam: University of Guam Press, 1997), 251.

109. Howe, *Where the Waves Fall*, 163.

110. It has been estimated that the syphilis, gonorrhea, influenza, tuberculosis, and typhoid introduced into the island from Cook's voyage onwards reduced the Hawaiian population from an estimated 500,000 in 1779 to 84,000 in 1853. In that year smallpox arrived and killed another 10,000. Jared Diamond, *Guns, Germs and Steel: A Short History of Everybody for the Last 13,000 Years* (London: Vintage, 1998), 214, based on the work of D. Stannard (1989) and O. A. Bushnell (1993).

111. P. V. Kirch and M. Sahlins, *Anahulu: The Anthropology of History in the Kingdom of Hawaii*, vol. 1: *Historical Ethnography*, 2 vols. (Chicago and London: University of Chicago Press, 1992), 1:134.

112. Ibid.

113. The first shipment comprised a modest 158 barrels. "Hawaii's History in Tabloid," *Honolulu Mercury*, 1 July 1929.

114. Kirch and Sahlins, *Anahulu*, 1:134.

115. Charles Bishop, reporting in 1883, stated that the cattle and goats "eat the young trees, trample upon the roots and in various ways weaken or destroy even the larger trees. The birds, accustomed to dense shade and quiet of the woods, desert the places opened to the glaring light and drying rays of the sun, and the myriads of insects have it all their own way." From a report coauthored with Sanford B. Dole. Quoted in Nelson Foster, *Bishop Museum and the Changing World of Hawaii* (Honolulu: Bernice P. Bishop Museum Press, 1993), 97.

116. G. Spatz, and D. Mueller-Dombois, "The Influence of Feral Goats on Koa Tree Reproduction in Hawaii Volcanoes National Park," *Ecology* 54 (1973): 870–876.

117. Eroarome Martin Aregheore, Country Pasture/Forage Resource Profile: French Polynesia, Internet publication (Apia: University of the South Pacific, 2002, updated 2006), www.fao.org/ag/AGP/AGPC/doc/Counprof/Southpacific/FrenchPolynesia.htm.

118. Institut d'Emission d'Outre-Mer, *La Polynésie Française En 2000* (Pape-'ete: l'agence IEOM/Imprimeries réunies de Nouméa, 2000), 8.

Chapter 5: Breadfruit Connections

1. The phrase was an African slave's and was rendered by Tobin as "de ship da hab de bush." Tobin, Journal, 290.

2. Grove, *Green Imperialism*, 300, quoting from Alexander Anderson, "Geography and History of St Vincent" (M5, Linnaean Society, c.1800), transcription ed. R. A. and E. S. Howard, Harvard College, 5.

3. Counting ten months at sea for the *Bounty* to reach Tahiti (23 Dec. 1787–26 Oct. 1788), five months at the island plus the additional sailing time, nearly a month, before the mutiny. Along with the twenty-two months spent by the *Providence* and *Assistant* from embarking at Deptford (22 June 1791) to their return (2 Aug. 1793), and not counting the five months spent in Jamaica assisting the war effort.

4. David Mackay, "Banks, Bligh and Breadfruit," *New Zealand Journal of History* 8 no. 1 (1974): 61.

5. Byron, *The Island*, canto 1, verse X. Quoted in Tobin, Journal, 228.

6. Peter Bellwood, *The Polynesians: Prehistory of an Island People* (London: Thames & Hudson, 1987), 27–28.

7. There is evidence for Polynesian-style horticulture in Samoan valleys by 300 BC, and breadfruit is presumed to have been one of the staples of Southeast Asian origin that was being cultivated from this era onwards. Polynesian settlers are generally accepted to have migrated from Samoa to the Society Islands, taking their staple plants with them. Ibid., 29, 35, 56.

8. This traveling food was still being used by eighteenth-century voyagers such as Ma'i and Hitihiti, who took it with them when they joined Cook's ships.

9. Oliver, *Ancient Tahitian Society*, 236.

10. Henry E. Baum, *The Breadfruit: Together with a Biographical Sketch of the Author. . . From the Plant World* (Washington: H. L. McQueen, 1904), 226.

11. Published in English for the first time by Alexander Dalrymple, *An Historical Collection of the Several Voyages and Discoveries in the South Pacific Ocean* (London: J. Nourse, T. Payne, and P. Elmsley, 1770), 70.

12. Giles Milton, *A New Voyage Round the World: The Journal of an English Buccaneer (1697)* (London: Hummingbird Press, 1998), 272–273. With thanks to Stewart Wicksteed for bringing this reference to my attention.

13. Ibid., 272.

14. George Anson, *A Voyage Round the World in the Years MDCCXL, I, II, III, IV* (London: John and Paul Knapton, 1749), 310.

15. Beaglehole, ed., *Banks Journal*, 1:341.

16. Ibid.

17. John Hawkesworth, *An Account of the Voyages Undertaken . . . by Commodore*

Byron, Captain Wallis, Captain Carteret, and Captain Cook (London: W. Strahan and T. Cadell, 1773).

18. And hurried Hawkesworth into a fatal decline. For more on Hawkesworth and his *Account,* see John Abbott, *John Hawkesworth: Eighteenth-Century Man of Letters* (Madison: University of Wisconsin Press, 1982).

19. Henry Hobhouse, *Seeds of Change: Six Plants That Transformed Mankind* (London: Pan Books, 1999), 74.

20. Ibid.

21. Grove, *Green Imperialism,* 277.

22. Hobhouse, *Seeds of Change,* 68–69.

23. Grove, *Green Imperialism,* 264.

24. Jenyns was the leading proponent of the proposition that deforestation led to desiccation. Ibid., 265.

25. W. Young, letter/order of 22 Feb. 1765 (PRO CO 106/9), quoted in ibid., 273.

26. Grove, *Green Imperialism,* 272–273.

27. W. Young: "The rains are less frequent and the sea air pure and salutary by reason of its not yet being infected in its passage over hot and reeking woods . . . the heat and moisture of the woods are likely to be the chief obstructions to the [speedy settlement of the colony]." W. Young, letter/order of 22 Feb. 1765 (PRO CO 106/9), quoted in ibid., 273.

28. Anonymous watercolor, "Beaucarnon [?] Vale in the Island of St Vincents, A.S. [?] Wm Youngs estate . . . 1791[?]," Institute of Commonwealth Studies, London (WIC-103-32).

29. Peter Cotgreave and Irwin Forseth, *Introductory Ecology* (Oxford: Blackwell Science, 2002), 18, 204–205.

30. It was soon common knowledge that Jamaica was suffering from not being able to maintain provision crops in the face of frequent violent storms. Tobin noted this point in his Journal, 298.

31. S. Taylor to Sir J. Taylor from Kingston, 9 Aug. 1784. Institute of Commonwealth Studies, London (TAYL/1A).

32. Ibid.

33. Mackay, "Banks, Bligh and Breadfruit," 65.

34. V. Morris to J. Banks, Piccadilly, 13 April 1772. BL (Add. Ms 33977.18).

35. Ibid.

36. Richard Drayton, *Nature's Government: Science, Imperial Britain, and the "Improvement" of the World* (New Haven, Conn.: Yale University Press, 2000), 114.

37. He withdrew from the second Cook expedition before its departure from London when the expanded accommodations on the *Resolution* he had demanded were dismantled. They made the ship unseaworthy, as Cook had predicted.

38. See for instance, G. Yonge to J. Banks, Stratford Place, 29 June 1786. Banks Correspondence, RBGK Archives (1.235); H. East to J. Banks, Kingston, Jamaica, 1789. Banks Correspondence, RBGK Archives (1.19, 1.168, 1.342).

39. See for instance, H. East to J. Banks, 27 April 1789, RBGK Archives (1.342); A. Anderson to J. Banks, 30 March 1796, Dawson Turner collection, NHM (10.[1].25–28).

40. G. Yonge to J. Banks, Stratford Place, 27 Aug. 1787. Banks Correspondence, RBGK Archives (1.281): "I have also receivd Parcels of various seeds, which appear to be valuable, and which I shall send, with yours, next week to S. Vincents."

41. Quoted in Linda Colley, *Britons: Forging the Nation 1707–1837* (New Haven, Conn., and London: Yale University Press, 1992), 59.

42. Ibid, 60.

43. Salmond, *Trial*, 11.

44. L. Auckland to J. Banks, The Hague, 29 Dec. 1790. Botany Library NHM (DTC 7.184–185).

45. John Ellis, *A Description of the Mangostan and the Bread-Fruit the First, Esteemed One of the Most Delicious, the Other, the Most Useful of All the Fruits in the East-Indies: To Which Are Added, Directions to Voyagers, for Bringing over These and Other Vegetable Productions, Which Would Be Extremely Beneficial to the Inhabitants of Our West India Islands* (London: Printed for the author, sold by Edward and Charles Dilly, 1775).

46. With thanks to Nicholas Thomas for uncovering this obscure reference in John Nichols, *Illustrations of the Literary History of the Eighteenth Century* (London: 1817), 1:154. See Thomas, *Discoveries*, 275.

47. Sir Henry T. Wood, *A History of the Royal Society of Arts* (London: John Murray, 1913), 95; see also Gascoigne, *Joseph Banks*, 206–207.

48. Yonge to Banks, 29 June 1786. RBGK Archives (1.235).

49. H. East to J. Banks, Hinton East, Kingston, 12 July 1784. Banks correspondence, RBGK Archives (1, 168–169).

50. Carey Miller, *Food Value of Bread Fruit, Taro Leaves, Coconut, Sugar Cane, &c. Bernice P. Bishop Museum Bulletin* 64 (1929): 23.

51. Dening, *Mr Bligh's Bad Language*, 11.

52. Ibid.

53. Thomas, *Man and the Natural World*, 220.

54. Janet Browne, "Botany in the Boudoir and Garden; the Banksian Context," in *Visions of Empire; Voyages, Botany, and Representations of Nature*, ed. David Miller and Peter Reill, 155–156 (Cambridge: Cambridge University Press, 1996).

55. Ibid., 159.

56. Emma C. Spary, *Utopia's Garden: French Natural History from Old Regime to Revolution* (Chicago: University of Chicago Press, 2000), 129.

57. Drayton, *Nature's Government*, 114, drawing on manuscripts in the Bibliothèque Central du Muséum National d'Histoire Naturelle: "Pièces relative au Projet d'une Correspondance Agriculto-Botanique . . . ," ms 308 and a letter from the Minister La Luzerne to Thouin, 5 Jan 1788, ms 308, 1–3.

58. André Thouin, "Instruction pour le Jardinier de l'Expédition autour du monde de M. D'Entrecasteux," 1791. Quoted in Spary, *Utopia's Garden*, 130.

59. M. Wallen to J. Banks, Cold Spring, Jamaica, 6 May 1784, BL (Add. Ms 33977.267).

60. Drayton, *Nature's Government*, 114.

61. G. Yonge to J. Banks, Stratford Place, 3 Feb. 1787. Banks Correspondence, RBGK Archives (1.258).

62. Ibid.

63. Mackay, "Banks, Bligh and Breadfruit," 68–69.

64. Ibid., 69.

65. Admiralty, Letter Book 1784–1793. PRO (HO 29/2), 63 and verso.

66. J. Banks, Letter Regarding the Breadfruit Project (Draft), 30 March 1787. RS Library (MM6.60), 4th page.

67. Ibid., 5th page.

68. Ibid.

69. Ibid.

70. Bligh, *Bounty*, 4.

71. Ibid., 73.

72. George Forster noted that "not less than ten" had been traded for red feathers during their stay. Thomas and Berghof, eds., *Voyage*, 361–362. One of these is at the British Museum (Oc,Tah.72). Other *parae* may have been secured on the third voyage.

73. Bligh, *Bounty*, 76–77.

74. Ibid., 77.

75. Ibid., 82–83.

76. Quote from Rutter, ed., *Log of the Bounty*, 380.

77. Bligh, *Bounty*, 85.

78. Rutter, ed., *Journal of James Morrison*, 201–202.

79. G. P. Wilder, *The Breadfruit of Tahiti. Bernice P. Bishop Museum Bulletin* 50 (1928): 8.

80. Rutter, ed., *Journal of James Morrison*, 215–216.

81. Ibid.

82. William Ellis, *Polynesian Researches, During a Residence of Nearly Eight Years in the Society and Sandwich Islands*, 4 vols. (London: Fisher, Son & Jackson, 1831) 1:43.

83. Oliver, *Ancient Tahitian Society*, 241.

84. Ibid, 236; Rutter, ed., *Journal of James Morrison*, 214.

85. Oliver, *Ancient Tahitian Society*, 238.

86. Beaglehole, ed., *Banks Journal*, 1:345.

87. Rutter, ed., *Journal of James Morrison*, 215.

88. Pétard, *Plantes Utiles*, 148–149.

89. Henry, *Ancient Tahiti*, 424–425.

90. Ibid., 425.

91. Ibid., 425–426.

92. Bligh, *Bounty*, 86.

93. Ibid., 139.

94. Dening, *Mr Bligh's Bad Language*, 61, 80–81, 83–84.

95. Bligh put the men on reduced rations as a punishment for their allegedly stealing some of his coconuts. During the mutiny, when Bligh confronted one of the armed mutineers with "This is a serious affair, Mr. Young," Young agreed, "Yes sir, it is a serious matter to be starved. I hope this day you get a belly full." Richard Hough. *Captain Bligh and Mr Christian: The Men and the Mutiny* (London: Arrow Books, 1974), 158.

96. Nigel Rigby, "The Politics and Pragmatics of Seaborne Plant Transportation, 1769–1805," in *Science and Exploration in the Pacific: European Voyages to the Southern Oceans in the Eighteenth Century*, ed. Margarette Lincoln, 87 (Woodbridge, Suffolk: Boydell Press with the National Maritime Museum, 1998).

97. Rutter, *Journal of James Morrison*, 53.

98. Ibid., 51–64.

99. Hough, *Captain Bligh and Mr Christian*, 204.

100. Rutter, *Journal of James Morrison;* Dening, *Mr Bligh's Bad Language*, 213.

101. They arrived at Timor on 12 June. Hough, *Captain Bligh and Mr Christian*, 159–161, 171.

102. Dening, *Mr Bligh's Bad Language*, 9.

103. Hough, *Captain Bligh and Mr Christian*, 218.

104. G. Yonge to Banks, from Stratford Place, Sept., year obliterated (1790). Banks Collection, RBGK Archive (2.182). Dawson catalogues this letter as 1797 and it is bound in the Kew volume run of 1797. The year is not fully visible. However, the king's suggestion of a second voyage had to have come after the *Bounty* returned, so after March 1790, and *before* the second breadfruit voyage departed in August 1791.

105. Ibid.

106. Hough, *Captain Bligh and Mr Christian*, 218.

107. Bligh, *Log of the Providence*, 14 April 1792.

108. Ibid., 13 April 1792.

109. Bligh selected a place convenient to the mouth of the Matavai River and by the beach where the boats could easily pull up. It was not far from the breadfruit plains, offering plenty of young breadfruit shoots spreading out from their parent trees. Ibid.

110. Ibid., 14 April 1792.

111. Ibid., 17 April 1792.

112. Ibid., 2 May to 7 June 1792.

113. Ibid., 26 May 1792.

114. Ibid.

115. Ibid., 18 June 1792.

116. Ibid., 5 June, 28 June 1792.

117. Ibid., 11 June 1792.

118. Ibid.

119. Ibid., 23 June 1792.

120. Bligh reporting Tu's statement, ibid., 23 June 1792.

121. Ibid., 9 July 1792.

122. Ibid., 12 June 1792.

123. Tobin, Journal, 200.

124. Ibid., 198.

125. Bligh, *Log of the Providence*, 16 July 1792.

126. Ibid., 18 July 1792.

127. Tobin, Journal, 241.

128. George Tobin, "In Oparrey Harbour, Island of O'tayhtey," watercolor, 1792. Album: "Sketches on HMS Providence," State Library of NSW, Sydney (PXA 563, f.47); Tobin, Journal, 290.

129. Tobin, Journal, 238.

130. Bligh, *Log of the Providence*, 18 July 1792.

131. Tobin, Journal, 267.

132. Ibid., 246.

133. Ibid., 247.

134. See Newell, "Pacific Travelers."

135. In which several islanders were wounded and perhaps killed and several crewmen were hit with arrows, one of whom died. Tobin, Journal, 257–278; Bligh, *Log of the Providence*, 7 Sept. 1792.

136. Bligh, *Log of the Providence*, 2 Oct. 1792.

137. J. Banks, Instructions to J. Wiles and C. Smith, Gardeners on the Providence, 25 June 1791. NHM (DTC 10).

138. Banks, *Log of the Providence*, 23 Jan. 1793.

139. Tobin, Journal, 288.

140. Of these, 623 went to the large island of Jamaica. Henry Shirley, *Letter to William Bligh, 20 March 1793, Kingston, Jamaica* (London: Society for the Encouragement of Arts, Manufactures, and Commerce, 1794), 317.

141. Paupo moved into a residence with the botanist J. Wiles. Maititi went to stay with a colonist, Mr. Raymond, near Port Henderson. Tobin, Journal, 296.

142. Ibid.

143. W. Bligh to the Society for the Encouragement of Arts, Manufactures, and Commerce, 26 October 1793, Durham Place, Lambeth. NLA (NK 9559).

144. Tobin, Journal, 297.

145. J. Wiles to J. Banks, 16 Oct. 1793, Bath, Jamaica. Banks Collection, RBGK Archives (2.103).

146. Dulcie Powell, "The Voyage of the Plant Nursery, H.M.S. Providence 1791–1793," *Bulletin of the Institute of Jamaica,* Science Series 15 no. 2 (1973): 36.

147. Oliver, *Return to Tahiti,* 258.

148. Shirley, *Letter to Bligh.*

149. Karen Nero and Nicholas Thomas, eds., *An Account of the Pelew Islands, by George Keate,* The Literature of Travel, Exploration and Empire series (London: Continuum, 2002).

150. George Keate, "To Captain Bligh," *European Magazine,* Aug. 1794, 140.

151. Tobin, Journal, 298.

152. F. Blumenbach to J. Banks, Göttingen, 29 June 1794. BL (Add. Ms 8098.218).

153. Campaigns began in the 1780s and had gained momentum by the 1790s. The act to abolish slavery was passed in Britain in 1807.

154. W. Bligh to J. Banks, near St Helena 16/25 Dec. 1792. Mitchell Library, SLNSW (MS A78/4).

155. J. Wiles to J. Banks, 16 Oct 1793, Bath, Jamaica, Banks Collection, RBGK Archives (2.103).

156. Report from Wiles and C. Smith to M. Flinders, 30 June 1799, Prince Wales Island. Flinders correspondence, NMM (FLI/1).

157. A. Anderson to J. Banks, 30 March 1796, St Vincent. Dawson Turner collection, NHM (10.[1].25–28).

158. E. Ellcock to J. Banks, 4 June 1793. Barbados. Banks Collection, RBGK Archive (2.96).

159. A. Anderson to J. Banks, 30 March 1796, St Vincent. Dawson Turner collection, NHM (10.[1].25–28).

160. J. Wiles to J. Banks, 16 May 1801, Linguanca, Jamaica. Banks Collection, Kew Gardens Library, Kew (2.248).

161. J. Banks to Sir George L. Staunton, 24 Feb. 1793, London. RS Library (MM.19.120).

162. Joseph Sturge and Thomas Harvey, *The West Indies in 1837: Being the Journal of a Visit to Antigua, Montserrat, Dominica, St. Lucia, Barbados, and Jamaica; Undertaken for the Purpose of Ascertaining the Actual Condition of the Negro Population of Those Islands* (London: Hamilton, Adams, & Co., 1838), 179.

163. Ibid.

164. William Hooker, *Paris Universal Exhibition: Report on Vegetable Products Obtained without Cultivation* (London: George E. Eyre and William Spottiswoode, 1857).

165. Jamaica Agricultural Society, *The Journal of the Jamaica Agricultural Society* 1 no. 1 (1897): appendix 9, 29.

166. Austin Clarke, *Pig Tails 'n Breadfruit* (Toronto: Random House, 1999), 113.

167. Ibid.

Chapter 6: Pigs, Muskets, and a New Order

1. Adams, *Memoirs*, 154.

2. For accounts of the battle, see Oliver, *Ancient Tahitian Society*, 1346–1350.

3. Procedure described by Gov. Philip Gidley King, Instructions to Lieut. Scott, 20 May 1801, *HRA* 3, 138.

4. John Jefferson, Journal of the Missionaries proceedings on Otaheite, Jan 1–July 30 1801. SSJ, LMS/Church World Mission Archive, SOAS (box 1 folio 10) 21 July, 39.

5. Which Tobin wrote as *"Wahēēney"* and *"Bōa."* Tobin, Journal, 164.

6. Thomas and Berghof, eds., *Voyage*, 16 Aug. 1773, 145.

7. Carrington, ed. *Discovery of Tahiti*, 179.

8. Corney, ed,. *Quest and Occupation*, 2:272.

9. Along with dogs and chickens. Bellwood, *Polynesians*, 27–28.

10. Colin Groves, *Ancestors for the Pigs: Taxonomy and Phylogeny of the Genus Sus. Technical Bulletin* 3 (Canberra: Department of Prehistory, Australian National University, 1981).

11. Leach et al., "Fishing . . . and Mammal Exploitation," 189.

12. Corney, ed., *Quest and Occupation*, 2:298.

13. Beaglehole, ed., *Cook Journals 1776–1780*, 29 Sept. 1777, 223.

14. Ibid., 30 Oct. 1777, 238–239 and 8 Dec. 1777, 253. The pigs left at Ra'iatea were likely to have been one of the gifts Cook left with his *taio*, the *ari'i* Orio. He also left two goats.

15. Rutter, ed., *Log of the Bounty*, 376.

16. Lt. Edward Bell, in Lamb, ed., *Voyage of Discovery*, 1:394 n. 2.

17. Vancouver recorded receiving pigs of between 150 to 200 pounds (68 to 90 kg). Lamb, ed., *Voyage of Discovery*, 435.

18. Ellis, *Polynesian Researches* 1829, 1:349.

19. Ibid.

20. Oliver, *Ancient Tahitian Society*, 272.

21. Thomas and Berghof, eds., *Voyage*, 205.

22. Rutter ed., *Journal of James Morrison*, 165.

23. W. Anderson, in Beaglehole, ed., *Cook Journals 1772–1775*, 157.

24. William Wilson, *A Missionary Voyage to the Southern Pacific Ocean, Performed in the Years 1796–1798, in the Ship Duff, Commanded by Captain James Wilson* (London: T. Chapman, 1799), 192.

25. Henry, *Ancient Tahiti*, 282.

26. Ibid, 282–284.

27. Jefferson, Journal 1801, 1 April, 11.

28. Henry, *Ancient Tahiti*, 383.

29. Ibid.

30. British Museum object Oc,LMS, 120. See BM website or Hooper, *Pacific Encounters*, cat. 134.

31. Henry, *Ancient Tahiti*, 303. Cook also describes this ceremony in detail, Beaglehole, ed., *Cook Journals 1776–1780*, vol. 2, 31–44.

32. Henry, *Ancient Tahiti*, 303.

33. Ibid., 289.

34. He was left uncured after this and "apparently despairing of assistance from his gods," wanted to try some of the bark in the missionaries' medicine chest. Jefferson, Journal 1801, 20.

35. Henry, *Ancient Tahiti*, 289.

36. Beaglehole, ed., *Cook Journals 1769–1771*, 85–86.

37. Tobin, Journal, 199.

38. Beaglehole, ed., *Cook Journals 1772–1775*, 212.

39. Ibid., 383.

40. H. E. Maude, "The Tahitian Pork Trade: 1800–1830: An Episode in Australia's Commercial History," in *Of Islands and Men: Studies in Pacific History* (Melbourne: Oxford University Press, 1968), 184.

41. Pork rations amounted to four pounds (1.8 kg) a week per person on the normal scale. 2,365 people were on full rations on 1 March 1802. Ibid.

42. King took up the governorship after Hunter and was succeeded by Bligh in 1806.

43. A. G. L. Shaw, "King, Philip Gidley (1758–1808)," *Australian Dictionary of Biography* (Melbourne: Melbourne University Press, 1967), 2:55–61.

44. Governor Arthur Philip, "Commission," *HRA* 7, 794; Bourke to Stanley, 30 June 1834, *HRA*, 17, 750.

45. Maude, "Tahitian Pork Trade," 207.

46. For more on this phase, see Inga Clendinnen, *Dancing with Strangers* (Melbourne: Text Publishing, 2003); and Val Attenbrow, *Sydney's Aboriginal Past: Investigating the Archaeological and Historical Records* (Sydney: University of New South Wales Press, 2003).

47. Maude, "Tahitian Pork Trade," 183.

48. Ibid., 184.

49. John Turnbull, *A Voyage Round the World in the Years 1800–1804*, 2nd ed. (London: 1813), 83.

50. Jefferson, Journal 1800, 29.

51. Jefferson, Journal 1801, reproduced in LMS Transactions 1801, 1; 213–214.

52. Jefferson, Journal 1801, 2 July, 29.

53. P. G. King to LMS Missionaries, Tahiti, 20 May 1801, quoted in Jefferson, Journal 1801, 26 June, 24–25.

54. Jefferson, Journal 1800, 1 April, 18 June, 25 June, 22, 23.

55. Ibid., 22.

56. Howe, *Where the Waves Fall*, 136.

57. "That our personal safety is more endangered by such an influx of fire-arms, must be obvious to every one who considers our peculiar situation," Letter to the Directors, 12 Dec. 1804, London Missionary Society, *Transactions Missionary Society to the end of the year 1812* (London: Directors of the Missionary Society, 1813), 3:36–37.

58. Jefferson, Journal 1801, 28 verso.

59. Howe, *Where the Waves Fall*, 138.

60. Jefferson, Journal 1800, 21 May, 10.

61. Ibid., 10, 25.

62. Ibid., 29 Oct., 25.

63. Ibid.

64. Jefferson, Journal 1801, 29 June, 28.

65. Ibid., 27 June, 28.

66. Maude, "Tahitian Pork Trade," 185–186.

67. Ibid., 186.

68. Ibid., 188.

69. The traders were gathering mature pigs ("hogs"), weighing 150 to 200 pounds (68 to 91 kg) as well as the lighter, younger "pigs" (at the time the term only applied to the young animals). Once an animal was butchered and the bones and offal removed along with any pieces of meat that had failed to take the salt, the number of pounds from each animal was considerably less than its original weight.

70. Jefferson, Journal 1801, 15.

71. Ellis, *Polynesian Researches* 1829,1:112–113.

72. *Sydney Gazette,* 1 March 1803, quoted in Maude, "Tahitian Pork Trade," 192.

73. Calculated from the totals of pounds imported, recorded by Maude, "Tahitian Pork Trade," Appendix D, 226–232.

74. Ibid., 188.

75. Captain Wilson's population estimate. Cited in Peltzer, *Chronologie*, 27.

76. Jefferson, Journal 1804, 22.

77. Ibid., 44.

78. Howe, *Where the Waves Fall*, 138. The missionaries' account of the incident is quoted in Oliver, *Ancient Tahitian Society*, 1311.

79. Maude, "Tahitian Pork Trade," 191.

80. Turnbull, *Voyage Round the World*, 264.

81. LMS, *Transactions 1812*, 36.

82. Ellis, *Polynesian Researches* 1829, 1:142. The mate of the *Venus* was killed and the crew held until Captain Campbell and Pomare made a counterattack in October 1809. Newbury, *Tahiti Nui*, 30–31.

83. Maude, "Tahitian Pork Trade," 185. For further discussion of ways of

interpreting the intersection of the Pomare's management of power and the impact of Europeans and European trade, see Newbury, *Tahiti Nui*, 31–32.

84. Oliver, *Ancient Tahitian Society*, 1336–1337.

85. Newbury, *Tahiti Nui*, 32.

86. They were painfully aware of Pomare's profligate lifestyle and homosexual practices, and his condoning of human sacrifice and abortion. London Missionary Society, *Transactions of the Missionary Society for the Year 1803* (London: T. Williams, 1804), 2:144; Niel Gunson, *Messengers of Grace: Evangelical Missionaries in the South Seas* (Melbourne: Oxford University Press, 1978), 196.

87. W. Henry, "Letter from the Rev. Mr. Henry, one of the Missionaries at Otaheite, then on a visit to New South Wales, to the Directors. Parramatta, 17 June 1813," in LMS, *Transactions to 1817*, 12.

88. J. Davies, Eimeo/Mo'orea, 1813–1814. LMS/CWM Archive, SOAS (box 3 folio 35), 17 April 1814, unpaginated.

89. LMS, *Transactions to 1817*, 148.

90. J. M. Orsmond to Rev. T. Cuzens, 1849. Orsmond Papers, Mitchell Library, Sydney (Ms A2606), cited in Maude, "Tahitian Pork Trade," 218.

91. LMS, "Extract of the Missionaries' Public Letter to the Directors," in *Transactions to 1812*, 37–38.

92. Maude, "Tahitian Pork Trade," 200; *Sydney Gazette*, 9 Nov. 1819.

93. A letter published in the *Sydney Gazette*, 4 Jan. 1817; Baron Field, "The Judge's Report [9 Dec. 1819] of the trial . . . 1 December 1817, wherein the Revd. Samuel Marsden, Principal Chaplain of the Colony, was Plaintiff, and John Thomas Campbell, Esqre., Secretary to His Excellency Governor Macquarie, was Defendant." *HRA* 10 (1821): 444.

94. Ibid.

95. Ibid.

96. For the rise of Port Jackson, American, and other traders visiting New Zealand for timber getting, sealing, whaling, and flax harvesting from the 1790s to the first decades of the nineteenth century, see Salmond, *Between Worlds*, chapters 9–13. On other islands, see Howe, *Where the Waves Fall*.

97. Maude, "Tahitian Pork Trade," 218.

98. W. P. Crook, Journal of William Crook, Tahiti, 1821, SSJ, LMS/CWM Archives, SOAS (box 4 folio 58), 6 Feb.

99. Ibid., 23 Mar. 1821.

100. Pomare to S. P. Henry, June 1820. J. M. Orsmond, Letter Book, 1–42. MS translated by R. G. White. Quoted in Niel Gunson, "Pomare II of Tahiti and Polynesian Imperialism," *JPH* 4 (1969): 69; Maude, "Tahitian Pork Trade," 201.

101. Peltzer, *Chronologie*, 36.

102. J. M. Orsmond, Journal at Tahiti, Raiatea and Bora Bora 1820–1821, LMS/CWM Archives, SOAS (box 4 folio 55), 6 Oct 1820, 9.

103. Pomare to S. P. Henry, June 1820. J. M. Orsmond, Letter Book, 1:42. Trans. R. G. White. Quoted in Gunson, "Pomare II," 69.

104. Ernest Dodge, *Whaling off Tahiti* (Paris: Société des Océanistes, 1971).

105. John Davies, W. P. Crook and W. Ellis, Tahiti 1817, LMS/CWM Archives, SOAS (box 4 folio 44), 1; John Gyles, Journal, Eimeo [Mo'orea] and Tahiti, 1818–1819, LMS/CWM Archives, SOAS (box 4 folio 51); Oliver, *Ancient Tahitian Society*, 174, 252.

106. He had fought against Pomare in 1808 in alliance with Pa'ofa'i. He was one of the chiefs of the coalition that dealt with French ultimatums in 1841 and signed the treaty of 1842. Peltzer, *Chronologie*, 46, 47.

107. Hitoi (Regent) to the Marquess of Londonderry, Principal Secretary for Foreign Affairs, 26 Aug. 1822. Consular Dispatches and Papers, Tahiti and Society Islands, Foreign Office Records. PRO (FO/58/14).

108. E.g.: regulations (1823) III Concernant des cochons; XXI Dommages causés par les chiens ou les porcs; XXII, Concernant les sangliers et les cochons errants. Vahi Sylvia Richaud, ed., *Code des lois* (Tahiti: Ministère de la Culture de Polynésie française, 2001).

109. Brassey and Stuart-Wortley, *Tahiti*, 49.

110. Personal communication, Robert Koenig (Président de la Société des Etudes Océaniennes), Archives Territoriales, Tiperui, Tahiti, 5 Dec. 2003.

Conclusion

1. Personal communication, Dr. Katrina Proust, Canberra, 2004; K. M. Proust, "Learning from the Past for Sustainability: Towards an Integrated Approach" (PhD thesis, The Australian National University, 2004).

GLOSSARY

Sources: Anne D'Alleva's glossary in "Art and the Body Politic," 1996; Hank Dreissen, "From Ta'aroa to 'Oro," 1994; T. Henry, *Ancient Tahiti,* 1928; Douglas Oliver, *Ancient Tahitian Society,* 1974; P. Pétard, *Plantes utiles de Polynésie,* 1986; B. Salvat, ed., *Flore et Faune Terrestres,* 1986.

ali'i	Hawaiian chief or member of a chiefly lineage.
Ao	The earthly, light world of the living, as distinct from the *Po,* the intangible, dark world of the spirit.
'Apa'apa	A season, the "descent into the time of scarcity," from late June to early July.
'arevareva	*Urodynamis taitensis,* long-tailed cuckoo.
ari'i	Tahitian chief or member of chiefly lineage.
Ari'ipaia	Tu's brother, born c.1758.
ari'i rahi	The highest-ranking title in a district; paramount chief.
'arioi society	A group of initiated men and women who devoted themselves to the worship of 'Oro, primarily through music, dance, dramatic, and often sexual performance. The society had eight grades and each district throughout the Society Islands had an *'arioi* lodge.
ata	An animal, plant or feature of the landscape selected by a god as a place to manifest physically.
atua	A god.
aute	*Broussonetia papyrifera,* paper mulberry.
'ava	*Piper methysticum,* root with narcotic qualities, used to make *kava.*
Borabora	See Porapora.
Eimeo	An early name for the island neighboring Tahiti, called Mo'orea by the early nineteenth century.
Fa'a'a	District in the west of Tahiti, formerly part of Atahuru with Puna'auia and Pa'ea.
fa'aipoipora'a	Wedding ceremony for members of the elite.

fare	A house or building.
fare atua	Literally, "house" of the *atua* (god), a carved, wooden keeping-place for the *to'o*, a wrapped figure for containing the *atua*.
fenua	A subdivision of a district.
fe'e	Octopus.
fei	*Musa troglodytarum*, cooking banana which grows in the highlands.
hapa'a	A type of *tapa* (barkcloth) with cut and pasted decoration.
heiva	Entertainment usually including dance, theatrical, and comic performances.
iho	The essence or nature of a person.
iho-iho-tupu	"Growing essences," that is, the living essences of people in the *Ao*.
'Itia	A high-ranking woman (1760–1814), wife of Tu, mother of Pomare II, *ari'i* of the Pare-'Aure district, end of the eighteenth century.
kava	Narcotic drink made of the *'ava* root. In the eighteenth century, a drink of elites.
Kuku peti	*Cyranoramphus zelandicus*, black-fronted parakeet.
Leeward Islands	The western group of Society Islands, comprising Ra'iatea, Taha'a, Huahine, Porapora (Borabora), Tupai, and Maupiti.
LMS	London Missionary Society.
Ma'a Tahiti	Traditional Tahitian food.
mahi	Fermented breadfruit paste.
Ma'i	Member of the *ra'atira* land-owning class of Ra'iatea, born c.1753. Traveled with the second Cook voyage to England, returned to the Societies on the third voyage, 1777. Died c.1780.
Maititi	*Teuteu* of the Pomares, accompanied Bligh on the *Providence* voyage. Died London 1793.
mana	Ancestral power, influence. A sacred power that flows through an ancestral lineage.
manahune	"Commoners." A social class ranking below the *ari'i* and *ra'iatira*, usually tenants and workers to those two classes.
Maohi	"People of the land," the word by which Society Islanders referred (and often still refer) to themselves.
marae	A highly sacred, open-air ceremonial site. Typically consisted of a stone platform (*ahu*) and a paved area, the paving furnished with carved wooden boards and wooden platforms for offerings. The site of requests and consultations with gods and ancestors.

maro 'ura and *maro tea*	Red-feather and yellow-feather girdles, respectively. One of the most sacred items of regalia, only worn by the *ari'i rahi*.
Matavai Bay	Sheltered bay on the northwest coast of Tahiti. Anchoring place of many eighteenth-century European ships.
Maui	High-ranking god/demigod, often said to have fished up islands out of the sea.
Meho	*Porzana tabuensis,* spotless crake (rail), previously thought to be extinct. Sighted 1998 in Pirae, but killed by two cats.
Melanesia	Cultural-geographic region in the western Pacific, including Papua New Guinea, Solomon Islands, New Caledonia, Vanuatu. Comprises much of the "Near Oceania" cultural-geographic grouping that is used by an increasing number of Pacific scholars.
Micronesia	Cultural-geographic region to the north of Melanesia, including Guam, Palau, Truk, the Caroline Islands, and others. Part of the "Remote Oceania" cultural-geographic grouping that is used by an increasing number of Pacific scholars.
miro	*Thespesia populnea,* rose wood.
mo'ora oviri	*Anas peocilorhyncha,* gray duck.
Mo'orea	Island to the northwest of Tahiti. The chiefly lineages of Tahiti and Mo'orea were closely related. Called Eimeo before the nineteenth century.
noa	Profane.
'Oro	God of war. In the late eighteenth century, 'Oro was reportedly being worshipped in Ra'iatea, Tahiti, Mo'orea, and Taha'a.
'oromatua	Disembodied familial spirit or inferior god, sometimes malignant.
'oromatua-maita'i	Benevolent familial spirit.
Otaheite/ Otahytey	Eighteenth-century spellings of Tahiti. Early visitors did not realize the article *o* was a separate word.
Papara	District in the south of Tahiti, home of the Teva lineage and people.
parae	Mourning dress, worn during rites for high-ranking people.
Pare-'Arue	Two districts, usually spoken of as one, in northern Tahiti. Base of the Pomare lineage.
Paupo	*Teuteu* of the Pomares, accompanied Bligh on the *Providence* voyage. Died in Jamaica, 1793.
Po	The spirit world, a hidden realm of darkness as opposed to the earthly, light world of the living, *Ao.*
Poeno	Chief of Matavai.

Point Venus	Located at the edge of Matavai Bay. The site eighteenth-century Europeans favored for setting up camp.
Polynesia	Cultural-geographic region, covering a triangle from Hawai'i in the northern Pacific to Easter Island in the far eastern Pacific down to New Zealand to the southwest. Includes the Society Islands. Part of the "Remote Oceania" cultural-geographic grouping that is used by an increasing number of Pacific scholars.
Porapora	or Borabora. Island northwest of Tahiti, militarily dominant in the Leeward Group in the eighteenth century.
pua'a	*Sus scrofa,* pig.
Puna'auia	District on Tahiti's west coast.
Purau	*Hibsicus tiliaceus,* hibiscus.
ra'a	Sacred, consecrated.
Ra'atira	"Gentry." A social class of independent landowners who ranked between the *ari'i* and *manahune.*
raau Tahiti	Traditional medical knowledge and practice of Tahiti.
rahui	Timed restriction on the consumption of particular resources.
Ra'iatea	Largest island of the Leeward Islands group, and Polynesian ancestral center and spiritual homeland. Spoken of in legends of creation as the source of the Society Islands and their inhabitants, as well as the people of the Hawaiian archipelago, Aotearoa/New Zealand, and others. Home of the Tamatoa lineage, the most prestigious lineage in the Societies.
Rauava	Tahitian shrub, branches of which were used in the *āmo'a* ("head-freeing") rite.
Tahaa	Island within the same reef as Ra'iatea.
Tahiti	Largest of the Society Islands, located in the Windward group. Composed of two parts, the larger, Tahiti-nui ("big Tahiti") and the smaller, Tahiti-iti ("little Tahiti," also called Taiarapu) connected by an isthmus.
tahua	Priest.
Taiarapu	Tahiti's smaller part (also named Tahiti-iti), joined to the island's large part (Tahiti-nui) by an isthmus.
taio	Bond friend, established through the formal exchange of gifts and personal names, who took on the role of a relative.
Ta'aroa	Creator god. Creator of the known universe and its inhabitants.
Tane	High-ranking god. Reported to be worshipped particularly in Huahine in the late eighteenth century.

tane	A man.
tapa	Barkcloth, made of the beaten inner bark of the paper mulberry, breadfruit, or other tree.
tapu	Restricted; consecrated. Can describe a person, object, or place that is in contact with the divine.
taro	*Colocasia esculenta*, staple root vegetable.
taui	Gift exchange, with connotation of compensation.
taura	"Oracle"/priest
Tetiaroa	Group of coral atolls to the north of Tahiti. Used by the Pomare lineage as a resort.
teuteu	Social class of hereditary servants to the *ari'i*. Often mistranslated as "slaves."
Teva	Chiefdom. Geographic and political division within which a chief holds authority.
Tevea	*Rallus pacificus*, Tahiti rail. Extinct bird species.
Tī	*Cordyline fruticosa*, cordyline, plant with protective spiritual qualities.
tiare	*Gardenia taitensis*. Native to the island, with white waxy flowers with seven petals. The national flower of Tahiti. Also called *tiare Maohi*.
tifaifai	Appliquéd quilt. The sewing of quilts was introduced by missionary women in the nineteenth century. They were soon taken over by Tahitian women as a distinctively Tahitian form of expression.
ti'i	"Fetcher"—a carved figure into which *'oromatua* (spirits) could be called.
Ti'i-potua-ra'au	"Back-to-back-wood-fetchers." Stacked *ti'i* carved of a single log from a *marae*, erected for an *ari'i* to mark a boundary (usually of sacred land) or a *rahui*.
Tō	1. *Saccharum officinarum*, sugar cane. 2. Conception.
to'o	Figure for temporarily housing a god, usually a wooden or stone core covered with a wrapping of knotted coconut fiber, often with face, ears, arms, and navel delineated in knotted fiber.
Torome/Tete	*Prosobonia leucaptera*, Tahitian sandpiper. Extinct.
Tu	(Tu-nui-e-a'a-i-te-Atua. Also named Pomare I, Tina, and Vaira'atoa) c.1750–1804. Chief of Pare-'Arue districts. Husband of 'Itia.
tupapa'u	A corpse or a ghost.
tupapa'u mere	Bier for the display and mummification of a corpse.
Tuvava/tuava	*Psidium guajava* or *Psidium cattleanium*, Guava.
'umera	*Ipomoea batatas*, sweet potato.
unu	Carved wooden boards placed on the stone platform of a

	marae. Usually depicting birds and prongs said to represent the hand of the god.
uri	Dog.
uru	*Artocarpus incisa.* Refers to both the breadfruit tree and its fruit.
'utafare	Household. The basic social unit of the Society Islands. Arranged largely by family ties, sharing a compound of huts, cooperating in producing food and clothing. Each had its own *marae.*
u'upa	*Ptilinopus purpuratus,* Pigeon vert or gray-green fruit dove.
va'atama'i	War canoe. Double-hulled canoe with decorated prow, stern, and fighting platform.
vahine	A woman.
Vaitepiha Bay	Bay on Tahiti's peninsula (Taiarapu or Tahiti-iti) where the Vehiatua lineage resided. The Spanish missionaries and Máximo Rodríguez stayed there in 1774–1775, and Cook visited there on his third voyage in 1777.
varua	Spirit of a dead person.
vi	*Spondias dulcis,* Pomme Cythère or Tahitian apple.
vini	*Vini peruviana,* parakeet. Extinct.
Windward Islands	The eastern group of the Society Islands, comprising Tahiti, Mo'orea, Tetiaroa, Meetia, and Maiao.

BIBLIOGRAPHY

Abbott, John. *John Hawkesworth: Eighteenth-Century Man of Letters.* Madison: University of Wisconsin Press, 1982.

Adams, Henry. *Memoirs of Arii Taimai e Marama of Eimeo, Teriirere of Tooarai, Terrinui of Tahiti, Tauraatua i Amo.* Paris: H. Adams, 1901.

Adams, Mark, and Nicholas Thomas, *Cook's Sites: Revisiting History.* Dunedin: University of Otago Press with Centre for Cross-Cultural Research, ANU, 1999.

Admiralty Records, ADM and HO series, Public Record Office, Kew (HO 29/2).

Aiton, W. T. *An Epitome of the Second Edition of Hortus Kewensis, for the Use of Practical Gardeners, to Which is Added, a Selection of Esculent Vegetables and Fruits Cultivated in the Royal Gardens at Kew.* London: Longman, Hurst, Rees, Orme and Brown, 1814.

Anson, George. *A Voyage Round the World in the Years MDCCXL I, II, III, IV.* London: John and Paul Knapton, 1749.

Aregheore, Eroarome Martin. Country Pasture/Forage Resource Profile: French Polynesia. Report, 2002. www.fao.org/ag/AGP/AGPC/doc/Counprof/Southpacific/FrenchPolynesia.htm.

Attenbrow, Val. *Sydney's Aboriginal Past: Investigating the Archaeological and Historical Records.* Sydney: University of New South Wales Press, 2003.

Babadzan, Alain. *Les Dépouilles des Dieux: Essai sur le religion tahitienne à l'époque de la découverte.* Paris: Fondation de la Maison des sciences de l'homme, 1993.

Banks, Joseph. Correspondence, British Library, London (Add. Ms 33977.18; 33977.267; 8098.218).

―――. Correspondence, Dawson Turner Collection. Natural History Museum, London, (DTC 10; 7.184–185; 10.[1].25–28; 11.213–214).

―――. Correspondence. Royal Botanic Gardens Kew Archives, Kew (1.19; 1.168–169; 1.235; 1.281; 1.342; 2.96, 2.103; 2.182; 2.248).

―――. Correspondence. Royal Society Library, London (MM6.60; MM.19. 120).

―――. Correspondence. State Library of NSW (MS A78/4).

Barratt, Glynn. *The Tuamotu Islands and Tahiti. Vol. 4 of Russia and the South Pacific, 1696–1840.* Vancouver: UBC Press, 1992.

Barrau, J. *Useful Plants of Tahiti.* Paris: Société des Océanistes, 1971.

Baum, Henry E. *The Breadfruit: Together with a Biographical Sketch of the Author . . . From the Plant World.* Washington: H. L. McQueen, 1904.

Beaglehole, J. C., ed. *The Endeavour Journal of Joseph Banks 1768–1771.* 2 vols. Sydney: Public Library of NSW and Angus & Robertson, 1963.

———, ed. *The Journals of Captain James Cook.* 4 vols. Vol. 1, *Journal of the Voyage of the Endeavour 1769–1771;* vol. 2, *Journal of the Resolution and the Adventure 1772–1775;* vols. 3 and 4, *The Voyage of the Resolution and Discovery 1776–1780.* Cambridge: Cambridge University Press and the Hakluyt Society, 1955–1967.

Bellwood, Peter. *The Polynesians: Prehistory of an Island People.* London: Thames & Hudson, 1987.

Bligh, William. Correspondence, 1793. Petherick Collection, National Library of Australia, Canberra.

———. Letter to the Society for the Encouragement of Arts, Manufactures, and Commerce, 26 October 1793, Durham Place, Lambeth. NLA (NK 9559).

———. *The Log of the* Bounty *1787–1789.* Facsimile edition. Guilford, Surrey: Genesis Publications, 1975.

———. Log of H.M.S. *Providence,* 1791–1793. PRO (ADM 55/151).

———. *The Log of H.M.S.* Providence *1791–1793.* Facsimile ed. Guilford, Surrey: Genesis Publications, 1976.

———. *A Voyage to the South Sea, Undertaken by Command of His Majesty, for the Purpose of Conveying the Breadfruit Tree to the West Indies, in His Majesty's Ship the* Bounty. London: G. Nicol, 1792.

Blin, Charles. *Voyage en Océanie.* Le Mans: Leguicheux Gallienne, 1881.

Borofsky, Robert, ed. *Remembrance of Pacific Pasts: An Invitation to Remake History.* Honolulu: University of Hawai'i Press, 2000.

Borsay, Peter. "The Culture of Improvement." In *The Eighteenth Century 1688–1815,* edited by Paul Langford, 183–210. Oxford: Oxford University Press, 2002.

Bowes, Arthur. Journal of Arthur Bowes, Surgeon of the Convict Transport *Lady Penrhyn* on a Voyage from Portsmouth to Botany Bay, 1787–1789. BL (Add. Ms 47966).

Brassey, Lady, and Colonel Stuart-Wortley. *Tahiti: A Series of Photographs Taken by Colonel Stuart-Wortley with Letterpress by Lady Brassey.* London: Sampson Low, Marston, Searle and Rivington, 1882.

Browne, Janet. "Botany in the Boudoir and Garden: The Banksian Context." In *Visions of Empire: Voyages, Botany, and Representations of Nature,* edited by David Miller and Peter Reill, 153–172. Cambridge: Cambridge University Press, 1996.

Bruner, Phillip L. *Field Guide to the Birds of French Polynesia.* Honolulu: Pacific Scientific Information Center, Bernice P. Bishop Museum, 1972.

Bryan, E. H. *The Hawaiian Chain.* Honolulu: Bishop Museum Press, 1954.

Byron, Lord George. *The Island: Or, Christian and His Comrades.* London: John Hunt, 1823.

Carrington, Hugh, ed. *The Discovery of Tahiti: A Journal of the Second Voyage of HMS* Dolphin *Round the World, under the Command of Captain Wallis, RN, in the Years 1766, 1767 and 1768, Written by Her Master, George Robertson.* London: Hakluyt Society, 1948.

Carter, Harold. "Note on the Drawings by an Unknown Artist from the Voyage of HMS *Endeavour.*" In *Science and Exploration in the Pacific: European Voyages to the Southern Oceans in the Eighteenth Century,* edited by Margarette Lincoln, 132–134. Woodbridge, Suffolk: Boydell Press with the National Maritime Museum, 1998.

Cathcart, Michael, Tom Griffiths, G. Houghton, V. Anceschi, L. Watts, and D. Goodman, eds. *Mission to the South Seas: The Voyage of the Duff, 1796–1799.* Melbourne University History Monographs 11. Parkville, Vic.: Melbourne University, 1990.

Chabouis, L. et F. *Petite Histoire Naturelle des Établissements Français de l'Océanie: Zoologie.* 2 vols. Cher: Imprimerie Bussière, 1954.

Chambers, Neil, ed. *The Letters of Sir Joseph Banks: A Selection, 1768–1820.* London: Imperial College Press, 2000.

Chard, Chloe, and Helen Langdon, eds. *Transports: Travel, Pleasure and Imaginative Geography 1600–1830.* New Haven, Conn., and London: Yale University Press, 1996.

Clarke, Austin. *Pig Tails 'n Breadfruit.* Toronto: Random House, 1999.

Clendinnen, Inga. *Dancing with Strangers.* Melbourne: Text Publishing, 2003.

Coffin, David. *The English Garden: Meditation and Memorial.* Princeton, N.J.: Princeton University Press, 1994.

Colley, Linda. *Britons: Forging the Nation 1707–1837.* New Haven, Conn., and London: Yale University Press, 1992.

Corney, Bolton Glanville, ed. *The Quest and Occupation of Tahiti by Emissaries of Spain During the Years 1772–1776, Told in Dispatches and Other Contemporary Documents.* 3 vols. London: Hakluyt Society, 1913–1919.

Cotgreave, Peter, and Irwin Forseth. *Introductory Ecology.* Oxford: Blackwell Science, 2002.

County of Hawaii Department of Research and Development. "County of Hawaii Data Book. Section 6: Land Use." 2004. www.hawaiicounty.com/databook _current/dbooktoc.htm.

Craighill Handy, E. S. *History and Culture in the Society Islands, Bernice P. Bishop Museum Bulletin* 79 (1971).

Crocombe, R. G. "Land Tenure in the South Pacific." In *Man in the Pacific Islands: Essays on Geographical Change in the Pacific Islands,* edited by R. Gerard Ward, 219–251. Oxford: Clarendon Press, 1972.

Cronon, William. *Changes in the Land: Indians, Colonists, and the Ecology of New England.* New York: Hill and Wang, 1983.

————. "A Place for Stories: Nature, History and Narrative." *Journal of American History* 78 (1992): 1347–1376.

————. *Uncommon Ground: Toward Reinventing Nature.* New York: W. W. Norton & Co., 1996.

Crook, W. P. Journal of William Crook, Tahiti, 1821. SSJ, LMS/CWM Archives, SOAS (box 4 folio 58).

Crosby, Alfred W. *Ecological Imperialism: The Biological Expansion of Europe 900–1900.* Cambridge: Canto, 1986.

Cuzent, Gilbert. *Îles de la Société: Considérations Géologiques, Météorologiques Et Botaniques Sur l'Île.* Pape'ete: Éditions Haere Po No Tahiti, 1983 (Orig. ed. 1860).

D'Alleva, Anne. "Continuity and Change in Decorated Barkcloth from Bligh's Second Breadfruit Voyage, 1791–1793." *Pacific Arts* 11–12 (1995): 29–42.

————. "Framing the 'Ahu Fara: Clothing, Gift-Giving and Painting in Tahiti." Paper presented on 23 June 2003 at the "Translating Things: Clothing and Innovation in the Pacific" conference, UCL, 23–25 June 2003.

————. "Shaping the Body Politic: Gender, Status and Power in the Art of Eighteenth Century Tahiti and the Society Islands." PhD dissertation, Columbia University, 1996.

Dalrymple, Alexander. *An Historical Collection of the Several Voyages and Discoveries in the South Pacific Ocean.* London: J. Nourse, T. Payne and P. Elmsley, 1770.

Daly, Martin. "'How Valuable a Horse Would Be Here': The Introduction of the Horse to Tonga." *Journal of Pacific History* 38 no. 2 (2003): 269–274.

Dancer, James. Abstract of an Oration Deliver'd at a Board of Directors under the New Act (1789) Respecting the Bath & the Botanic Garden in Jamaica by J. Dancer M.D. Island Botanist, 1 March 1790. BL (Add. Mss 22678).

D'Arcy, Paul. *The People of the Sea: Environment, Identity and History in Oceania.* Honolulu: University of Hawai'i Press, 2006.

Darnton, Robert. *The Great Cat Massacre: And Other Episodes in French Cultural History.* New York: Vintage Books, 1985.

Davies, John. Eimeo/Mo'orea 1813–1814. SSJ, LMS/CWM Archive, SOAS (box 3 folio 35).

————. A Journal of the Missionaries Proceedings on Tahiti, 1807–1808. SSJ, LMS/CWM Archive, SOAS (box 3 folio 31).

Davies, John, W. P. Crook, and W. Ellis. Tahiti 1817, LMS/CWM Archives, SOAS (box 4 folio 44).

Daws, Gavan. *A Dream of Islands: Voyages of Self-Discovery in the South Seas: John Williams, Herman Melville, Walter Murray Gibson, Robert Louis Stevenson, Paul Gauguin.* Milton, Qld.: Jacaranda Press, 1980.

Day, A. Grove. *History Makers of Hawaii: A Biographical Dictionary.* Honolulu: Mutual, 1984.

Dening, Greg. "Ethnohistory in Polynesia." In *Essays from the Journal of Pacific History*, edited by Barrie MacDonald, 49–68. Palmerston North, N.Z., 1979.

———. *Islands and Beaches: Discourse on a Silent Land. Marquesas 1774–1880.* Honolulu: University of Hawai'i Press, 1980.

———. *Mr Bligh's Bad Language: Passion, Power, and Theatre on the* Bounty. Cambridge: Cambridge University Press, 1992.

———. *Performances.* Chicago: University of Chicago Press, 1996.

Denoon, Donald, Stewart Firth, and Jocelyn Linnekin, eds. *The Cambridge History of the Pacific Islanders.* Cambridge: Cambridge University Press, 1997.

Diamond, Jared. *Guns, Germs and Steel: A Short History of Everybody for the Last 13,000 Years.* London: Vintage, 1998.

Dodge, Ernest. *Whaling Off Tahiti.* Paris: Société des Océanistes, 1971.

Drayton, Richard. *Nature's Government: Science, Imperial Britain, and the "Improvement" of the World.* New Haven, Conn.: Yale University Press, 2000.

Driessen, Hank. "From Ta'aroa to 'Oro: An Exploration of Themes in the Traditional Culture and History of the Leeward Society Islands." PhD thesis, ANU, 1991.

———. "Outriggerless Canoes and Glorious Beings: Pre-contact Prophecies in the Society Islands." *Journal of Pacific History* 17 (1982): 3–28.

Dunmore, John. *Visions and Realities: France in the Pacific 1695–1995.* Waikane, Hawai'i: Heritage Press, 1997.

———, ed. *The Pacific Journal of Louis-Antoine De Bougainville 1767–1768.* London: Hakluyt Society, 2002.

Ehrlich, Celia. "'Inedible' to 'Edible': Firewalking and the *Ti* Plant (Cordyline Fructicosa [L.] A. Chev.)" *Journal of the Polynesian Society* 110 no. 4 (2000): 371–400.

Elder, James, and Charles Wilson, Journal Round Tyerrabboo [Taiarapu], 28 June–1 August, 1803, SSJ, LMS/CWM Archive, SOAS (box 1 folio 14), 30 July 1803, 13.

Ellis, John. *A Description of the Mangostan and the Bread-Fruit the First, Esteemed One of the Most Delicious, the Other, the Most Useful of All the Fruits in the East-Indies: To Which Are Added, Directions to Voyagers, for Bringing over These and Other Vegetable Productions, Which Would Be Extremely Beneficial to the Inhabitants of Our West India Islands.* London: Edward and Charles Dilly, 1775.

———. *Directions for Bringing over Seeds and Plants, from the East Indies and Other Distant Countries in a State of Vegetation: Together with a Catalogue of Such Foreign Plants as Are Worthy of Being Encouraged in Our American Colonies, for the Purposes of Medicine, Agriculture, and Commerce.* London, L. Davis, 1770.

Ellis, William. *An Authentic Narrative of a Voyage Performed by Captain Cook and Captain Clerke.* 2 vols. London: Robinson et al., 1782.

———. *Polynesian Researches, During a Residence of Nearly Eight Years in the Society and Sandwich Islands.* 4 vols. London: Fisher, Son & Jackson, 1831.

————. *Polynesian Researches, During a Residence of Nearly Six Years in the South Sea Islands.* 2 vols. London: Fisher, Son & Jackson, 1829.

Ewusie, J. Yanney. *Elements of Tropical Ecology: With Reference to the African, Asian, Pacific and New World Tropics.* London: Heinemann, 1980.

Farrell, B. H. "The Alien and the Land of Oceania." In *Man in the Pacific Islands,* edited by R. G. Ward, 34–73. Oxford: Clarendon, 1972.

Field, Baron. "The Judge's Report (1819) of the Trial . . . 1 December 1817, Wherein the Revd. Samuel Marsden, Principal Chaplain of the Colony, Was Plaintiff, and John Thomas Campbell, Esqre, Secretary to His Excellency Governor Macquarie, Was Defendant." *Historical Records of Australia* 10 (1821): 443–447.

Fitzpatrick, Martin, Nicholas Thomas, and Jennifer Newell, eds. *The Death of Captain Cook and Other Writings by David Samwell.* Cardiff: University of Wales Press, 2007.

Flinders, Matthew. Personal Letters, 1800–1814. NMM (FLI/1).

Florence, Jacques. *Flore de la Polynésie française.* Paris: Éditions de l'Orstom, 1997.

Foster, Nelson. *Bishop Museum and the Changing World of Hawaii.* Honolulu: Bernice P. Bishop Museum Press, 1993.

Fothergill, John. *Directions for Taking up Plants and Shrubs and Conveying Them by Sea.* London, 1796.

Gascoigne, John. *Joseph Banks and the English Enlightenment: Useful Knowledge and Polite Culture.* Melbourne: Cambridge University Press, 1994.

Gilpin, William. *Three Essays: On Picturesque Beauty; on Picturesque Travel; and on Sketching Landscape.* London: R. Blamire, 1792.

Grenfell Price, A. *The Western Invasions of the Pacific and Its Continents: A Study of Moving Frontiers and Changing Landscapes, 1513–1958.* Oxford: Clarendon Press, 1963.

Griffiths, Tom. *Forests of Ash: An Environmental History.* Cambridge and Melbourne: Cambridge University Press, 2001.

————. "The Voyage." In *Mission to the South Seas: The Voyage of the Duff, 1796–1799,* edited by M. Cathcart et al., 33–52. Melbourne University History Monographs 11 (1990).

Griffiths, Tom, and Libby Robin, eds. *Ecology and Empire: Environmental History of Settler Societies.* Edinburgh: Keele University Press, 1997.

Grove, Richard. *Green Imperialism: Colonial Expansion, Tropical Island Edens and the Origins of Environmentalism 1600–1800.* Cambridge: Cambridge University Press, 1995.

Groves, Colin. *Ancestors for the Pigs: Taxonomy and Phylogeny of the Genus Sus.* Technical Bulletin 3. Canberra: Department of Prehistory, Australian National University, 1981.

Gunson, Niel. "Gyles, John (–1827)." In *Australian Dictionary of Biography,* 1:495–496. Carlton: Melbourne University Press, 1966.

———. *Messengers of Grace: Evangelical Missionaries in the South Seas.* Melbourne: Oxford University Press, 1978.

———. "Pomare II of Tahiti and Polynesian Imperialism." *Journal of Pacific History* 4 (1969): 65–82.

Gyles, John. Journal, Eimeo [Moʻorea] and Tahiti, 1818–1819, LMS/CWM Archives, SOAS (box 4 folio 51).

Hammond, L. Davis, ed. *News from New Cythera: A Report of Bougainville's Voyage 1766–1769.* Minneapolis: University of Minnesota Press, 1970.

Hassall, Rowland. Account of the Tahitian Mission, 1796–1799. SSJ, LMS/CWM Archives, SOAS (box 1 folio 2).

Hauʻofa, Epeli. "Our Sea of Islands." *Contemporary Pacific* 6 (1994): 146–161.

———. "Pasts to Remember." In *Remembrance of Pacific Pasts,* edited by R. Borofsky, 453–471. Honolulu: University of Hawaiʻi Press, 2000.

———. *Tales of the Tikongs.* Honolulu: University of Hawaiʻi Press, 1994.

———. *We Are the Ocean: Selected Works.* Honolulu: University of Hawaiʻi Press, 2008.

Hawkesworth, John. *An Account of the Voyages Undertaken by the Order of His Present Majesty, for Making Discoveries in the Southern Hemisphere, and Successively Performed by Commodore Byron, Captain Wallis, Captain Carteret, and Captain Cook.* London: W. Strahan and T. Cadell, 1773.

Hayward, James, Henry Nott, William Scott, and Charles Wilson. A Journal of the Proceedings at Taheite after the Departure of the Perseverance 10 November 1808 to 7 January 1809. SSJ, LMS/CWM Archives, SOAS (box 3 folio 34).

Henry, Teuira. *Ancient Tahiti, by Teuira Henry Based on Material Recorded by J. M. Orsmond. Bernice P. Bishop Museum Bulletin* 48 (1928).

Henry, William. Early Days on Tahiti, 1797. SSJ, LMS/CWM Archives, SOAS (box 1 folio 3).

Hereniko, Vilsoni, prod. *The Land Has Eyes/Pear ta ma 'on maf,* feature film. Honolulu: Te Maka Productions, 2004.

Hitoi (Regent) to the Marquess of Londonderry, Principal Secretary for Foreign Affairs, 26 Aug. 1822. Consular Dispatches and Papers, Tahiti and Society Islands, Foreign Office Records. PRO (FO/58/14).

Hoare, Michael E., ed. *The Resolution Journal of Johann Reinhold Forster: 1772–1775.* 4 vols. London: Hakluyt Society, 1982.

Hobhouse, Henry. *Seeds of Change: Six Plants That Transformed Mankind.* London: Pan Books, 1999.

Honolulu Mercury. "Hawaii's History in Tabloid." 1 July 1929, 91–96.

Hooker, Sir William. *Paris Universal Exhibition: Report on Vegetable Products Obtained without Cultivation.* London: George E. Eyre and William Spottiswoode, 1857.

Hooper, Beverley, ed. *With Captain James Cook in the Antarctic and Pacific: The*

Private Journal of James Burney Second Lieutenant of the Adventure on Cook's Second Voyage 1772–1773. Canberra: National Library of Australia, 1975.

Hooper, Steven. *Pacific Encounters: Art and Divinity in Polynesia, 1760–1860.* London: British Museum Press, 2006.

Hough, Richard. *Captain Bligh and Mr Christian: The Men and the Mutiny.* London: Arrow Books, 1974.

Howe, K. R. *Nature, Culture and History: The "Knowing" of Oceania.* Honolulu: University of Hawai'i Press, 2000.

———. *Where the Waves Fall: A New South Sea Islands History from First Settlement to Colonial Rule.* Pacific Islands Monograph Series. Honolulu: University of Hawai'i Press, 1984.

Hulme, Peter, and Ludmilla Jordanova, eds. *The Enlightenment and Its Shadows.* London: Routledge, 1990.

Institut d'Emission d'Outre-Mer. *La Polynésie Française En 2000.* Pape'ete: l'agence IEOM/Imprimeries réunies de Nouméa, 2000.

Irwin, Geoffrey. "Voyaging and Settlement." In *Vaka Moana: Voyages of the Ancestors: The Discovery and Settlement of the Pacific,* ed. K. R. Howe, 55–91. Auckland: Auckland War Memorial Museum and David Bateman, 2008.

ISSG. Global Invasive Species Database. Web database. http://www.issg.org/database/species/.

Jacquier, H. "Enumérarion des Plantes Introduites à Tahiti Depuis le Découverte Jusqu'en 1885." *Bulletin de la Société des Études Océaniennes* 1 no. 5 (1960): 117–146.

Jamaica Agricultural Society. *Journal of the Jamaica Agricultural Society* 1 no. 1 (1897).

Jefferson, John. Journals of the Missionaries Proceedings on Otaheite 1799–1804. SSJ, LMS/CWM Archives, SOAS (box 1 folios 6, 7, 10, 13, and box 2 folio 22).

Joppien, Rüdiger, and Bernard Smith. *The Art of Captain Cook's Voyages.* 3 vols. New Haven, Conn., and London: Paul Mellon Centre for Studies in British Art and Yale University Press, 1985–1988.

Keate, George. "To Captain Bligh." *European Magazine,* Aug. 1794.

King, Gov. Philip Gidley. Instructions to Lieut. Scott, 20 May 1801, *Historical Records of Australia,* 3, 138.

——— to Portland, 1 March 1802, *Historical Records of Australia,* 3, 432–433.

Kippis, Andrew. *A Narrative of Voyages Round the World, Performed by Captain James Cook, with an Account of His Life, During the Previous and Intervening Periods.* London: Carpenter & Son, 1814 (1st ed. 1788).

Kirch, Patrick V. "Epilogue: Islands as Microcosms of Global Change?" In *Historical Ecology in the Pacific Islands: Prehistoric Environmental and Landscape Change,* edited by Patrick V. Kirch and Terry L. Hunt, 284–286. New Haven, Conn., and London: Yale University Press, 1997.

———. "Introduction." In *Historical Ecology in the Pacific Islands: Prehistoric Envi-*

ronmental and Landscape Change, edited by Patrick V. Kirch and Terry L. Hunt, 1–21. New Haven, Conn., and London: Yale University Press, 1997.

———. *The Wet and the Dry: Irrigation and Agricultural Intensification in Polynesia.* Chicago and London: University of Chicago Press, 1994.

Kirch, Patrick V., and Marshall Sahlins. *Anahulu: The Anthropology of History in the Kingdom of Hawaii,* vol. 1: *Historical Ethnography.* 2 vols. Chicago and London: University of Chicago Press, 1992.

Kirch, Patrick V., and Terry Hunt, eds. *Historical Ecology in the Pacific Islands: Prehistoric Environmental and Landscape Change.* New Haven, Conn., and London: Yale University Press, 1997.

Koerner, Lisbet. "Nature and Nation in Linnean Travel." In *Visions of Empire: Voyages, Botany, and Representations of Nature,* edited by David Miller and Peter Reill, 117–135. Cambridge: Cambridge University Press, 1996.

Lamb, Jonathan. "The Place of Property in the South Seas Narrative." Paper given at the Exploring Text and Travel Conference, National Maritime Museum, Greenwich, 12 March 2005.

———. *Preserving the Self in the South Seas 1680–1840.* Chicago and London: University of Chicago Press, 2001.

——— et al., eds. *The South Pacific in the Eighteenth Century: Narratives and Myths.* Special Issue of *Eighteenth Century Life* 18 no. 3 (1994).

Lamb, W. Kaye. *A Voyage of Discovery to the North Pacific Ocean and Round the World, 1791–1795* [by George Vancouver]. 4 vols. London: Hakluyt Society, 1984.

Langdon, Robert. "The Banana as a Key to Early American and Polynesian History." *Journal of Pacific History* 28 no. 1 (1993): 15–35.

———. "When the Blue-Egg Chickens Come Home to Roost." *Journal of Pacific History* 24 (1989): 164–192.

Lavondès, Anne, ed. *Encyclopédie de la Polynésie,* 5. Pape'ete: Christian Gleizal/ Multipress, 1986.

Leach, B. F., M. Intoh, and I. W. G. Smith. "Fishing, Turtle Hunting, and Mammal Exploitation at Fa'ahia, Huahine, French Polynesia." *Journal de la Société des Océanistes* 40 no. 79 (1984): 183–197.

Le Clerc, G. L. *Barr's Buffon: Buffon's Natural History, Containing a Theory of the Earth, a General History of Man, of the Brute Creation, and of Vegetables, Minerals, &c.* English ed. London: H. D. Symonds, 1797.

Lepofsky, Dana Sue. "Prehistoric Agricultural Intensification in the Society Islands, French Polynesia." PhD dissertation, University of California at Los Angeles, 1995.

Levy, Robert. *Tahitians: Mind and Experience in the Society Islands.* Chicago: University of Chicago Press, 1973.

Lincoln, Margarette, ed. *Science and Exploration in the Pacific: European Voyages to the Southern Oceans in the Eighteenth Century.* Woodbridge, Suffolk: Boydell Press with the NMM, 1998.

Lobban, C. S., and M. Schefter, *Tropical Pacific Island Environments*. Mangilao, Guam: University of Guam Press, 1997.

London Missionary Society. Journal of the Missionaries Proceedings at Tahiti, 1808. SSJ, LMS/CWM Archives, SOAS (box 3 folio 33).

————. *Narrative of the Mission at Otaheite and Other Islands in the South Seas; Commenced by the London Missionary Society in the Year 1797*. London: J. Dennett, 1818.

————. *Transactions of the Missionary Society for the Year 1803*, 2. London: T. Williams, 1804.

————. *Transactions of the Missionary Society to the End of the Year 1812*, 3. London: J. Dennett, 1813.

————. *Transactions of the Missionary Society to the End of the Year 1817*. London: Directors of the Missionary Society, 1818.

[Lucett, E.]. *Rovings in the Pacific from 1837 to 1849; With a Glance at California, By a Merchant Long Resident at Tahiti*. 2 vols. London: Longman, Brown, Green and Longmans, 1851.

Mackay, David. "Banks, Bligh and Breadfruit." *New Zealand Journal of History* 8 no. 1 (1974): 61–77.

Marshall, P. J., and Glyndwr Williams. *The Great Map of Mankind: British Perceptions of the World in the Age of Enlightenment*. London, Melbourne, Toronto: J. M. Dent and Sons, 1982.

Martin, Captain Henry Byam. *The Polynesian Journal of Captain Henry Byam Martin, R.N., in Command of HMS Grampus, 50 Guns, at Hawaii and on Station in Tahiti and the Society Islands August 1846 to August 1847*. Salem, Mass.: Peabody Museum of Salem, 1981.

Maude, H. E. *Of Islands and Men: Studies in Pacific History*. Melbourne: Oxford University Press, 1968.

————. "The Tahitian Pork Trade: 1800–1830: An Episode in Australia's Commercial History." In *Of Islands and Men*, edited by H. E. Maude, 178–232 (Melbourne: Oxford University Press, 1968).

McCalman, Iain. "Introduction." In *An Oxford Companion to the Romantic Age: British Culture 1776–1832*, edited by Iain McCalman, 1–11. London: Oxford University Press, 1999.

McCormick, E. H. *Omai: Pacific Envoy*. Auckland: Auckland University Press, Oxford University Press, 1977.

McNeill, J. R., ed. *Environmental History in the Pacific World*. 18 vols. The Pacific World, vol. 2. Aldershot: Ashgate, 2001.

Menzies, Archibald. Journal of Vancouver's Voyage, 1790–1794. BL (Add. Ms 32641).

Miller, Carey. *Food Value of Bread Fruit, Taro Leaves, Coconut, Sugar Cane, &c. Bernice P. Bishop Museum Bulletin* 64 (1929).

Milton, Giles. *A New Voyage Round the World: The Journal of an English Buccaneer (1697)*. London: Hummingbird Press, 1998.

Ministère chargé de l'Environnement. "Les Plantes Envahissantes en Polynésie Française" Brochure. Pape'ete: Delegation à l'Environnement, c.2003.

Mitchell, Andrew. *The Fragile South Pacific: An Ecological Odyssey*. Austin: University of Texas Press, 1989.

Moffat, Hugh. "George Tobin, RN." *Sea Breezes* 39 (1965): 592–596.

Monnier, Jeanne, Anne Lavondés, Jean-Claude Jolinon, Pierre Elouard. *Philibert Commerson: Le découvreur du Bougainvillier*. Châtillon-sur-Chalaronne: Association Saint-Guignefort, 1993.

Montémont, Albert. *Bibliothèque universelle des voyages*. Paris: Armand-Aubrée, 1834.

Montgomery, James. *Journal of Voyages and Travels by the Rev. Daniel Tyerman and George Bennet, Esq . . . 1821–1829*. Boston: Crocker and Brewster, 1832.

Moorehead, Alan. *The Fatal Impact: An Account of the Invasion of the South Pacific*. Harmondsworth: Penguin Books, 1987 (Orig. pub. 1966).

Moschner, Irmgard, ed. *A Missionary Voyage to the Southern Pacific Ocean 1796–1798*. Graz: Akademische Druck, u. Verlagsanstalt, 1966.

Musée de Tahiti et ses Îles/Te fare Manaha, *Nōhea mai mātau?: Destins d'objets polynésiens*. Tahiti: STP Multipress, 2007.

Nero, Karen, and Nicholas Thomas, eds. *An Account of the Pelew Islands, by George Keate*. The Literature of Travel, Exploration and Empire. London: Continuum, 2002.

Newbury, Colin, ed. *The History of the Tahitian Mission, 1799–1830. Written by John Davies, Missionary to the South Seas Islands*. London: Cambridge University Press, 1961.

———. *Tahiti Nui: Change and Survival in French Polynesia 1767–1945*. Honolulu: University of Hawai'i Press, 1980.

Newell, Jennifer. "Exotic Possessions: Polynesians and Their Eighteenth-Century Collecting." *Journal of Museum Ethnography* 17 (2005): 75–88.

———. "Irresistible Objects: Collecting in the Pacific and Australia in the Reign of George III." In *Enlightenment: Discovering the World in the Eighteenth Century*, edited by Kim Sloan, 246–257. London: British Museum Press, 2003.

———. "Pacific Travelers: The Islanders Who Voyaged with Cook." *Commonplace* (web journal) 5 no. 2 (2005): www.common-place.org.

———. "Revisiting Cook at the British Museum." *Journal of the History of Collections* (forthcoming).

Nichols, John. *Illustrations of the Literary History of the Eighteenth Century*. Vol. 1. London, 1817.

Nugent, Maria. *Botany Bay: Where Histories Meet*. Crows Nest, N.S.W.: Allen & Unwin, 2005.

———. *Captain Cook Was Here*. Melbourne: Cambridge University Press, 2009.

Nunn, Patrick D. *Pacific Islands Landscapes*. Suva: Institute of Pacific Studies, University of the South Pacific, 1998.

Obeyesekere, Gananath. *The Apotheosis of Captain Cook: European Mythmaking in the Pacific.* Princeton, N.J.: Princeton University Press, 1992.

O'Brien, Gerard. "Ponsonby, William, second Earl of Bessborough (1704–1793)." In *Oxford Dictionary of National Biography.* Oxford: Oxford University Press, 2004.

Oliver, Douglas. *Ancient Tahitian Society.* 3 vols. Canberra: ANU Press, 1975.

———. *The Pacific Islands.* Honolulu: University of Hawai'i Press, 1989.

———. *Return to Tahiti: Bligh's Second Breadfruit Voyage.* Melbourne: Melbourne University Press, 1988.

O'Reilly, Patrick. *La vie à Tahiti au temps de la Reine Pomare.* Paris: Société des Océanistes, 1975.

Orliac, Michel. "Human Occupation and Environmental Modifications in the Papeno'o Valley, Tahiti." In *Historical Ecology in the Pacific Islands: Prehistoric Environmental and Landscape Change,* edited by Patrick V. Kirch and Terry L. Hunt, 200–229. New Haven, Conn., and London: Yale University Press, 1997.

Orsmond, John Muggridge. Journal at Tahiti, Raiatea and Bora Bora 1820–1821, LMS/CWM Archives, SOAS (box 4 folio 55).

———. to Rev. T. Cuzens, 1849. Orsmond Papers, Mitchell Library, SLNSW (MS A2606).

Owen, J. "Rabbit Production in Tropical Developing Countries: A Review." *Tropical Science* 18 no. 4 (1976): 203–210.

Pálsson, Gísli. "The Idea of Fish: Land and Sea in the Icelandic World-View." In *Signifying Animals: Human Meaning in the Natural World,* edited by Roy Willis. London: Unwin Hyman, 1990.

Park, Geoff. *Ngā Uruora, The Groves of Life: Ecology and History in a New Zealand Landscape.* Wellington: Victoria University Press, 1995.

Peltzer, Louise. *Chronologie des Événements Politiques, Sociaux et Culturels de Tahiti et des Archipels de la Polynésie Française.* Pirae, Tahiti: Au vent des îles, 2002.

Pétard, Paul. *Plantes Utiles de Polynésie: Raau Tahiti.* Pape'ete: éditions Haere po no Tahiti, 1986.

Philip, Governor Arthur. "Commission." *Historical Records of Australia,* 7, 794.

Pocock, J. G. A. "Nature and History, Self and Other: European Perceptions of World History in the World of Encounter." In *Voyages and Beaches: Pacific Encounters, 1769–1840,* edited by Alex Calder, Jonathan Lamb, and Bridget Orr, 25–44. Honolulu: University of Hawai'i Press, 1999.

Ponting, Clive. *A Green History of the World.* London: Penguin, 1992.

Powell, Dulcie. "The Voyage of the Plant Nursery, H.M.S. Providence 1791–1793." *Bulletin of the Institute of Jamaica,* Science Series 15 no. 2 (1973).

Price, Martin L., and Fremont Regier. *Rabbit Production in the Tropics.* Web publication (North Ft. Myers, Fla.: ECHO, 1982). http://echotech.org/mambo/images/DocMan/RabitPro.PDF

Pritchard, George. "The Aggressions of the French at Tahiti and Other Islands in the Pacific." Photocopied typescript. University of Auckland Library, New Zealand and Pacific collection, Auckland, n.d. (post-1843).

Proust, Katrina M. "Learning from the Past for Sustainability: Towards an Integrated Approach." PhD Thesis, ANU, 2004.

Puget, Peter. Log Book of the *Chatham* Tender, Lt. W. R. Broughton Commander, Jan.–Sept. 1791. BL (Add. Ms 17,542).

Rendle-Short, Francesca, ed. *Cook and Omai: The Cult of the South Seas.* Canberra: National Library of Australia, 2001.

Richaud, Vahi Sylvia, ed. *Code des Lois.* Tahiti: Ministère de la Culture de Polynésie française, 2001.

Rickman, John. *Journal of Captain Cook's Last Voyage to the Pacific Ocean on Discovery* (London: E. Newbery, 1781).

Rigby, Nigel. "The Politics and Pragmatics of Seaborne Plant Transportation, 1769–1805." In *Science and Exploration in the Pacific: European Voyages to the Southern Oceans in the Eighteenth Century,* edited by Margarette Lincoln, 81–100. Woodbridge, Suffolk: Boydell Press with the National Maritime Museum, 1998.

Robin, Libby. *Defending the Little Desert: The Rise of Ecological Consciousness in Australia.* Melbourne: Melbourne University Press, 1998.

Rodenhurst, T. *A Description of Hawkstone the seat of Sir Richard Hill,* 6th ed. London: John Stockdale, 1799.

Rosenman, Helen, ed. *Voyage au Pole Sud et dans l'Oceanie sur les Corvettes l'*Astrolabe *et la* Zélée, *by Jules Sébastien César Dumont d'Urville.* English ed. Honolulu: University of Hawai'i Press, 1988.

Russell, C. F. *A History of King Edward VI School Southampton.* Cambridge: Cambridge University Press, 1940.

Russell, Samuel. *Tahiti and French Oceania: A Book of Reliable Information for the Traveller, the Sportsman, the Yachtsman, and the Resident in the South Seas.* Sydney: Pacific Publications Ltd, 1935.

Rutter, Owen, ed. *The Journal of James Morrison, Boatswain's Mate of the Bounty Describing the Mutiny & Subsequent Misfortunes of the Mutineers Together with an Account of the Island of Tahiti.* London: The Golden Cockerel Press, 1935.

———. *The Log of the Bounty: Being Lieutenant William Bligh's Log of the Proceedings of His Majesty's Armed Vessel Bounty in a Voyage to the South Seas, to Take the Breadfruit from the Society Islands to the West Indies.* London: Golden Cockerel Press, 1937.

Salmond, Anne. *Aphrodite's Island: The European Discovery of Tahiti.* Auckland: Penguin Books, 2009.

———. *Between Worlds: Early Exchanges between Maori and Europeans 1773–1815.* Auckland: Viking, 1997.

———. *The Trial of the Cannibal Dog: Captain Cook in the South Seas.* London: Penguin Books, 2004.

————. *Two Worlds: First Meetings between Maori and Europeans 1642–1772*. Honolulu: University of Hawai‘i Press, 1992.

Salvat, Bernard, ed. *Flore et Faune Terrestres*. Vol. 2, *Encyclopédie de la Polynésie*, edited by Christian Gleizal. Pape‘ete: Multipress, 1986.

Samson, Jane. *Imperial Benevolence: Making British Authority in the Pacific Islands*. Honolulu: University of Hawai‘i Press, 1998.

Schama, Simon. *Landscape and Memory*. London: Harper Collins, 1995.

Schiebinger, Londa, and Claudia Swan, eds. *Colonial Botany: Science, Commerce, and Politics in the Early Modern World*. Philadelphia: University of Pennsylvania Press, 2004.

————. *Plants and Empire: Colonial Bioprospecting in the Atlantic World*. Cambridge, Mass.: Harvard University Press, 2004.

Schreiber, Roy, ed. *Captain Bligh's Second Chance: An Eyewitness Account of his Return to the South Seas by Lt George Tobin*. Sydney: University of New South Wales Press, 2007.

Shaw, A. G. L. "King, Philip Gidley (1758–1808)." In *Australian Dictionary of Biography*. Melbourne: Melbourne University Press, 1967, 2:55–61.

Shelley, William. Ship Porpoise from Otaheite towards Port Jackson, 1801. SSJ, LMS/CWM Archives, SOAS (box 1 folio 12).

Shineberg, Dorothy. *They Came for Sandalwood: A Study of the Sandalwood Trade in the South-West Pacific, 1830–1865*. Melbourne: Melbourne University Press, 1967.

Shipley, Conway. *Sketches in the Pacific: The South Sea Islands*. London: T. McLean, 1851.

Shirley, Henry. *Letter to William Bligh, 20 March 1793, Kingston, Jamaica*. London: Society for the Encouragement of Arts, Manufactures, and Commerce, 1794, 311–317.

Sloan, Kim. *"A Noble Art": Amateur Artists and Drawing Masters c. 1600–1800*. London: British Museum Press, 2000.

Smith, Bernard. "Constructing 'Pacific' Peoples." In *Remembrance of Pacific Pasts*, edited by R. Borofsky, 152–168. Honolulu: University of Hawai‘i Press, 2000.

————. *European Vision and the South Pacific*. 2nd ed. Melbourne: Oxford University Press, 1989.

Société d'ornithologie de Polynésie française. *Manu: les Oiseaux de Polynésie*. Pirae: Tahiti Books, 1999.

Spary, Emma C. *Utopia's Garden: French Natural History from Old Regime to Revolution*. Chicago: University of Chicago Press, 2000.

Spatz, G., and D. Mueller-Dombois. "The Influence of Feral Goats on Koa Tree Reproduction in Hawaii Volcanoes National Park." *Ecology* 54 (1973): 870–876.

Sturge, Joseph, and Thomas Harvey. *The West Indies in 1837: Being the Journal of a Visit to Antigua, Montserrat, Dominica, St. Lucia, Barbados, and Jamaica;*

Undertaken for the Purpose of Ascertaining the Actual Condition of the Negro Population of Those Islands. London: Hamilton, Adams, & Co., 1838.

Taylor correspondence, Institute of Commonwealth Studies, London (TAYL/ 1A).

Teaiwa, Katerina. "Our Sea of Phosphate: The Diaspora of Ocean Island." In *Indigenous Diasporas and Dislocations,* edited by G. Harvey and C. Thompson, 169–192. Aldershot, Hampshire: Ashgate, 2005.

Teaiwa, Teresia K. "Mānoa Rain." In *Pacific Places, Pacific Histories: Essays in Honor of Robert Kiste,* edited by Brij V. Lal, 216–236. Honolulu: University of Hawai'i Press, 2004.

Thomas, Keith. *Man and the Natural World: Changing Attitudes in England 1500– 1800.* Harmondsworth, Middlesex: Penguin, 1984.

Thomas, Nicholas. *Discoveries: The Voyages of Captain Cook.* London: Allen Lane/ Penguin Books, 2003.

———. *Entangled Objects: Exchange, Material Culture, and Colonialism in the Pacific.* Cambridge, Mass: Harvard University Press, 1991.

———. "Exploration." In *An Oxford Companion to the Romantic Age: British Culture 1776–1832,* edited by Iain McCalman, 345–353. Oxford: Oxford University Press, 1999.

Thomas, Nicholas, and Oliver Berghof, eds. *A Voyage Round the World by George Forster.* Honolulu: University of Hawai'i Press, 2000.

Thomas, Nicholas, Harriet Guest, and Michael Dettelbach, eds. *Observations Made During a Voyage Round the World by J. R. Forster.* Honolulu: University of Hawai'i Press, 1996.

Tobin, George. Journal on HMS *Providence* 1791–1793, 1797. Mitchell Library, SLNSW (MLA 562).

———. Log of H.M. Ship *Providence,* Wm Bligh Esq Comdr. . . . 1791. PRO (ADM 55/94).

———. Sketches on HMS *Providence,* including some sketches from later voyages on Thetis and Princess Charlotte, 1791–1811. Mitchell Library, SLNSW (PXA 563).

Torrence, Robin, and Anne Clarke, eds. *The Archaeology of Difference: Negotiating Cross-Cultural Engagements in Oceania.* London: Routledge, 2000.

Turnbull, John. *A Voyage Round the World in the Years 1800–1804.* 2nd ed. London, 1813.

Ward, R. Gerard, ed. *Man in the Pacific Islands: Essays on Geographical Change in the Pacific Islands.* Oxford: Clarendon Press, 1972.

Warner, Oliver, ed. *An Account of the Discovery of Tahiti: From the Journal of George Robertson Master of HMS Dolphin.* London: Folio Press, J. M. Dent, 1973.

Watson, J. S. "Feral Rabbit Populations on Pacific Islands." *Pacific Science* 15 (1961): 591–593.

Wendt, Albert. "Novelists and Historians and the Art of Remembering." In *Class and Culture in the South Pacific,* edited by Antony Hooper, 78–91. Suva:

Centre for Pacific Studies, University of Auckland and Institute of Pacific Studies, University of the South Pacific, 1987.

West, Morris. *The Shoes of the Fisherman*. London: Heinemann, 1963.

Wilder, G. P. *The Breadfruit of Tahiti. Bernice P. Bishop Museum Bulletin* 50 (1928).

Wilkinson, Francis. Log of Francis Wilkinson on HMS Dolphin, Book 2: 19 June–22 October 1767. PRO (ADM 51/4541/96).

Williams, Glyndwr. *The Great South Sea: English Voyages and Encounters 1570–1750*. New Haven, Conn., and London: Yale University Press, 1997.

———. "Tupaia: Polynesian Warrior, Navigator, High Priest—and Artist." In *The Global Eighteenth Century*, edited by Felicity A. Nussbaum, 38–51. Baltimore; London: Johns Hopkins University Press, 2003.

Willmott, John. *An Alphabetical Enumeration of the Plants Contained in the Hortus Kewensis*. London: Plummer, 1798.

Wilson, David. *The British Museum: A History*. London: British Museum Press, 2002.

Wilson, William. *A Missionary Voyage to the Southern Pacific Ocean, Performed in the Years 1796–1798, in the Ship Duff, Commanded by Captain James Wilson*. London: T. Chapman, 1799.

Wood, Sir Henry T. *A History of the Royal Society of Arts*. London: John Murray, 1913.

Wright, Shane, and Annette Lees. "Biodiversity Conservation in the Island Pacific." In *The Origin and Evolution of Pacific Island Biotas, New Guinea to Eastern Polynesia: Patterns and Processes*, edited by Allen Keast and Scott Miller, 443–461. Amsterdam: SPB Academic Publishing, 1996.

INDEX

politics and ecological exchange, 52, 103–104, 190
Polynesia, 14
Pomare family, 16–18, 34, 109, **131,** 156, 162, 176; contrast with Kamehameha in Hawai'i, 133; and missionaries, 126–129 passim, 181–182, 186–187; in power struggles, 120–121, 127, 159, 161, 163 (*see also under* Pomare II); reign ended by France, 130
Pomare I. *See* Tu
Pomare II, 18, 128, 154, **189,** 206; birth, 18, 205, 229n.45; conversion to Christianity, 86, 127, 186–187, 211; marriage, 186, 209; personal habits, 186, 265n.86; role in trade, 178, 184–185, 188–190; as shipowner, 189–190; struggles with rivals, 171, 184, 185–187, 209–210; thrust for power, 182, 185, 189–190; death, 190, 211
Pomare III, 190, 191, 211, 212
Pomare IV. *See* Aimata
population levels, 110, 113, 211, 212, 249n.116, 254n.110
Porapora (Borabora), 2, 103, 157, 185, 205
pork trade. *See under* pigs
Port Jackson, 172, 180, 184, 188–191 passim
poultry, 7, 104. *See also* chickens *(mo'a)*
power structures, 36–37, 137, 190, 196
predator animals, 100–101, 103, 107, 112
priests *(tahua),* 17, 37, 120, 171
Pritchard, George, 129
property, cultural conceptions of, 11–13, 85
Providence, 42, 160, 163–164, 166. *See also* Tobin, George
provisioning, 25–36, 38–39, 40–41, 54–55, 113, 173, 235nn.115–116; breeding livestock for future, 94; counting and record-keeping, 77–78; ecological and social impacts, 53–54, 55–56; main trade again in 1820s, 190
Purea ("Queen Oberea"), 49, 71, 178, 183, 203, 205; dealings with Wallis, 7, **32,** 34–36, 103; pet-keeping, 112

Quiros, Ferdinand de, 144

rabbits: on other islands, 101, 198, 245n.45; in Tahiti, 100–101, 194
rahui (formal restrictions), 47–49, 80
Ra'iatea, 111, 120, 128, 157, 174, 176, 185, 186; Banks' visit (1769), 62
rats: European, 111, 112, 113; Polynesian, 103, 112
Resolution, **12,** 118–119, 121, 150, 173, 204–205
resource management by Tahitians, 19, 45–49, 102–105
Reti (chief), 38–39
Robertson, George, 29, 33, 35, 48, 173
Rodríguez, Máximo, 117
Romantic movement, 61–62
Royal Admiral, 183
Royal Botanic Gardens (at Kew), 63, 163, 166, 237n.26
Royal Society, 40, 63, 141, 150, 166, 198
Rua-ta'ata, 157

sacred objects and places, 13, 16, 33, 79–83, 184; cattle in Hawai'i, 134–135
Salmond, Anne, 3, 14, 30, 97, 113
sandalwood, 189, 197
scarcity, times of, 46, 53, 102, 179
science as motivation, 62, 65–67
Scott, Captain William, 172, 181, 182
scurvy, 26–27, 38, 99
seasons in Tahitian year, 46
seed planting (by Europeans), 36, 39, 105, 107–108
settlement by Maohi, 9, 103. *See also* migration in Pacific
settlers (European), 84, 130–131, 158–160, 191. *See also* missionaries
sexual exchanges, 6, 36, 39, 49, 111–112, 129, 158
sheep, 7, 99, 100, 197, 245n.39
Smith, C. (botanist), 164
Smith, Harrison, 19
social changes, 41–44, 51–52
Société des Etudes Océaniennes, 192–193
Society Islands, 2, **4,** 130
Solander, Daniel, 62–65
South Africa, 109. *See also* Cape of Good Hope
Spanish visits, 16, 100, 116–119; occu-

ABOUT THE AUTHOR

DR. JENNIFER NEWELL is a Pacific historian and curator. She has
been a curator at the British Museum and is now a research fellow at the National Museum of Australia. She obtained a doctoral
degree at the Australian National University in 2006. She has published on aspects of cross-cultural encounters in the Pacific and the
material culture of the region. Her museum work has brought her
into close contact with people and places across both the contemporary and historic Pacific.

Production Notes for
NEWELL / TRADING NATURE

Designed by Josie Herr with text and display in New Baskerville

Composition by Josie Herr

Printing and binding by The Maple-Vail Book Manufacturing Group

Printed on 60# Maple Recycled Opaque, 408 ppi